RXpert SERIES
Student's Companion

Scale Up and Technology Transfer

Dulal Krishna Tripathi Ex-Director
Santosh Rungta Group of Institutions,
Bhilal, CG.

PharmaMed Press
An imprint of BSP Books Pvt. Ltd.
4-4-309/316, Giriraj Lane,
Sultan Bazar, Hyderabad - 500 095.

Scale Up and Technology Transfer
by **Dulal Krishna Tripathi**

Published by

PharmaMed Press
An imprint of BSP Books Pvt. Ltd.
4-4-309/316, Giriraj Lane, Sultan Bazar, Hyderabad - 500 095.
Phone: 040-23445688; Fax: 91+40-23445611
E-mail: info@pharmamedpress.net
www.bspbooks.net/www.pharmamedpress.net

ISBN: 978-93-48734-10-5 (Hardback)

Preface

Among the various research-intensive industries, pharmaceutical industry is one. Pharmaceutical industries are also extensively regulated by regulatory authorities. The research is conducted in various directions. Moreover, the industries are supposed to follow Good Manufacturing Practice as per ICH guidelines. Any formulation of a drug whether new or existing is supposed to be basic outcome of formulation development studies and the result must be reproducible, and consistent. Before according the permission for commercial manufacturing and marketing there lies another step called as **Scale Up and Technology Transfer**. In this the manufacturer is supposed to produce data showing that the results are consistently within the limits and proper care has been taken for validation of the equipment, process, stability of the product and method. Hence, permission for regular commercial manufacture and marketing must be accorded from the respective drug regulatory authority.

Therefore, scale up and technology transfer is a common process of transferring the technology to production department. Whether it is OTC product, commonly marketed or it is a new product to be newly introduced to the market. In each pharmaceutical industry there must be a pilot plant wherein the products are manufactured using the same equipment, used for regular commercial manufacturing but their size is small. Each process, or technology at the end must be validated, because validation is considered to be an essential part of GMPs. The concept of profit is basic element of any business, and the industries do business to earn money. The cost of a product must be reduced to minimal to increase the profit, this is the driving principle of any business. Pharmaceutical industries fall also on the same line. Accordingly, for reduction of the cost of a product, formulation development/ research & development department work throughout the year. Whatever the process or component is used, based on the availability in the market. There is continuous development in those areas. also, where the ingredients/ components either are being manufactured and sold. Hence, development is a dynamic state, not a static one.

In fact, earlier to 2017 different educational institutions of this country affiliated to various Universities had different syllabus for their respective M. Pharmacy courses. But, from the academic session 2017 – 2018, the Pharmacy Council of India have done a revolutionary work by according the permission from the Government of India for implementing a common syllabus for across the country. Therefore, all the academic Institutions including their affiliating Universities are bound to implement the syllabus.

This book, **Scale Up and Technology Transfer** has been prepared as per the syllabus for M. Pharm course with specialization in Industrial Pharmacy, I1st semester. The contents have been prepared with as per as possible simple languages, so that the reader can understand easily. The book has six chapters in accordance with the syllabus, such as, Pilot plant design, Scale up, Validation, Equipment qualification, Process qualification, and Industrial safety. At the end of each chapter, some model questions such as multiple-choice questions, short questions and long questions have been provided. There are some references also. During preparation of the book adequate care has been taken to avoid any mistake; however, if any mistake is found later kindly inform the publisher or the undersigned. So that, during subsequent printing error can be corrected.

Dulal Krishna Tripathi

Acknowledgement

The author is thankful to Shirsho Chakrabartty, Saswati Chakrabartty and Nirmalya Tripathi for extending their expertise in MS Office. The author expresses his sincere gratitude to his better half, Mrs. Bimala Tripathi without her support the book could not have been completed.

Dulal Krishna Tripathi

Contents

CHAPTER - 6

Industrial Safety

CHAPTER - 1

Pilot Plant Design

Introduction, Basic Requirements for Design, Facility, Equipment Selection for Tablets, Equipment Selection for Capsules, Equipment Selection for Liquid Orals, Equipment Selection for Parenterals, Equipment Selection for Semisolid Preparation

INTRODUCTION

Pilot plant is *a place where the 5 M's like money, material; man, method and machine are utilized to perform the manufacturing of the products.* A pilot plant is a pre-commercial production system. It employs new production technology and/or produces small volumes of new technology-based products, mainly for the purpose of learning about the new technology. The technology obtained is then used for design of full-scale production systems and commercial products, as well as for identification of further research objectives and support of investment decisions. Other purposes include gaining public support for new technologies and questioning government regulations. Pilot plant studies must include a close examination of formula to determine its ability to with stand batch scale and process modifications; it must include a review of range of relevant processing equipment, also availability of raw materials meeting the specification of product. During the scale up efforts in the pilot plant production and process control are evaluated, validated and finalized.

The necessity of pilot plants development in pharmaceuticals has been felt extensively. The dispute comes out primarily on the need for piloting the processes is the production of organic chemicals. Baekeland's[1] famous comment, *Commit your blunders on a small scale and make your profit on a large scale*, can be applied to this situation where the pilot plant represents an intermediate stage between the laboratory studies and the industrial/ commercial plant. The necessity of the pilot plant will depend on the complexity of the formulation and the experience available. The pilot plant must be understood just not as a scale-up of laboratory equipment[2], but as a small scale simulation of the future industrial operations. Results of the laboratory studies will be used to choose the most suitable process and will lead to the selection of the equipment for each stage of the flow sheet. If the laboratory studies are positive and the pilot plant studies are necessary. The pilot plant will be designed to simulate the industrial operations. It is not always necessary that the pilot plant include all of the flow sheets, but it must include at least those which

a) Require equipment not frequently used;
b) Fair and markedly different from conventional practice
c) Have caused some problems at the laboratory scale; and
d) Have some elements, even trace elements, that might build up in some streams, for example in solvent extraction.

In pilot plants for new chemical processes it is usually desirable to use the same materials of construction that will be used in the industrial plant.

Pilot plant is defined as a *part of the pharmaceutical industry where a laboratory formula is transformed into a viable product by the development of liable practical procedure for manufacture.*

As per the definition given above, a pilot plant is a pre-commercial production system that uses new production technology and/or produces small volumes of new technology-based products, mainly for the purpose of learning about the new technology. The knowledge obtained is then used for design of full-scale production systems of commercial products, as well as for identification of further research objectives and support of investment decisions. The schematic development of final of drug product from R & D to commercial production has been shown in Fig,1.1 below.

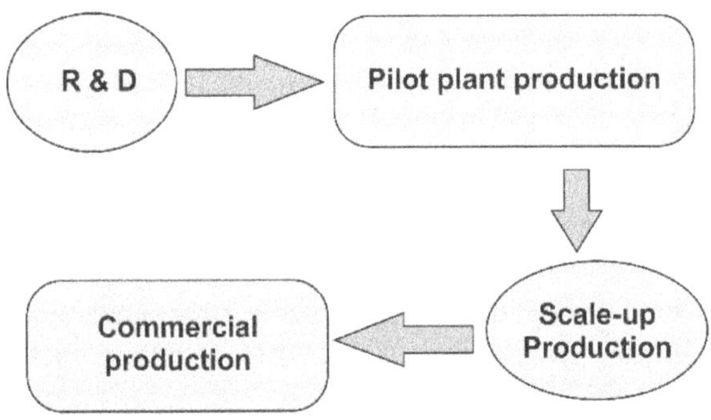

Fig.1.1 Schematic diagram of processes involved in design of pilot plant.

During the scale up experiments in the pilot plant production and process control are evaluated, validated and finalized[3].

- A pilot plant allows investigation of a product and the process on an intermediate scale before large full-scale production.
- It is usually not possible to predict the effects of a many-fold increase in scale.
- It is not possible to design a large complex drug/ drug product processing plant from laboratory data alone with any degree of success.

Therefore, pilot plant can be designed for

- Evaluation of the results of laboratory studies and making the product and process corrections and improvements.
- Production of small quantities of the product for sensory, chemical, microbiological evaluations. Limited market testing or furnishing samples to potential customers, shelf-life and storage stability studies.
- Generating data that can be used in making a decision on whether or not to proceed to a full-scale production process. In case of a positive decision, designing and constructing a full-size plant or modifying an existing plant.
- Type and size of a pilot plant depends on the goals, evaluation of product and process; producing samples of product for evaluation.
- Close liaison between R&D and pilot plant is essential.
- Labour requirements and costs of staff, skilled operators and maintenance staff-pilot plant costs may exceed those of usual plant production costs.
- The pilot plant may be used for training of personnel for a full- scale plant.

To attempt a process on a model of proposed plant before committing large sum of money on a production unit[4].

The significance of a pilot plant is[3] to

- Standardize a formulae.
- Review the range of relevant processing equipment.
- Optimize and control of production rate.
- Inform about the infrastructure of equipment during the scale up batches and about the physical space required.
- Identify the critical features to maintain quality of a product.
- Maintain the appropriate records and reports to support GMP.

Objectives of pilot plant

The main objective of the pilot plant is to check on a reduced scale, the process developed in laboratory studies. The decision to proceed with the full scale plant project should be based on a proven process, which gives a more reliable and economic estimate. Hence, to design correctly the full scale production, pilot plant and simulated full scale production using equipment of smaller capacity would be necessary. This is not only the purpose of a pilot plant. There are other objectives which should be fulfilled simultaneously and in some cases these objectives may provide the definitive considerations for the decision to build the pilot plant. Therefore, the objectives of a pilot plant, can differ depending on the specific circumstances of each project, and the decision for its conversion can include one or several of the following objectives:

- To optimize the operating parameters of the process,
- To study the effects of recirculating the process and accumulation of impurities over long periods.
- To obtain the process information necessary to specify and design the full scale plant,
- To test process control systems and procedures,
- To test materials of production,
- To optimize the requirement of the equipment.
- To obtain sufficient information to prepare a detailed and reliable estimates of capital and operating costs and to prepare a reliable economic evaluation of the project.
- To gain operating experience and to train the personnel that will operate the full scale plant,.
- To identify hazards in the process and ensure safety in design and operation, including the disposal of wastes[5-7]

In general, the products are prepared in the commercial scale after laboratory scale has been shown in Fig.1.2.

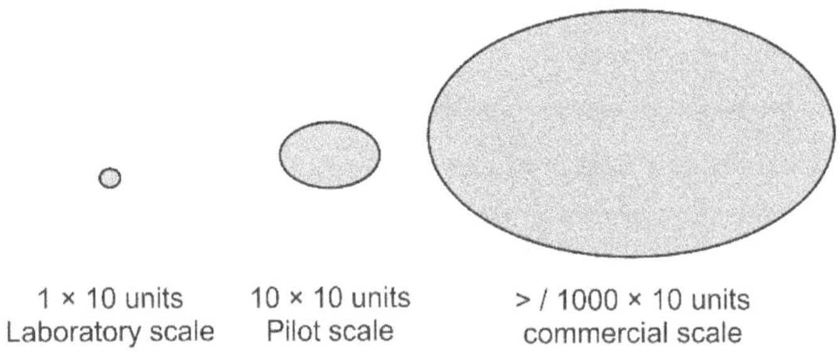

Fig.1.2 Progression of batches from laboratory to commercial scale.

BASIC REQUIREMENTS FOR DESIGN

Pilot plant can be viewed as a commercial manufacture of pharmaceuticals in miniature form. For preparation of any dosage form, the type and size of instruments/ equipment would not be same, for example, for making solution and blending for tablets[7], mixing is a common step but different type of mixers are required.

The design data required for each process can be classified under six heads:

- Data available from past experience.
- Data given in the laboratory report or which can be derived from the laboratory results.
- Data available in the literature.

- Data which can be approximated sufficiently and closely for design purpose by means of thermodynamic relations, the theorem of corresponding states, or some of the many empirical or semi empirical correlations that have appeared in recent year.
- Data which could be obtained by further research in the laboratory.
- Other practical felt to be necessary for design purpose.

Another important objective of a pilot plant is the training of personnel, especially in countries where similar processes do not exist. In this case, the personnel would be trained not only for operation of the different types of equipment, but only for control of the process.

FACILITY

Plant is a place where the 5's such as money, material, man, machine and method are brought together for the manufacturing of the product and pilot plant is a part of the pharmaceutical industry. A lab scale formula is transformed into viable product through the development of practical method of manufacture in a pilot plant.

The multi-functional facility will comprise a total area of about 50,000 sq. yard. It should be added substantial capacity to the current chemical development and API manufacturing capabilities of the company.

It will have facilities for testing of raw materials, intermediates and finished products. A separate quality assurance department will ensure that the output-quality meets established cGMP standards and manufacturing is carried out following the standard operating procedures.

Additional space should be made available for further expansions to support any increase in commercial manufacturing activities[8-10].

- Plant design should be made as per WHO-GMP norms.
- Uni-directional for Man and material flow should be provided.
- Separate and dedicated area for each activity based on respective formulation should be provided.
- In-house dedicated product testing facility should be there.
- The complete plant area should be centrally air-conditioned. The independent supply systems are fed with separated air handling units to avoid cross air contamination. Humidity, temperature and pressure gradients should also be maintained.
- For avoiding contamination in production area epoxy flooring is considered.
- Separate entry should be made for personnel and material in each critical production area to avoid cross contamination.

The following are the capacity of three common streams of the formulation and packaging plant:

Machine activity	Capacity
Capsule filling & sealing	500 caps./min (500 mg).
Semi-automatic capsule filling and sealing machine	60,000 caps/hr
Capsule Polishing Machine Empty capsule sorter	
Tablet compression	500 Tabs./min (500 mg)
Tablet compression Rapid Mixer Granulator (RMG)	15/30 kg
Fluid bed drier (FBD)	30 kg
Roller compactor	20 Kg
Tablet compression machine	16 station
Auto coater	28" with 20" and 18" pan
Blister packing machine	100 blister/hr
Strip packing machine	100 strip/hr.
Liquid filling machine	40 bottles/min (100 ml)
Liquid online preparation tank	500ltr.
Bottle washing machine	3000-6000 Bottles/hr.
Bottle filling and sealing machine	40 bottles/hr.

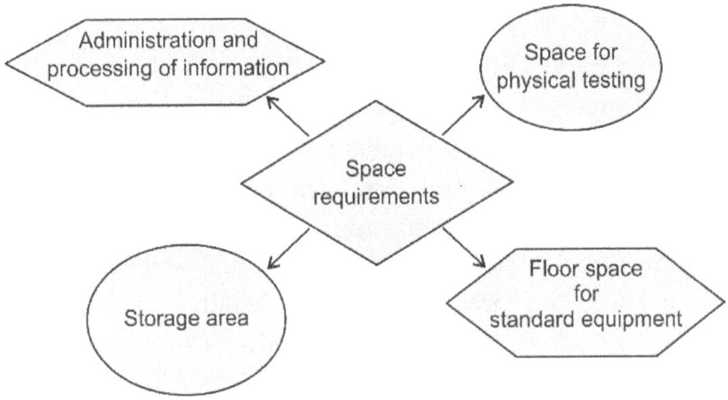

Fig.1.3 Schematic diagram for space required in pharmaceutical pilot plant.

In a large pharmaceutical organization, the development team may be made responsible for the transfer of new formulations to produce. A well-equipped space for conducting scale-up runs should also be provided. Such a developmental team may report administratively to the head of pharmaceutical research and development or the production head.

The various types of organizational structures that may exist in pharmaceutical pilot development, these are mentioned below.

- Research Pharmacist Responsible for Initial Scale-Up and Initial Production Runs
- Pharmaceutical Pilot Plant Controlled by Pharmaceutical Research
- Pharmaceutical Pilot Plant Controlled by the Production Division

Whatever may be the type of pharmaceutical pilot plant, the personnel working must be of very good educational background and must have some previous experience on pilot plant functioning. Let us discuss on a new tablet product.

A typical floor plan is shown in Figure 1.4; the floor plan reference is shown in Table 1.1. A typical floor plan for a small pilot plant is shown in Figure 1.5, and its reference is shown in Table 1.2. The variety of equipment installed must be narrow because of space limitations[11-13.] However, efficient use of such limited space can be made by borrowing from the production division, as required, portable tablet presses, mills, and coating pans.

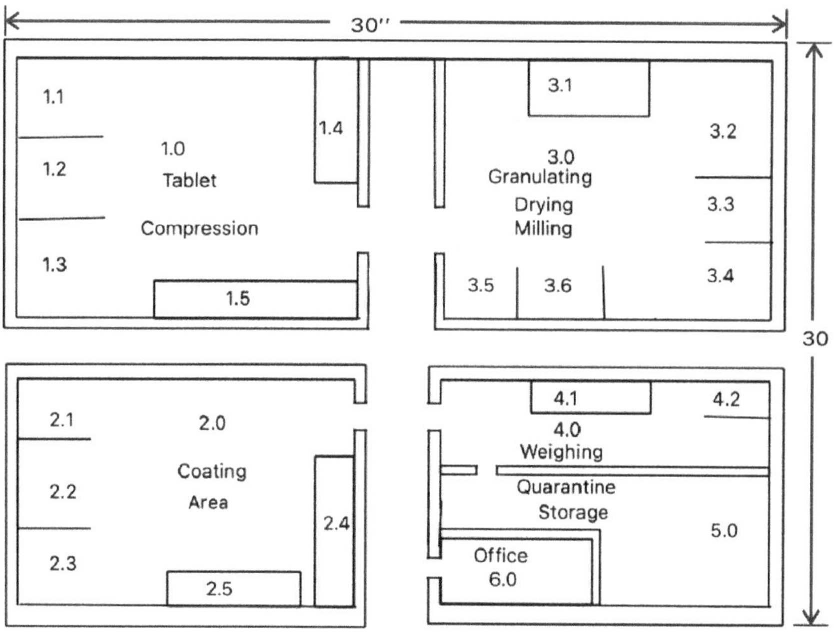

Fig.1.4 Floor plan for a small pilot plant for tablet development.

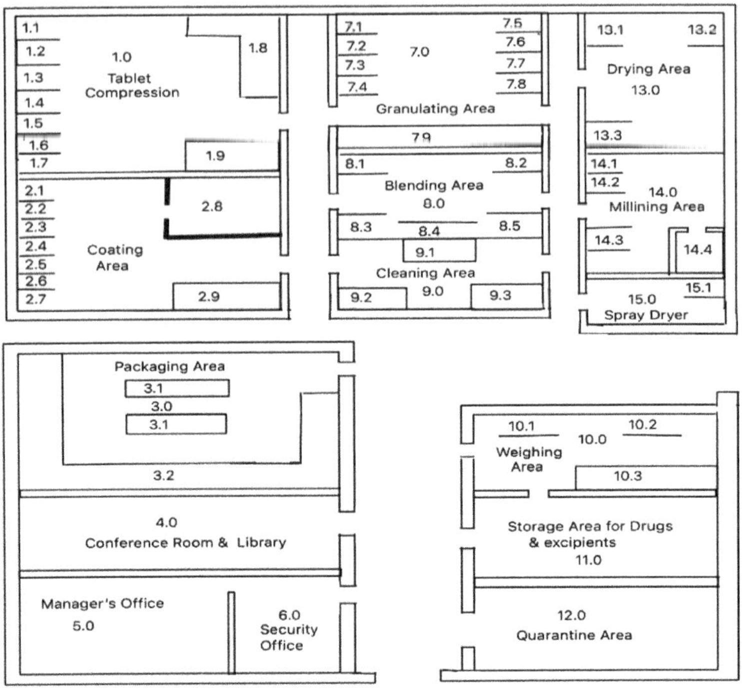

Fig.1.5 Floor plan of a pilot for development of a tablet.

Table 1.1 Floor plan for small pilot plant for Tablet manufacturing.

Sl. No.	Area specified for equipment	Sl. No	Area specified for equipment
1.0	Tablet compression room	3.0	Granulating, drying, and milling area
1.1	Tablet press, single-punch	3.1	Tray and truck dryer
1.2	Rotary tablet press 16 stations	3.2	Hobart mixer
1.3	Tablet deduster	3.3	Comminuting mill
1.4	Blench top with wall cabinets Ancillary equipment: Balances, Fibrilator, Dis-integration testing apparatus, Dissolution testing apparatus, Hardness tester	3.4	Hammer mill
1.5	Blench top with wall cabinets Ancillary supplies: Tools, Vacuum cleaner	3.5	Fluidized bed dryer

Table 1.1 ***contd...***

Sl. No.	Area specified for equipment	Sl. No	Area specified for equipment
2.0	Coating area	3.6	V-shaped blender with intensifier bar
2.1	Polishing pan, 36-in diameter	4.0	Weighing area
2.2	Coating pan, 36-in diameter	4.1	Bench top with wall cabinets
2.3	Airless spray equipment	4.2	Scale
2.4	Area for preparing syrups, Solutions, and suspensions for sugar or film coating	5.0	Quarantine and storage area
2.5	Sink	6.0	Office

Table 1.2 Floor plan (reference to Fig 1.5) of development of a tablet dosage form.

Sl. No	Area specified for equipment	Sl. No	Area specified for equipment
1.0	Tablet compression room	7.6	Comminuting equipment
1.1	Heavy-duty tablet press for dry granulation	7.7	Extractor
1.2	Rotary tablet press, 54 stations	7.8	Chilsonator
1.3	Rotary tablet press, 16 stations	7.9	Bench top with wall cabinets
1.4	Compression-coating tablet press	8.0	Blending area
1.5	Single-punch tablet press	7.6	Comminuting equipment
1.6	Tablet deduster	7.7	Extractor
1.7	Storage cabinet for the punches and dies	8.1	V-shaped blender with intensifier bar, 1 ft^3 capacity
1.8	Bench top with wall cabinets Ancillary equipment: balances, friabilator, disintegration-testing apparatus, dissolution-testing apparatus, hardness tester	8.2	V-shaped blender with intensifier bar, 5 ft^3 capacity
1.9	Bench top with wall cabinets Ancillary supplies: tools, vacuum cleaner	8.3	V-shaped blender with intensifier bar, 20 ft^3 capacity
2.0	Coating area	8.4	Ribbon blender
2.1	Coating pan. 36-in diameter	8.5	Lodige blender
2.2	Coating pan, 30-in diameter	9.0	Cleaning area
2.3	Coating pan, 20-in diameter	9.1	Sink
2.4	Perforated coating pan. 24-in diameter	9.2	Ultrasonic cleaner

Table 1.2 *contd...*

Sl. No	Area specified for equipment	Sl. No	Area specified for equipment
2.5	Polishing pan	9.3	Bench top with wall cabinets
2.6	Fluidized bed coating apparatus	10.0	Weighing area
2.7	Airless spray equipment	10.1	Scale
2.8	Area for preparing syrups, solutions, and suspensions for sugar or film coating	10.2	Scale
2.9	Bench top with wall cabinets	10.3	Bench top with wall cabinets Small scales and balances positioned on bench top
3.0	Packaging area	11.0	Storage area for drugs and excipients
3.1	Working tables	12.0	Quarantine area
3.2	Storage cabinets containing packaging supplies	13.0	Drying area
4.0	Conference room & library	13.1	Tray and truck dryer
5.0	Manager's Office	13.2	Fluidized bed dryer
6.0	Secretarial Office	13.3	Freeze dryer
7.0	Granulating area	14.0	Milling area
7.1	Comminuting mill	14.1	Hammer mill
7.2	Sigma blade mixer	14.2	Ball mill3
7.3	Planetary-type mixer	14.3	Muller
7.4	Tornado mill	14.4	Fluid energy mill (micronizsrs) 2 in diameter
7.5	Fluidized bed spray granulator	15.0	Spray-drying area
		15.1	Spray-dryer

Communication between pilot plant (Research) and Quality Control and Production Department

When a formulation say, a tablet formulation has been developed at the pilot scale, it becomes responsibility of the tablet formulator to issue clearly in written instructions for its manufacture' for example, the use of micronized drug may be specified. Moreover, the analytical specifications for the ingredients must be thoroughly described unambiguously. The in-process control steps describing the milling conditions to be followed must also be written down. Moreover, the particle size characterization of the micronized material must be included. In other cases, the characterization would be included as a responsibility of research team to inform the quality control or purchased micronized bulk drug. The tablet formulator should be well aware of the necessity to use micronized material on the basis of dissolution studies conducted during the early stages of formulation development. When bulk drug specifications are being established, such information becomes related to the members of the quality control and production divisions[14,15]. A raw material (RM) number is designated for the micronized bulk drug along with any physical or chemical information considered significant. Melting point is not only an important indication of the purity of a compound, it serves as an additional checkpoint for the desired polymorphic form on a crystalline compound. A stringently low trace metal content may be specified in some cases, if improved drug stability desires it. A typical specification sheet for ascorbic acid has been shown in Table 1.3. There may be several grades of particle sizes of ascorbic acid within the company. It is important to remember to specify the desired grade (Table 1.4 - 1.6) demonstrate manufacturing instructions for tablets containing 50 mg of hydrochlorothiazide. The sheet, Table. 1.5 listed the ingredients with mention of the amounts per tablet, and the amounts of each ingredient required for the batch size. In the Table 1.4 and Table 1.5 there may be the words "product code number." Such designation will help to avoid confusion by the various departments involved in the manufacture and release of the finished tablets. There may be hydro-chlorothiazide tablet potencies other than 50mg also being manufactured in the company. When a new drug is to be marketed in a tablet dosage form a new product code number is assigned and subsequently used. There are columns headed by the words "compounded by" and "checked by". When each ingredient is weighed, the individual who has weighed, puts his or her initials alongside the ingredient weight. The observer of this operation also puts his or her initial as a double check on the accuracy of the weighing operation. A similar procedure is followed for each step in the compounding operation. Such double checking is required by the Food and Drug Administration for all new drug application-type products. Such a double-checking procedure should be followed to ensure that there are no weighing or compounding errors.

In the list of ingredients, the lot number of each ingredient and the code number allotted to each ingredient, may be active ingredient or excipient, used must be recorded. Such recordings are of special importance when one attempts to trace the history of a particular batch of tablets. Troubleshooting can be simplified in some cases by tracing the source of a raw material. A typical problem that may arise can be due to a particular lot number of a substandard excipient that could have been unintentionally used.

On the sheet of the proposed manufacturing instructions (Table. 1.4) the stepwise procedure to be followed (instructions) is required to be described. The words selected and written should be readily understood by the individuals who will be reading these instructions. Thus, the personnel of quality control department can consider the establishment of in-process controls, pilot, and production operators who are supposed to follow the procedure for the first time. One should not be confused by cryptic phrases containing technical words and can easily understand. The tablet formulator should consider that his or her manufacturing procedure may also be circulated to foreign manufacturing organizations. Manufacturing instructions that are clearly written are also advantageous because they avoid confusion which may cause errors. Table 1.6 represents a list of specifications for the finished tablets indicating the product code and lot number. There are three forms which become a part of the file for the lot number of the batch of tablets prepared[17-19]. These three sheets work as a historical record. Attachments that are included, for example, would be the clearance data from the quality control department and a record of the physicians receiving the material for clinical study.

Table 1.3 Specification sheet for ascorbic acid.

Description	**Specification**
Ingredients	Ascorbic acid
Synonym	Vitamin C; L-Ascorbic acid, 3-Oxo-L--gulofuranolactone
Formula	$C_8H_8O_6$
Molecular weight	176.13
Product Code	SPVCOS
CAS No.	50-81-7
Properties	
Self-life	36 months
Description	White/ almost white crystals/ crystalline powder
Assay (GC)	99.0 - 100.5%
Melting point	190 - 192^{0}C
Loss on drying	$\geqq$ 0.4%
Colour of solution	$\geqq$ BY_7
Clarity of solution	Clear
Optical rotation	+ 20.5 - +21.5^0
Density at 20^{0}C	1.65 g/ cm^3
pH (5% solution)	2.1 - 2.6
pH (2% solution)	2.4 - 2.8
Sulphated ash	$\geqq$0.1%

Table 1.4 A sample of manufacturing instructions to prepare hydrochlorothiazide Tablets.

Name of the Product: Hydro-chlorthiazide tablets Strength: 50 mg	**Product Code Number**	**Lot Number**	**Page 1**
Steps	Manufacturing Instructions	Compound by	Checked by
1.	Pass items 1, 2 and 3 through a #16 screen using a comminuting mill to break up any lumps		
2.	Blend the three Ingredients in a V shaped blender for 1 hour.		
3.	Add the magnesium stearate and continue blending for 15 mins.		
4.	Subdivide the blended material into polyethylene lined drums. Submit representative samples to the Quality Control division to determine the homogeneity of blend.		
5.	After receipt of clearance from Quality Control, tablet the blend with 5/16 standard, round concave puncres on the 54 station, rotary tablet machine.		
6.	Submit representative samples of the finished tablets to the Quality Control division for final release.		

Table 1.5 List of ingredients used in manufacturing hydrochlorothiazide tablets (50 mg).

Product and Strength Hydrochlorthiazide Tablets, 50 mg	Product Code Number		Lot Number				Page 2
	Batch Size 50,00,000			Starting Date			Completion Date
	Prepared By			Production Approval		Quality Control Approval	
Number Ingredient	Grade	Grams/ Tablet	Grams/ Batch	Compounded by	Checked by	RM	Lot
1. Hydrochlor-thiazide	U.S.P.	0.050	250.000				
2. Microcrystalline Cellulose (PH 101)	N.F.	0.050	250.00				
3. Dicalcium phosphate, dihydrate	N.F.	0.099	495.000				
4. Magnesium Stearate	N.F.	0.001	5,000				
Total		0.200	10,00,000				

Table 1.6 An example of tablet specifications of hydrochlorthiazide tablets.

Name of the Product: Hydrochlorthiazide Tabs. **Strength:** 50 mg	**Product Code Number**	**Lot Number**	**Page 3**
Tablet Specifications			
Each tablet weighs: 0.200 g Range of weight : 0.190 – 0.210 g Strength : 50 mg per Tablet Range of strength : 46.25 – 53.75 mg per Tab. Hardness of the tab : 7 – 9 (Strong-Cobb Units) Disintegration Time: Less than 5 mins. (USP method) Dissolution Rate : 60% of the labelled claim (potency) shall dissolve within 30 mins (USP method) Colour of the Tabs. : White			

EQUIPMENT SELECTION FOR TABLETS

With the development of pharmaceutical companies worldwide, pharmaceutical machinery manufacturers have also developed high tech machinery to meet the demands of pharmaceutical products. Tablets are one of the most convenient way to consume medicines. Hence, manufacturing machinery of tablet is one of the most important segment of pharmaceutical machinery. As a result of the technological evolution and growth of the pharmaceutical industry, a wide range of advanced machines is available for various applications in the tablet manufacturing process[20].

In the tablet manufacturing process, various types of machines are used for different applications at different stages from production to packaging. Applications of some of the major equipment used for pilot plant study for tablet are mentioned below:

Tablet Press Machine, Double Cone Blender and Rapid Mixer Granulator

Different models of tablet press machine, like Single Sided Rotary Tablet Press Machine, Double Sided Rotary Tablet Press Machine and High Speed Rotary Tablet Press Machine are used for the production of the tablets of different shapes and size. The production capacity and features of these machines may vary based on their type. For the mixing of dry powders and granules, companies mostly use Double Cone Blender. Similarly, Rapid Mixer Granulator is used for mixing of the ingredients and wet granulation.

Fluid Bed Dryer, Multi Mill, Octagonal Blender and V Cone Blender

Drying is one of the very important stages in the tablet manufacturing process and Fluid Bed Dryer is used for drying the product like wet powder at a desired temperature. Multi Mill is a versatile machine which is used for granulating, pulverizing, mixing, shredding and chopping of materials at high speed. For the blending of different types of materials, the pharmaceutical companies mostly use advanced machines like Octagonal Blender and V-Cone Blender. These machines are also widely used in the food and cosmetic industries for mixing the materials[21].

Vibro Sifter, Conventional Coating Pan and Automatic Tablet Coater

Vibro Sifter is a hightech machine mainly used for separating mass composition of solids, liquid from solid. Another important application of it is gradation of materials as per particle sizes. Masking the smell and taste of the drug is very important for the pharmaceutical companies and this process is effectively executed by Conventional Coating Pan. With constantly increasing demands of the pharmaceutical products, most of the companies use Automatic Tablet Coater for tablet coating.

Besides, machines such as Mass Mixer, Vacuum Tray Dryer, Starch Paste Kettle, Tablet De Duster, Ribbon Blender, and Tablet & Capsule Inspection Machine are also used in different stages of the tablet manufacturing process. Over the years, there has been good research and development in this area and today, an extensive range of tablet manufacturing machine is available for the pharmaceutical industry.

There are six things to think before selection of an equipment for tablet making.

1) **Scalability**

   Scaling up a tableting process from R&D to production can be challenging, with formulation problems likely to arise in the form of tablet defects. Advanced R&D processes help to prevent issues by mimicking the tablet compression characteristics of high-speed production equipment. Compaction simulators, for example, can replicate the punch movement and speed of a rotary tablet press, mimicking compression time, dwell time, and strain rate.

   "This allows formulation scientists to develop tablets as if they were using production equipment, so there is less surprise when they move to industrialisation.

2) **Return on investment (ROI)**

   Price is important for pharmaceutical laboratories, but ROI is what matters most. The right tablet press should result in significant cost savings for your business. It is important to select a system with comprehensive data acquisition and analysis software. This can help to evaluate tablet quality and develop more robust formulations, meaning less defects and downtime during production.

   With compaction simulation technology, companies can avoid performing experimental development work on their production equipment. Beyond the obvious benefit of freeing up the industrial press for commercial manufacturing, this can result in several cost savings.

   A CDMO (Contract Development and Manufacturing Organization) specialising in oral solid dosage forms, notable reductions in costly product waste is an advantage. The CDMO can also calculate the significant time savings when using the compaction simulator. The reduced time in the assembly and cleaning phases, experiments that would have taken 168 hours on an industrial press, took just 24 hours on the compaction simulator.

   A compaction simulator can also be beneficial during production. For example, if quality control is registering a high number of reject tablets, the technology can be used for troubleshooting formulation issues, thus helping the companies in reducing downtime while optimising output[22].

3) Versatility

A versatile R&D tablet press is key for flexible drug development. This is where compaction simulation really shines. With one compaction simulator, one can have access to several production processes in one place. One can simulate all the high-speed production presses or roller compactors on the market, this means versatility.

Versatility and flexibility is a way to secure the investment for the next 10 to 15 years. It is critical to find an R&D press that can not only answer the needs of current project but also those far into the future, whether they may be multi-layer tablets or tab-in-tab.

4) Ease of use

Tablet compression and powder characterisation technology is primarily complex, but it should not seem so to users. Most vendors will claim to offer intuitive software, so it is important to consider what actions are to be taken during development to ensure this.

The complexity of the equipment in the technical areas is hidden and can make it easy for a beginner in compression or an expert. This goes from set-up of the experiment to cleaning and dismantling, not forgetting analysis. The software is made flexible, whether it is desired to look at simple graphs or go deeper into the raw data.

5) Operator safety

Insufficient toxicology data during the early stages of drug development means new molecules should be treated as dangerous until more is known. With increasing use of highly potent active pharmaceutical ingredients (HPAPIs) by pharmaceutical companies, purchasing tablet presses with containment features is becoming more and more critical.

When selecting a system, it is essential to first evaluate the user safety level (i.e. OEB level) the products necessitate. After that, make sure to balance safety against ergonomics, as the introduction of large isolator boxes has the potential to turn a nifty tablet press into a huge, cumbersome machine.

6) Strong service network

Maintenance is necessary to keep the tablet press running smoothly throughout a long service life. This is usually a simple calibration or a quick change of wear parts. In the time-pressured environment of pharmaceutical R&D, slow service from the tablet press partner could set back in time and money.

The company now has tableting experts positioned across the world to service machines, and help the customers to get the most from their purchases. It is the quality of a vendor's service and the scientific expertise behind their machines that the buyers should value the most. The team should speak the same language as the scientists.

In general, the equipment used in commercial manufacturing of tablets, are used in pilot plant but with lower capacity[23].

EQUIPMENT SELECTION FOR CAPSULES

Capsule is the most versatile of all dosage forms. Capsules are solid dosage forms in which one or more active ingredient(s). Inert ingredients are enclosed in a small shell or container usually made of gelatine. There are two types of capsules, "hard" and "soft". The hard capsule is also called "two pieces" as it consists of two pieces in the form of small cylinders closed at one end, the shorter piece is called the "cap" which fits over the open end of the longer piece, called the "body". The soft gelatine capsule is also called as "one piece". Capsules are available in many sizes to provide dosing flexibility. Unpleasant drug tastes and odours can be masked by the tasteless gelatine shell. The administration of liquid and solid drugs enclosed in hard gelatine capsules is one of the most frequently utilized dosage forms.

Properties of empty capsule: Empty capsules contain a significant amount of water that acts as a plasticizer for the gelatine film and is essential for their function. The specification for standard moisture content for hard gelatine capsules is between 13 % w/w and 16 % w/w. This value can vary depending on the environmental conditions to which they are exposed, that is at low humidity they will lose moisture and become brittle, and at high humidity they will gain moisture and soften. The moisture content can be maintained within the correct specification by storing them in sealed containers at a specified temperature and humidity. Capsules are readily soluble in water at 37°C. When the temperature falls below this, their rate of solubility decreases. At below about 30°C they are insoluble and simply absorb water, swell and distort. This is an important factor to take into account during disintegration and dissolution testing. Because of this, most Pharmacopoeia have set a limit of 37°C ± 1°C for the media for carrying out these tests. Capsules made from have different solubility profile, being soluble at temperatures as low as 10°C.

Types of materials for filling into hard gelatine capsules:

- Dry solids – powders, pellets, granules or tablets
- Semisolids – suspensions or pastes
- Liquids – non-aqueous liquids

The standard sizes, volume, locked length and external diameter of two pieces capsules are given in Table 1.7.

Table 1.7 Standard sizes of two pieces capsule.

Size	Volume (ml)[A]	Locked length (mm)[A]	External diameter (mm)[A]
5	0.13	11.1	4.91
4	0.21	14.3	5.31
3	0.3	15.9	5.82
2	0.37	18	6.35
1	0.5	19.4	6.91
0	0.68	21.7	7.65
0E	0.7	23.1	7.65
00	0.95	23.3	8.53
000	1.37	26.14	9.91
13	3-2	30	15.3
12	5	40.5	15.3
12el	7.5	57	15.5
11	10	47.5	20.9
10	18	64	23.4
7	24	78	23.4
Su07	28	88.5	23.4

One-piece shell capsules are formed, filled, and sealed in a single process on the same machine and are available in a wide variety of sizes, shapes, and colours. The most common type of one-piece capsule is that produced by a rotary die process that results in a capsule with a seam. The soft gelatine shell is somewhat thicker than that of two-piece capsules and is plasticized by the addition of polyols such as glycerine, sorbitol, or other suitable material. Depending on the nature of the fill material, the ratio of the plasticizer to the gelatine can be varied to change the flexibility of the shell its intended usage, or environmental conditions. In most cases, one-piece capsules are filled with liquids. Typically, APIs are dissolved or suspended in a liquid vehicle. Classically, an oleaginous vehicle such as a vegetable oil has been used. However, the nonaqueous, water-miscible liquid vehicles such as the lower molecular weight polyethylene glycols now are more common. The physicochemical properties of the vehicle can be selected to ensure stability of the API and to influence the release profile from the capsule shell.

The equipment should be selected for plant activities according to the equipment to be used for commercial manufacture of capsules. Same equipment of less capacity are used for pilot scale manufacturing. The completely automatic machine most commonly used for capsule production consists of mechanisms for automatically dipping, spinning, drying, stripping, trimming, and joining the capsules.

- Stainless steel pins are used on which the capsule is formed and controls some of the final critical dimensions of the capsule.
- One hundred and fifty pairs of these pins are dipped in to gelatine sol of carefully controlled viscosity to form caps and bodies simultaneously. The pins are usually rotated to distribute the gelatine uniformly, during which time the gelatine may be set or gelled by a blast of cool air.
- The pins are moved through a series of controlled air drying kilns for the gradual and precisely controlled removal of water. The capsules are striped from the pins by bronze jaws and trimmed to length by stationary knives while the capsule halves are being spun in chucks or collets. After being trimmed to exact length, the cap and body sections are joined and ejected from the machine. The entire cycle of the machine lasts approximately 45 min.
- Thickness of the capsule wall is controlled by the viscosity of the gelatine solution and the speed and time of dipping. Mould pin dimensions, precise drying, and machine control relating to cut lengths are matters that are critical to the final dimensions. Precise control of drying conditions is essential to the ultimate quality of the cast film.

Industrial scale filling: the machines for industrial-scale filling of hard gelatine capsules come in great variety of shapes and sizes, varying from semi- to fully automatic and ranging in output from 5000 to 15000 per hour. Automatic machines can be either continuous in motion, like a rotary tablet press, or intermittent, where the machine stops to perform a function and then indexes round to the next position to repeat the operation on a further set of capsules. The capsule filling process is illustrated in figure 1.6 and 1.7.

EQUIPMENT SELECTION FOR LIQUID ORALS

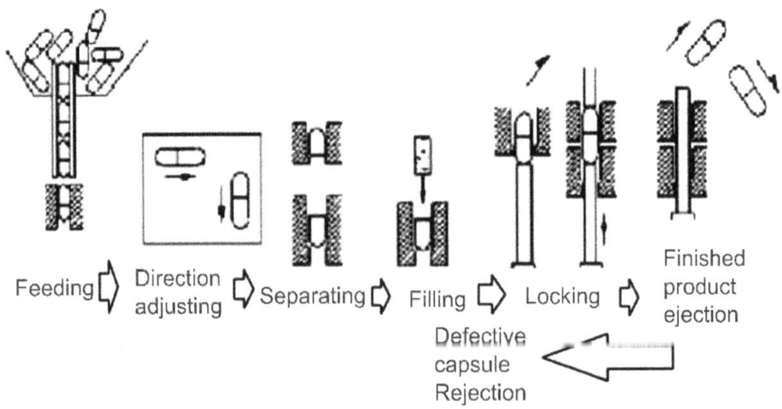

Fig.1.6 Flow diagram of capsule filling.

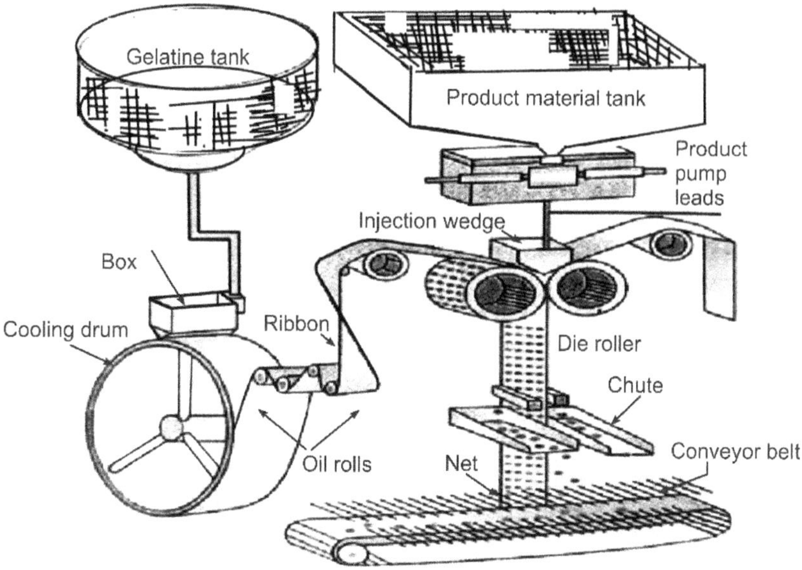

Fig.1.7 Schematic diagram of automatic soft gelatin capsule filling machine.

The liquid dosage forms may be classified as per their application as follows:

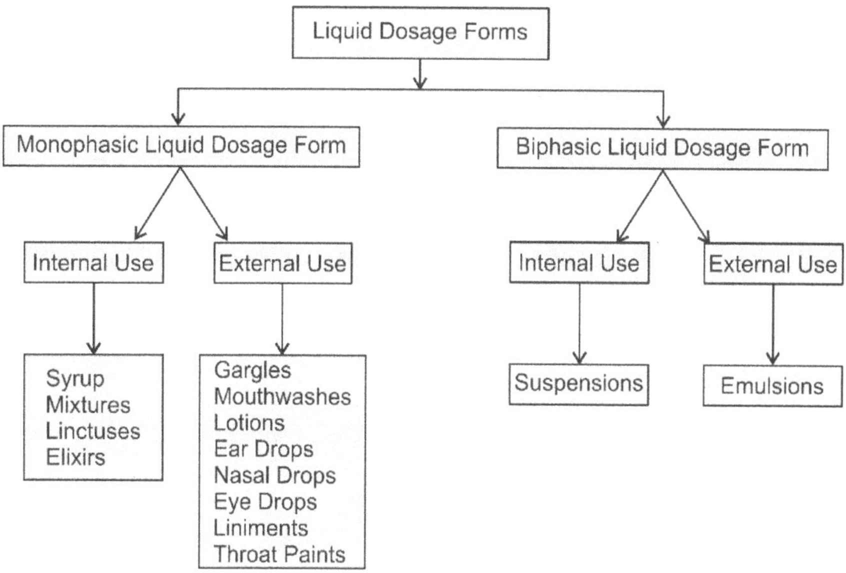

Fig.1.8 Classification of liquid dosage form.

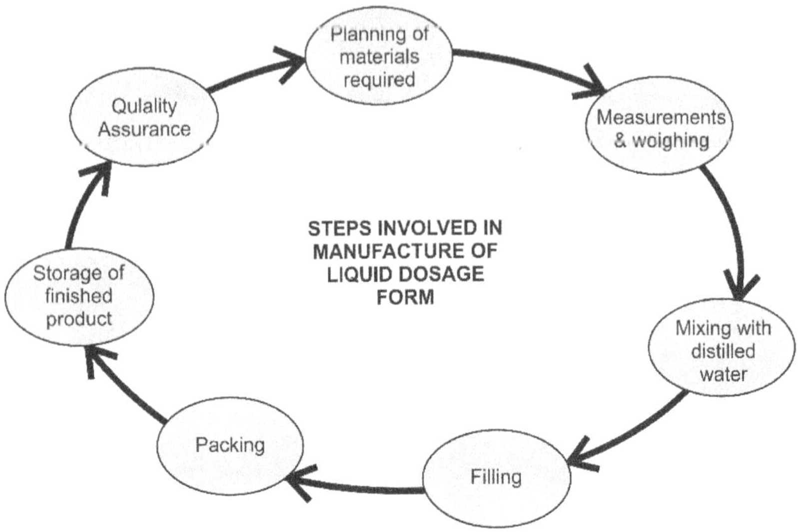

Fig.1.9 Schematic diagram of steps involved in manufacture of liquid dosage form.

Steps involved in liquid manufacturing process:

- Planning of material needs.
- Measurements and weighing
- Filling and Packing.
- Quality assurance.
- Critical features of liquid manufacturing
- Physical Plant.
- Heating, ventilation and air regulating system.

The impact of extended processing durations at suboptimal temperatures should be evaluated in terms of repercussions on the physical or chemical stability of components as well as product.

Solution: The parameters to be considered are for scaling up of solutions are;

- Impeller diameter.
- Tank size (diameter)
- Number of impellers.
- Impeller type.
- Mixing capabilities of impeller.
- Rotational speed of the impeller.
- Height of the filled capacity of the tank.
- Number of baffles.
- Transfer system.
- Clearance between Impeller Blades and wall of the mixing tank.

Filtration device should remove desirable elements but should not eliminate active or adjuvant substances. It should remove desired materials but should not remove active or adjuvant ingredients. Passivation of Stainless Steel (Pre-reacting the SS with acetic acid or nitric acid solution to eliminate. the surface alkalinity of the Stainless Steel. Pre-reacting the SS with acetic acid or nitric acid solution removes the surface alkalinity of the Stainless Steel.

Suspension:

The criteria to be considered are for scaling up of suspension are;

- Versator that avoids air entrapment prevent air entrapment
- Wetting of suspending agent.
- Addition and dispersion of suspending agents.
- Selection of the equipment according to batch size.
- Time and temperature necessary for hydration of the suspending agent.
- Mixing speeds, high speed should not be utilised since it leads to air entrapment.
- Mesh size should be able to remove the foreign particles and sieve determines depending on the manufacturing batch size testing.

Emulsion:

The parameters to be examined are for scale up of emulsion are:

- Homogenizing equipment.
- Temperature.
- Mixing equipment
- Phase densities.
- In-process or final product filters.
- Phase volumes.
- Screens, pumps and filling equipment.
- Phase viscosities.

The following equipment are recommended for the manufacture of oral/internal use preparations i.e. Syrups, Elixirs, Emulsions and suspensions, whichever is applicable, namely: -

1) Mixing and storage tanks (stainless steel),
2) Jacketed Kettle / Stainless steel tank (steam, gas or electrically heated).
3) Portable stirrer (electrically operated)
4) A colloid mill or suitable emulsifier (electrically operated)
5) Suitable filtration equipment (electrically operated)
6) Semi-automatic/automatic bottle filling machine

7) Pilfer proof cap sealing machine.

8) Water distillation unit or deioniser

9) Clarity testing inspection units.

A minimum area of thirty square meters for basic installation and ten square meters for Ancillary area is recommended.

EQUIPMENT SELECTION FOR PARENTERALS

The whole operation of manufacture of parenteral preparations (small volume injectables and large volume parenterally in glass and[24,25] plastic containers may be divided into the following separate areas/rooms, namely

Parenteral preparations in glass containers:

1) Water management area: this includes water treatment and storage
2) Containers and closures preparation area: This includes washing and drying of ampoules, vials, bottles and closures.
3) Solution preparation area: This includes preparation and filtration of solution.
4) Filling, capping and sealing area: This includes filling and sealing of ampoules and/or filling, capping and sealing of vials and bottles.
5) Sterilization area
6) Quarantine area
7) Visual inspection area
8) Packaging area

The following equipment is recommended for above-mentioned areas, namely

(a) Water management area,
   1) De-ionised water treatment unit
   2) Distillation (multi-column with heat exchangers) unit.
   3) Thermostatically controlled water storage tank.
   4) Transfer pumps.
   5) Stainless steel service lines for carrying water into user areas.

(b) Containers and closures preparation area,
   1) Automatic rotary ampoule/vial/bottle washing machine having separate air, water distilled water jets.
   2) Automatic closures washing machine,
   3) Storage equipment for ampoules, vials, bottles and closures.
   4) Dryer/sterilizer (double ended)
   5) Dust proof storage cabinets.
   6) Stainless steel benches/stools.

(c) Solution preparation area.
   1) Solution preparation and mixing stainless steel tanks and other containers.
   2) Portable stirrer

EQUIPMENT SELECTION FOR SEMISOLID PREPARATION

The following parameters have to be addressed during the scale up of semisolids:

- Mixing speed.
- Mixing apparatus (Could be able to transport semisolid substance from outer walls to the middle and from bottom to top of the kettle) (Could be able to move semisolid mass from outside walls to the centre and from bottom to top of the kettle).
- Motors (Drive mixing system with proper handling system at its most viscous stage) (Drive mixing system with appropriate handling system at its most viscous stage).
- Heating and cooling procedure.
- Component homogenization.
- Product transfer.
- Addition of active ingredients.
- Working temperature range.
- Shear during handling and transfer from manufacturing to holding tank to filling lines.
- Transfer pumps (Easily must transport viscous material without producing excessive shear and free of entrapped air) (Easily must move viscous material without applying excessive shear and free of entrapped air).
- Pumping rate.
- Pumping pressure necessary should be considered.
- Product compatibility with the pump surface.

The following equipment is recommended for different above-mentioned areas, for example:

a) Water management area
   1) De-ionised water treatment unit
   2) Distillation (multi-column with heat exchangers) unit.
   3) Thermostatically controlled water storage tank.
   4) Transfer pumps.
   5) Stainless steel service lines for carrying water into user areas.

b) Containers and closures preparation area
   1) Automatic rotary ampoule/vial/bottle washing machine having separate air, water distilled water jets.
   2) Automatic closures washing machine,
   3) Storage equipment for ampoules, vials, bottles and closures.
   4) Dryer/sterilizer (double ended)
   5) Dust proof storage cabinets.
   6) Stainless steel benches/stools.
c) Solution preparation area
   1) Solution preparation and mixing stainless steel tanks and other containers.
   2) Portable stirrer.
   3) Filtration equipment with cartridge and membrane filters/ bacteriological filters.
   4) Transfer pumps.
   5) Stainless steel benches/stools
d) Filling, capping and sealing area
   1) Automatic ampoule/vial/bottle filling, sealing and capping machine under laminar air flow workstation.
   2) Gas line (Nitrogen, Oxygen, Carbon dioxide) wherever required.
   3) Stainless steel benches / stools
e) Sterilization area
   1) Steam sterilizer preferably with computer control for sterilization cycle along with trolley sets for loading/unloading containers before and after sterilization).
   2) Hot air sterilizer (preferably double ended).
   3) Pressure leak test apparatus.
f) Quarantine area
   1) Storage cabinets.
   2) Raised platforms/steel racks.
g) Visual inspection area
   1) Visual inspection units (preferably conveyor belt type and composite white and black assembly supported with illumination).
   2) Stainless steel benches/stools.
h) Packaging area
   1) Batch coding machine (preferably automatic)
   2) Labelling unit (preferably conveyor belt type)
   3) Benches/stools

Exercise

Multiple Choice Questions

1. Fill in the blank with correct word given below

   Pilot plant is a ——- where 5M's like money, material, man, method & machine are utilised to produce the product

   a) Place b) Room

   c) Area d) Plant

2. Fill in the blank with correct word given below

   During scale up experiment in a pilot plant production & process control are evaluated, ——- and finalised.

   a) Done b) Evaluated

   c) Calibrated d) None of the above

3. Which of the following statements is correct?

   a) The main objective of a pilot plant is to prepare the product

   b) The main objective of a pilot plant is to optimise the operating parameters of the process

   c) The main objective of a pilot plant is to measure the process parameters

   d) The main objective of a pilot plant is to develop the method

4. Which of the following statements is correct?

   a) Pilot plant should be designed as per requirements of the company

   b) Pilot plant should be designed as per factory rules

   c) Pilot plant should be designed as per the WHO-GMP norms

   d) Pilot plant should be designed as per the pollution control norms

5. Which of the following statements is correct?

   a) Research pharmacist is responsible for initial scale up & initial production run

   b) Pharmaceutical Research team is responsible for pilot plant scale up technology

   c) Production department is responsible for pilot plant & scale up technology

   d) All the above

6. Which of the following statements is correct?

   a) The manufacturing sheet must be signed by any two no production personnel

b) The manufacturing sheet must be signed by two persons, one from manufacturing and other from Quality Control departments

c) The manufacturing sheet must be signed by two persons, one from manufacturing and other from R & D department

d) The manufacturing sheet must be signed by one who is directly responsible for manufacturing and other who is responsible for check up

7. Which of the following six things are to be thought before selecting equipment for manufacturing a tablet

   a) Scaleability, return of investment, versatility, ease of use, operator safety & strong service network

   b) Scaleability, return of goods, operator safety, ease of use, versatility & strong service network

   c) Scaleability, return of investment, ease to use, versatility, operator safety, & strong service network

   d) Scaleability, return of goods, ease to reprocess, operator safety, versatility, & strong service network

8. Which of the following liquid preparations is filled into a hard gelatine capsule?

   a) Aqueous liquid

   b) Nonaqueous liquid

   c) Mixture of aqueous and non-aqueous liquid

   d) None of the above

9. Fill in the blank with suitable word given below

   The specification for standard moisture content of hard gelatine capsules——- to ——-

   a) 13 percent to 16 percent b) 13 percent to 15 percent

   c) 10 percent to 15 percent d) 9 percent to 15 percent

10. Fill in the blank with suitable word given below

   A versatile R & D tablet press is ———— for flexible drug development

   a) Important b) Frequent

   c) Casual d) Required

11. What for CDMO stands?

   a) Construction of Drug Manufacturing Organisation

   b) Construction, Development & Manufacturing Office

   c) Contract Development & Manufacturing Organisation

   d) Contract Drug Manufacturing Office

12. Fill in the blank with a suitable word given below

    A significant amount of water present in capsule shell acts as ——- to the gelatine film.

    a) Coat
    b) Lubricant
    c) Disintegrant
    d) Plasticizer

13. Fill volume of standard 5 size capsule is….?

    a) 0.13 ml
    b) 0.15 ml
    c) 1.3 ml
    d) 0.21 ml

14. Fill in the blanks with suitable words given

    The most common type of one piece capsule is produced by —— ——- process

    a) Die and pin
    b) Rotating die and pin
    c) Rotary die
    d) Multiple dies

15. what is a criterion for scaling of suspension?

    a) Mixing equipment
    b) wetting of suspending agent
    c) In process or final product filler
    d) Phase volume

16. Which of the following criteria is related to emulsion manufacturing?

    a) Time and temperature necessary for hydration of the suspending agent
    b) Addition and dispersion of suspending agent
    c) Temperature
    d) Wetting of suspending agent

17. What is the minimum area required for installation of basic equipment?

    a) Fifteen square meters
    b) Thirty square foot
    c) Thirty square meters
    d) Fifteen square foot

18. Which of the following equipment is placed in water management area?

    a) Transfer pump
    b) Dust proof storage cabinet
    c) Portable stirrer
    d) Product transfer

19. Which of the following equipment is required for solution preparation area?

    a) Steriliser
    b) De-ionised water treatment unit
    c) Transfer pump
    d) Stainless steel benches

20. What is the equipment required for quarantine area?

    a) Storage tank
    b) Batch coding machine
    c) Pressure leak test apparatus
    d) Storage cabinets

Short Questions

1. What is pilot plant, define it. Do you think that pilot plant must mimic all the flow sheets? If not, what does it include? A pilot plant should be designed for what?
2. What are the significance of a pilot plant? What are the objectives of a pilot plant?
3. What are the basic requirements for designing a pilot plant?
4. Write down the activities of the machine for capsules, tablets and liquid filling and mention their capacities.
5. Give a floor plan for small pilot plan for tablet manufacturing, mention the areas required for each equipment.
6. Give a floor plan for tablet dosage form, not small one.
7. What do you mean by the specification sheets for active ingredients? Explain with the help of a specific example.
8. What are the main characteristics for selecting the equipment for tablet manufacturing. Briefly explain these.
9. What are the parameters for producing emulsion and suspension.
10. How do you select the equipment for manufacturing the parenteral products?

Long Questions

1. What is a pilot plant? How is it relevant to pharmaceutical industry? Explain the silent feature of a pilot plant.
2. What are the facilities required for a pharmaceutical pilot plant?
3. Explain how the communication between pilot plant and Quality Control and Production departments take place.
4. Explain how the equipment required for tablet manufacturing can be selected.
5. Write down how the equipment can be selected for liquid orals manufacturing.
6. How can you select the equipment for manufacturing the capsules and parenterals?
7. Discuss how can the equipment be selected for manufacturing of semisolid preparations.
8. Explain the preparation of a floor plan for manufacturing the tablets with the help of the relevant diagram.
9. Present in a tabular form the manufacturing instructions to prepare tablet and also the list of ingredients required.
10. Prepare the list of final tests to be performed for different types of Pharmaceutical products.

Answers

1	2	3	4	5	6	7	8	9	10	11	12	13	14	15	16	17	18	19	20
a	b	b	c	d	d	c	b	a	a	c	d	a	c	b	c	c	a	b	d

References

1. Baekeland, L.H., J. Ind. Eng. Chem. 8, 184, 1916.
2. Constant, L.G., Pilot plants for medium-sized companies, Chem. Eng. Prog. 56, Feb. 1984.
3. Floter, W., "Pressure leaching", Uranium Extraction Technology: Current Practice and New Developments in Ore Processing, OECD, Paris; 54-58, 1983.
4. Lowenstein, J.G., The pilot plant, Chem. Eng. 92 25, 62-76, 1985.
5. Leon Lachman, Herbert A Lieberman, Joseph L Kanig: The Theory and Practice of Industrial Pharmacy: Section IV: Chapter 23: Pilot Plant Scale-Up Techniques: 3rdedition, published by Varghese Publishing house,; 681-710, 2009.
6. James Swarbrick, James C Boylan: Encyclopaedia of Pharmaceutical Technology: Pilot Plant Design, Volume 12 New York,; 171-186, 2001.
7. Gomez AL, Strathy WA. Engineering Aspects of Process Scale-Up and Pilot Plant Design. In: Michael Levin, editor. Pharmaceutical Process Scale-Up. New York: Marcel Dekker Inc; p.311-324, 2002.
8. Roop K Khar, Farhan J Ahmad, A Vashishtha, S. Harder, GV Buskirk, JV Battista. Pilot Plant Scale-up and Production Management. In: Roop K Khar, SP Vyas, Farhan J Ahmad, Gaurav K Jain, Editors. Industrial Pharmacy. 4 th edition. New Delhi: CBS Publishers & Distributors Pvt Ltd,; pp. 947-1002, 2013.
9. Dhobale AV, Mahale AM, Shirsat M, Pethkar S, Chakote V. Recent Advances in Pilot Plant Scale Up Techniques - A Review. Indo Am J Pharm Res; 8(4): 1060-1068, 2018.
10. Gomez AL, Strathy WA. Engineering Aspects of Process Scale-Up and Pilot Plant Design. In: Michael Levin, editor. Pharmaceutical Process Scale-Up. New York: Marcel Dekker Inc; p. 311-324, 2002.
11. Pharmaceutics – The Science of Dosage form Design by M.E. Aulton, 2 nd Edition, Page no: (515-538).
12. Remington – The Science and Practice of Pharmacy, 20 th Edition, Volume – 1, Page no: (918-922).
13. The Theory and Practice of Industrial Pharmacy by Leon Lachman, Page no: (374-411).

14. Shah VP, Skelly JP, Barr WH, Malinowski H, Amidon GL. Scale-up of Controlled Release Products - Preliminary Considerations. Pharm Technol; 16(5):35-40, 1992.
15. FDA. Center for Drug Evaluation and Research, Guidance for Industry: Immediate Release Solid Oral Dosage Forms. Scale-up and Post-Approval Changes: Chemistry, Manufacturing and Controls, In Vitro Dissolution Testing, and In Vivo Bioequivalence Documentation [SUPAC-IR]; 1995.
16. Walker, S. E., et al.: The filling of molten and thixotropic formulations into hard gelatine capsules. J. Pharm. Pharmacol. 32, 389-393, 1980.
17. Bauer, K. H.: Die Herstellung von Hart- und Weich gelatine kapseln, in: Die Kapsel, ed. Fahrig, W., Hofer, U., Wissenschaftliche Verlagsgesellschaft mbH Stuttgart, 1983.
18. Cole, E.T.: Liquid filled and sealed hard gelatine capsules. Capsugel Library, BAS 210 2000.
19. Mounica, NVN, Sharmila, RV, Anusha, S, Evangeline, L, Nagabhushanam, MV, Nagarjuna Reddy, D; Scale up and Post approval changes (SUPAC) Guidance for Industry: A Regulatory note. Int J Drug Regul Aff.; 5(1): 13-19, 2017.
20. Sherman R. Technology & Product Architectures. In: Business Intelligence Guidebook. Science Direct; 2015.
21. Ogura T, Furuya Y, Matuura S. HPMC capsules: an alternative to gelatine. Pharm Tech Europe.; 10(11): 32-42, 1998.
22. D. Aviad Shapira, M.ASCE; and Marat Goldenberg Associate Professor, Dept. of Civil and Environmental Engineering, Technion–Israel Institute of Technology, Haifa 32000, Israel. Submitted: 11 November, 2003.
23. Marcelo M. Azambuja; and William J. O'Brien Assistant Professor, Dept. of Construction, Southern Illinois University Edwardsville.
24. David Arditi, Member, ASCE, Prof., Dept. of Civ. and Arch. Engineering, Illinois Inst. of Technol., Chicago, IL 60616.
25. Serdar Kale and Martino Tangkar Grad. Student, Dept. of Civ. and Arch. Engineering., Illinois Inst. of Technol., Chicago, IL. Published: 01 December 1997.

CHAPTER - 2

Scale Up

Importance, Scaling up, Technology Transfer from R&D to Pilot Plant to Plant Scale, Process Scale up for Tablets, Process Scale up for Capsules, Scale-up and Post Approval Changes (SUPAC), Process Scale Up for Liquid Orals, Process Scale Up for Semisolids, Process Scale Up for Parenterals, Process Scale Up for NDDs Products, Niosomes, Stress Formulas, Stress on Equipments, Stress on Product Uniformity, Stress on Stability, Stress on Raw Materials, Stress on Physical Layout, Stress on Input, Stress on In-process and Finished Product, Specifications, Problems Encountered during Transfer of Technology

IMPORTANCE

The integrity of a drug during a pharmaceutical manufacturing is maintained through scale-up. It is essential for producers who wish to grow their operation while ensuring high standards and legal compliance.

During the transition from R&D to manufacturing, the operators scale up their operation several times. Each time it is made sure that they set safe and realistic goals. A successful product goes through the scaling process several times before its commercial manufacturing.

At larger scales powder handling is being recognised as a new headache to manage because it completely changes the whole process. To do this new single use technologies that were not part of the original smaller scope need to be validated. The primary conditions are to make sure that (1) the powder is not getting into places where it should not go and (2) there is no chance of contamination risk. The single use solutions also need to be convenient and safe for the users.

One of the leaders in single use powder handling is that whose powder handling products are designed to be compatible with pharmaceutical manufacturing operations of numerous capacities.

Across the globe around 300,000 successful product installations for which pharmaceutical and biopharmaceutical companies rely on for their powder transfer systems every day, from cGMP to nanogram levels.

One of the major concerns pharmaceutical manufacturers face during transitioning from a small-scale to a largescale operation is that they face a higher risk of contamination of the product when they get to grips with new processes. To minimise risk of contamination, the entire pharmaceutical processing system must be closed. Single and multiple-use containment systems keep powdered materials contained inside a specially formulated film. In this way, the product can be made significantly less likely to come into contact with foreign contaminants.

Single-use solutions are beneficial. They are disposed of after each use. This minimises time wasted on cleaning validations, weigh and dispense steps, and concerns about powder contaminations.

- The importance of quality by design (QbD) for risk management, cost reduction, and meeting regulatory requirements in product and process development has been explained in the pharmaceutical industry over the past decade[1]. The primary goal of QbD is to develop pharmaceutical products. This can consistently satisfy patient's healthcare needs in terms of safety, efficacy, and performance. This is defined in the quality target product profile (QTPP)[2]. For this reason, QbD can be divided into several steps: Critical quality attributes (CQAs), which are directly linked to the safety and efficacy of pharmaceutical products, are adopted in the QTPP through critical assessment, such as prior knowledge and pre-clinical or clinical studies.
- Risk assessment (RA) is performed to assess the degree of risk for material attributes and process parameters on CQAs. Critical material attributes (CMAs) and critical process parameters (CPPs) are identified.
- The effects of CMAs and CPPs on CQAs can be quantified to identify their relationship. This step can be performed through design of experiments (DoE).
- A multi-dimensional design space consisting of a combination of CMAs and CPPs ensures that desirable CQAs are derived through the DoE. A control strategy is established based on this design space to ensure the safety, efficacy, and performance of pharmaceutical products[1-5]. Initially, the research on the development of the pharmaceutical manufacturing process was performed through DoE at the laboratory-scale to establish an efficient control strategy. A multi-dimensional design space containing a combination of CPPs was obtained on the basis of the laboratory-scale experimental data. However, the process variability—batch size or manufacturing equipment changes—during the scale-up process makes it difficult to transform the design space to a larger scale, for example, pilot-scale or commercial scale[6,7]. Hence, an alternative approach is found necessary for pharmaceutical QbD to establish a control strategy for efficient scale-up of the manufacturing process. Recently, the simulation of manufacturing process, performed using a physics-based model, has been applied in the pharmaceutical industry[8-10].

Physics-based models have been preferred because they can provide a detailed scientific explanation of the manufacturing process[9]. Moreover, these models are somewhat predictable, even outside the areas of the experimental space. These can easily be scaled up. These are based on the equations of mass, momentum, and energy conservation in the manufacturing processes[11].

Physics-based models include the discrete element method (DEM), computational fluid dynamics (CFD), and finite element method (FEM). Out of these DEM is a numerical method that simulates the dynamic behaviour of particles in a system[12]. CFD provides insights into the mathematical physics of fluid flow[13]. FEM predicts the behaviour of particles by dividing the process into finite elements or volumes. Both models are located in the field of continuum mechanics. DEM is commonly used to simulate pharmaceutical manufacturing processes, such as blending, granulation, and coating.

Blending is an important and common manufacturing process used to prepare a solid dosage form of pharmaceutical drugs[14]. Blending is performed mainly in rotating devices, such as V-blenders, double-cone blenders, and cubic blenders[15]. The mixture of powders should have a degree of homogeneity during blending to ensure the quality of solid dosage forms, such as tablets and capsules. The homogeneity of the powder mixture is affected by several factors, such as (1) material attributes, for example, particle density, shape, size distribution, surface properties, and cohesive strength, (2) process parameters, for example, design of blender, rotational speed, filling level, and blending time[16]. These factors can affect the agglomeration and segregation of the mixture during the blending process, which further affect the mixture's homogeneity. However, sufficient number of experiments are not performed to confirm changes in the agglomeration and segregation of the mixture caused by these factors. Simulations of blending can provide deeper insights to understand the material attributes, process parameters, and blending mechanisms for the blending process[17]. A DEM simulation might be useful in that it would provide detailed information that could not be obtained through experiments on the blending process.

Intermediate critical quality attributes (IQAs) and CPPs for the blending process have been identified in the QbD approach. The operating space has been produced by performing a laboratory-scale DoE in a V-blender. Changes in operating space can occur during the scale-up process, including batch size and equipment changes, etc. These are validated using the DEM model. Pilot-scale blending simulations are performed in a V-blender and double-cone blender, and the results are statistically evaluated with experimental results. The QbD-based DEM model developed can be an efficient alternative approach to the scale-up strategy of the pharmaceutical manufacturing process. In addition, this study can provide the basis for further studies regarding scale-up strategy in other pharmaceutical manufacturing processes.

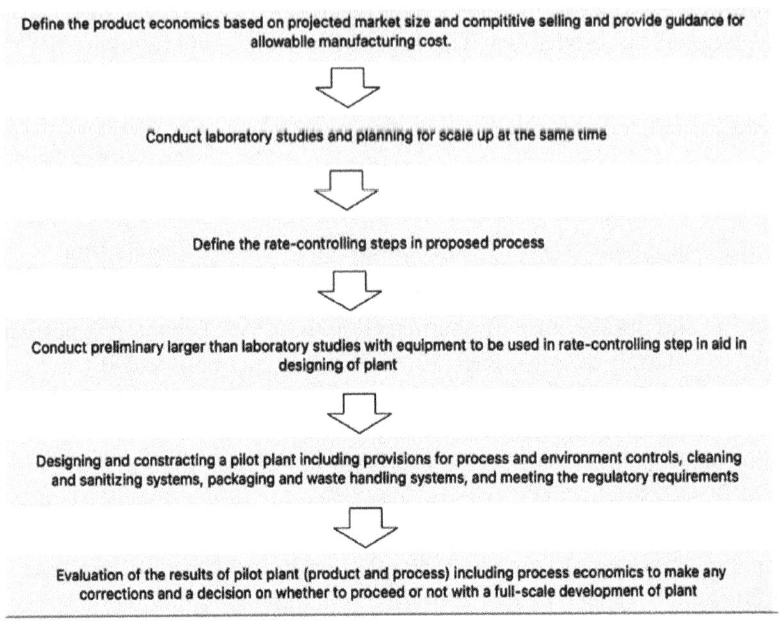

Fig.2.1 Schematic diagram of steps involved in scale up technology.

SCALING UP

Technology transfer (scaling up) in pharmaceutical industry is done for following reasons:

- To find out necessary information to transfer technology from R&D to actual manufacturing by sorting out various information obtained during R&D.
- To find out necessary information related to transfer of technology on existing products between various manufacturing places.
- To illustrate specific procedures and points of concern for the two reasons of technology transfer to contribute to smooth technology transfer. This applies to the technology transfer through R&D. The production of drug substances or drug products and the technology transfer, related to post-marketing, changes in the manufacturing places.

Technology transfer has the following importance as extended benefits of R&D to the society:

1) In the pharmaceutical industry, designing of dosage form the requirements to scale up at several stages have been taking place; such as pilot scale from 0.5-2 kg batch can be scaled up to 5-10 kg and while commercial production is more than 100 kg. Production scale typically ranges from 200 kg to 1000 kg. It involves the manufacturing of drug products with increasing their batch sizes with the help of larger equipment.

2) Scale-up involves the transfer of technology and the knowledge that has been gathered during the small-scale development of products and processes. Usually, research has been carried out on a small scale before it is produced for a large-scale commercial batch. Technology transfer is important for research activities to materialize on a large scale for commercialization especially in the case of developing a drug product.
3) To elucidate necessary information for transfer the technology from R&D to actual manufacturing by sorting out various information obtained during R&D.
4) Necessary information are being transferred for the technology transfer of existing products between various manufacturing places.
5) Commercialization of university-discovered technologies works as a driver of economic growth and the universities plays a major role in bringing innovative ideas from inventions to market.

Transfer of technology can potentially generate revenues for the universities, to create research in collaboration with industry. Therefore, the regional economic growth can improve. The development and transfer of knowledge and technology has been found critical for success in all types of industries[12]. Recently, the awareness has grown that an appropriate transfer of manufacturing technologies (technology transfer) is important to upgrade quality of drug as designed during R&D. This refers to the final product during manufacture as well as to assure the stability of quality of products. For many reasons, technology is being transferred between the contract giver and contract acceptor during manufacture.

- The knowledge is more effectively shared within an organization, the more efficiently the organization can operate.
- Continuous improvement is possible through increase of knowledge.
- New information may then become explicit knowledge; that is, the knowledge that can be set down in procedures, handbooks or process maps.
- Transfer of knowledge within a company can be called as "organizational learning". Traditionally, it refers to the handbooks, policies, SOP's and even E-mail. It can facilitate organizational learning, but additional means must be considered to share the knowledge more effectively.
- Technology transfer team represents all stake holders, from development to engineering to production.
- Technology transfer team includes professionals, representing supply chain management, packaging, health and safety.
- It encourages use of technology developed using taxpayer to benefit society.
- It demonstrates relevant research program and value.

- It allows researchers to partner with the private sector, leverage resources, and share the ideas in a protected environment.
- It gives increased visibility to researchers and enables them to generate and earn royalty income.
- Innovative R&D.
- Drug Approvals.
- Compliant and effective commercialization.
- It ensures safety, purity and effective drug product.
- It provides consistent interpretation of GMP regulations.
- Brings new, more effective products to market faster.
- Cost effective production and distribution.
- Superior return on investment to shareholders / stakeholders.

WHO Guiding Principles of Technology Transfer

WHO has been guiding principles on transfer of technology. These are used to serve as a framework which can be applied in a flexible manner rather than a strict rigid guidance. Attention has been given to the quality aspects, in line with WHO's mandate.

a) At some stage in the life-cycle of most products, transfer of processes to an alternative site occurs from development, scale-up, manufacturing, production and launch, to the post-approval phase.

b) Transfer of technology is defined as "*a logical procedure that controls the transfer of any process together with its documentation and professional expertise between development and manufacture or between manufacturing sites*".

c) The ever-changing business strategies of pharmaceutical companies have increasingly involved intra- and inter-company transfers of technology for the reasons such as need for additional capacity, relocation of operations or consolidations and mergers.

d) The WHO Expert Committee on Specifications for Pharmaceutical Preparations recommended in its forty-second report that WHO address this issue through preparation of WHO guidelines in this area.

e) Transfer of technology requires a documented, planned approach/process using trained and knowledgeable personnel working within a quality system, with documentation of data covering all aspects of development, production and quality control. Usually there is a sending unit, a receiving unit and the unit managing the process which may or may not be a separate entity.

f) For successful transfer, the following general principles and requirements should be met:

- The project plan should include the quality aspects of the project and be based on the principles of quality risk management.
- The capabilities of the sending unit (SU) and at the receiving unit (RU) should be similar, but not necessarily identical, and facilities that an equipment should operate according to similar operating principles;
- A comprehensive technical gap analysis between the SU and RU including technical risk assessment and potential regulatory gaps, as required.
- Adequate trained staff should be made available or the personnel should be trained at the Receiving unit;
- Regulatory requirements in the countries of the SU and the RU, and in any country where the product is prepared for supply, should be taken into account and interpreted consistently throughout any transfer programmed project.
- There should be effective process and product knowledge transfer
- Technology transfer can be considered successful, if there is documented evidence that the RU can routinely reproduce the transferred product, process or method against a predefined set of specifications as agreed with the Sending unit.
- In the event that the RU identifies particular problems with the process during the transfer, the RU should communicate those back to the SU to ensure continuing knowledge management.
- Technology transfer projects, between different companies, have legal and economic implications. If such issues may include intellectual property rights, royalties, pricing, conflict of interest and confidentiality, are expected to impact on open communication of technical matters in any way. They should be addressed before and during planning and execution of the transfer.
- Any lack of transparency may lead to ineffective transfer of technology.
- Some of the principles outlined in this document may also be applicable to manufacturing investigational pharmaceutical products for clinical trials as a part of research and development, but this is not the main focus of this guidance and has been excluded due to the complexity of the processes.

TECHNOLOGY TRANSFER FROM R&D TO PILOT PLANT TO PLANT SCALE

In the pharmaceutical industry, the technology transfer may broadly refer to the processes required for successful movement from drug discovery to product development, clinical trial and fullscale commercialization. Usually, it is defined as transferring of technical know-how for manufacturing the product from the development in laboratories or in the pilot plant into full commercial scale manufacturing facilities. In cases, where a secondary commercialization becomes necessary, it also involves transfer to different facilities in multiple regions and countries. Appropriate technology transfer includes the transfer of scientific information, capability, technological basis of the product and process, and analytical test methods from a knowledge centre (donor) to the manufacturing plant (receptor). For a typical research-based pharmaceutical company, drug discovery and development into distinct stages are clearly described in Figure 2.2.

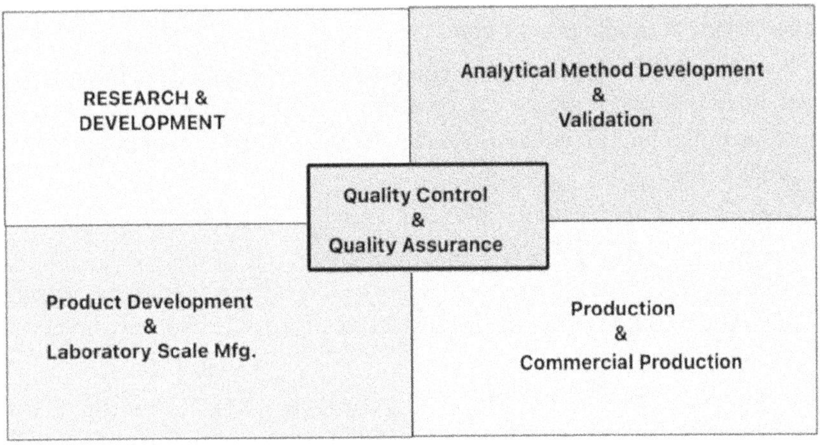

Fig.2.2 Steps involved in technology transfer from R&D to commercial production.

It is the process by which an original innovator of technology makes its technology available to commercial partner. This will exploit the technology. So, there are 3 standards in the definition of technology:

- First, knowledge must be systematic. This means that it must be organized in terms of providing solutions to problems.
- Second, knowledge must exist in certain places like in someone's head or in documents, and must be able to be presented, so it must be able to be transferred from one person to another.
- Third, it must have purpose-orientation, so that it can be utilized for useful purposes in industry, farming, and commercial fields[18].

Technology transfer is the process by which the developers of technologies make the technology available to a commercial partner, who exploits the technology. There are two types of Technology Transfer, (1) vertical and (2) horizontal. Vertical Technology transfer refers to transfer of technology from basic research to development and production respectively, whereas Horizontal Technology transfer refers to the movement and application of technology used in one place or context to another place. According to the WHO, Transfer of technology is defined as *a logical procedure. It controls the transfer of any process together with its documentation and professional expertise between development and manufacture or between manufacture sites.* It is a systematic procedure that is followed to pass the documented knowledge and experience gained during development and/ or commercialization to an appropriate, responsible and authorized party. Technology transfer embodies both the transfer of documentation and the demonstrated ability of the receiving unit (RU) to effectively perform the critical elements of the transferred technology, to the satisfaction of all parties and any applicable regulatory bodies[19]. The development and transfer of knowledge and technology has been and will continue to be critical for success in pharmaceutical industry. The transfer of technology is considered as both fundamental and significant to the drug discovery and development process for any new medicinal entity. This process is important for to elucidate necessary information for technology transfer from R & D (Research & Development) to PDL (product development laboratory).

Technology Transfer in Pharmaceutical Industry has been viewed from the perspective of Innovation and Research & Development. Since research is carried out in laboratories on small scale before it could be produced on commercial scale. Thus, Technology Transfer is important for such research to materialize on a larger scale for commercialization in case of developing and under developing countries. Technology Transfer is an integral part of New Drug Discovery and development of new medicinal products. Thus if Technology Transfer process to production site is carried out at an affordable cost, the cost of product development would not raise during pilot scale up. For successful technology transfer of a product, the Departments responsible in a pharmaceutical industry are:

- Research & Development,
- Production,
- Engineering,
- Quality Control and
- Quality Assurance

Technology Transfer is the intersection between business, science, engineering, law and government. Technology transfer is the process by which basic science research and fundamental discoveries are developed into practical and commercially relevant applications and products. Whether a tablet, a transdermal patch, a topical ointment, or an injectable, the transformation of a pharmaceutical prototype into a successful product requires the cooperation of many individuals[20]. Traditionally, technology transfer teams were charged with moving a physical process from research and development into production while that the role remains critical, today's transfer team plays a larger part, helping the company attain its strategic goals throughout the product life cycle[21]. The research is also intended to propose some regulations to realize technology transfer necessary for high quality and stable manufacturing of developed products and existing products by reviewing technology transfer based on the following ideas.

- The technology transfer means actions to transfer information and technologies necessary to realize quality of design of drugs during manufacturing
- Appropriate technology transfer is important to upgrade the quality of design to be the quality of product, and ensure stable and high quality of the product.
- It should be noted that drugs may influence human lives and health, and their raw materials, compositions and manufacturing methods are changed during their long term manufacturing and marketing.
- To assure the drug quality, it is desired to make sure 5 W's and 1 H, that is what, when and why information should be transferred to where and by whom and how to transfer, then share knowledge and information of the drug product between transferring and transferred parties.
- The technology transfer does not mean one time actions taken by the transferring party toward the transferred party, but means continuous information exchange between the both parties to maintain the product manufacturing[22].

The successful technology transfer from research and development (R&D), the transferring site, to the commercial Production site, the receiving site, is a critical process in the development and launch of a new medicinal product. It can be extremely costly for a company if things go wrong during the transfer process, resulting in delays to launching a new product on the market and lost sales. Also, it can take increased resource, time and cost to make corrective actions following an unsuccessful transfer. Progressive pharmaceutical companies are therefore placing more attention to streamlining and optimizing their technology transfer process to ensure the rapid and successful introduction of a new medicinal product to market.

a) The transfer of technology from R & D (sending unit) to manufacturing site (Receiving unit) is the key step to getting a high quality to the marketplace.
b) A thorough review, manufacturing modes of operation (including batch size and recommended equipment) can be proposed for the initial scale up batches.
c) R & D should recommend any in process tests and tentative finished product specification, which have optimized for the formula.
d) During initial scale up batches, all processing parameters and finished product specification should be challenged.

e) Once a final manufacturing has been established, key process data and product specification should be tracked closely to establish normal process variability.

PROCESS SCALE UP FOR TABLETS

The art for designing of prototype using the data obtained from the pilot plant model is called scale up.

Objectives

- To try the process on a model of proposed plant before committing large sum of money on a production unit.
- To identify the critical feature of the process.
- Guidelines for production and process control.
- To provide master manufacturing formula with instructions for manufacturing procedure.
- To avoid the scale - up problems.
- Evolution and validation of process and equipment's

Process scale up:

Scale-up is generally defined *as the process of increasing the batch size.* Scale-up of a process can also be viewed as a procedure for applying the same process to different output volumes. There is a subtle difference between these two definitions: batch size enlargement does not always translate into a size increase of the processing volume. In mixing applications, scaleup is indeed concerned with increasing the linear dimensions from the laboratory to the plant size. On the other hand, processes exist (such as, tableting) for which "scale-up" simply means enlarging the output by increasing the speed. To complete the picture, one should point out special procedures (especially in biotechnology) in which an increase of the scale is counterproductive and "scale-down" is required to improve the quality of the product. In moving from R&D to production scale, it is sometimes essential to have an intermediate batch scale. This is achieved at the so-called pilot scale, which is defined as the manufacturing of drug product by a procedure fully representative of and simulating that used for full manufacturing scale. This scale also makes possible the production of enough product for clinical testing and samples for marketing. However, inserting an intermediate step between R&D and production scales does not in itself guarantee a smooth transition. A well-defined process may generate a perfect product in both the laboratory and the pilot plant and then fail quality assurance tests in production[23]. It is procedure of transferring the results of R&D obtained on laboratory scale to the pilot plant and finally to production scale. Process scale up can also be viewed as procedure for applying the same process to different output volume.

Process of changing the equipment ,machine speed or process steps to enable large scale manufacturing scale up of a process that involve powder handling is especially difficult because the dynamic behaviour of powders is not very well understood. Process scale up is done to give the quality to the product and for extensive scientific knowledge of the physiochemical process that transform the incoming materials into the finals products, hence Scale up gives a clear cut idea about the formulations and help us to control the critical process parameters by proper process optimization. When scale up is applied to granulation process, the effects of the operational variable on powder properties and granule growth is not clearly known. So, scale up process of material in the solid state can be based on dimensional analysis, mathematical modelling, and computer simulation, most of the work in this field still depends on trial and error and the principles of geometric similarity. Ratio of some variables in small scale equipment should be equal to that of similar variables in equivalent larger-scale equipment. Dimensional analysis is a algebraic treatment of variables affecting a process. It does not result in a numerical equation, but experimental data are fitted to an empirical process equation that result in scale up being achieved more readily. Scale up gives us the various information about the product like physically and chemically stable therapeutic dosage forms, evaluate the formulation and process suitability for large scale, review of processing equipment, to identify the production and process control parameters, to identify the critical features of product and process, to provide the master formula and formulation evaluation for assessing criticality of ingredients. Identify the role of ingredient in formulation - decide criticality. HPMC film coating material or rate controlling polymer in matrix. b) Starch- diluents or disintegrate. c) Aesthetic or reservoir CR system. Scale up provide us the process monitoring and its control like complex city of process/formulation, process time limit, reproducibility, Simplicity for execution and Identifying processing stress on product quality, example a) Loss of viscosity during colloid milling, b) Evaporation of alcohol during processing. c) Capping during high speed compression. Stages of production of tablets:

- Material handling
- Dry blending
- Granulation
- Drying
- Reduction of particle size
- Blending
    - Dry blending
    - Direct compression
    - Slugging (dry granulation)

Material Handling

In laboratory, materials are scooped, dumped or poured by hand. It may work well for small or intermediate scale productions. For large scale productions, mechanical means is necessary. The simple means are: post hoist devices, devices for lifting and tilting drums but the sophisticated ones are: vacuum loading systems, screw feed system and meter pumping systems. The type of system selected depends upon the characteristics of the material such as density. Material handling system should cause no/minimal loss of material. The lengthy the transfer, the more is material loss. If one system being used for more than one material cross contamination should be avoided, accomplished by using validated cleaning procedures[24]

In the dry blending process using a binary cohesive-powder mixture which contains two different sizes, it is well known that finer particles adhere preferentially on the surface of the coarse particles. This type mixture has been called an interactive mixture. The blending of fine and coarse particles breaks down the agglomerates of fine and coarse powders, and produces an electric charge by contact and collision between particles. Fine and coarse particles do not revert to the former agglomerates. The blending operation produces new agglomerates in which fine particles are adhered to the surface of the coarse particles. In the first step, however, the coating particles randomly adhere onto the surface of the core particles. Problems of improper blending:

- Flow problem through the equipment
- Non- reproducible compression
- No content uniformity screening and/or milling of the ingredients before blending is done to make the process more reliable and reproducible.

The equipment used for blending are:

- V-blender
- Double cone blender
- Ribbon blender
- Slant cone blender
- Bin blender
- Orbiting screw blenders vertical and horizontal high intensity mixer

Scale up considerations:

- Time of blending
- Blender loading
- Size of blender

Granulation

Granulation process is a "*process whereby small particles are gathered into larger, masses in which the original particles can still be identified.*" Pharmaceutical granulation is the rapid breakdown of agglomerates is important to maximize the available surface area and aid in solution of the active drug. In ancient times the granulation process has been used within the pharmaceutical industry but in recent time, granulation technology has been widely used by a wide range of industries, such as Pharmaceutical, Food industries. The term "granulated" material is derived from the Latin word "granulatum," meaning grained. The fundamental research on mixing, segregation mechanisms of powder, surface chemistry, and material science are necessary to develop the theoretical framework of granulation technology. The granulated material can be obtained by direct size enlargement of primary particles, or size reduction from dry compacted material. These industries use agglomeration techniques to reduce dust, provide ease of handling, and enhance the material's ultimate utility. Granulation is process of particle designing[25].

Granulation methods

These are of two types

1. Wet methods utilizes some form of liquid to bind the primary particles.
2. Dry methods minimizes the granulation technical risks.

1. Wet granulation technology:

It is used on the low-shear mixers or the mixers/blenders normally used for dry blending such as ribbon mixers. There are a number of products currently manufactured using these low-shear granulators. The process control and efficiency has increased over the years. However, the industry has embraced high-shear granulators for wet granulation because of its efficient and reproducible process and modern process control capabilities[26].

2. Dry granulation methods:

Dry compaction technique like roller compaction is commonly used in the Pharmaceutical industry. There are a number of drug substances which are moisture sensitive and cannot be directly compressed. Pharmaceutical granulation process is used for tablet and sometimes for capsule dosage forms; however, the process is used to produce spherical granules for the modified release indications or to prepare granules as sprinkles to be used by paediatric patients. Pharmaceutical compounds are granulated done:

- To increase the uniformity of drug distribution in the product
- To increase the density of the material
- To enhance the flow rates and rate uniformity

- To facilitate metering or volumetric dispensing
- To reduce dust
- To improve the appearance of the product.
- Granulation encountered the incomplete description behaviour of powders in general.

Various Drying Techniques used for granulation in pharmaceutical manufacturing include wetting and nucleation, coalescence or growth, consolidation, and attrition or breakage. Initial wetting of the feed powder and existing granules by the binding fluid is strongly influenced by spray rate or fluid distribution and feed formulation properties.

Role of binders in wet-granulation process may be adhesives that are added to solid dosage formulations. The primary role of binders is to provide the cohesiveness essential for the bonding of the solid particles under compaction to form a tablet. In case of wet-granulation process, the binders promote size enlargement to produce granules and thus improve flowability of the blend during the manufacturing process. Binders may also improve the hardness of the tablets by enhancing intragranular as well as intergranular forces. In a direct compression process, binders often act as fillers and impart compressibility to the powder blend. The cohesive properties of binders may reduce friability of the tablets and thus help in their durability and elegance. Commonly used binders are Starch, Pregelatinized Starch, PVP, Methyl cellulose, HPMC New Natural and Synthetic binders: Khaya gum, Leucaena leucocephala seed gum, Anacardium occidentale gum, Gellant gum, Combination of detarium gum and vee gum. New synthetic binders used are Maltrodextrins, Chitosan derivative. The choice of granulation technique depends on various factors such as chemical and physical stability of the final dosage form, intended biopharmaceutical performance.

- High- and low-shear granulation
- Roller compaction
- Spray drying
- Fluid-bed granulation
- Extrusion spheronization
- Melt granulation and Pelletization

Effervescent Granulation Characterization

Granulation is a process used to prevent segregation of formulation components in a powder blend, bulk volume of granulation, improve blend flow, content uniformity, compressibility, and other properties. Chemical properties are equally important due to their impact on specifications of a dosage form such as content uniformity, chemical purity, and *in vitro* and *in vivo* performances such as bioequivalence. It is done to determine whether a pivotal bioequivalency batch passes or fails. Granule Size affect the dissolution performance which ultimately affect bioequivalence study. Physical characterization can be performed at molecular, particulate, or bulk (macroscopic) levels.

Drying is the most common and conventional method. It involves circulating hot air oven, which is heated by either steam or electricity. Scale up considerations for oven drying operation depends on:

- Air flow
- Air temperature
- The depth of the granulation on the trays

Too deep or too dense bed makes the drying process inefficient and if soluble dyes are involved, migration of the dye to the surface of the granules take place.

Drying times at specified temperatures and air flow rates must be established for each product and for each particular oven load. Fluidized bed dryers are an attractive alternative to the circulating hot air ovens. The important factor to be considered for scale up of fluidized bed dryer are, (1) optimum loads, (2) rate of airflow, (3) inlet air temperature and (4) humidity. Reduction of particle size: Particle size influences many properties of particulate materials and is a valuable indicator of quality and performance. This is true for powders, suspensions, emulsions, and aerosols. The size and shape of powders influences flow and compaction properties. Problems encountered due to improper particle size are:

- Too large particle size leads to the insufficient filling of the die cavity that results in weight variation of the tablets.
- In case of coloured granulation the coarser the granulation, greater are the chances of mottling.
- The very fine particle size leads to the flowability problem that results in the weight variation of the tablets.
- Capping (also occurs if the speed of the press is increased) Equipment used are:
- Oscillating granulator (for not too hard oversize granulation)
- Hammer mill
- Mechanical sieving device
- Screening device

Therefore, particle size distribution needs to be small enough to go through an 18 mesh screen. While machine type and condition play a role, the following list of items should also be considered.

Flowability:

Generally speaking, the smaller is the particle the better is the flow. Compare powdered sugar with granular sugar. But, the fine particles in powdered sugar aide dissolution but not flow.

Feeder clearance:

Particle size must be larger than the feeder clearance to prevent leakage.

Die table run-out:

If die table run-out increases, feeder clearance and particle size must also increase proportionately. To check the run-out, use a dial indicator to determine the variation of the die table.

Die fill:

Wide variations in particle sizes can cause inconsistent fill volumes.

Weight control:

Final volume is final weight. Larger particles pulled out of the die can reduce the final weight. Fine particles require more precise scrape-off and increase the need for a good scraper blade. *Compressibility:*

This is improved with increased particle size and decreases as particles become smaller and smaller. Small particles have less ability to lock together during compaction.

Hardness:

Smaller particles are more sensitive to over-compression.

Ejection force:

Small particles decrease interstitial space and increase drag and friction.

***Lubrication levels*:**

In general, higher percentages of small particles require increased quantities of lubricant. Magnesium stearate is the most commonly used lubricant and should be de-agglomerated before use.

Effects of particle size

Small particles decrease disintegration time, and increase dissolution.

- *Friability*

  Larger particles usually lock together better which results in reduced friability, while small particles often increase the potential for failure (higher friability).

- *Electro Static effects:*

  Electro static charge is increased as the percentage of small particles increases.

- *Dust control:*

  Fine particles create a dusty operation, creating a need for frequent production stoppages and press clean-ups.

- *Environmental conditions:*

  Many products are hygroscopic and sensitive to heat. Variations in room conditions can cause poor flow, compression and ejection conditions.

- *Lamination & Capping*:

  Small particles are responsible for the most common defects.

- *Punch lubrication:*

  Dust and super fine particles become airborne and combine with the oils and greases which can produce black specks in the tablets.

- *Tooling condition:*

  Punch tip and die clearance are designed to control air release allowing for improved compaction. *Machine condition:*

  Cleaning and maintenance are downtime issues. A high percentage of fine particles and dust increases the chance for greater wear, increased cleaning frequency, reduced yield, greater particle segregation, and more tablet defects.

- *Cost:*

  Fines (small dusty particles) increase the operating costs, require increased levels of dust collection, decreased yields, increased frequency of cleaning, and generate greater machine and tool wear. Reducing fines will improve tablet quality[27].

- *Blending:*

Blending in solid dose manufacturing has two objectives:

1) To achieve blend uniformity: The blend step(s) are designed to achieve homogeneity of all components prior to the final blend of the lubricant
2) To distribute the lubricant: Blending powders is more of a challenge due to particle size, moisture content, structure, bulk density and flow characteristics.

The first step, in achieving predictable results in a blend is to introduce the proper particle profile within a range, between 40 – 180 mesh for most oral solid dosages. Any particles larger than 20 mesh can try to hard the limit of percentage of fines (smaller than 200 mesh) to less than 20%. The next step is to complete pre-blending steps in a carefully planned order of addition.

Characteristics of material:

- *Fragile particles* or agglomerates: more readily abrade, more fines are produced, this results in improper mixing, causing flow problems; fill problems, content uniformity problems.
- *Particle abrasion* is more when high shear mixing with spiral screws or blades are used. For prolonged mixing tumble blenders can be used.
- *Bulk density* of raw materials is considered in selection of the blender and determining optimum blender load.
- *Excessive granulation* can results in poor content uniformity, poor lubrication, and improper colour dispersion.
- *Direct compression* is defined as the process by which tablets are compressed directly from powder mixture of API and suitable excipients. No pre-treatment of the powder blend by wet or dry granulation procedure is required 28.

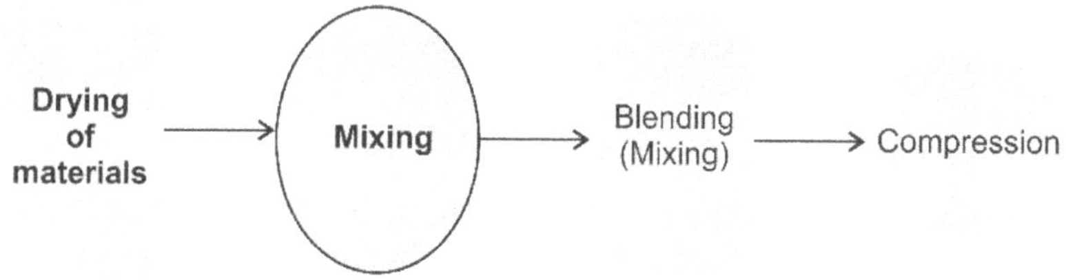

Fig.2.3 Steps involved in direct compression method.

Manufacturing Steps for Direct Compression with control factors are shown in Fig 2.3.

During granulation, the powder particles circulate within the product chamber and provide a constant flow of bed particles through a defined spray granulation zone. At the spray granulation zone, a fine spray of liquid binder is usually atomized and deposited onto the fluidizing particles. Particle wetting brings about granule formation. Partial drying of the wetted particles by the fluidizing air occurs continuously during granulation. When the spraying of liquid binder is completed, the granules are quickly dried by the hot air stream and complete drying is achieved[28].

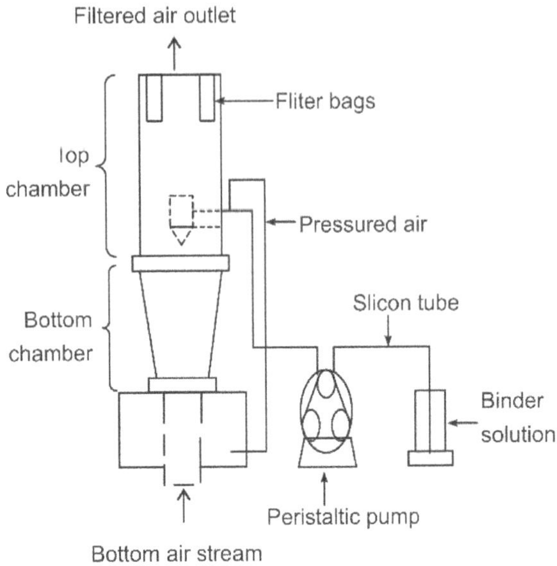

Fig.2.4 Schematic diagram of fluidized bed dryer.

PROCESS SCALE UP FOR CAPSULES

In bringing a new product to the market, scale-up from the initial development batches to commercial manufacturing is an important activity. Scale-up is generally defined as *the process of increasing batch size.* In moving from research and development (R&D) to production scale, it is sometimes essential to have an intermediate place of work.

Capsules are solid dosage forms in which the drug substance either alone or mixed with other suitable excipients is enclosed either in hard or soft gelatine capsule or shell.

Steps involved in capsule manufacturing are:

- Mixing of ingredient(s)
- Granulation and lubrication
- Filling of capsules
- Sealing of capsules
- Testing of content of uniformity
- Packaging and labelling

The method of manufacture of capsule is same to that of tablet. Both tablet and capsules are prepared from the ingredients, which are either dry blended or wet granulated to produce a dry powder or dried mixer of granules with uniformly dispersed active ingredient(s). To produce capsules using high speed equipment/ machine, the particle size distribution of the powder blend should be uniform. The bulk density and compressibility of the powders/ granules should be checked and within the acceptable limit. The flow property of the powder mix should also be adequate and when measured it should be within the acceptable limit, so that the compacts of right size and sufficient cohesiveness of the filled in powders can be obtained.

The mixing of ingredients should be evaluated for obtaining at least three information: (1) duration of mixing, (2) speed of mixer, and (3) uniformity of mixing.

Manufacturing of Hard Gelatine Capsules Shell

Gelatine is prepared by the hydrolysis of collagen. There are two basic types of gelatine: Type-A and Type-B. The two types can be differentiated by their isoelectric points (7.0 - 9.0 for type-A and 4.8 - 5.0 for type-B) and by their viscosity and film forming characteristics. Combination of pork skin and bone gelatine is often used to optimize shell characteristics. The physicochemical properties of gelatine of most interest to manufactures shell are the bloom strength and viscosity.

- *Colorants:* Various soluble synthetic dyes (coal tar dyes) and insoluble pigments are used. Colorants not only play a role in identifying the product, but also play a role in improving patient compliance.
- *Opaquing agents:* Titanium dioxide may be included to render the shell opaque. Opaque capsules may be used to provide protection against light or to conceal the contents.
- *Preservatives:* The preservatives used are parabens, often selected.

Shell Manufacturing

- *Dipping:* Pairs of the stainless-steel pins are dipped into the dipping solution simultaneously to form the caps and bodies. The pins are at ambient temperature; whereas the dipping solution is maintained at a temperature of about 50°C in a heated, jacketed dipping pan. The duration of time to cast the film has been reported to be about 12 sec.
- *Rotation:* After dipping, pins are elevated and rotated ½ - 2 times until they are facing upward. This rotation helps to distribute the gelatine over the pins uniformly and to avoid the formation of a bead at the capsule ends.
- *Drying:* The racks of gelatine coated pins are then passed into a series of four drying ovens. Drying is mainly done by dehumidification. A temperature elevation to only a less degrees is permissible to prevent film melting. Under drying will leave the films too sticky for subsequent operation.
- *Stripping:* A series of bronze jaws strip the cap and body portions of the capsules from the pins.

- *Trimming:* The stripped cap and body portions are delivered to collects in which they are firmly held. As the collects rotate, knives are brought against the shells to trim them to the required length.
- *Joining:* The cap and body portions are aligned concentrically in channels and the two portions are slowly pushed together.
- *Sorting:* The moisture content of the capsules as they are from the machine will be in the range of 15-18% w/w. During sorting, the capsules pass on a lighted moving conveyor are examined visually by inspectors. Defects are generally classified according to their nature and potential to cause problems in use.
- *Printing:* In general, capsules are printed before filling. Generally, printing is done on offset rotary presses having throughput capabilities as high as three-quarter million capsules per hour.
- *Sizes and Shapes:* For human use, empty gelatine capsules are manufactured in eight sizes, ranging from 000 to 5. The largest size normally acceptable to patient is a No. 0. Three larger sizes are available for veterinary use– 10, 11, and 12 having fill volume capacities of about 18, 10, and 7.5 ml, respectively. The standard shape of capsules is traditional, symmetrical bullet shape. Some manufactures have used distinctive shapes. For example, Lilly's pulvule tapers to a bluntly pointed end, Smith Kline Beacham's spansule capsules taper at both the cap and body ends.
- *Sealing*: Capsules are sealed and somewhat reshaped in the Etaseal process. This thermal welding process forms an indented ring around the waist of the capsule where the cap overlaps the body.
- *Storage:* Finished capsules normally contain an equilibrium moisture content of 13-16% to maintain a relative humidity of 40-60% when handling and storing capsules. Filling of Hard Gelatine Capsules[29].

Equipment used in capsule filling operations involve one often of two types of filling systems: (i) Zanasi or Martellien capsulator: Forms slugs in a dosatar which is a hollow tube with a plunger to eject capsule plug. (ii) Hofliger-Karg machine: Forms compacts in a die plate using tamping pins to form a compact.

- In both these systems, the scale-up process involves bulk density, powder flow, compressibility and lubricant distribution. Overly lubricated granules are responsible for delaying capsule disintegration and dissolution.
- The ratio of dry plasticizer to dry gelatine, determines the "hardness" of the shell and can vary from 0.3-1.0 for very hard shell to 1.0-1.8 for very softshell.
- Up to 5% sugar may be included to give a "chewable" quality to the shell.
- The residual shell moisture content of finished capsules will be in the range of 6- 10%.

Formulation:

- Formulation for soft gelatine capsules involves liquid, rather than powder technology. Materials are generally formulated to produce the smallest possible capsule consistent with maximum stability, therapeutic effectiveness and manufacture efficiency. The liquids are limited to those that do not have an adverse effect on gelatine walls. The pH of the lipid can be between 2.5 and 7.5. Emulsion cannot be filled because water released from it will affect the shell.
- The types of vehicles used in soft gelatine capsules fall into two main groups: (i) Water immiscible, volatile or more likely more volatile liquids such as vegetable oils, mineral oils, medium-chain triglycerides and acetylated glycerides. (ii) Water miscible, non-volatile liquids such as low molecular weight PEG has been used recently because of their ability to mix with water readily and accelerate dissolution of dissolved or suspended drugs. All liquids used for filling must flow by gravity at a temperature of 35°C or less. The sealing temperature of gelatine films is 37°C - 40°C. Manufacture Processes: 1. Plate Process: The process involves:
- Placing the upper half of a plasticized gelatine sheet over a die plate containing numerous die pockets. Vacuum is applied to draw the sheet into the die pockets, filling the pockets with liquor or paste, Folding the lower half of gelatine sheet back over the filled pockets, and Inserting the "sandwich" under a die press where the capsules are formed and cut-out.

Rotary Die-Press:

- In this process, the die cavities are machined into the outer surface of the two rollers.
- The die pockets on the left-hand roller form the left side of the capsule and the die pockets on the right-hand roller form the right side of the capsule.
- Two plasticized gelatine ribbons are continuously and simultaneously fed with the liquid or paste fill between the rollers of the rotary die mechanism.
- As the die rolls rotate, the convergence of the matching die pockets seals and cuts out the filled capsules.

Ability to withstand batch-scale.

- Process modification.
- Compatibility of the equipment with the formulation.
- Cost factor.
- Physical space required.
- Market requirement.
- Layout of the related functions.
- Availability of the raw materials meeting the specifications.

Pilot Plant Consideration for semi-solid dosage forms

Following parameters are to be considered during the scale up of semisolid products:

Mixing speed: Mixing equipment (Could be able to move semisolid mass from outside walls to the centre and from bottom to top of the kettle). Motors (Drive mixing system with appropriate handling system at its most viscous stage).

Heating and cooling process. Component homogenization. Product transfer. Addition of active ingredients. Maintain the working temperature range, shear during handling and transfer from manufacturing to holding tank to filling lines. Transfer pumps (must easily move the viscous material without applying excessive shear and free of entrapped air). Following parameters must be consider during choosing the size and type of pump,

- Pumping rate.
- Pumping pressure required should be considered.
- Product compatibility with the pump surface.
- Product viscosity.

Validation:

- o Design specification.
- o Installation qualification.
- o Operational qualification.
- o Performance qualification.
- o Compliance with cGMP and FDA standards.

Training:

- o Technical skills and knowledge.
- o Safety and environment responsibility.
- o Compliance with GMP. Compliance with SOPs.

Engineering Support:

- o Design of facility.
- o Co-ordination scheduling.
- o Direction of ongoing operations.
- o Validation of facility.
- o Construction of facility.

Maintenance and Calibration:

- To ensure the integrity and equipment reliability and research.
- To meet cGMP norms. Computerized System:

- o Material control
- o Labelling (GMP-GLP)
- o Inventory
- o Orders (FIFO)

Process and Manufacturing Activities:

1) Formulation and process development studies.
2) Technology evaluation scale up and transfer.
3) Clinical supply and manufacture.

Quality Assurance:

* Auditing pilot plant.
* Auditing and approval of component supplies.
* Reviewing approval and mainframe batch records for clinical supplies.
* Sampling and release of raw material.
* Release of clinical supplies.
* Maintaining and distributing facility and operating procedure(SOPS).
* Review and approval of validation.
* Engineering documentation.

Quality Control:

- o Release testing of finished product.
- o Physical, chemical and microbiological testing of finished clinical products, components required for supplies.
- o Testing for validation and revalidation.
- o QC in process testing during development scale-up and technology transfer.

SCALE-UP and POST APPROVAL CHANGES (SUPAC)

FDA and American association of pharmaceuticals scientist (AAPS) provided the scientific foundation for the scale-up and post approval changes required for immediate release product called SUPAC. It provides guidelines for post approval changes in the following: 1) Components, 2) Compositions, 3) Site of manufacturing, 4) Process and equipment Significance of Pilot Plant:

- Examination of formulae.
- Review of range of relevant processing equipment.
- Production rate adjustment.

- Idea about physical space required.
- Appropriate records and reports to support GMP.
- Identification of critical features to maintain quality.

PROCESS SCALE UP FOR LIQUID ORALS

The Physical form of a drug product that is pourable can display Newtonian or non-Newtonian flow behaviour and conforms to its container at room temperature. Liquid dosage forms may be dispersed systems or solutions. In dispersed systems there is two or more phase; where one phase is distributed in another.

Pharmaceutical liquid dosage forms are those preparations that contains a combination of active drugs and excipients (emulsifying, dispersing, solubilizing, stabilising, suspending, wetting, thickening agent, preservative, sweetening agent, flavouring agent, and colouring agent) that are dissolved or suspended in appropriate solvents and used as a drug or medication[30]. It is the simplest type of pharmaceutical preparations for high absorption of drugs and rapid onset in which two components are enhanced to complete a liquid dosage form solute (a component that dissolves) and solvents (the medium in which the solute will dissolve). In pharmaceutical liquid preparations, parenteral routes are available in sterile forms, whereas oral liquids are non-sterile and can be administered via oral or parenteral routes (Injectable, inhalation, otic, tropical, nasal and ophthalmic). Monophasic liquid dosage forms are the liquid solutions that comprise two or more components in a single phase. True solutions, which are homogeneous mixtures created by dissolving solute in long-term solvents, are also known as true solutions[31].

The oral liquid dosage forms classify as Monophasic and Biphasic. The Monophasic is of simple solutions. The Biphasic is suspension and emulsion. Liquid preparation for oral use is usually Solutions, Emulsions or Suspensions containing one or more drug forms in suitable vehicle. The preparation for oral use are either supplied in finished form or with excipients or it may also be prepared just before use by dissolving the powder in vehicle stated on the label. The liquid preparation for oral use consists of antimicrobial preservative, antioxidants, dispensing agent, suspending agent, thickening agent, emulsifying agent, buffering wetting, solubilizing, stabilizing, flavouring and sweetening with suitable colouring agent. They may be single dosage or multiple dosage preparation. The devices used are spoon or cup, oral syringe, dropper, etc. The liquid of should be uniformity of mass, uniformity of mass of doses delivered by measuring devices, container with proper labelling. The Oral suspension consists of active ingredient suspended in suitable liquid or vehicle. It should be readily dispersed when shaken and stable to give or enable correct dose to be delivered. Oral emulsion is active ingredients which are stabilized in oil in water dispersion or water in oil dispersion. It also readily disperses while shaking. Oral drops which are used in small volumes with the help of suitable measuring device. The drops should be free from precipitate. The instability can be seen through flocculation, sedimentation, change in colour, etc. Powders for oral solutions consists of one or more dose preparation consisting of solid loose, dry particle with high degree of fitness. It should be readily disperse in solution and should not form cake and the instability can be checked through texture. Examples are clumping. Presentation for granules for oral solutions are intended to be issued to patient as granules to be swallowed, as such to be chewed or taken through water. They are dry aggregate of powder particles sufficiently resistant to withstand handling. It has noticeable changes in physical appearance when there is disability in the drug.

Formulation aspects of liquid orals are suspensions, emulsions, solutions.

They are facilitating the connection between API and Vehicle. Steps involved in manufacturing process include planning of material requirements, liquid preparation, filling and packing, quality assurance. The Equipment used are mixers or mixing tank, homogenizer, filtration assembly, bottling assembly. The mixing tank and storage tank for liquid oral contains a bottom out let with electric or steam heating facility also available. Storage tank is manufactured from stainless steel 304/stainless steel 316 and is argon welded. They are made up with suitable thickness with smooth finish. It has a valve at bottom and lid at the top. It has capacity of 50-10000 litres. The tank will be mounted on 4 legs with casted for movement. It is used for proper mixing of drug and excipients. Stainless steel tank with stirrer is available with stainless steel steam jacket and insulating with stainless cladding. They are different types of stirrer such as paddle/anchor/propeller. The electric heating of liquid is possible for small scale. It has capacity of 100-10000 litres. Colloidal mill is used for superfine grinding and simultaneous emulsifying, dispersing and homogenizing within one process. The homogenizer spring crude mixture inlet outlet homogenized liquid valve cover, valve seating. It is used for making suspension and emulsion. It consists of head of spring arrangement made out of stainless steel ultrasonifier inlet orifice vibrating blade outlet. The filter press is used where the liquid is to be filtered and pumped to tank. Bottle washing machine makes four inner and one outer wash. The first wash with water, second wash with detergent then two washes with demineralized water and dry in inverted position or dried under hot air oven. The liquid packaging area as per schedule 'M' include bottle washing area, filling and capping area, bottle labelling and box filling area. In the bottle washing area, a tank is provided with filled fresh demineralized water and then places in bottle into aluminium tray and then put in hot air oven. The bottles should be inspected and rejected. Then the correct size should be chosen and fix on stainless steel platform and washing process is semiautonomous platform and washing process is semi-automatic. The washed bottles should be inverted on empty nozzlcs and then unloading of washed bottle in aluminium clean perforated tray in inverted position. So the water should be drained completely then dried at oven for 120°C for 1 hour. The filling and capping area contains the bulk containers which are used for filling. Only washed bottles and cleaned caps are used. The filled volumes record should be recorded and maintained as prescribed. The box filling area consists of the sealed and filled bottles are passed through convey belt and filled boxes consists labelling. The layout of pilot plant of liquids consists of the equipment such as tanker, mixer, homogenizer, filtration assembly.

Solutions

Solid materials are dissolved in an appropriate solvent, which are homogeneous mixture containing one or more chemical compounds. Solutions are one of the oldest dosage forms and are made by dissolving a solid, liquid, or gas into a solvent in which the solute molecules are dissolved into a solvent such as water, alcohol or carbonated beverages[32].

Syrup

Syrup is sugar-in-water saturated aqueous solution with or without medicinal, ingredients. Syrups have a high percentage of sucrose (66.7% w/w I.P. and 85% w/v USP). Prepare sucrose 66.7% w/w syrup in filtered water, stirring constantly while heating. It's crucial not to let the temperature climb above 1600°C while heating. After cooling, it's kept in a cool, dry area in a tightly sealed container to keep moisture and foreign particles out. Vitamins, sedatives, saline medicines, and antibiotics all use syrups in their compositions.

Linctus

Linctus is a viscous, monophasic liquid solution with a high syrup concentration that is used to treat cough and sore throat. It's made by dissolving citric acid in chloroform, adding peppermint water, amaranth solution, and syrup (as a carrier) to reach the desired volume. However, the majority of linctus comprises chemicals that have expectorant, sedative, and antibacterial properties.

Elixirs

An elixir is a sweet fragrant liquid mixture. It is administered orally for medical purposes. It contains a variety of active substances, including ethyl alcohol, propylene glycol, water, glycerine, and flavouring agents, all of which are necessary for elixir manufacture. The elixirs available are of two types medicated elixirs and non-medicated. Non-medicated elixirs are used as vehicles or solvents for medicated elixirs, which include potent medications as antihistaminic, antibiotics, hypnotics, and sedatives, and should be kept in a light-resistant, firmly closed container away from sunlight[33].

Biphasic liquid dosage forms

Biphasic liquid dosage forms are ones that have two phases in them. This comprises the medicine that has been dissolved as well as the solvent (vehicle). There are two types of biphasic liquid dosage forms.

- Suspension
- Emulsion

Suspension:

Suspensions are biphasic liquid dosage forms of medication in which the internal phase is uniformly distributed with finely divided solid particles in a liquid dispersion medium over a period of 0.5 to 5 minutes. In pharmaceutical solutions, solid particles act as a disperse phase, while liquid vehicles act as a continuous phase. The external phase, also known as the suspending medium. Pharmaceutical suspension formulations are done for the following reasons.

- To improve the drug stability of the suspensions.
- To reduce the bitterness.
- The medication is insoluble in the delivery medium in this formulation.
- To achieve long term medication release (sustained release).

Classification of suspension:

Suspensions are categorised using the following basis: Based on the route of administration

- Oral
- Parenteral
- Topical
- Based on the nature of solid particles electro kinetics
- Flocculated suspension
- Deflocculated suspension

Oral suspensions

For oral administration, an oral suspension consists of undissolved particles and active substances suspended in sweetening, flavouring, or viscous vehicles with therapeutic agents. Oral suspensions are commonly used to treat oral fungal infections. "Oral suspensions allow for dose flexibility and are cost-effective when a patient requires dose titration, however many pharmaceutical medications are not available as oral suspensions. Insoluble components are suspended in a dispersion media with suspending agents to create oral suspensions. Suspending agents are used to help disperse powders evenly throughout the preparation and avoid particle flocculation.

Types of emulsion

The two basic types of emulsions such as

O/W (oil dispersed in water)

W/O (water dispersed in oil).

Oil-in-water emulsions (O/W), pharmaceutical emulsions are made up of a mixture of oil droplets scattered throughout the aqueous phase. Fats and oils for oral administration are always manufactured as oil-in-water (O/W), whether as carriers for oil-soluble medications or as medicines in their own right. These are non-greasy and easy to wipe away from the skin's surface[34]. They are applied physically to provide a cooling effect and internally to mask the oil's unpleasant taste.

Water-in-oil emulsions (W/O), water-in-oil emulsions (W/O emulsions) are medicinal emulsions in which water is scattered as globules in oil continuous phase. Water-in-oil emulsions have an occlusive action, which hydrates the stratum corneum and prevents the evaporation of eccrine secretions. These are oily but not water soluble, and these are used to maintain moisture from evaporating from the skin's surface while cleansing it of oil-soluble dirt, for example, Cold cream. Knowledge of API, excipients, their interactions, and process parameters is essential for a successful pharmaceutical formulation. Ideal qualities of excipients are

- Excipients perform well in their intended applications.
- They have to be physiologically inactive.
- They must be physically and chemically stable.
- They should be less affected by machinery and processes.
- They have to be non-toxic.
- They must be acceptable in terms of organoleptic qualities.
- There is no effect on medication bioavailability.
- Excipients must not include pathogenic bacteria.
- They must meet the requirements of the regulating agency.
- They must be cost-effective.

Excipients utilised in liquid dosage form formulation Excipients are categorised according to the function they perform; however, different excipients respond differently at different concentrations, and one excipient might be employed for numerous purposes depending on the dosage form's requirements. Oral liquid formulations are prepared by mixing various chemicals to accomplish activities such as wetting and solubilization, stability, and the addition of appropriate colour, taste, and viscosity for compatible, non-reactive, and stable formulations. The following excipients are commonly used in liquid formulations:

- Vehicles
- Solubilizers
- Preservatives
- Stabilizers
- Organoleptic agents.

Vehicles/ Solvents

In liquid pharmaceutical formulations, vehicles are important components that serve as a base for dissolving or dispersing drugs and other excipients. They work by breaking bonds and reducing effective charge on ions, increasing solute-solvent attraction forces, which eventually outnumber solute-solute and solvent-solvent attraction forces. In hydro-alcoholic liquid systems, polyhydric alcohols, acetic acid, ethyl acetate, and buffers are examples of such substances. Thin liquids, thick syrupy liquids, mucilage, and hydrocolloid bases are all possibilities. Vegetable oils, mineral oils, organic oily bases or emulsified bases are examples of oily vehicles.

Co-solvents

Co-solvents are *organic solvents that are water miscible and are utilised in liquid medicine formulations to boost the solubility of weakly water soluble compounds or to improve the chemical stability of a drug.* A co-solvent boosts a drug's solubility. The dielectric constant of an ideal co-solvent should be between 25 and 80. A water/ethanol blend is the most generally utilised solution that will handle this range. When administered for oral or parental use, it should not cause toxicity or irritancy. Sorbitol, glycerol, propylene glycol, and syrup are some of the other co-solvents.

PROCESS SCALE UP FOR SEMISOLIDS

The scarcity of published studies or data on scale-up—particularly for non-parenteral semisolids—suggests otherwise. On the other hand, one could argue that the scarcity of published studies or data is nothing more than a reflection of the need to maintain a competitive advantage through secrecy. One could also argue that this deficiency in the literature attests to the complexity of the unit operations involved in pharmaceutical processing. If pharmaceutical technologists view scale-up as little more than a ratio problem, whereby

$$\text{scale-up ratio} = \frac{\text{large-scale production rate}}{\text{small-scale production rate}} \qquad \text{.....(1)}$$

then the successful resolution of a scale-up problem will remain an empirical, trial-and-error method, rather than a scientific one. In 1998, in a monograph on the scale-up of disperse systems, Block[35] noted that due to the complexity of the manufacturing process that involves more than one type of unit operation, such as, mixing, transferring, process scale-up from the bench or pilot plant level to commercial production is not a simple extrapolation: The successful linkage of one unit operation to another defines the functionality of the overall manufacturing process. Each unit operation as such may be scalable, in accordance with a specific ratio. But the composite manufacturing process may not be the effective scale-up ratios. This may be different from one unit operation to another. Unexpected problems in scale-up are often a reflection of the separation between unit operation scale-up and process scaleup. Furthermore, commercial production introduces problems that are not a major issue on a small scale; for example, storage and materials handling may become problematic only when large quantities are involved. Heat generated in the course of pilot plant or production scale processing may overcome the system's capacity for dissipation to an extent not anticipated based on prior laboratory-scale experience. Moreover, unit operations may function in a rate-limiting manner as the scale of operation increases. A clue to the resolution of the scale-up problem for semisolids resides in the recognition that their processing invariably involves the unit operation of mixing. It is important to the effective processing scale-up is the understanding of microscale and macroscale transport phenomena, that is, diffusion and bulk flow, respectively. Transport by diffusion involves the flow of a property (e.g., mass, heat, momentum, electromagnetic energy) from a region of high concentration to a region of low concentration as a result of the microscopic motion of electrons, atoms, molecules, etc. Bulk flow, whether convection or advection, however, involves the flow of a property as a result of macroscopic or bulk motion induced artificially (e.g., by mechanical agitation) or naturally (e.g., by density variations).

Full-scale tests using production equipment and involving no scale-up studies whatsoever are sometimes turned to when single-phase low-viscosity systems and processing is considered to be predictable and directly scalable. By and large, these are unrealistic assumptions when viscous liquids, dispersions, or semisolids are involved. Moreover, the cost related to full-scale testing is substantial. Commercial-scale equipment is relatively inflexible and costly to operate. In full-scale processing involve error in large amounts of material. Insofar as most liquids or semisolids have been considered then, full-scale tests are not an option. On the other hand, scale-up studies involving relatively low scale-up ratios and few changes in process variables are not necessarily a reasonable alternative to full-scale testing. For this reason, experimental designs using little, incremental, changes in processing equipment and conditions are unacceptable. These consume time, an irreplaceable resource that must be utilized to its maximum advantage, hence, these alternative test modes are unacceptable. Appropriate process development, reduced costs and accelerated lead times, plays an important role in product development performance. In the development factory:

unlocking the potential of process innovation, the author Gary Pisano[36] argues that while pharmaceuticals compete largely on the basis of product innovation, there is a hidden leverage in process development and manufacturing competence. This provides more degrees of freedom, in developing products, to more skilful organizations than to their less expert competitors. Although Pisano focuses on synthesis of drug and biotechnology process scale-up, his conclusions translate effectively to the manufacturing processes for drug and delivery systems/ dosage forms. Actually, the scale-up issues need to be addressed jointly by pharmaceutical engineers and formulators as soon as a dosage form or delivery system becomes commercially viable. Scale-up studies should not be downgraded to the final stages of product development, whether initiated at the command of the FDA (to meet regulatory requirements) or marketing and the sales divisions (to meet marketing directives or the sales quotas). The worst scenario would require the delay of scale-up studies until after commercial distribution (to accommodate unexpected market demands).

Modular scale-up involves the scale-up of individual components or unit operations of a manufacturing process. The interactions among these individual operations comprise the potential scale-up problem, i.e., the inability to achieve sameness when the process is conducted on a different scale. When the physical or physicochemical properties of system components are known, the scalability of some unit operations may be predictable.

Known scale-up correlations thus may allow scale-up when laboratory or pilot plant experience is minimal. The fundamental approach to process scaling involves mathematical modelling of the manufacturing process and experimental validation of the model at different scale-up ratios. Virtually no guidelines or models for scale-up have generally been available that have stood the test of time, insofar as the scale-up of pharmaceutical liquids (especially disperse systems) and semisolids is concerned. Uhl and Von Essen[37], referring to the variety of rules of thumb, calculation methods, and extrapolation procedures in the literature, stated that unfortunately, the enormous literature and attributions to the subject of scale-up seemed to have served more to surprise. Some allusions are specious, most rules are extremely limited in application, examples give too little data and limited analysis. Not surprisingly, then, the trial-and-error method is the one most often employed by formulators. As a result, serendipity and practical experience continue to play large roles in the successful pursuit of the scalable process.

PROCESS SCALE UP FOR PARENTERALS

The term *parenteral* is applied to preparations administered by injection through one or more layers of skin tissue. The word has been derived from the Greek words *para* and *etheron,* meaning "outside of the intestine," is used for those dosage forms administered by routes other than the oral route. Because the administration of injectables, by definition, requires circumventing the highly protective barriers of the human body, the skin, and the mucous membranes, the dosage form must achieve an exceptional purity. This is generally accomplished by strict adherence to good manufacturing practices. One of the most important processes involved in the scale-up of liquid parenteral preparations is mixing. For liquids, mixing can be defined as a transport process. This occurs simultaneously in three different scales. During this one substance (*solute*) achieves a uniform concentration in another substance (*solvent*). On a large, visible scale, mixing occurs by *bulk diffusion,* in which the elements are blended by the pumping action of the mixer's impeller. On the microscopic scale, elements that are in proximity, are blended by eddy currents. They create drag, where local velocity and shear-stress differences act on the fluid. On the smallest scale, final blending occurs through molecular diffusion, whose rate is unaffected by the mechanical mixing action. Therefore, large-scale mixing depends primarily on flow within the vessel. While small-scale mixing is dependent mostly on shear. This approach focuses on large-scale mixing using three viable approaches, specifically concentrating on the scale-of-agitation method.

Dimensionless-Numbers Method

This method, for achieving appropriate scale-up of mixing, uses dimensionless numbers to predict scale-up parameters. The use of dimensionless numbers simplifies design calculations by reducing the number of variables. The dimensionless-number method has been used with good success in heat transfer calculations and to some extent in gas dispersion (mass transfer) for mixer scale-up. Usually, the primary independent variable in a dimensionless-number correlation is the Reynolds number:

$$N_{Re} = \frac{D^2 \rho N}{\mu} \qquad .....(2.1)$$

where, N_{Re} is the Reynolds number, N is the shaft speed (sec^{-1}), D is the propeller blade diameter (cm), ρ is density of solution dispersion (g/cm^3), and μ is the viscosity of solution dispersion (g/[cm /sec]).

Other dimensionless numbers are used widely for various scale-up applications. One example is the Froude number:

$$N_{Fr} = \frac{DN^2}{g} \qquad .....(2.2$$

where *g* is acceleration due to gravity in cm/sec^2.

The Froude number compares inertial forces to gravitational forces inside the system.

Another example is the Power number, which is a function of the Reynolds number and the Froude number:

$$N_P = \frac{Pg_c}{\rho N^3 D^5} \qquad .....(2.3)$$

where P is power, g_C is a gravitational conversion factor. This number relates density, viscosity, rotational speed, and the diameter of the impeller. The power number correlation has been used successfully for impeller geometric scale-up. Approximately half a dozen other dimensionless numbers are involved in the various aspects of mixing, heat and mass transfer, etc.

Both of the preceding methods belong to a traditional fluid mechanical approach known as *dimensional analysis*. Unfortunately, these methods cannot always achieve results in certain manufacturing environments. Therefore, a third method is introduced, which can be applied easily to the various research and pro- duction situations. This method actually is a combination of the first two methods.

is a combination of the first two methods.

Scale-of Agitation approach for parenteral suspensions

The basis of the scale-of-agitation method is a geometric scale-up with the power law exponent, n =1. This provides for equal fluid velocities in both large- and small-scale equipment. Moreover, several dimensionless groups have been used to relate the fluid properties to the physical properties of the equipment being considered. In particular, the bulk-fluid velocity comparisons are made around the largest blade in the system. This method is the best suited to turbulent flow agitation in which tanks are assumed to be vertical cylinders.

Although good success may be achieved in applying this technique to marine-type propeller systems, the original development was based on low-rpm, axial, or radial impeller arrangements. Because the most intensive mixing occurs in the volume immediately around the impeller, this discussion focuses on this particular region of mixing. Table 2 describes the nomenclature used to develop the theory behind the approach.

The analysis proceeds as follows: First, determine the D/T ratio of the tank, based on the largest impeller, in which the original (usually R&D) batches had been compounded. It is also necessary to know the rotational speed and the horse- power of the mixer used.

The only two product physical properties needed are density and viscosity. Generally, parenterals, like most solution-type products, will follow Newtonian fluid behaviour and may also be considered incompressible. Therefore, point densities and viscosities can be used satisfactorily.

The next step in the analysis is to calculate the impeller Reynolds number achieved during this original compounding using Eq. (5). The impeller Reynolds number must be greater than 2000 to proceed with the analysis. Mixing achieved in the initial R&D processing must be in the turbulent range. If the impeller Reynolds number is less than 2000, then mixing in the pilot tank was either inadequate or represented some other special case, such as moderately viscous fluids. In these situations, another *D/T* ratio curve must be used.

Proceeding further, obtain the value of the terminal pumping number in the R&D pilot process by using the following formula:

$$N_Q = 1.1283 - 1.07118\left(\frac{D}{T}\right) \qquad .....(2.4)$$

The Table 2.1 shows the nomenclature.

Table 2.1 Nomenclature.

Symbol	Explanation
Q	Effective pumping capacity or volumetric pumping flow, in cm^3/sec
N	Shaft speed, in sec^{-1}
N_{Re}	Impeller Reynolds number, dimensionless
N_Q	Pumping number, dimensionless
D	Diameter of the largest mixer blade, in cm
ρ	Density of the fluid, in g/cm^3
μ	Viscosity of the fluid, in g/[cm/sec]
vb	Bulk fluid velocity, in cm
T	Diameter of the tank, in cm
A	Cross-sectional area of the tank, in cm^2

The above eqn. no.4 shows an empirical relationship obtained by the linear regression between D/T and the terminal pumping number. It is important to note that a family of curves exists for each D/T ratio when N_Q (pumping number) is plotted against the impeller Reynolds number. In the turbulent range (N_{Re} > 2000), the N_Q curves flatten out and thus are independent of the Reynolds number. The terminal pumping number, $N_Q / _{Re>2000}$, plotted against the D/T ratio results in the above eqn. The cross-sectional area of the pilot-size tank is determined by using Eq. 5:

$$A = \frac{\pi T^2}{4} \qquad .....(2.5)$$

Then the value of the effective pumping capacity for the pilot-size mixer is calculated using Eq.6:

$$Q = N_Q N D^3 \ cm^3/sec \qquad .....(2.6)$$

Finally, the value for bulk-fluid velocity around the largest impeller of the system is obtained:

$$V_b = \frac{Q}{A} \text{ cm /sec} \qquad .....(2.7)$$

The bulk-fluid velocity can be inserted into Table 3 to determine the level of agitation achieved in the original R&D pilot batch. The larger-size production tank and mixer are then designed so that the scale of agitation produced in the larger vessel matches that required for the pilot-size batches. The scale-of-agitation approach was first developed in the mid-1970s by engineers at Chemineer, Inc. The Table 2.2 provides the summary of the scale-of-agitation parameters and provides a qualitative description of the type of mixing related to the various levels. According to this approach, mixing is a similar process if the calculated bulk-fluid velocities for the production-size vessels lie within ±1 unit level of the scale of agitation required from an analysis of the R&D pilot batches. It is quite easy to match the required scale of agitation by simply adjusting the rpm when working with variable-speed equipment. Thus, a given tank equipped with a variable-speed mixer will generally be capable of several agitation levels. Let us explain the phenomenon with the help of an example.

The actual application of the scale-of-agitation approach to scale-up, the method has been applied to the scale-up of typical injectables solution from a 378 litre pilot batch to a 3780 litre production-size batch. The example product is a Newtonian fluid with density of 1.018 g/cm^3 and a viscosity of 0.0588 g/(cm/sec)(5.88 cps). The tank used in the manufacturing of the pilot batch had the following parameters:

T = diameter of the tank = 74.6 cm

A = cross-sectional area = 4371 cm^2

The agitation was accomplished with a turbine-type mixer, and the largest axial impeller was 40.64 cm. The pilot batch was mixed at 90 rpm (1.5 sec^{-1}). From the initial known data the D/T ratio was determined:

$$\frac{D_{378L}}{T_{378L}} = \frac{40.64\text{cm}}{74.60 \text{ cm}} = 0.54$$

The value of the impeller Reynolds number is obtained by plugging known values into Eq.1:

$$N_{Re3785L} = \frac{D^2_{378L}\rho.N_{378L}}{\mu} = \frac{(40.64\text{cm}^2)(1.018\text{g/cm}^3)(1.5\text{Sec}^{-1})}{0.0588\text{g/(cm/Sec)}}$$

$$= 44449$$

Because the value of the Reynolds number is greater than 2000, eq.4 is used to obtain the pumping number. The pumping number is inserted into eq.6 to obtain the effective pumping capacity:

$$Q_{378L} = (N_{Q(378L)})(N_{378L})(D^3_{370L}) = (0.55)(1.5Sec^{-1})(40.64cm)^3$$
$$= 55375cm^3/Sec$$

Knowing the effective pumping capacity of agitation and the cross-sectional area of the pilot-batch tank, bulk-fluid velocity is obtained by using eq.7:

$$v_{b378L} = \frac{Q_{378L}}{A_{378L}} = \frac{55375cm^3/Sec}{4371cm^2} = 12.6\ cm/Sec$$

Inserting this bulk-fluid velocity into Table 3, one can calculate the level of agitation used in the pilot batch of indictable solution as 4, which is described as characteristic of fluid velocities in most chemical process industries' agitated batches.

Now the appropriate shaft speed for scaled-up production equipment can be calculated. The tank used for production batches has a capacity of 3780 L. It is equipped with a turbine-type agitator, which has a shaft speed range of 20–58 rpm. The diameter of this tank is 167 cm. The diameter of the largest axial impeller is 87 cm. Given the diameter of the production tank, the cross-sectional area can be determined as

$$A_{3780L} = \frac{\pi T^2_{3780L}}{4} = \frac{\pi(167cm)^2}{4} = 21{,}904cm$$

The next step is solving eq. 6 for effective pumping capacity in the larger vessel:

$$Q_{3780L} = (v_{b(378L)})(A_{3780L}) = (12.6cm/Sec)(21904cm^2)$$
$$= 275990cm^3/Sec$$

Earlier, the analysis established that the mixing of this product occurs in the turbulent flow regime because the Reynolds number obtained far exceeds the minimally required 2000. Therefore, the pumping number can be calculated for the 3780-L tank by using eq.4 to obtain

$$N_{Q(3780L)} = 1.1283 - [(1.07118)(\frac{87cm}{167cm})] = 0.57$$

Finally, eq. 6 is rearranged to solve for the appropriate shaft speed to be used in a 3780-L batch:

$$N_{3780L} = \frac{Q_{378L}}{N_{Q(3789L)}D^3_{3780L}} = \frac{275990cm^3/Sec}{(0.57)(87cm)^3} = 0.73Sec^{-1} = 44\ rpm$$

The shaft speed value obtained is well within the rpm range of the 3780-L tank agitator. To determine the rpm range for production batches, start with level-3 agitation at the low rpm end and level-5 agitation at the high rpm end. Table 2.2 provides bulk velocities for levels 3 and 5. In turn, these are used to calculate the respective pumping capacities, defined via eq. 7. The low and high speeds are then calculated, as described earlier, by rearranging eq.6.

This method can easily be used to show the logic behind the scale-up from original R&D batches to production-scale batches. Although scale-of agitation analysis has its limitations, especially in the mixing of suspension, non-Newtonian fluids and gas dispersions, similar analysis could be applied to these systems, provided that pertinent system variables were used. These variables may include superficial gas velocity, dimensionless aeration numbers for gas systems, and terminal settling velocity for suspensions.

Table 2.2 Process Requirements Set the Degree of Agitation for Solids Suspension.

Scale of agitation	**Bulk fluid Velocity (cm/sec)**	**Description of mixing**
1	3	Agitation levels 1 and 2 are characteristic of applications requiring minimum fluid velocities to achieve the product result
2	6	Agitators capable of level 2 will: a) Blend miscible fluids to uniformity if specific gravity differences are less than 0.1 and if the viscosity of the most viscous is less than 100 times that of the other b) Establish complete fluid-batch control c) Produce a flat but moving fluid-batch surface
3	9	Agitation levels 3–6 are characteristic of fluid velocities in most chemical (including pharmaceutical) industries agitated batches
4	12	Agitation levels 3–6 are characteristic of fluid velocities in most chemical (including pharmaceutical) industries agitated batches
5	15	Agitation levels 3–6 are characteristic of fluid velocities in most chemical (including pharmaceutical) industries agitated batches
6	18	Agitators capable of level 6 will: a) Blend miscible fluids to uniformity if specific gravity differences are less than 0.6 and if the viscosity of the most viscous is less than 10,000 times that of the other b) Suspend trace solids (<2%) with settling rates of 2–4 ft/min c) Produce surface rippling at lower viscosities
7	21	Agitation levels 7–10 are characteristic of applications requiring high fluid velocities for process result, such as mixing of the high-viscosity suspension preparations

Table 2.2 ***contd...***

Scale of agitation	Bulk fluid Velocity (cm/sec)	Description of mixing
8	24	Agitation levels 7–10 are characteristic of applications requiring high fluid velocities for process result, such as mixing of the high-viscosity suspension preparations
9	27	Agitation levels 7–10 are characteristic of applications requiring high fluid velocities for process result, such as mixing of the high-viscosity suspension preparations
10	30	Agitators capable of level 10 will: a) Blend miscible fluids to uniformity if specific gravity differences are less than 1.0 and if the viscosity of the most viscous is less than 100,000 times that of the other b) Suspend trace solids (<2%) with settling rates of 4–6 ft/min c) Provide surging surface at low viscosities

PROCESS SCALE UP FOR NDDS PRODUCTS

There are several different carriers with benefits made on the basis types in the novel drug delivery systems (NDDS). The traditional dosage forms display high dose and low availability, in-stability, first- pass effect, fluctuation of plasma drug levels, and fast release of medicinal products. By performance, protection, compliance with patients, and product shelf life. NDDS will mitigate the problems.

Types of Novel Drug Delivery System (NDDS)

Phytosome

Phytosomes, also called phyto-phospholipid complexes, are the vesicular systems formed by the interaction between hydrophilic parts of phospholipids and the phyto-active constituents resulting in the formation of hydrogen bonds between them. The structural difference between liposomes and phytosomes is that liposomes have their active ingredient inside the hydrophilic cavity or within the layers of membranes while in phytosomes, those components are a part of the membrane itself. Phytosomes are synthesized by complexing these active ingredients with phospholipids in the defined stoichiometric ratios under the predefined conditions. The resulting complex helps these active ingredients to pass through the outer membrane of gastrointestinal cells and reach their functional site. Due to this, the absorption of these components is greatly increased and their bioavailability becomes much greater as compared to the original component. Phytosomes have been found to significantly enhance the bioavailability of many plants extracts like curcumin, *Ginkgo biloba*, silymarin, ginseng, and polyphenolic compounds found in olive oil, green tea and grape seeds. The successfully formulated phytosome loaded with quercetin using phosphatidylcholine and cholesterol resulted in its better release and bioavailability, thus proves its potential to be used in formulation of fortified food products containing water insoluble antioxidants. In fact, for several decades, medicinal herbs and their active constituents have been utilized to treat different diseases[38].

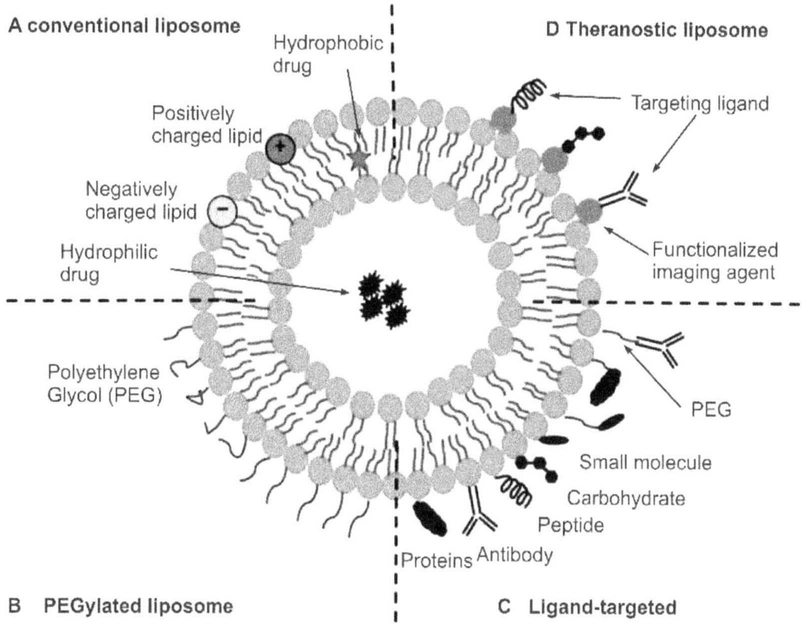

Fig.2.5 Schematic diagram of a typical noisome.

Liposomes

Liposomes are condensed bilayered vesicles with a completely contained aqueous volume. It is a lipid membrane bilayer consisting mainly of natural or synthetic phospholipids. The liposomes are named from two Greek words: 'Lipos' which means fat, 'Soma' the flesh. A liposome can be produced in a range of sizes as single or multi-lamella house, and its name concerns its building blocks, phospholipids, not its dimension. A liposome has no lipophobic substance, for example water, even if it does not contain. Artificial vesicles consisting of bilayer lipid are liposomes. Drugs may be filled into the liposomes and can be used to administer in cancer and other diseases as medicines. Biological membranes such as sonic disruption can be prepared. They are microparticulate or colloidal carriers, typically 0.05-5.0 μm in diameter, spontaneously forming in aqueous media such as lipids hydrate. DDSs involve delivering the potentially active drug to the site of action *via* a nano-vehicle to enhance the pharmacological properties of free drugs and cover their undesirable features through improving drug pharmacokinetics and biodistribution, as well as acting as drug reservoirs[39]. Liposomes are made up a relatively bio-compatible, biodegradable and aqueous material. An amount of natural and/or synthetic lipids are entangled in one or more bilayers. A large variety of medications can be administered through liposomes. In liposomes, either in phospholipids bilayer, varying lipophilicity can be encapsulated or at the interface of the two layers the captured amount of aqueous substances remain.

NIOSOMES

Niosomes are one of the best among these carriers. The self-assembly of non-ionic surfactants into vesicles was first reported in the 70s by the researchers in the cosmetic industry. Niosomes (non-ionic surfactant vesicles) obtained on hydration are microscopic lamellar structures formed upon combining non-ionic surfactant of the alkyl or dialkyl polyglycerol ether class with cholesterol. The non-ionic surfactants form a closed bilayer vesicle in aqueous media based on its amphiphilic nature using some energy, for example heat, physical agitation to form this structure. In the bilayer structure, hydrophobic parts are oriented away from the aqueous solvent, whereas the hydrophilic heads remain in contact with the aqueous solvent. The properties of the vesicles can be changed by varying the composition of the vesicles, size, lamellarity, tapped volume, surface charge and concentration. Various forces act inside the vesicle, such as, van der Waals forces among surfactant molecules, repulsive forces emerging from the electrostatic interactions among charged groups of surfactant molecules, entropic repulsive forces of the head groups of surfactants, short-acting repulsive forces, etc. These forces are responsible for maintaining the vesicular structure of niosomes. But, the stability of niosomes are affected by type of surfactant, nature of encapsulated drug, storage temperature, detergents, use of membrane spanning lipids, the interfacial polymerisation of surfactant monomers *in situ,* inclusion of charged molecule. Due to the presence of hydrophilic, amphiphilic and lipophilic moieties in the structure, these can accommodate drug molecules with a wide range of solubility. These may act as a depot, releasing the drug in a controlled manner. The therapeutic performance of the drug molecules can also be improved by delayed clearance from the circulation, protecting the drug from biological environment and restricting effects to target cells. Noisome made of alpha, omega-hexadecyl-bis-(1-aza-18-crown-6) (Bola-surfactant)-Span 80-cholesterol (2:3:1 molar ratio) is named as Bola-Surfactant containing noisome[40]. The surfactants used in niosome preparation should be biodegradable, biocompatible and non-immunogenic. A dry product known as pro-niosomes may be hydrated immediately before use to yield aqueous niosome dispersions. The problems of niosomes such as aggregation, fusion and leaking, and provide additional convenience in transportation, distribution, storage, and dosing. Niosomes behave *in vivo* like liposomes, prolonging the circulation of entrapped drug and altering its organ distribution and metabolic stability. As with liposomes, the properties of niosomes depend on the composition of the bilayer as well as method of their production. It is reported that the intercalation of cholesterol in the bilayers decreases the entrapment volume during formulation, and thus entrapment efficiency. The structure of the niosome has been shown in figure 2.6.

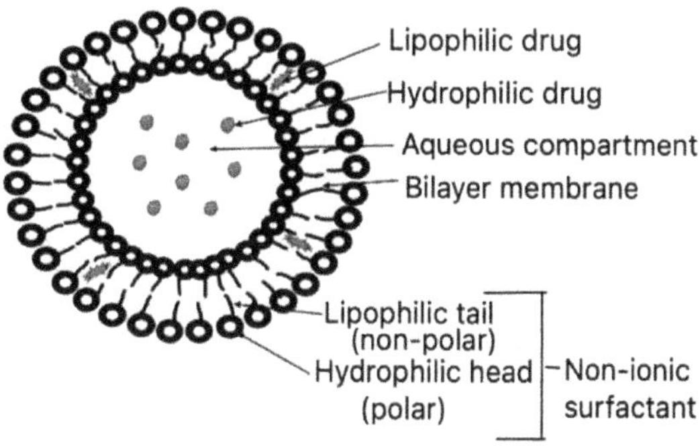

Fig.2.6 Schematic diagram of a neosomes.

Transfersomes

Gregor Cevc introduced the definition and idea of transferosome in 1991. An efficacious, successful therapeutic treatment cannot be done in most cases, often due to many reasons, such as the occurrence of hepatic first-pass metabolism, adverse side effects, the rejection of invasive treatments and poor patient compliance[41]. Therefore, several drug delivery systems have been developed and studied over the past decades to overcome these problems. One promising approach is the use of transdermal delivery systems, as they are minimally invasive methods without first-pass effects. However, the barrier function of the skin that prevents or dampens the transdermal delivery of therapeutic agents has to be addressed. Nanoencapsulation using a lipid-based vesicular system such as liposomes has been used to overcome the aforesaid challenge. Liposomes facilitate drug transport through the skin by three possible mechanisms: adsorption to the skin surface with a subsequent transferring of the drug directly from vesicles to skin, fusion with the lipid matrix of the stratum corneum, thereby increasing drug partitioning into the skin, and lipid exchange between the liposomal membrane and cell membrane, facilitating the diffusion of the drug across the membrane. However, the problem with conventional liposomes is that they do not deeply penetrate into the viable skin and blood circulation. Therefore, liposomes have been widely used as drug carriers for dermal delivery and not for transdermal delivery. Conventional liposomes also have limitations, such as the poor encapsulation efficiency of hydrophilic drugs, an unstable membrane that results in leaky behaviour and a short half-life. These major obstacles have led to the discovery and development of other novel vesicles such as niosomes, sphingosomes, bilosomes, chitosomes, transfersomes, ethosomes and invasomes.

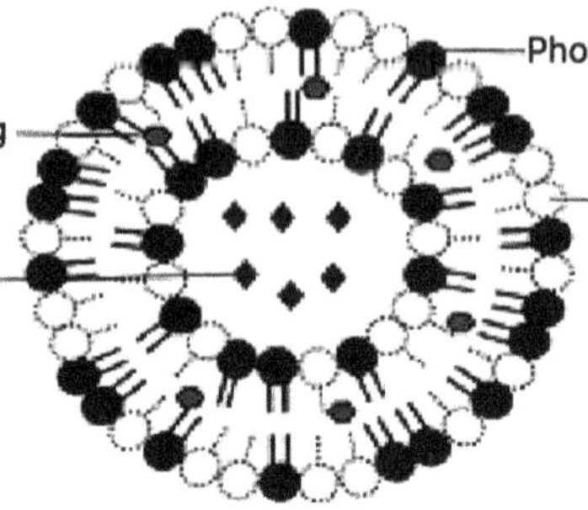

Fig.2.7 Schematic representation of transfersome.

Stability on storage of Nanoparticles

The need and degree of purification depend on the final purpose of the formula. Gel filtration, ultra-centrifuge, dialysis and, recently, cross-flow filtering are the most frequently mentioned procedures. Freeze-drying appears to be a highly stabilizing method. The technique involves freezing of the suspension and subsequent reduction of the water content by sublimation by lower pressures. Freezing is the most aggressive step in this regard. A complete preclusion must be avoided by adding certain additives. In order to prevent alteration of the suspension it is therefore necessary to enhance the resistance of an anoparticles by adding a cryoprotector. At times the glucose, trealose, mannitol, and sorbitol cryoprotectants were added to ensure redistribution or to permit the suspension to be vitrified in refreshment and to prevent liquid suspension crystallization.

STRESS FORMULAS

When a material is subjected to an external force, a resisting force is set up in the component. The internal resistance force per unit area acting on a material is called the stress at a point. It is a tensor quantity having unit of N/m^2 or Pascal.

It may be necessitated to analyse the kinds of forces that are exerted on each of the load-carrying members before one can design them. This calls for the use of the principles of statics in which one should have already gained competence. The following discussion provides a review of some of the key principles one will need in this course. The work as a designer proceeds as follows:

1) Analysis of the forces that are exerted on each load-carrying member using the principles of statics.

2) Identification of the kinds of stresses that each member is subjected to by the applied forces.
3) Proposal for the general shape of each load-carrying member and the material from which each is to be made.
4) Completing the stress analysis for each member to determine its final dimensions.

Let us work through steps 1 and 2 now, as a review of statics. One can improve the ability to do steps 3 and 4 by reviewing the strength of materials and adding competencies that build on that foundation.

One major goal of stress analysis is to determine the point within a load-carrying member that is subjected to the highest stress level. One should develop the ability to visualize a stress element, a single, infinitesimally small cube from the member in a highly stressed area, and to show vectors that represent the kind of stresses that exist on that element. The orientation of the stress element is critical, and it must be aligned with specified axes on the member, typically called x, y, and z. There are examples of stress elements with two basic fundamental kinds of stress: Normal (tensile and compressive) and shear. The complete three dimensional cube and the simplified, two-dimensional square forms are shown for the stress elements. The square is one face of the cube in a selected plane. The sides of the square represent the projections of the faces of the cube that are perpendicular to the selected plane. It is recommended that one can visualize the cube form first and then represent a square stress element showing the stresses on a particular plane of interest. In some problems with more general states of stress, two or three square stress elements may be required to depict the complete stress condition. Tensile and compressive stresses, called normal stresses, are acting perpendicularly to opposite faces of the stress element. Tensile stresses tend to pull on the element, whereas compressive stresses tend to crush it. Shear stresses are created by direct shear, vertical shear in beams, or torsion. In each case, the action on an element subjected to shear is a tendency to cut the element by exerting a stress downward on one face while simultaneously exerting a stress upward on the opposite, parallel face. This action is that of a simple pair of shears or scissors. But note that if only one pair of shear stresses acts on a stress element, it will not be in equilibrium. Rather, it will tend to spin because the pair of shear stresses forms a couple. To produce equilibrium, a second pair of shear stresses on the other two faces of the element must exist, acting in a direction that opposes the first pair.

Types of stress

Stress can be defined as the internal resistance offered by a unit area of a material to an externally applied load. Normal stresses (s) are either tensile (positive) or compressive (negative). For a load-carrying member in which the external load is uniformly distributed across the cross-sectional area of the member, the magnitude of the stress can be calculated from the direct stress formula:

Normal stress

Direct Tensile or Compressive Stress

$$\sigma = \text{force/area} = F/A$$

The units for stress are always force per unit area.

Common units in the U.S. Customary system and the SI metric system follow.

U.S. Customary Units	SI Metric Units
lb/in2 = psi	N/m2 = pascal = Pa
kips/in2 = ksi	N/mm2 = megapascal
Note: 1.0 kip = 1000 lb	= 10^6 Pa = MPa
1.0 ksi = 1000 psi	

The conditions on the use of above equation are as follows:

1. The load-carrying member must be straight.
2. The line of action of the load must pass through the centroid of the cross section of the member.
3. The member must be of uniform cross section near where the stress is being computed.
4. The material must be homogeneous and isotropic.
5. In the case of compression members, the member must be short to prevent buckling.

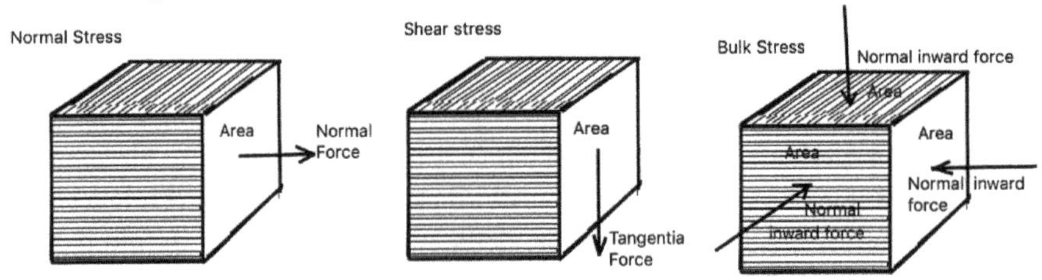

Fig.2.8 Schematic representation of types of stress.

$$\text{Normal stress} = \frac{\text{Normal Force}}{\text{Area}}$$

or,

$$\sigma_n = \frac{F_n}{A}$$

Shear stress

Direct shear stress occurs when the applied force tends to cut through the member as scissors or shears do or when a punch and a die are used to punch a slug of material from a sheet. Another important example of direct shear in machine design is the tendency for a key to be sheared off at the section between the shaft and the hub of a machine element when transmitting torque. Figure 3–7 shows the action. The method of computing direct shear stress is similar to that used for computing direct tensile stress because the applied force is assumed to be uniformly distributed across the cross section of the part that is resisting the force. But the kind of stress is shear stress rather than normal stress. The symbol used for shear stress is the Greek letter tau (τ). The formula for direct shear stress can thus be written as

$$\text{Shear stress} = \frac{\text{Tangential force}}{\text{Area}}$$

or,

$$\sigma_t = \frac{F_t}{A}$$

Bulk stress

$$\text{Bulk stress.} = \frac{\text{Normal inward force}}{\text{Areaa}}$$

or,

$$\sigma_B = P$$

True stress

The true stress is defined as the ratio of the load to the cross section area at any instant.

$$(\sigma_r) = \frac{\textbf{Load}}{\textbf{Instantaneous area}} = \boldsymbol{\sigma}\ \mathbf{(1 + \boldsymbol{\varepsilon})}$$

Where σ and ε is the engineering stress and engineering strain respectively.

STRESS ON EQUIPMENTS

One of the most important issues in keeping membrane structures in good condition is to maintain the proper tension distribution over the membrane. However, it is not easy to determine the real stress level in the membrane quantitatively after completion of the structures. Fluttering by strong wind or ponding caused by rain water may cause severe damage to the membrane structure itself. Therefore, it is very important to know the magnitude of existing stress in membrane structures for their maintenance and management. In this paper, the authors propose a new method that can measure membrane stress using sound waves, and hold experimental tests of membrane stress measurement that use the sound external excitation with sine wave and white noise[42].

Charge accumulation on the spacer surface in gas insulated equipment is very severe under DC field, leading to flashover easily, which restricts the application of DC GIS/GIL. Therefore, the knowledge about the charge accumulation characteristic in gas insulated equipment at DC stress is essential. In this paper, we have reviewed the research methods and the characteristics of charge accumulation on spacer. A summary of charge measurement methods and setups are presented. And the surface charge inversion algorithms are introduced. Then the simulation model for charge accumulation and dc field is reviewed. Subsequently, the charge accumulation mechanisms and phenomenon, the influence factor of surface charge accumulation and the influence of accumulated charge on spacer insulation characteristics are summarized. In addition, some suppressions methods of surface charge accumulation are discussed. Finally, based on the understanding of charge accumulation on spacer, some suggestions on the further studies are presented to aid the design of a better spacer free from surface charges[43]. Multi-physics process-based understanding of the subsurface (0–4 km depth) is increasingly enabling society to address many significant challenges through existing and newly developing technology. Examples include low and high temperature geothermal energy extraction techniques, recovery of conventional and unconventional hydrocarbons, the storage isolation of substances such as CO_2 and toxic radioactive waste[44], energy storage and the subsurface injection of liquid wastes. Sustainable management of the subsurface requires the ability to understand, predict and monitor the physical response of the geo-reservoirs and the surrounding rock mass to changes in fluid pressure, stress, temperature, fluid composition and biological activity. These physical responses are often described as combinations of thermal (T), mechanical (M), hydraulic (H), chemical (C), and micro-biological processes (B). Experimental approaches provide an opportunity to gain better understanding of process interactions and provide quantitative values that underpin the development and calibration of behavioural laws. A primary motivation for the experimental apparatus development reported here is to progress the capability for experimental investigation of coupled THM processes in geo-reservoirs under *in-situ* condition controls that are beyond the current state of the art. The design goals for this development emphasise large samples to allow more complexity of the fracture(s) within the sample, the capability of achieving rotatable, true-triaxial stress states, the ability to heat the sample in the apparatus and the ability to investigate fluid flow through the sample under controlled conditions. To date this has not been possible within a single experiment. This paper describes the new apparatus and initial operational outcomes that demonstrate its capabilities.

STRESS ON PRODUCT UNIFORMITY

The innovator drug product containing clopidogrel hydrogensulfate (named hereafter clopidogrel) was discovered by Sanofi. It is marketed by Sanofi–Synthelabo and BMS worldwide under the brand names PLAVIX® and ISCOVER®. Clopidogrel is an antiplatelet agent which selectively inhibits the binding of adenosine diphosphate (ADP) to its platelet receptor and blocks the subsequent ADP-mediated activation of the glycoprotein GPIIb/IIIa complex, thereby inhibiting platelet aggregation. The clinical benefits of clopidogrel have been demonstrated in trials involving more than 30,000 patients and it is used worldwide for the long term prevention of atherothrombotic events (myocardial infarction, stroke, peripheral arterial disease, acute coronary syndrome, cardio-vascular death). Several copies of PLAVIX®/ISCOVER® have been brought onto the market in some Asian and South American countries.

The molecule is a thienopyridine derivative containing an assymetric carbon leading to the existence of two enantiomers (R and S) as shown in Fig 2.9. Studies from Sanofi–synthelabo showed that the active compound clopidogrel is the S-enantiomer. This implies that the content of the R-enantiomer must be carefully controlled in clopidogrel bulk substance and drug products, as required by health authorities. It should be noted that there is currently no official Pharmacopoeia monograph that would set official limits to the impurities and content of clopidogrel bulk samples. According to the ICH guidance (ICH Q3B) entitled "impurities in new drug products", the level of the impurities contained in the drug product should also be carefully controlled and the upper level of the impurities should be determined and supported by adequate data in the dossier filed for registration of a new drug.

Few methods for the determination of clopidogrel have been reported in the literature. A non-stereospecific liquid chromatographic (LC) method for the determination of clopidogrel in oral dosage forms has been validated and used for degradation studies under stress conditions[45]. The chiral inversion of clopidogrel in vivo was investigated using a chiral HPLC procedure while a non-stereospecific assay method was applied to monitor the hydrolysis of clopidogrel. A capillary zone electrophoretic method using cyclodextrins for the enantio-separation of drugs also evaluated clopidogrel.

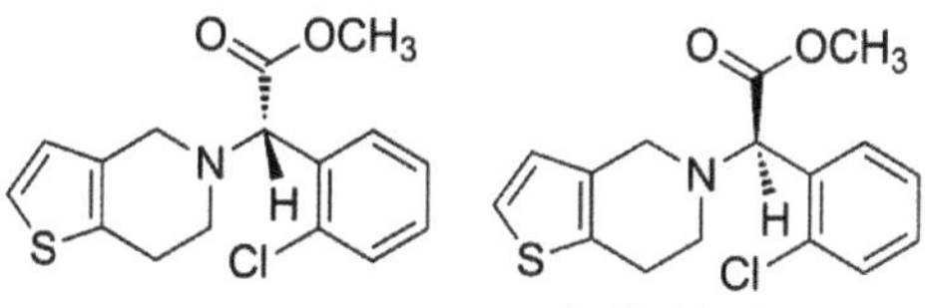

Fig.2.9 S-Clopidogrel.

Another important part of the quality control is the release of the active from its pharmaceutical formulation, in this case a tablet. In most cases an in vitro dissolution test using paddles is performed to check whether a minimum percentage is dissolved at a predetermined time point. However, dissolution profiles with an equal percentage dissolved at a certain time point can have a different shape before reaching that time point, which, from a pharmacokinetic point of view, can lead to a difference in plasma concentrations. So, for comparison, it is advisable to check multiple time points.

In this paper, the quality of 18 copies is described and compared to the quality of the original drug product (PLAVIX®/ISCOVER®). The mass uniformity, the purity and content using a chiral LC separation method and the dissolution profiles were examined. Samples were analysed at different time points: first at time point zero and then after 3 months in their original packaging at 40 °C and a relative humidity of 75% to check the influence of these stress conditions on the impurity profile.

A high level of impurities was found in many copies; over 60% of the copies contained more than four times the amount of hydrolysis product or R-enantiomer compared to the reference drug product. In addition, 50% of the samples did not comply with the 95–105% limits for content. It should be noted that there is no Pharmacopoeia monograph at the moment of writing this document that would set limits to the impurities and content in clopidogrel bulk substance. Although most copies passed the dissolution specifications at 30 min, no adequate dissolution profiles were obtained for most of them. Differences in excipients led to different tablet masses and they also had an influence, together with the packaging of the tablets, on the stability during 3 months under stress conditions. Most of the copies are not of equivalent quality compared to the innovator drug product.

STRESS ON STABILITY

Stress testing of the drug substance can help identify the likely degradation products, which can in turn help establishing the degradation pathways and the intrinsic stability of the molecule and validate the stability indicating power of the analytical procedures used. The nature of the stress testing will depend on the individual drug substance and the type of drug product involved. Stress testing is likely to be carried out on a single batch of the drug substance. It should include the effect of temperatures in 10°C increments such as, 50°C, 60°C, etc. above that for accelerated testing, humidity, such as, 75% RH or greater where appropriate, oxidation, and photolysis on the drug substance. The testing should also evaluate the susceptibility of the drug substance to hydrolysis across a wide range of pH values when in solution or suspension. Photostability testing should be an integral part of stress testing. The standard conditions for photostability testing are described in ICH Q1B. Examining degradation products under stress conditions is useful in establishing degradation pathways and developing and validating suitable analytical procedures. However, it may not be necessary to examine specifically for certain degradation products if it has been demonstrated that they are not formed under accelerated or long term storage conditions. Results from these studies will form an integral part of the information provided to regulatory authorities.

Data from formal stability studies should be provided on at least three primary batches of the drug substance. The batches should be manufactured to a minimum of pilot scale by the same synthetic route as, and using a method of manufacture and procedure that simulates the final process to be used for, production batches. The overall quality of the batches of drug substance placed on formal stability studies should be representative of the quality of the material to be made on a production scale. Other supporting data can be provided.

Specification, which is a list of tests, reference to analytical procedures, and proposed acceptance criteria, is addressed in ICH Q6A and Q6B. In addition, specification for degradation products in a drug substance is discussed in Q3A. Stability studies should include testing of those attributes of the drug substance that are susceptible to change during storage and are likely to influence quality, safety, and/or efficacy. The testing should cover, as appropriate, the physical, chemical, biological, and microbiological attributes. Validated stability-indicating analytical procedures should be applied. Whether and to what extent replication should be performed will depend on the results from validation studies.

Animals and plants evolved in the context of immense microbial diversity. Multicellular life forms only a small and highly derived portion of universal trees of life, with the rest occupied by bacteria, archaea and microbial eukaryotes. In keeping with their phylogenetic diversity, these ancient microbial lineages have developed great genomic and metabolic diversity. Exceeding even the immense diversity of cellular microorganisms is the vast array of phages, viruses and other transmissible genetic elements (conjugative transposons, integrative and conjugative elements, addiction plasmids, and so on) that infect them. This wilderness of microorganisms, viruses and parasitic genetic elements was already long established before the emergence of animals and plants. Thus, the ecological context in which animals and plants emerged both necessitated defence against exploitation by opportunistic microorganisms, and provided many opportunities to benefit from microbial metabolic innovations through mutualistic symbioses. Reflecting this heritage, symbiosis with microorganisms is ubiquitous in metazoans, influencing host health, development, disease susceptibility, and even behaviour. As symbiotic microbial communities and their associated gene pools (microbiomes) influence many aspects of fitness, animals and plants regulate them. Animal mechanisms for microbiome regulation are diverse—ranging from the specialized light organs of the Hawaiian bobtail squid to production of microbiome-targeted oligosaccharides in human breastmilk.

They have in common the aim of both preventing invasions by pathogens and managing symbiotic microorganisms to maximize their benefit to the host. These activities partially overlap, as mutualisms with beneficial microorganisms often provide animal hosts a measure of defence against pathogens through mechanisms such as competition for resources, antibiotic production, metabolic inhibition and spatial occlusion, as well as through feedbacks with host immunity. Recent evidence suggests that even phages may have been recruited by hosts as defensive mutualists on animal mucosal surfaces—an especially important and flexible defence for animals lacking a host-derived adaptive immune system. Predicting when and how normal regulation of microbiomes breaks down is at the heart of many important problems in microbial ecology. Under normal circumstances, the defensive activities of animal hosts, and their typical microbiota and phages, are thought to restrict microbiome membership, avoiding the many detrimental possibilities in favour of a smaller range of beneficial microbiome configurations. A corollary of this observation is that stressors need not, at least in principle, shift a microbiome to a specific dysbiotic configuration in order to reduce host fitness—they need only release of normal regulation of microbiome membership. Currently, most microbial ecology workflows attempt to identify a specific microbiome configuration associated with stress or disease. Overall community changes in host microbiomes are typically examined using high-throughput marker gene or shotgun metagenomic data. Commonly measured microbial community properties include richness (diversity of species within a sample), evenness (distribution of counts between one or many species), and β-diversity (turnover of species between samples). Analysis of β-diversity has been particularly useful in microbial ecology. While β-diversity was originally defined as species turnover along a habitat gradient, microbial ecologists have applied measures of β-diversity to examine differences in communities separated by health status, the passage of time, or divergence in the evolutionary history of their host. These differences are visualized by computing a matrix of β-diversity distances between samples, then using ordination methods such as non-metric multidimensional scaling (NMDS) or principal coordinates analysis (PCoA) to represent this multidimensional matrix in two or three dimensions. In many cases, the microbial communities associated with diseased hosts will form distinct clusters in such two- or three-dimensional ordination spaces, indicating a correlation between microbiome change and degraded host health (for example, chronic periodontitis, corals challenged by turf algal competition, and so on). Additional experiments, such as microbiome transplants, test the direction of causation underlying these correlations. In many cases, important host phenotypes, ranging from increased energy harvest (and weight gain) to the capability to digest otherwise poisonous foods, are conferred by distinct microbial communities that are reflected by clusters in ordination space. However, despite their well-understood importance, these patterns of microbial community change may not reflect the full range of dynamics needed to understand the contribution of microorganisms to host health and disease. In this Perspective, we examine findings in diverse systems from threatened coral reefs to simian immunodeficiency virus (SIV)-infected chimpanzees where host stress or disease produces stochastic rather than deterministic changes in the microbiome. These stochastic changes often induce dispersion, rather than location, effects on microbial community composition. That is, rather than shift the microbiome to a new discrete configuration, producing clusters, these stressors allow the microbiomes of stressed individuals to take on a wider range of possible configurations than healthy controls, producing a constrained 'core' of control microbiomes surrounded by a large 'halo' or 'smear' of stressed or diseased microbiomes. Observations of microbiome variability associated with disease have led several workers to propose an Anna Karenina principle (AKP) for animal microbiomes. The principle derives from the opening line of Tolstoy's Anna Karenina: "all happy families are all alike; each unhappy family is unhappy in its own way". It was popularized by Diamond in reference to the many reasons why animals might prove undomesticable. Translated into a hypothesis for host-associated microbiomes, the AKP predicts that certain stressors have stochastic rather than deterministic effects on community composition. In these cases, 'all healthy microbiomes are similar; each dysbiotic microbiome is dysbiotic in its own way'. Giongo and colleagues proposed that microbial changes during autoimmune misregulation in type 1 diabetes followed the AKP. Independently, in applying a new method (Dirichlet multinomial mixtures) for clustering microbial samples into enterotypes, Holmes and colleagues noted that obese gut microbiomes may be associated with a broader range of configurations than lean[46]. On this basis, they suggested that there may be an AKP for human microbiomes, in that samples from obese patients are explained by a mixture of more enterotypes than samples from healthy patients. Later, Dey et al. made similar observations in investigating the microbiome of Crohn's disease. Despite this remarkable convergence in findings, interpretation, and even metaphor across diverse specialties, AKP effects are little discussed in the microbiological literature. This situation makes it challenging for workers to compare notes. Indeed, even the above publications describing AKP effects in specific systems do not reference the other works, and these effects are not well known outside of specialized publications on particular diseases. We argue that AKP effects in animal microbiomes are common, important, and often linked to declining host health. We synthesize observations of microbiome dispersion in diverse systems into testable predictions, and show how the predicted patterns, although often quite clear, are easily missed—or dismissed as statistical artifacts—by the most commonly applied workflows. We describe different types of community dynamics that could produce apparent AKP effects (Box 1) and present methods that can help distinguish them. We also discuss scenarios that appear to decrease inter-individual variation relative to healthy controls (see 'Anti-AKP effects', Box 1). We then address new empirical and theoretical avenues for exploring the microbiome opened by these emerging perspectives, and discuss their broader importance for personalized medicine.

Testing Frequency

For long-term studies, frequency of testing should be sufficient to establish the stability profile of the drug substance. For drug substances with a proposed re-test period of at least 12 months, the frequency of testing at the long term storage condition should normally be every 3 months over the first year, every 6 months over the second year, and annually thereafter through the proposed re-test period. At the accelerated storage condition, a minimum of three time points, including the initial and final time points, such as, 0, 3, and 6 months), from a 6-month study is recommended. Where an expectation (based on development experience) exists that results from accelerated studies are likely to approach significant change criteria, increased testing should be conducted either by adding samples at the final time point or by including a fourth time point in the study design. When testing at the intermediate storage condition is called for as a result of significant change at the accelerated storage condition, a minimum of four time points, including the initial and final time points (e.g., 0, 6, 9, 12 months), from a 12-month study is recommended.

Storage condition

In general, a drug substance should be evaluated under storage conditions (with appropriate tolerances) that test its thermal stability and, if applicable, its sensitivity to moisture. The storage conditions and the lengths of studies chosen should be sufficient to cover storage, shipment, and subsequent use. The long term testing should cover a minimum of 12 months' duration on at least three primary batches at the time of submission and should be continued for a period of time sufficient to cover the proposed re-test period. Additional data accumulated during the assessment period of the registration application should be submitted to the authorities if requested. Data from the accelerated storage condition and, if appropriate, from the intermediate storage condition can be used to evaluate the effect of short term excursions outside the label storage conditions (such as might occur during shipping). Long term, accelerated, and, where appropriate, intermediate storage conditions for drug substances are detailed in the sections below. The general case applies if the drug substance is not specifically covered by a subsequent section. Alternative storage conditions can be used if justified.

Different storage conditions are required for pharmaceuticals. To ensure the stability of a pharmaceutical preparation for the period of its intended shelf life, the product must be stored in proper conditions. The labelling of each product includes the desired conditions of storage. The terms generally employed in such labelling have meanings defined by the USP. For example,

- Storage at freezer refers to a place in which the temperature is maintained between −25° and −10° (−13° and 14 °F).
- Refrigerated storage refers to a cold place in which the temperature is maintained between 2° and 8° (36° and 46 °F).
- Cold storage refers to a cold place in which the temperature does not exceed 8°C (46°F).
- Storage at cool place refers to a cold place in which any temperature between 8° and 15° (46° and 59 °F).
- Storage at controlled cold temperature is defined as temperature maintained thermostatically between 2° and 8° (36° and 46°F), that allows for excursion in temperature between temperature between 0° and 15°C (32° and 59°F) that may be experienced during storage, shipping, and distribution such that allowable calculated mean kinetic temperature is not more than 8° (46°F). Transient spikes up to 25°C (77° F) may be permitted if the manufacturer so instructs and provided that such spikes do not exceed 24 hours unless supported by stability data or the manufacturer instructs otherwise.
- Storage at room temperature means temperature prevailing in a working area.
- Storage at controlled room temperature refers to the temperature maintained thermostatically that encompasses at the usual and customary working environment of 20° – 25°(68° – 77°F). The following conditions also apply. Mean kinetic temperature not to exceed 25°. Excursions between 15° and 39° (59° and 86°F) that are experienced in pharmacies, hospitals, and warehouses, and during shipping are allowed. The mean kinetic temperature does not exceeding 25°, spiking up to 40° are permitted as long as they do not exceeding 24 h. Spiking above 40° may be permitted only if the manufacturer so instructs.
- Articles may be labelled for storage at 'controlled room temperature' or at 'up to 25°', or other wording based on the same mean kinetic temperature.
- An article for which storage at Controlled room temperature is directed may, alternatively, be stored and shipped in a cool place or refrigerated, unless otherwise specified in the individual monograph or on the label.
- Storage at warm condition refers to any place temperature between 30° and 40°C(86° and 104°F).
- Storage at excessive hot temperature refers to any temperature more than 40°C(104°F).
- Storage at dry place means a place that does not exceed 40% average relative humidity at 20° (68 °F) or the equivalent water vapor pressure at other temperatures. The determination may be made by direct measurement at the place or may be based on reported climatic conditions.

Determination is based on NLT 12 equally spaced measurements that encompass either a season, a year, or, where recorded data demonstrate, the storage period of the article. There may be values of up to 45% relative humidity provided that the average value does not exceed 40% relative humidity. Storage in a container validated to protect the article from moisture vapor, including storage in bulk, is considered a dry place.

- Storage with protection from freezing means the place, where, in addition to the risk of breakage of the container, freezing subjects an article to loss of strength or potency, or to destructive alteration of its characteristics, the container label bears an appropriate instruction to protect the article from freezing.
- Protection from light means the place, where light subjects an article to loss of strength or potency, or to destructive alteration of its characteristics, the container label bears an appropriate instruction to protect the article from light.

Evaluation

The purpose of the stability study is to establish, based on testing a minimum of three batches of the drug substance and evaluating the stability information (including, as appropriate, results of the physical, chemical, biological, and microbiological tests), a re-test period applicable to all future batches of the drug substance manufactured under similar circumstances. The degree of variability of individual batches affects the confidence that a future production batch will remain within specification throughout the assigned re-test period. The data may show so little degradation and so little variability that it is apparent from looking at the data that the requested re-test period will be granted. Under these circumstances, it is normally unnecessary to go through the formal statistical analysis; providing a justification for the omission should be sufficient. An approach for analysing the data on a quantitative attribute that is expected to change with time is to determine the time at which the 95% one-sided confidence limit for the mean curve intersects the acceptance criterion. If analysis shows that the batch-to-batch variability is small, it is advantageous to combine the data into one overall estimate. This can be done by first applying appropriate statistical tests, such as, p values for level of significance of rejection of more than 0.25 to the slopes of the regression lines and zero time intercepts for the individual batches. If it is inappropriate to combine data from several batches, the overall retest period should be based on the minimum time a batch can be expected to remain within acceptance criteria. The nature of any degradation relationship will determine whether the data should be transformed for linear regression analysis. Usually the relationship can be represented by a linear, quadratic, or cubic function on an arithmetic or logarithmic scale. Statistical methods should be used to test the goodness of fit of the data on all batches and combined batches, where appropriate, to the assumed degradation line or curve. Limited extrapolation of the real time data from the long term storage condition beyond the observed range to extend the re-test period can be undertaken at approval time, if justified. This justification should be based on what is known about the mechanism of degradation, the results of testing under accelerated conditions, the goodness of fit of any mathematical model, batch size, existence of supporting stability data, etc. However, this extrapolation assumes that the same degradation relationship will continue to apply beyond the observed data. Any evaluation should cover not only the assay, but also the levels of degradation products and other appropriate attributes.

STRESS ON RAW MATERIALS

In 2008, the European Commission launched the Raw Materials Initiative, based on three main pillars: to ensure the access to raw materials on world market at undistorted conditions; to foster sustainable supply of raw materials from European sources and to reduce the EU's consumption of primary raw materials. To prioritize the policy initiatives in the field of resource security, the EC identified the materials facing the highest supply risk with respect to the whole economy. The topic of resource criticality is also mentioned in the Flagship Initiative "Resource Efficient Europe", which includes the goal of reducing the use of materials through enhancing the efficiency in the resource use. In this context, "measure to take life cycle impacts more into account, to avoid waste, reuse and recycling more, improved research and innovation and other measures to improve market structure" are pointed out as main strategies. The European Innovation Partnership on Raw Materials has been launched to foster the technological advances for increasing the internal supply of raw materials, substituting the critical ones and improve their recyclability. The objectives of this Partnership include (1) the achievement of up to ten pilot plants for the exploration, extraction and processing, collection and recycling of raw materials; (2) the substitution for at least three key applications of critical and scarce raw materials; (3) the enhancement of efficiency in material use and in prevention, (4) the re-use and recycling of valuable raw materials from waste streams (especially for materials whose production implies high environmental impacts) and (5) a dynamic modelling system linking trends in supply and demand with economically exploitable reserves and (6) a full life cycle analysis.

- **Security of supply**

  The ad hoc working group that compiled the EU study on Critical Raw Materials considered supply risk and economic importance of different materials as the two main variables. Many other criticality assessments have been published in recent years and different methodologies for their identification have been proposed and debated. Some studies have been conducted also at sectorial level, with reference to the energy sector that requires many technology metals, especially in the case of low-carbon technologies[47].

In these studies, the indicators used to assess the materials criticality vary, but they usually take into account different components: geological, economic, technological, social and regulatory, geopolitical. Aspects like the supply concentration, the economic importance of materials, their substitutability and recycling potential are the most commonly included in these assessments.

- **Resource Scarcity**

  A different perspective on resource depletion looks at the population growth and the economic development of emerging countries, which are driving the demand of raw materials to unprecedented levels, as main threats for future resource availability. This concern rises especially when a principle of ecological and social justice in the use of resources (both between different geographical areas and between present and future generations) is taken into account. Scarcity of abiotic resources is a matter of concern also for the related environmental impacts. The exploitation of lower grade deposits, in fact, implies higher impacts on ecosystems. As soon as a lower grade of resource becomes available, extraction implies increasing energy consumption, emissions, water requirements, waste, bigger impacts on landscape as well as the exploration of ecologically sensitive areas.

  Therefore, increased scarcity can imply higher costs for environmental protection. These costs are reduced when operating in developing countries, having low governance and poor environmental regulation. At the same time, such conditions favour the rise of conflicts related to the control of natural resources and lead to an increased risk, both for producers and downstream users.

- **Resources and sustainability Assessment**

  Life Cycle Assessment (LCA) is an internationally standardised methodology for assessing the impacts of products, both goods and services, along their supply chains. Resources consumed and emissions that are associated with the supply, use, and end-of-life of products are compiled in an inventory phase. These are then further assessed in terms of environmental, health, and resource related burdens through the use of indicators in an impact assessment.

All of the models used in LCA have an anthropocentric approach, as they focus on the use value for humans, but are based on different theoretical approaches, classification methods and purposes. The (ILCD) International reference Life Cycle Data grouped the different methods in four categories: the ones focusing on an inherent property of the resource; the ones measuring scarcity; the methods for water and the methods accounting the future consequence of resource extraction. The ILCD recommended a method based on resource scarcity, thus accounting the ratio between resource extraction and reserve. None of the endpoint methods that estimate, such as, impacts at the Area-of-Protection level were recommended, since there is no consensus on the proper methodology for assessing the future consequences of the resource use and scarcity.

STRESS ON PHYSICAL LAYOUT

Facility layout planning (FLP) involves the process of physically arranging all the production factors that make up the production system so it can suitably and efficiently comply with the organisation's strategic objectives. As part of business operational strategies, FLP is considered one of the most important design decisions. It also significantly affects the efficiency of production systems and their productivity level Figure 1 depicts a general framework of FLP, which can also be used by the reader as a guiding thread throughout this article.

Efficient FLP must ensure that production schedules are met in the short, mid and long terms and at a lower cost, while adequately using space and guaranteeing, in turn, a certain degree of flexibility for future re-layouts and minimum health/security risks at work. Conversely, inefficient layouts can simultaneously lead to bottlenecks, congestion and poorly used space, and too much work underway can accumulate, while job posts can become idle or overloaded. All this can entail anxiety and ill ease for workers, accidents at work, and make the control of operations and personnel management difficult. Moreover, if a good closeness level is lacking among the organisation's working centres, the working day in transport activities cannot be put to the best use, which contributes no value. This is one of the main reasons why production times increase and work productivity levels lower.

Despite its importance, FLP is no easy problem to solve. The most convenient generation and selection of facility layouts for an organisation involve a complex and iterative process that depends on rating the elements shaping the goods/services production system. According to the computational complexity theory, FLP is considered an NP-hard (non-polynomial hard problem) optimisation problem because no solution algorithms exist that provide an optimum solution in a reasonable polynomial time[48]. Despite their high degree of complexity, several authors have dealt with these problems by contributing acceptable solutions in realistic calculation times. It is stressed that when FLP is planned by assuming demand remains constant throughout the planning horizon, this problem is known as static or single-period FLP (SFLP). In many production systems however, considering a single design may not be practical because the material flow is not likely to remain invariable with time. Conversely, when demand is seasonal or vastly varies, it might be more worthwhile considering a different FLP for each time period, in which case the planning approach is either dynamic or multiperiod (DFLP).

Since the second half of the twentieth century, FLP has been a broadly discussed scientific subject because it has been considered one of the most important classic operations management and industrial engineering problems. Some literature reviews have dealt with it in more or less depth. Most have centred on specific dimensions of the problem[49], but others have covered them more generally. Despite such wide scientific coverage, research into many FLP aspects is still in its early days. This is because physical layout requirements in industry constantly change to adapt to the technological changes related to the fourth industrial revolution, the proliferation of cyber-physical systems, increasingly more demanding market requirements, a shift to more flexible manufacturing styles that permit large product nomenclatures in increasingly smaller lots, and the development of health and safety guidelines in the workplace, which are all motivations to keep contributing to its understanding. This article presents a literature review of 232 articles published in science journals of known prestige in their category. FLP classification system based on the review of 186 bibliographic sources published between 1987 and 2016. According to these authors, FLP decisions depend on the layout evolution, characteristics of workshops, formulating the problem and its resolution approaches. Here we produced a new taxonomy to extend this proposed classification by including new classification criteria based on the most recent literature review in the FLP context; namely: problem type, approach and planning phase, characteristics of production facilities, materials handling system configuration, approaches employed to generate FLP alternatives and assessment approaches. The taxonomy also deals with characteristics of FLP mathematical modelling approaches as regards model type, objective function type, data type, certain or uncertain demand, distance metrics and considered solution approach. Consequently, the main contribution of this article was detailed, accurate and structured FLP conceptualisation, contextualisation and description.

Assessments are important for identifying the best layout among a finite set of alternatives generated by some of the above-described approaches, or to even detect improvement opportunities in an already existing production system's productivity. The FLP approaches in the literature have focused on generating layout alternatives and very few advances have been made in the assessment stage. This is probably why very little attention has been paid to the re-layout of existing facilities because re-layout decisions are usually made as a result of an assessment process when an existing layout does not allow the objectives set by an organisation to be met.

STRESS ON INPUT

Several excellent and widely cited reviews have been written on this topic of stress and depression in the past 15 years[50]. Therefore, one challenge of the current chapter is to provide a useful brief summary of the state of the field, yet include coverage that is forward-looking enough to avoid duplication of prior reviews. Accordingly, particular attention is devoted to emerging topics in this field, or to highlighting interesting topics with significant conceptual or empirical gaps admittedly subjective decisions. A second challenge is that this is a huge field, with major works emerging not only in clinical psychology, but also in sociology, psychiatry, and public health/ epidemiology. Hundreds of articles have been published in just the past few years. Thus, it is necessary to be selective, with no pretense of comprehensive and exhaustive reporting. Coverage focuses on relatively more recent work, mostly based on longitudinal studies, addressing adult unipolar depressive disorders rather than symptom outcomes. (There are some exceptions if relevant work is distinctive, informative, or illustrative of key points.) The chapter starts with an affirmation of the empirical link between stress and depression, and the methodological issues in stress measurement, followed by sections that address several questions in the stress-depression relationship.

Research has supported a strong association between stress and depression, but the overarching question remains: Why do some people get depressed following stressful experiences and others do not? Promising explorations of this question from cognitive, developmental, biological, personality, and contextual approaches have been pursued, with much left to be done to resolve the question to the point of yielding treatment and prevention implications. As we build future efforts on previous accomplishments, several challenges are noteworthy. One fundamental issue is recognition of the empirical limitations of the field: the extent to which most stress-depression research has been based on largely female samples, mostly on episodic stressors, and mainly on cross-sectional designs, with few tests of mediation. Expansion of research populations and longitudinal designs, and conceptualization and measurement of chronic stress, would improve the validity and completeness of our models and their empirical support. A challenge to the field is the need for multivariate, complex models with different levels of variables, possibly yielding different pathways to depression (e.g., Kendler et al. 2002). Such studies are enormously difficult and require considerable resources, but seem necessary to capture the complexities of the stress depression process. Such work calls for integrative biological-developmental psychosocial research, and offers an exceptional opportunity for interdisciplinary efforts. A further challenge to the field is to characterize and account for the possibility of progressive, changing processes over time and clinical course, and for the mutual and transactional relationships between the person and the environment. Issues such as stress generation, effects of childhood adversity on later susceptibility to stress, onset versus recurrence, and stress sensitization and kindling processes are all examples of research that deepens our appreciation that a dynamic rather than static process occurs in the stress-depression relationship.

STRESS ON IN-PROCESS AND FINISHED PRODUCT

Pharmaceutical aerosols are products that are packaged under pressure and contain therapeutically active ingredients which are released upon activation of an appropriate valve system. The term ''aerosol'' refers to the fine mist of spray that results from most pressurized systems. They are intended for topical application on the skin as well as local application into the nose (nasal aerosols), mouth (lingual aerosols), or lungs (inhalation aerosols). These products may be fitted with valves enabling either continuous or metered-dose delivery. Inhalation aerosols are fine suspensions or dispersions of solid particles in a gas, intended for local action in the respiratory tract. Various types of inhalers such as nebulizers, metered dose inhalers (MDIs) and dry powder inhalers (DPIs) are available. Various factors such as actuator tube design, orifice diameter, and concentration of surfactant in the system, vapor pressure of propellants, and efficiency of valve crimping and particle size of the plume emerging from the inhaler etc. affect the therapeutic performance of aerosols. Exceptional aspect of pharmaceutical aerosols is the presence of propellants, whose properties like flash point, viscosity and density also modify the aerosol performance. Quality control (QC) is the part of GMP (Good Manufacturing Practice) that is concerned with sampling, specifications, testing and with the organization, documentation and release procedures which ensure that the necessary and relevant tests are actually carried out and that materials are not released for use, sale or supply, until their quality have been judged to be satisfactory according to specifications. The process of QC is carried out to confirm an expected level of quality in a product by eliminating errors at every stage in production. QC is a team work and we have to keep in mind that quality must be incorporated into a drug product during product and process design[51]. So, it is possible patently be apprehended that, quality is not an accident but a result of intelligent efforts. The total quality of the product is assured by the in process quality control (IPQC) and finished product quality control (FPQC) tests. IPQC tests are carried out at regular intervals before the manufacturing process is completed. The function of IPQC involves monitoring and if necessary adaptation of the manufacturing process with a view to comply with pharmacopoeias. FPQC tests are performed when the manufacturing process is completed in order to check qualitative and quantitative characteristics along with test procedures and their acceptance limits, by which the finished product must comply throughout its valid shelf-life. The total dealing process (IPQC and FPQC tests) represents rigorous QC tests to make products completely indefectible before they are launched into the market. In terms of pharmaceutical development and manufacture, the regulatory entities are continually developing their requirements to meet the challenges of these new technologies and to ensure their safety, quality and efficacy in the global marketplace. The ultimate responsibility for the safety, quality and efficacy of medicines and medical devices lies with the various national regulatory bodies designated to safeguard public health. In Europe, in the USA and in the UK this function is performed by the European Medicines Agency (EMA), Food and Drug Administration (FDA) and Medicines and Healthcare products Regulatory Agency (MHRA) respectively. In USA, as the FDA has a command that the marketed drug product should be safe and effective; the drug product must conform particular criteria for quality and purity. In 2002, the FDA launched a new initiative "Pharmaceutical cGMPs (current Good Manufacturing Practices) for the 21st century" in which it proposed a new approach to pharmaceutical manufacturing.

The main role of the pharmacopoeias is to define the standards with which medicines shall comply and the methods by which compliance will be adjudged. There are diverse types of pharmacopoeias such as British Pharmacopoeia (BP), United States Pharmacopoeia-National Formulary (USP-NF), European Pharmacopoeia (PhEur), International Pharmacopoeia (PhInt), Japanese Pharmacopoeia (JP) and Indian Pharmacopoeia (IP) in different parts of the world and the role of these pharmacopoeias are to embellish quality specifications for active pharmaceutical ingredients (APIs), finished pharmaceutical products (FPPs) and general requisites, e.g. for dosage forms. So, it is momentously incumbent to maintain the quality of aerosols by variegated numbers evaluation, based on the series of tests carried out during the formulation development and finished product testing stages[52]. The purpose of this study is to give an outline about the in-process and finished product quality control tests for pharmaceutical aerosols based on pharmacopeial standards and specifications.

SPECIFICATIONS

It is very difficult to estimate the number of online pharmacies and people buying online, the volume of drugs traded, and the revenue and profits generated by such a hidden business. Moreover, the geographical distribution of the phenomenon seems to be very heterogeneous. With regard to the number of online pharmacies, Mark Monitor in a 2009 press release claimed to have found nearly 3000 websites selling prescription medicines, while a 2010 review by the US National Association of Boards of Pharmacy (NABP) investigated the characteristics of 5859 Internet outlets selling prescription medications. Regarding access to drugs online, the 2006 Online Health Search, a US survey by the Pew Internet & American Life Project, showed that "prescription or over-the-counter drugs" was the fifth most widely searched health topic on the Internet. Another US telephone survey concluded that 4% of Americans had purchased prescription drugs on the Internet. Very few estimates regarding the revenue and profits of this phenomenon are available, there being great variability in methods and numbers. Besides economic aspects, there is a legal issue and jurisdictional consequences: cases of law enforcement acts and legal prosecutions have been reported in the literature. This new market has undoubted advantages for patients: access to drugs for the disabled or housebound, access 24 hours a day, a virtually unlimited number of products available, relative privacy, which may encourage patients to ask questions about embarrassing issues, and more affordable prices. But direct access to health services, especially drugs, poses a hazard to consumers because it is difficult to determine whether drugs purchased online are counterfeit, unapproved, or illegal. Besides, the inappropriate use of medicines, the limited or non-existent opportunity for advice (which blurs the line between wilful abuse and unknowing misuse), and the risk of increased antibiotic resistance arising from their misuse have also been suggested as negative consequences of online purchase of medication. What is more, the chance to circumvent prescription boundaries can be a potential disruptor at several levels, at both an individual and a public health level. At an individual level, this phenomenon can influence the doctor–patient relationship. At a public health level, since each country has a unique system, access to drugs from abroad can disrupt the delicate equilibrium that leads to a certain drug price on the basis of taxation, co-payment, reimbursement, and negotiation with industry. Articles regarding only over-the-counter medicines, complementary medicines, herbal remedies, supplements, and drugs of abuse were excluded. If the researchers analysed websites selling prescription and over-the-counter drugs, we considered websites selling prescription drugs if it was possible to identify them. We decided to deal only with prescription drugs, although over-the-counter substances can also have negative effects on people's health, despite the no-harm claims made by their producers, as several clinical cases demonstrate. Although examining non-prescription drugs was not an objective of this review, it should be borne in mind that some case reports showed the presence of prescription drugs even in products that did not claim to contain them[54]. This means that prescription of drugs can be distributed through channels in which the active substances do not appear. As an additional inclusion criterion, we selected articles in English that had the abstract or the full text available. We included only scientific articles, which means that we excluded popular articles published in daily newspapers, and in weekly and monthly magazines

PROBLEMS ENCOUNTERED DURING TRANSFER OF TECHNOLOGY

Implementation of efficient technological transfer is gaining strategic importance under the current conditions of accelerated transformation of socio-economic processes caused by rampant technological development. In such an environment, technology transfer (TT) becomes an important factor for improving companies' competitiveness through technological advancement and innovations[55], and contributes to socio-economic development of regions and countries[56]. There are various TT models presented and evaluated in the literature[57]. Let us explain the topic with the help of an example.

There may be many reasons for lack of technology transfer successes in the past. The one which is of great interest to the research community is that the algorithms developed in the past are not considered adequate for operational use. In the speech recognition area, word recognition error rates are intolerably high unless the speech source is limited vocabulary, isolated word, wide band width and free of background noise. Moreover, applications are limited to the simplest uses. There is little understanding of how to apply language processing results to speech. In the text processing area, problems being addressed are often severely constrained in terms of vocabulary, grammar and application. But it is verbally impossible to find real-world problems that are constrained enough to allow application of the newly developed techniques. The substantial progress that has been made by the research community has changed this situation. The current state-of-the-art, clearly inadequate for very general problems, has great prospects for certain moderately specialized applications. An additional problem that has impeded technology transfer has been the high cost and limited capability of the data and signal processing equipment required to implement the algorithms researchers developed. In the speech processing area, researchers used to be restricted to general purpose hardware which is tens or hundreds of time slower than real time, or of using special, fixed-point signal processors with very limited memory and dynamic range which are programmed in assembly language. Use of more modern computer languages such as LISP allows faster design and implementation of experiments, but even with machines specially designed for that environment, processing is very slow. Moreover, the graphics required for a good user interface is limited in display speed and resolution. The net result of these limitations is that, except for the simplest algorithms, it is impractical to transfer research successes into operational use. However, while the thirst of researchers for ever greater computing, storage, networking and display capability still exists, it is greatly slackened. The explosive progress of computing over the past decade, led by the development of modern, high-performance, low cost, graphics workstations, now allows real-time or faster operation of fairly computational and memory intensive algorithms on floating point processors programmed in high-level languages. Another fundamental problem has been that the customer processing environment do not contain the infrastucture required for the introduction of the techniques being developed. New digital speech processing systems could not be easily introduced into systems in which speech signals are being processed as analog signals and stored on analog tape. Text processing systems cannot be made to operate in an environment in which textual information is still being handled on paper and data bases are on file cards. Again, thanks to major advances in data networks, low-cost terminals, optical character recognition, data base software, A/D and D/A conversion, and other technologies. Many offices now contain the backbone of the system required to make use of new text or speech processing techniques. Moreover, the adoption of standards for programming languages, operating systems, windowing systems and network protocols often is resulting in the users obtaining computing systems. These are compatible or which can easily be made compatible with the systems on which the processes are being developed. Thus, standardization will result in technology transfer being an easier job. The problems described so far may be classed as technical problems. As stated above, these technical problems are rapidly decreasing. However, there is one technical problem that still must be overcome before technology transfer can occur on a widespread basis. Unfortunately this remaining major technical problem has received little attention to date, probably because of the way in which the research problem has been structured. That is, the problems reported that the conference are primarily defined by two things: (1) the selected (or created) and marked training and test data, or corpus, and (2) a criterion or criteria for testing the researchers system against that corpus. This standardization of problem domain, goals and test criteria has been a powerful tool of the research managers. It has focussed the researchers attention onto relatively specific goals and objectives. Since the performance of the algorithms produced by different researchers can be directly compared, it has simultaneously created an environment of constructive competition. However, this narrow focus has resulted one critical area of work: the study of the process of converting an algorithm or process from one domain, that is supported by a well-defined and documented corpus, to a different, operational domain, which may have little marked training or testing data. The result is there has been little work to even formally define the process necessary to convert from one domain to another and from one objective function to another one, much less to automate or semi-automate that process. In other words, there has been insufficient emphasis on or efforts to achieve technology transfer. There are also a number of political, managerial or psychological problems which need to be addressed, if the transfer of language processing techniques into operational use is to be successful. All of these nontechnical problems are associated with the potential customers of the research. It is important to recognize that in general, the customers are not the sponsors of the research. The sponsors are usually other researchers or research managers who are supposed to represent the customers. The true customers are the people or organizations that will be the end user of any new product or capability that results from the research effort. The first problem involving the potential customer is that the customer usually not directly involved in the research efforts of the human language technology program. On the other hand, most researchers are not sufficiently familiar with the customers' requirements and operating procedures to know whether a test corpus is truly representative of real data and whether the research goals will solve any real problem. Government customers also tend to be relatively conservative and sometimes even suspicious of new ideas and new technology. They frequently have developed a well understood routine and procedure for doing their jobs and are reluctant to change. In other words, there is often a lot of inertia which may only be overcome through the use of force. In this context, one such force which comes from demonstrated success. But since the voice and text processing technology is (and probably always will be) imperfect, success, like beauty will be defined in the eye of the beholder. Since customers will be the ultimate judge of our products, it is required to ensure that those products are demonstrated in the best possible manner. Another force for change results from budget reductions. The conflicting pressures of less resources and desire to maintain capability tends to make some customers much more open to accepting new, imperfect technology.

The current program of research must be continued. There has been substantial progress in understanding the fundamental problems of language processing and in developing ever better techniques for addressing those problems. This progress must continue if we are to have any hope of success against the less constrained problems. However, the goal of this research program should be broadened to explicitly include technology transfer. The task of adapting speech and text understanding processes from one domain to another needs to be specified as one of the program goals. Algorithms need to be developed which can be easily converted from one task to another without requiring years of additional work by highly trained scientists. Techniques need to be developed which will allow supervised adaptation to new situations. One implication of broadening the program to extend across domains is the need to increase the dimensionality of the research corporation, so they also extend across domains. Instead of having data for a single situation which is segmented into portions for training, test and validation. This single set should be considered as the training portion for one domain, with another similar set for a different. But related domain could be used to test how well the algorithm performs on the new domain. Possibly a third set of data from yet a third domain to validate the results of the domain transfer test.

Moreover, the researchers need to spend more time working with customers to better understand the manual processes. Currently being used so they can better understand what is needed in order to produce a successful language processing capability.

Finally, the overall goal of the program should be broadened. Funding is to be provided to produce pilot or prototype systems. These have been designed to be moved into operational situations and used for extended periods of time. Experimental operational prototypes are an absolutely necessary step in any long-term research effort. The trick is to determine the time for that step.

Exercise

Multiple Choice Questions

Fill in the blank with an appropriate word given below.

1. A successful product goes through the scaling process .... times before its commercial manufacturing.

   a) several b) two

   c) three d) four

2. The primary goal of QbD is to develop pharmaceutical..............

   a) process b) analysis

   c) products d) production

3. Risk .... is performed to assess the degree of risk for material attributes and process parameters on CQAs.

   a) Management b) assessment

   c) Analysis d) none of these

4. Which of the following statement is correct?

   a) The effects of CQAs and CPPs on CMAs can be quantified to identify their relationship.

   b) The effects of CMAs on CPPs can be quantified to identify their relationship.

   c) The effects of CPPs on CMAs can be quantified to identify their relationship.

   d) The effects of CMAs and CPPs on CQAs can be quantified to identify their relationship.

5. Which of the following statement is correct?
   a) For the blending process in the QbD approach intermediate critical quality attributes (IQAs) has been identified.
   b) For the blending process in the QbD approach intermediate critical quality attributes (IQAs) and CPPs have been identified.
   c) For the blending process in the QbD approach CPPs has been identified.
   d) For the blending process in the QbD approach intermediate critical quality attributes (IQAs) and CPPs have not been identified.
6. Which of the following statement is correct?
   a) The batch size during scaling up of technology in pharmaceutical industries varies from 0.5kg to 5kg.
   b) The batch size during scaling up of technology in pharmaceutical industries varies from 5kg to 15kg.
   c) The batch size during scaling up of technology in pharmaceutical industries varies from 2kg to 10kg.
   d) The batch size during scaling up of technology in pharmaceutical industries varies from 5kg to 100kg.
7. Which of the following statement is correct?
   a) Continuous improvement is possible through increase of knowledge.
   b) Continuous improvement is not possible through increase of knowledge.
   c) All the above
   d) None of the above
8. Which of the following statement is correct?
   a) Improvement within a company can be called as "organizational learning".
   b) Transfer of knowledge within a company can be called as knowledge.
   c) Transfer of process within a company can be called as knowledge.
   d) Transfer of knowledge within a company can be called as "organizational learning".
9. Which of the following statement is correct?
   a) Technology transfer team represents QC, QA, Production and Service departments.
   b) Technology transfer team represents QC, and Production.
   c) Technology transfer team represents all stake holders.
   d) Technology transfer team represents QC, QA, and Production.

10. Which of the following statement is correct?
    a) Technology transfer does not ensure safety, purity and effective drug product.
    b) Technology transfer ensures effective drug product.
    c) Technology transfer ensures safety, and purity.
    d) Technology transfer ensures safety, purity and effective drug product.
11. Any lack of transparency may lead to .... transfer of technology.
    a) Ineffective
    b) effective
    c) worst
    d) best
12. Dry granulation .... the uniformity of drug distribution in the product.
    a) Decreases
    b) increases
    c) slightly decrease
    d) negligible increase
13. Which of the following statement is correct?
    a) The choice of granulation technique depends on roller compaction.
    b) The choice of granulation technique depends on fluid-bed granulation.
    c) The choice of granulation technique depends on intended bio-pharmaceutical performance.
    d) The choice of granulation technique depends on melt granulation and palletisation.
14. Which of the following statement is correct?
    a) The important factor to be considered for scale up of fluidized bed dryer is chemical property.
    b) The important factor to be considered for scale up of fluidized bed dryer is mechanical sieving device.
    c) The important factor to be considered for scale up of fluidized bed dryer is screening device used.
    d) The important factor to be considered for scale up of fluidized bed dryer is humidity.
15. Which of the following statement is NOT correct?
    a) Steps involved in capsule manufacturing is granulation and lubrication.
    b) Steps involved in capsule manufacturing is excessive granulation.
    c) Steps involved in capsule manufacturing is mixing of ingredient(s).
    d) Steps involved in capsule manufacturing is filling of capsules.

16. Which of the following statement is NOT correct?
    a) Various insoluble synthetic dyes and pigments are used to colour the capsule shell.
    b) Gelatine is prepared by the hydrolysis of collagen.
    c) The duration of time to cast the film has been reported to be about 12sec.
    d) Titanium dioxide may be included to render the shell opaque.
17. Which of the following statement is NOT correct?
    a) For human use, empty gelatine capsules are manufactured in eight sizes, ranging from 000 to 5.
    b) The moisture content of the capsules as they are from the machine will be in the range of 15-18% w/w.
    c) The moisture content of the capsules as they are from the machine will be in the range of 10-14% w/w.
    d) Three larger sizes available for veterinary use are - 10, 11, and 12.
18. Which of the following statement is correct?
    a) Suspensions are monophasic liquid dosage forms
    b) Suspensions are prepared only for topical use.
    c) The dielectric constant of an ideal co-solvent should be between 20 and 60.
    d) The term parenteral is applied to preparations administered by injection.
19. Which of the following statement is NOT correct?
    a) Liposomes are condensed bilayered vesicles with a completely contained aqueous volume.
    b) Several drug delivery systems have not been developed and studied over the past decades to overcome these problems.
    c) Niosomes are one of the best among these carriers.
    d) A dry product known as pro-niosomes may be hydrated immediately before use to yield aqueous niosome dispersions.
20. Which of the following statement is correct?
    a) At an individual level, this phenomenon can influence the doctor–patient relationship.
    b) At a public level, this phenomenon can influence the doctor–patient relationship.
    c) The prescription of drugs cannot be distributed through channels in which the active substances appear.
    d) It is very easy to estimate the number of online pharmacies and people buying online.

Short Questions

1. Explain the statement, 'A multi-dimensional design space consisting of a combination of CMAs and CPPs ensures that desirable CQAs are derived through the DoE.'
2. What are reasons for Technology transfer (scaling up) in pharmaceutical industry is done?
3. What are reasons for which the technology is being transferred between the contract giver and contract acceptor during manufacture.
4. How the batch size can be increased through technology transfer process?
5. Describe the characteristics of process scale up for capsule.
6. What are the transferosome?
7. Discuss in brief the stress on physical layout.
8. Discuss in short, the problems encountered during transfer of technology.
9. Discuss in short, stress on in-process and finished product.
10. What do you understand by specification?

Long Questions

1. Explain different types of granulation technology.
2. How do you characterize the effervescent granulation technology?
3. Explain the process scale up for liquid orals.
4. Describe the two basic types of emulsions.
5. Discuss on the process scale up for semisolids.
6. Explain the dimensionless-number method.
7. What are nanoparticles? Write a note about niosomes.
8. Explain the stress on equipment.
9. Discuss on stress on product uniformity.
10. 'Stress testing of the drug substance can help identify the likely degradation products, which can in turn help establishing the degradation pathways and the intrinsic stability of the molecule and validate the stability indicating power of the analytical procedures used.' explain the statement.

Answers

1	2	3	4	5	6	7	8	9	10	11	12	13	14	15	16	17	18	19	20
a	c	b	d	b	c	a	d	c	d	a	b	c	d	b	a	c	d	b	a

References

1. Barrasso D., Eppinger T., Pereira F.E., Aglave R., Debus K., Bermingham S.K., Ramachandran R. A multi-scale, mechanistic model of a wet granulation process using a novel bi-directional PBM–DEM coupling algorithm. *Chem. Eng. Sci.* 2015;123:500–513.
2. Djuris J., Djuric Z. Modeling in the quality by design environment: Regulatory requirements and recommendations for design space and control strategy appointment. *Int. J. Pharm.* 2017;533:346–356.
3. Gilchrist M., Van Dyck W. *Transforming Industrialization, a New Paradigm for Pharmaceutical Development.* IBM Corp.; Somers, NY, USA: 2005. p. 438. IBM Institute for Business Value, Publication G510-3997-00.
4. Lawrence X.Y. Pharmaceutical quality by design: Product and process development, understanding, and control. *Pharm. Res.* 2008;25:781–791.
5. S., Suzzi D., Radeke C., Khinast J.G. An integrated quality by design (QbD) approach towards design space definition of a blending unit operation by discrete element method (DEM) simulation. *Eur. J. Pharm. Sci.* 2011;42:106–115.
6. Dumarey M., Talwar S., Yahyah M., Peterson J. *Computer Aided Chemical Engineering.* Volume 38. Elsevier; Amsterdam, The Netherlands: 2016. Empirical modelling to support scale up of primary pharmaceutical processes; pp. 2241–2246.
7. Björn I.N., Jansson A., Karlsson M., Folestad S., Rasmuson A. Empirical to mechanistic modelling in high shear granulation. *Chem. Eng. Sci.* 2005;60:3795–3803.
8. Ketterhagen W.R., am Ende M.T., Hancock B.C. Process modeling in the pharmaceutical industry using the discrete element method. *J. Pharm. Sci.* 2009;98:442–470.
9. Wassgren C., Curtis J.S. The application of computational modeling to pharmaceutical materials science. *MRS Bull.* 2006;31:900–904.
10. Pandey P., Bharadwaj R. *Predictive Modeling of Pharmaceutical Unit Operations.* Woodhead Publishing; Sawston/Cambridge, UK: 2016
11. Rogers A., Ierapetritou M. Challenges and opportunities in modeling pharmaceutical manufacturing processes. *Comput. Chem. Eng.* 2015;81:32–39.
12. Cundall P.A., Strack O.D. A discrete numerical model for granular ssemblies. *Geotechnique.* 1979;29:47–65.
13. Norton T., Sun D.-W. Computational fluid dynamics (CFD)—An effective and efficient design and analysis tool for the food industry: A review. *Trends Food Sci. Technol.* 2006;17:600–620.
14. Zheng Q.J., Yu A.B. Modelling the granular flow in a rotating drum by the eulerian finite element method. *Powder Technol.* 2015;286:361–370.
15. Diarra H., Mazel V., Busignies V., Tchoreloff P. Fem simulation of the die compaction of pharmaceutical products: Influence of visco-elastic phenomena and comparison with experiments. *Int. J. Pharm.* 2013;453:389–394.

16. Yamamoto M., Ishihara S., Kano J. Evaluation of particle density effect for mixing behavior in a rotating drum mixer by DEM simulation. *Adv. Powder Technol.* 2016;27:864–870.
17. Börner M., Michaelis M., Siegmann E., Radeke C., Schmidt U. Impact of impeller design on high-shear wet granulation. *Powder Technol.* 2016;295:261–271.
18. Freireich B., Kumar R., Ketterhagen W., Su K., Wassgren C., Zeitler J.A. Comparisons of intra-tablet coating variability using DEM simulations, asymptotic limit models, and experiments. *Chem. Eng. Sci.* 2015;131:197–212.
19. Vanarase A.U., Osorio J.G., Muzzio F.J. Effects of powder flow properties and shear environment on the performance of continuous mixing of pharmaceutical powders. *Powder Technol.* 2013;246:63–72.
20. Mahdi Y., Mouhi L., Guemras N., Daoud K. Coupling the image analysis and the artificial neural networks to predict a mixing time of a pharmaceutical powder. *J. Fundam. Appl. Sci.* 2016;8:655–670.
21. Moakher M., Shinbrot T., Muzzio F.J. Experimentally validated computations of flow, mixing and segregation of non-cohesive grains in 3d tumbling blenders. *Powder Technol.* 2000;109:58–71.
22. Cleary P.W., Sinnott M.D. Assessing mixing characteristics of particle-mixing and granulation devices. *Particuology.* 2008;6:419–444.
23. Mendez A.S.L., de Carli G., Garcia C.V. Evaluation of powder mixing operation during batch production: Application to operational qualification procedure in the pharmaceutical industry. *Powder Technol.* 2010;198:310–313.
24. Chaudhuri B., Mehrotra A., Muzzio F.J., Tomassone M.S. Cohesive effects in powder mixing in a tumbling blender. *Powder Technol.* 2006;165:105–114.
25. Arratia P.E., Duong N.-h., Muzzio F.J., Godbole P., Lange A., Reynolds S. Characterizing mixing and lubrication in the bohle bin blender. *Powder Technol.* 2006;161:202–208.
26. 26 Manish SM, Bharat P, Yakub S, Technology Transfer in Pharmaceutical Industry; Facts and Steps Involved, American Journal of Pharmatech Research, 2012; 2(4):78.
27. Biruk A, Biruk Abate, Technology transfer in pharmaceutical industries through product development and scale-up approaches: Challenges and opportunities for developing countries, International Journal of Emerging Technology and Advanced Engineering, 2016; 6(7): 232-243
28. Patil RP: Technology Transfer in Pharmaceutical Industry: objectives, Issues & Policy Approaches. Int J Pharm Res Dev 2010; 2(10): 43-48.
29. Le Trong Vu, P. Eng, Technology Transfer Challenges in Pharmaceutical Industry, Joint CVG/ Therapeutic Products Directorate International Convention & Exhibition, Toronto, Canada, Octo. 5-6, 2006 pg no-1-6. 10
30. Culler, S. (2016). A bioengineering platform to industrialize biotechnology. *Chemical Engineering Progress, 112*, 42–51.

31. The theory & practice of industrial pharmacy by Leon Lachman, Herbert A. Lieberman, Joseph L. kenig, 3rd edition, published by Varghese Publishing house.

32. Rambali B, Baert L, Using experimental design to optimize the process parameters in fluidized bed granulation on a semi-full scale, International Journal of Pharmaceutics,220,2001,149-160.

33. Aulton ME Pharmaceutics: The Science of Pharmacy, Churchil Livingstone Pub, 13th Edition.

34. Michael Levin,Metropolitan Computing Corporation,East Hanover, New Jersey, Pharmaceutical Process Scale-Up, Marcel Dekker, Inc,2001.

35. L. H. Block. Scale-up of disperse systems: Theoretical and practical aspects. In: H. A. Lieberman, M. M. Rieger, and G. S. Banker, eds. Pharmaceutical Dosage Forms: Disperse Systems. 2nd ed. Vol. 3. New York: Marcel Dekker, 1998, p 363.

36. G. P. Pisano. The Development Factory: Unlocking the Potential of Process Innovation. Boston: Harvard Business School Press, 1997.

37. V. W. Uhl and J. A. Von Essen. Scale-up of equipment for agitating liquids. In: V. W. Uhl and J. B. Gray, eds. Mixing Theory and Practice. Vol. III. New York: Academic Press, 1986, p 200.

38. Lu M, Qiu Q, Luo X, et al. Phyto-phospholipid complexes (phytosomes): a novel strategy to improve the bioavailability of active constituents. *Asian J Pharm Sci.* 2019;**14**(3):265–274.

39. Khater D., Nsairat H., Odeh F., Saleh M., Jaber A., Alshaer W., Al Bawab A., Mubarak M.S. Design, preparation, and characterization of effective dermal and transdermal lipid nanoparticles: a review. *Cosmetics.* 2021;8

40. Kaur IP, Garg A, Singla AK, Aggarwal D. Vesicular systems in ocular drug delivery: An overview. *Int J Pharm.* 2004;269:1–14.

41. Chaurasiya P., Ganju E., Upmanyu N., Ray S.K., Jain P. Transfersomes: A novel technique for transdermal drug delivery. *J. Drug Deliv. Ther.* 2019;9:279–285.

42. Sang-W. J. and Hiroshi O.; Development of membrane stress measurement equipment for membrane structures: proposal of measuring method and its experimental verification; Meas. Sci. Technol. 22 (2011).

43. G. M. Ma, C. Shi, W. Q. Qin, Y. B. Li, H. Y. Zhou, and C. R. Li, "A Non-Intrusive Electrical Discharge Localization Method for Gas Insulated Line Based on Phase-Sensitive OTDR and Michelson Interferometer," IEEE Transactions on Power Delivery, pp. 1-1, 2019.

44. Birkholzer, J. T. *et al.* DECOVALEX-2015: an international collaboration for advancing the understanding and modeling of coupled thermo-hydro-mechanical-chemical (THMC) processes in geological systems. *Environ. Earth Sci.* **77**(14), art. 539 (2018)

45. A. Mitakos, I. Panderi, J. Pharm. Biomed. Anal. 28 (2002) 431–438.

46. Gilbert, J. A., Holmes, I., Harris, K. & Quince, C. Dirichlet multinomial mixtures: generative models for microbial metagenomics. PLoS ONE 7, e30126 (2012).
47. RL Moss, E Tzimas, H Kara, P Willis, J Kooroshi; The potential risks from metals bottlenecks to the deployment of Strategic Energy Technologies. Energy Policy 55:556–564; 2013.
48. Grobelny, Jerzy, and Rafał Michalski. "A Novel Version of Simulated Annealing Based on Linguistic Patterns for Solving Facility Layout Problems." *Knowledge-Based Systems* 124 (May): 55–69, 2017.
49. Pérez-Gosende, Pablo, Josefa Mula, and Manuel Díaz-Madroñero. "Overview of Dynamic Facility Layout Planning as a Sustainability Strategy." *Sustainability* 12 (19): 8277, 2020.
50. Paykel ES.; Life events and affective disorders.; Acta Psychiatr. Scand.; 108:61–66, 2003
51. Uddin MS, Mamun AA, Tasnu T, Asaduzzaman M. In-process and finished products quality control tests for pharmaceutical tablets according to pharmacopoeias. J of Chemi and Pharmace Res. 2015;7(7):180-181.
52. Brambilla G, Ganderton D, Garzia R, Lewis D, Meakin B, Ventura P. Modulation of aerosol clouds produced by pressurized inhalation aerosols. International Journal of Pharmaceutics. 1999;186:53-61.
53. Müller D, Weinmann W, Hermanns-Clausen M. Chinese slimming capsules containing sibutramine sold over the Internet: a case series. Dtsch Arztebl Int; Mar;106(13):218-222, 2009.
54. Nguyen MH, Ormiston T, Kurani S, Woo DK. Amphetamine lacing of an Internet-marketed neutraceutical. Mayo Clin Proc; 81(12):1627-1629, 2006.
55. T. Nicodemus, J.A. Egwakh; Technology transfer and competitive advantage: The managers' perspective; Eur. J. Bus. Manag.; 11, 2019, pp. 66-75
56. K. De Moortel, T. Crispeels; International university-university technology transfer: Strategic management framework; Technol. Forecast. Soc. Chang., 135 (2018), pp. 145-155
57. E. Villani, E. Rasmussen, R. Grimaldi; How intermediary organizations facilitate university—Industry technology transfer: A proximity approach; Technol.; Forecast. Soc. Chang.; 114 (2017), pp. 86-102.

CHAPTER - 3

Validation

Introduction, General Concept of Validation, Types of Validation, Procedures of Validation, Protocols of Validation, Documentation of Validation, Validation Master Plan (VMP), Analytical Method Validation, Cleaning Validation, Vender Qualification

INTRODUCTION

The basic objective of any pharmaceutical industry is to manufacture the drug products of required forms with consistent quality, at the lowest possible cost. Since long, validation studies have been performed in pharmaceutical industry. Due to increasing interest in validation and industry's greater emphasis in recent years on quality assurance program, is an efficient production operation[1]. Validation is a concept evolved in the united states in 1978. The concept of validation has expanded through the years to embrace a wide range of activities from analytical methods used for the quality control of drug substances and drug products to computerized systems for clinical trials, labelling or process control. Validation is founded on, but not prescribed by regulatory requirements and is best observed as an important and integral part of cGMP[2]. The word validation simply means assessment of validity or action of proving effectiveness. Validation is a team effort where it involves people from various disciplines of the plant. This principle includes the understanding that the following conditions exist:

Quality, Safety, and Efficacy are designed or built into the product. Quality cannot be adequately assured merely by in-process and finished product inspection or testing each step of a manufacturing process is controlled to assure that the finished product meets all properties of quality including specifications. The development of a drug product is a lengthy process involving drug discovery, laboratory testing, animal studies, clinical trials and regulatory registration. Process controls include inspection of raw materials, in-process controls and targets for final product. The purpose is to monitor the online and off-line performance of the manufacturing process and then, validate it. After manufacturing process is validated, current good manufacturing practice also requires that a well-written procedure for process controls is established to monitor its performance[3]. On the basis of validation, FDA regulations describing current good manufacturing practice (cGMP) for finished pharmaceuticals are given in 21 CFR parts 210 and 211. The cGMP regulations require that manufacturing processes should be designed and controlled to assure that in-process materials and the finished products meet predetermined quality requirements and do so consistently and reliably. Process validation is required, in both general and specific terms, by the cGMP regulations mentioned in parts 210 and 211[4].

Two FDA (Food and Drug Administration) officials, Ted Byers and Bud Loftus, proposed the concept of validation first in the mid-1970s to improve the quality of pharmaceutical products[5.6]. It has been proposed as a direct response to the large volume of problems of parenteral sterile products. The first validation activities focused on the processes involved in making these products, but they spread rapidly across all pharmaceutical production processes[7]. The purpose of validation is to test the quality of the system at each, as validation activities include checks on production materials, operating procedure, training of the persons involved and monitoring of the system during production. U.S.F.D.A (United States Food and Drug Administration) pioneered the validation process concept, but until September 29, 1978, the definition of the validation process did not appear in any of the USFDA literature, no cGMP's law has spoken about the validation process[8]. The concept of validation has expanded during last few years in a wide range of activities, from the methods of analysis used to control the quality of medical substances and drugs to computerized systems, the validation process has become an important and integral part of cGMPs[9]. Validation is a method with applicability in various fields: medicine, sales, economics, psychology, chemistry, biology, etc. In fact, the validation concept can be applied in most areas. Validation of a new or improved method must ensure the integrity and quality of the method in terms of precision, accuracy, detection limit, limit of determination, selectivity, linearity field, and last but not least the transferability of the method[10-12]. Process validation can be defined as ' establishing documented evidence that provides a high degree of assurance that a certain system of equipment and processes that are consistently linked meet approved specifications and products with predetermined quality attributes'[13]. The word validation means 'evaluating validation actions or proving effectiveness'. Process validation can be defined as collecting and evaluating data from the product design phase and throughout the process, which establishes by scientific evidence that the process can consistently deliver quality products.

GENERAL CONCEPT OF VALIDATION

The concept of validation was first proposed to improve the quality of pharmaceuticals. In direct response to several problems in the sterility of large volume parenteral market, it was proposed. The first validation activities were focused on the processes involved in making these products, but quickly spread to associate the process oof pharmaceuticals. USFDA was the pioneer in advocating the concept of process validation, till 29th September 1978 the definition of process validation did not appear in any part of literature of USFDA no cGMP regulations talked anything about process validation[14].

Table 3.1 Definitions of validation as per different authorities.

Institution	Definition
European Commission, 1991	Validation – "Act of proving in accordance with GMPs that any ..." process actually leads to expected results.
European Commission, 2000	"Evidence that this process, operated within established parameters, can perform efficiently and reproducibly to produce a drug substance meeting its predetermined specifications and quality attributes"
US FDA	"The process validation is the establishment of evidence to ensure a high degree of certainty for a specified process to consistently produce a product that meets its predefined specifications and documented quality characteristics." (FDA, 1998).
ICH	Process validation represents the means of ensuring and providing supporting documents specifying their design parameters by whom they are capable repeatedly and reliably produce a finished product of the required quality."(ICH, 2011).
WHO	"The document proves that any procedure, process, equipment, material, activity or system can lead to the expected result."

Validation is an integral part of quality assurance system. It involves the systematic study of systems, facilities and processes aimed at determining whether they perform their intended functions adequately and consistently as specified. A validated process has been demonstrated to provide a high degree of assurance to produce uniform batches. These batches meet the required specifications and formally approved. Validation does not improve the processes but confirms that the processes have been properly developed and are under control[18]. In fact, a process that is well understood and in a state the confidence, control of quality of the product manufactured cannot be assured without validation.

Cost Reduction

Since each step in validation is constantly monitored, there have been lesser amount of rejects and reworks which would ultimately result in effective cost reduction.

Government Regulation

Validation is considered to be an essential part of GMPs. Throughout the world validation requirements have been made necessary for obtaining approval to manufacture and to introduce new products. The FDA's cGMP have been referred to the concepts of the validation in 211.110 and 211.113 sections. According to the section 211.110, such controlled procedures shall be established to monitor the output and to validate the performance of the manufacturing processes. These processes may be responsible for causing variability in the characteristics of in-process materials and drug products. The accuracy, sensitivity, specificity and reproducibility of test methods used by the company shall be recorded and treated as established documents.

A general requirement for process validation is contained in the cGMP for medical device, regulation, under section 820.100(b)(1). This regulation states that, 'where deviations from specifications for device could occur due to the manufacturing process itself, there shall be written procedures describing any processing controls required to assure conformance to specifications.' Pharmaceutical validation is a vast area of work. It practically covers every aspect of pharmaceutical processing activities, hence it becomes a very difficult task to define the scope of validation.

When a systematic look at the pharmaceutical operations is maid, it will point out at least the following areas for pharmaceutical validation[19].

- Analytical
- Instrument Calibration
- Process Utility services
- Raw materials
- Packaging materials
- Equipment
- Facilities
- Manufacturing operations
- Product Design
- Cleaning
- Operators

Importance of Validation

- Assurance of quality
- Time bound
- Process optimization
- Reduction of quality cost
- Nominal mix-ups, and bottle necks

- Minimal batch failures, improved efficiently and productivity
- Reduction in rejections
- Increased output
- Avoidance of capital expenditures
- Fewer complaints about process related failures
- Reduced testing in process and in finished goods
- More rapid and reliable start-up of new equipment
- Easier scale-up form development work
- Easier maintenance of equipment
- Improved employee awareness of processes
- More rapid automation
- Government regulation (Compliance with validation requirements is necessary for obtaining approval to manufacture and to introduce new products)[20,21].

TYPES OF VALIDATION

Based on the type and timing of validation, the following types of validation can be distinguished as follows:

- Prospective or perspective validation,
- Concurrent validation,
- Retrospective or retroactive validation, and
- Revalidation[22].

Prospective validation represents all the activities performed before the distribution of new products to ensure compliance with the initial (legislative/ proposed/ etc.) conditions by the product's characteristics.

Prospective validation is defined article as the documented evidence that a system does what it is supposed to perform.

Concurrent validation is issued for establishing documented evidence during actual imputation of the process to show that the process is in a state of control.

Retrospective process validation is based on a review of historical manufacturing and testing data, and the analysis of accumulated results from past production to assess the consistency of a process. It is assumed that the composition, procedures and equipment remained unchanged. During retrospective validation results of in-process and final control tests are evaluated. All difficulties and failures recorded are analysed to determine limits of process parameters and product-related problems.

The retrospective validation is not considered to be a quality assurance measure. It should not be applied to new processes or products.

Revalidation is exploratory review of the current performance of the validation effect to confirm the validated status of the facilities, systems, equipment, manufacturing processes and software. Revalidation is necessary for the products that need to be reviewed in time.

- **Prospective Validation**

It is defined as the established documented evidence that a system does what it supposed to do on the basis of a pre-planned protocol. This validation usually carried out before distribution either of a new product or a product made under a revised manufacturing process. It is performed on at least three successive production-sizes (consecutive batches). In prospective validation, the validation protocol is executed before the process is put into commercial use. During the product development phase, the process of production should be categorized into individual steps. Each step should be evaluated on the basis of experience or theoretical considerations to determine the critical parameters. This may affect the quality of the finished product. A series of experiment should be designed to determine the criticality of these factors. Each experiment should be planned and documented fully in an authorized protocol. All equipment, production environment and the analytical testing methods to be used should have been fully validated. Master batch documents can be prepared only after the critical parameters of the process have been identified and machine setting, component specifications and environmental conditions have been determined. Using this defined process a series of batches should be produced. In theory, the number of process runs carried out and observations made should be sufficient to allow the normal extent of variation and trends to be established to give sufficient data for evaluation. It is generally considered acceptable that three consecutive batches/ runs within the finally agreed parameters. This should give the product of the desired quality which would constitute a proper validation of the process. In practice, it may take some considerable time to accumulate these data. Some considerations should be exercised when selecting the process validation strategy. Among these should be the use of different lots of active raw materials and major excipients, batches produced on different shifts, the use of different equipment and facilities dedicated for commercial production, operating range of the critical processes, and a thorough analysis of the process data inn case of Requalification and revalidation. During the processing of the validation batches, extensive sampling and testing should be performed on the product at various stages, and should be documented comprehensively. Detailed testing should also be done on the final product in its package. Recommendations should be made on the extent of monitoring and the in-process controls necessary for routine production. These should be incorporated into the batch manufacturing and packaging record or into appropriate standard operating procedures. Limits, frequencies and action to be taken in the event of the limits being exceeded should be specified. Prospective validation should include, not be limited to the following:

- Short description of the process
- Summary of the critical processing steps to be investigated.
- List of the equipment/facilities to be used (including measuring, monitoring/recording equipment) together with its calibration status.
- Finished product specifications for release.
- List of analytical methods, as appropriate.
- Proposed in-process controls with acceptance criteria.
- Additional testing to be carried out, with acceptance criteria and analytical validation, as appropriate.
- Sampling plan.
- Methods for recording and evaluating results.
- Functions and responsibilities.
- Proposed timetable.

Batches made for process validation should be the same size as the intended industrial scale batches. If it is intended that validation batches are sold or supplied, the conditions under which these are produced should comply completely with the requirements of Good Manufacturing Practice, including the satisfactory outcome of the validation exercise and the marketing authorization.

- **Concurrent Validation**

It is similar to prospective, except the operating firm will sell the product during the qualification runs, to the public at its market price, and also similar to retrospective validation.

- This validation involves in-process monitoring of critical processing steps and product testing. This helps to generate and documented evidence to show that the production process is in a state of control.
- In exceptional circumstances it may be acceptable not to complete a validation programme before routine production starts.
- The decision to carry out concurrent validation must be justified, documented and approved by authorized personnel.
- Documentation requirements for concurrent validation are the same as specified for prospective validation.

- **Retrospective Validation**

  Retrospective validation is defined as the established documented evidence that a system does what it appears to do on the review and analysis of historical information. This is achieved by the review of the historical manufacturing testing data to prove that the process has always remained in control. This type of validation is a process for a product already in distribution. Retrospective validation is only acceptable for well-established processes and will be inappropriate. There have been recent changes in the composition of the product, operating procedures or equipment. Validation of these processes should be based on historical data. These steps require the preparation of a specific protocol and the reporting of the results of the data review, leading to a conclusion and a recommendation. The source of data for this validation should include, not limited to batch processing and packaging records, process control charts, maintenance logbooks, records of personnel changes, process capability studies, finished product data, including tendency of cards and storage stability results. Batches selected for retrospective validation should be representative of all batches made during the review period. Any batches failed to meet the specifications, and should be sufficient in number to demonstrate process consistency. Additional testing of retained samples may be needed to obtain the necessary amount or type of data to retrospectively validate the process. For retrospective validation, generally data from ten to thirty consecutive batches should be examined to access process consistency, but fewer batches may be examined.

Some of the essential elements for Retrospective Validation

Batches manufactured for a defined period is minimum of 10 last consecutive batches. That is, the number of lots released per year would be ten.

- Batch size/strength/manufacturer/year/period.
- Master manufacturing/packaging documents.
- Current specifications for active materials/finished products.
- List of process deviations, corrective actions and changes to manufacturing documents.
- Data for stability testing for several batches.
- **Revalidation**

Revalidation gives the evidence that changes in a process and/or the process environment that are introduced do not adversely affect process characteristics and product quality. Documentation requirements will be the same as for the initial validation of the process.

Facilities, systems, equipment and processes, including cleaning, should be periodically evaluated to confirm that they remain valid. Where no significant changes have been made to the validated status, a review with evidence that facilities, systems, equipment and processes meet the prescribed requirements fulfils the need for revalidation. Revalidation becomes necessary in certain situations. Some of the changes that require validation are as follows:

- Changes in raw materials (physical properties such as density, viscosity, particle size distribution and moisture etc that may affect the process or product).
- Changes in the source of active raw material manufacturer.
- Changes in packaging material (primary container/closure system)
- Changes in the process (mixing time, drying temperatures and batch size)
- Changes in the equipment (addition of automatic detection system).
- Changes of equipment which involve the replacement of equipment on a "like for like" basis would not normally require revalidation except that this new equipment must be qualified.
- Changes in the plant/facility. A decision not to perform revalidation studies must be fully justified and documented[23,24].

PROCEDURES OF VALIDATION

Drugs are critical elements in health care. A dosage form is the physical form of a dose of a chemical compound used as a drug or medication intended for therapeutic activity. Dosage form must be manufactured to the highest quality levels. The main objective of dosage form design is to achieve predicable therapeutic response to a drug included in a formulation. It is capable of large scale manufacturing with reproducible product quality. Various processes involved in the development of a drug product into a dosage form are drug discovery, laboratory testing, animal studies, clinical trials and regulatory registration. Before releasing the product into the market various product quality features like identity, chemical, physical stability, suitable preservation against microbial contamination if appropriate, strength, quality, purity, uniformity of dose of drug, stability, acceptability to users including prescriber and patient as well as suitable packing, labelling and validation are required. Process validation and process controls are two important key parameters which can ensure the above said parameters in the manufacturing process. In pharmaceutical organisation validation is a fundamental segment that supports a company commitment to quality assurance. Validation is a tool of a quality assurance which provides confirmation of the quality in equipment systems, manufacturing process, software and testing methods[25].

Pharmaceutical Process Validation is the most important and recognized parameters of cGMPs. The requirement of process validation appears of the quality system (QS) regulation. The goal of a quality system is to consistently produce the products. Those are fit for their intended use[26]. Process validation is a key element in assuring that these principles and goals are met. The process validation is standardization of the validation documents that must be submitted with the submission file for marketing authorization. The process validation is intended to assist manufacturers in understanding the quality management system (QMS) requirements concerning process validation and has general applicability to manufacturing process. According to FDA, Assurance of product quality is derived from careful and systemic attention to a number of importance factors, including: selection of quality process through in-process and end product testing[27]. The basic principle for validation may be stated as follows[27, 28]:

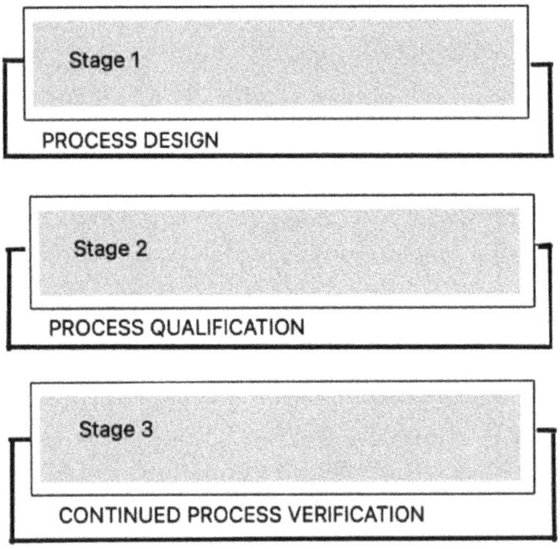

Fig.3.1 Approaches to process validation.

Installation Qualification (IQ)

Establishing by objective evidence that all key aspects of the process equipment and ancillary system installation adhere to the manufacturer's approved specification. The recommendations of the supplier of the equipment are suitably considered. IQ considerations are:

- Equipment design features (i.e. material of construction clean ability, etc.)
- Installation conditions (wiring, utility, functionality, etc.)
- Calibration, preventative maintenance, cleaning schedules.
- Safety features.
- Supplier documentation, prints, drawings and manuals.
- Software documented.
- Spare parts list.
- Environmental conditions (such as clean room requirements, temperature, and humidity).

Fig.3.2 Phases in process validation.

Operational Qualification (OQ)

The objective of operational qualification is to establish the evidence of process control limits and action levels. This results in product that all predetermined requirements. OQ considerations include:

- Process control limits (time, temperature, pressure, line speed, setup conditions, etc.)
- Software parameters.
- Raw material specifications
- Process operating procedures.
- Material handling requirements.
- Process change control.
- Training.
- Short term stability and capability of the process, (latitude studies or control charts).
- Potential failure modes, action levels and worst-case conditions.
- The use of statistically valid techniques such as screening experiments to optimize the process can be used during this phase.

Performance Qualification (PQ)

Establishing by objective evidence that the process, under anticipated conditions, consistently produces a product which meets all predetermined requirements. PQ considerations include:

- Actual product and process parameters and procedures established in OQ
- Acceptability of the product.
- Assurance of process capability as established in OQ.
- Process repeatability, long term process stability.

Requalification

In case of modification to, or relocation of equipment should be satisfactorily reviewed. The proposal for change control should be properly documented through the change control procedure. The formal review of this proposal includes consideration of requalification of the equipment. However, minor changes or changes that have no direct impact on final or in-process product quality can be handled through the documentation system of the preventive maintenance program.

In the early 1970s, the concept of process validation came through the regulatory aspects associated with cGMP regulations. The application thereof is considered to different analytical, quality assurance, pilot plant, production, and sterile product and solid dosage forms. During early 1990s, the concept of pre-approval inspection (PAI) came into existence and become important to quality assurance system. The approved validation protocols and schedules have generated the system of comprehensive development, scale-up, and bio batch. The commercial batch validation data were also required to achieve a successful regulatory PAI audit. There are ample of reasons for validating a product and/ or process.

- The manufacturers are required to conform to cGMP relations by law.
- A good business requires that the manufacturer avoids the possibility of rejected or recalled the batches.
- Validation can help to ensure the uniformity of product, reproducibility and quality of the product.

Although, originally the focus of validation was directed towards the prescription drugs. The FDA Modernization Act of 1997 expanded to inspect the establishments manufacturing over-the-counter (OTC) drugs, by the agencies, to ensure compliance with cGMP. Once this concept enabled to predict the ability of performance of process to meet the users' requirements, FDA regulatory officials established that there would be a legal basis for requiring process validation. The cGMP regulations for finished pharmaceuticals, 21 CFR 210 and 211, were prepared and enforced the requirements of the act. FDA possesses the authority and responsibility to inspect and evaluate the process validation performed by the manufacturers. For validating pharmaceutical (drug) manufacturing the cGMP regulations require that drugs/ drug products are being produced with a high degree of quality assurance, meeting all the quality parameters they are supposed to possess [21 CFR 211.100(a) and 211.110(a)]. Under the Section 501(a) (2) (B) of the FD & C Act, it has been stated that a drug is considered to be adulterated, if the method used in, or the facilities or controls used for, its manufacture, processing, packing, or holding do not conform to or are not operated or administrated in conformity with cGMP. Assurance must be given that the drug should meet the requirements of the act as to safety and would have identity and strength and meet the quality and purity characteristics that it is supposed to or represented to possess. Under the same section of the act, the requirements for premises and process validation for both finished products and active pharmaceutical ingredients, have been clearly stated. The active pharmaceutical ingredients are considered as drug under the act. For finished pharmaceuticals, the cGMP regulations have been stated to enforce the requirements of the act, under 21 CFR 210 and 211. These regulations do not include the definition for process validation. The requirement is completely stated in the language of 21 CFR 210 and 211as 'There shall be written procedures and process control designed to assure that the drug products have the identity, quality, and purity they purport or are represented to possess[29,30.]'

According to the FD & C Act, the following activities are to maintained:

- Process Development Designee shall review the product development report, data from pilot scale, scale up batch and proposed master formula document of product intended for manufacturing.
- Process Development Designee shall review/ ensure the availability of analytical method transfer report to the plant and plant preparedness for conducting validation testing and routine testing; function shall co-ordinate with QC/ QA in this regard[31].
- Process Development Designee shall prepare commercial/ exhibit batch production and control records which include the operational limits and overall strategy for process control based on development report.
- The Process Validation is performed after facility, utility, equipment, and laboratory test methods have been validated and released for process validation activities. Where compendial method is used only limited analytical method validation shall be conducted.
- All raw material and packaging material specification shall be obtained from approved vendors and shall be tested in Quality Control laboratory for approval.

- All the equipment and instrument to be utilized shall be calibrated and preventive maintenance program should be in place.
- Relevant SOPs are in place and training is completed on equipment, operation, manufacturing instruction and sampling strategy.
- Key process steps and process variables are identified and their operating ranges have been established.
- All the master formula, manufacturing instruction, packaging instruction, testing procedure and specification shall be approved before execution of process validation batches.
- The cleaning of the area and equipment should be completed before the initiation of process validation.
- The validation team and operational team should be trained from process engineer[32].

PROTOCOLS OF VALIDATION

The goal of the Funding Opportunity Announcement (FOA) should be reflected in the work demonstrated during the validation process. The validation process is intended to assess technical performance and cost improvements within the context of the FOA goals, as defined in the negotiated award. It is understood that research on such processes is ongoing and that consequently some changes to the overall integrated process that do not directly relate to the larger FOA goal itself may occur over the course of the project. In such cases, the recipient must provide and the validation team with adequate information about the modified process, including any proposed changes to cost and performance assumptions, and the basis for these, in order to enable the validation of the key performance and cost metrics. The recipient must also demonstrate that any improvements based on sources other than those expressly included within the approved project scope were not paid[33] or project cost-share funds. Change control protocols must be followed before implementing any changes in the feedstock, process, cost, or project plan during the project. The recipient needs to describe any proposed changes to the feedstock, process, or project plan relative to what was described in the application, and the recipient must submit this information in the form of a change request before adoption for a determination as to the level of change control that must be followed. Any changes to the process—including equipment, materials used, and cost estimates—must be described in quarterly reports or by other written means no later than three to four weeks before the next on-site validation team visit.

As appropriate, revised performance metrics may also be proposed and on the basis of assumptions for each revised metric must be described. Changes to project scope, technical targets/tables, schedule, or budget that impact the award may need to be approved by the contracting officer. Changes that do not rise to that level need to be approved by the project officer, and they may require changes to the project's project management plan. Both the validation team and the recipient when the changes have been accepted. The recipient is required to submit revised Tech Fin tables with revised benchmark and/or target data that represent the updates (as well as any appropriate supporting documentation) along with a detailed description of how the process changes differ from what was specified in the original application or negotiated award. Any changes to the project targets, research plan, methods, or the statement of project objectives must have prior approval and must be described in detail in quarterly reports or by other written means at least three to four weeks before scheduling the next on-site validation visit.

The validation team[34] contacts the recipient within 10 business days of the official start date of the project, which is the day the award is signed by the contracting officer. The initial on-site validation is performed to (1) validate technical benchmark data, (2) replicate the benchmark performance data before improvements funded through the project, and (3) (after the benchmark process performance has been confirmed or re-established) replicate the benchmark process details and techno-economic information, with the recipient using the project's approved techno-economic calculation methods. At the initial validation, feedstock material (raw and/or pre-treated) for use throughout the validation process needs to be segregated as a lot and labelled, and adequate tracking must be maintained so that the validation team can verify that the same feedstock material is being used during each phase of the validation process. The validation team reviews the protocol for feedstock tracking during the first site visit. If new lots of feedstock material (raw or pre-treated) are obtained or made during the project, their composition (and, if pre-treated, the conditions under which they were produced) must be provided to the validation team in the quarterly reports or by other written means before scheduling the next on-site validation visit. Any materials made via a new process must be analysed and controlled as per the feedstock control methodology described above.

The validation protocol should be numbered, signed and dated, and should contain as a minimum the following information:

Technical Performance Verification

The recipient is required to perform the full proposed process operations described in the application and/or negotiated in the award. A complete analysis is used to determine the performance of the benchmark process or processes. It is expected that new (validated) benchmark data should be able to replicate the data presented in the application (or agreed to during award negotiations) to within a 5% coefficient of variation. Improvements to process economics made during the project are measured against the benchmark performance verified during the initial validation phase. Key aspects of this part of the validation procedure include:

1. The recipient, validation, and the teams schedule an on-site visit or visits by the validation team to observe all experiments.
2. Validation experiments for each process must occur at least in duplicate and preferably in triplicate (if equipment and available resources allow).
3. Compositional analysis of relevant process streams must be provided in sufficient detail to demonstrate the mass balance.
4. Analytical procedures for determining the composition of all necessary streams (or for analysing time point samples obtained from a batch process) must be provided.
5. A stock (or stocks) of the feedstock, enzyme preparation(s) (or enzyme production strain), and fermentation strain(s) or catalyst(s) used in the initial benchmarking validation experiments must be maintained (as appropriate) to enable direct comparisons to be made with the improved process or processes to be developed and evaluated during the intermediate validation and final validation phases.
6. A summary of experimental results, including data tables and product conversion yields is sent to the validation team once data analysis is complete.
7. If technical performance or replication of application data cannot be verified during the on-site visit, the recipient, and validation team may agree to a period of time to develop the data in question, followed by a second review by the validation team.

Process Design and Cost Validation

Again, the approach follows that described for the initial validation, with the validation team reviewing cost estimates obtained during the intermediate validation against both the original (benchmark) project target and the intermediate project target. For this phase of the validation, the recipient updates the technical and economic tables, detailing the current (intermediate) results based on the actual process improvements. The recipient also provides appropriate supporting information (e.g., updated energy and material balances, sizing calculations, and performance calculations) sufficient to enable the validation team to validate the accuracy of the technical and economic tables. The validation team again determines whether any information required for fully understanding and verifying the proposed improvements is missing or lacking. If experimental data, process details, or cost estimates cannot be verified because of incomplete information, the recipient,

The validation team may agree to a period of time to develop the missing information to enable a second review by the validation team. The validation is typically rescheduled to occur within three to four weeks after the date of the first intermediate validation. Ultimately, a file of the documentation used to validate the project's process improvement progress is created and stored. In the event of an unsuccessful initial validation.

The primary purpose of the initial techno-economic validation is to verify the benchmark process data and the techno-economic assumptions and methodology, including process details and cost estimates related to the overall process and individual process steps. Key aspects of this part of the validation procedure include:

1. The recipient provides the technical and economic tables showing the (1) benchmark, intermediate, and final targets and (2) supporting information based on the results of the benchmark technical validation experiments. Supporting information should include, at a minimum, the mass and energy balance data, process flow diagrams, and costing information used to complete the tables provided in the application.
2. The project and validation teams review the tables along with supporting documentation for the benchmark process. The validation team determines whether any additional information is needed to fully understand the benchmark or to perform subsequent validations (e.g., lack of or insufficient details regarding material balances, process flow diagrams, or costs).
3. If process details and cost estimates cannot be verified because of insufficient information, the recipient, and validation team may agree to a period of time to develop the missing information, followed by a second review by the validation team. The validation team determines whether any information required for fully understanding and verifying the proposed improvements is missing or lacking. If experimental data, process details, or cost estimates cannot be verified because incomplete information, the recipient, and validation team may agree to a period of time to develop the missing information to enable a second review by the validation team. The rescheduled validation is typically scheduled to occur within three to four weeks after the date of the first initial validation. Ultimately, a file of the documentation used to validate the project's process improvement progress is created and stored.

The recipient again prepares and provides to the validation team updated technical and economic tables showing the final project results in addition to the benchmark and intermediate validation data and targets. In support of these updated tables, the recipient provides an updated package of supporting information (material and energy balances, new equipment sizing calculations, new yield calculation, etc.) based on the results of the final validation demonstrations. As before, any changes to the process or process step(s) also must be documented, and new supporting documentation provided as necessary. If process details or cost estimates cannot be verified due to a lack of information, validation team may allow the recipient to develop the missing information over a defined period of time to enable a second review by the validation team to occur, ideally within three to four weeks after the date of the first final validation. A file of the documentation used to validate the project's final process performance improvement progress is created and stored.

Protocol for Intermediate Validation

The intermediate validation is scheduled approximately 12–18 months after the project is initiated but before the go/no-go or stage gate decision point as determined by the project schedule. This second on-site validation is performed by the validation team to document (1) improvements to the process or processes and (2) improvements in outside process or processes that impact the performance of the project's applicable process steps, and (3) progress of the project as measured by intermediate targets. The process design and cost validation takes place with the technical performance validation experiments, and it incorporates the demonstrated experimental data—by applying the project's cost estimation methodology—to determine the level of process cost reduction achieved. Any changes to the process or process steps developed since the initial on-site validation must be highlighted in communications to the validation team before the intermediate site visit. In such cases, appropriate additional supporting documentation may need to be provided to the validation team. Any changes to the process outside of the project scope are reviewed at this time, along with any new supporting documentation.

Technical Performance Validation

The methodology is identical to that employed for the initial validation, as described above, including the key aspects of the validation procedure spanning scheduling of an on-site visit by the validation team through obtaining a detailed summary of experimental data and data work-up into target performance metrics.

Protocol for Final Validation

The third and final on-site validation is conducted within two months of the completion date of the award (before or after, as is feasible), following procedures that are similar to those used in the previous phases of the project validation. The purpose of this final validation is to assess the final performance of the process improvements addressed within the scope of the award. This validation also documents improvements in processes impacting the performance and cost attributes of the overall improved system. Results from these final validation demonstrations are compared to the initial and intermediate validation results. The recipient must reserve sufficient project funds to allow this final validation and associated site visit to occur.

Technical Performance Validation

The project, and validation teams schedule an on-site visit during which validation team members observe all final process performance and validation demonstrations. The required supporting documentation (which is similar to what was provided in the previous validations) must be supplied to support this final validation, and a summary of the validation test results including data tables must be provided to the validation team after completing the experimental data analysis.

Protocol for Dealing with Unsuccessful Validations

In the event that any validation demonstrations do not meet the agreed validation criteria during a site visit, the recipient discusses the options for addressing the failure.

Validation could involve remediation steps, including a return visit by the validation team to repeat the validation demonstrations. Not more than one return visit is allowed during any phase of the validation process. Examples of validation phase failure include but are not limited to:

1. Inability to repeat results achieved in earlier experimental demonstrations
2. Unreliable data quality as the result of inadequate implementation of quality assurance and quality control procedures
3. Inability to meet the project target or targets specified in the application or agreed to during award negotiation.

The magnitude of performance variance constituting a failed validation demonstration is defined after the validation team has determined the level of variance associated with the instruments and methods used to measure performance. Typically, the return visit is scheduled within three to four weeks of the original visit. If the return visit must be delayed for more than four weeks, the schedule and the reasons for the extended time must be submitted for approval. If the project is unable to achieve all of the key performance metrics after two visits, the metrics are considered not to have been met and the validation is deemed unsuccessful. When return visits are required to complete the technical performance and process economics elements of a specific phase of project validation, the validation report must also contain:

1) An explanation of why the return visit was required
2) The appropriate data gathered from both validations visits
3) An analysis or description of any impacts the return visit had on the project (scope, schedule, or budget)

4) Any recommendations for increased monitoring of the project or corrective actions that could be considered discussing with the recipient to reduce the return validation visits, are needed later on in the life of the project.

- Title
- Objective and Scope
- Responsibility
- Protocol Approval
- Validation Team
- Product Composition
- Process Flow Chart
- Manufacturing Process
- Review of Equipment / Utilities
- Review of Raw Materials and Packing Materials
- Review of Analytical and Batch Manufacturing Records
- Review of Batch Quantities for Validation (Raw Materials)
- Review of Batch Quantities for Validation (Packing Materials)
- HSE Requirements
- Review of Process Parameters Validation Procedure
- Sampling Location
- Documentation
- Acceptance Criteria
- Summary
- Conclusion

The strategy selected for process validation should be simple and straightforward. The following five points gives strategy for process validation:

1) The use of different lots of raw materials should be included. That is, active drug substance and major excipients.
2) Batches should be run in succession and on different days and shifts (the latter condition, if appropriate).
3) Batches should be manufactured in the equipment and facilities designated for eventual commercial production.
4) Critical process variables should be set within their operating ranges and should not exceed their upper and lower control limits during process operation. Output responses should be well within finished product specifications.

5) Failure to meet the requirements of the Validation protocol with respect to process input and output control should be subjected to process requalification and subsequent revalidation following a thorough analysis of process data and formal discussion by the validation team.

Process validation can be defined *as the collection and evaluation of data, from the process design stage through commercial production, which include scientific evidence that a process is capable of consistently delivering quality product.*

This guidance describes the process validation activities in three stages.

Stage 1: Process Design: The commercial manufacturing process is defined during this stage based on knowledge gained through development and scale-up activities.

Stage 2: Process Qualification: During this stage, the process design is evaluated to determine whether the process is capable of reproducible commercial manufacturing.

Stage 3: Continued Process Verification: Ongoing assurance is to be gained during routine production that the process remains in a state of control.

Before any batch from the process is commercially distributed for use by consumers, a manufacturer should have gained a high degree of assurance in the performance of the manufacturing process such that it will consistently produce APIs and drug products meeting those attributes relating to identity, strength, quality, purity, and potency. The assurance should be obtained from objective information and data from laboratory-, pilot-, and/or commercial-scale studies. Information and data should demonstrate that the commercial manufacturing process is capable of consistently producing acceptable quality products within commercial manufacturing conditions.

A successful validation program depends upon information and knowledge from product and process development. This knowledge and understanding is the basis for establishing an approach to control of the manufacturing process that result in products with the desired quality attributes. Manufacturers should:

- Understand the sources of variation
- Detect the presence and degree of variation
- Understand the impact of variation on the process and ultimately on product attributes
- Control the variation in a manner commensurate with the risk it represents to the process

Stage 1: Process Design Process design is *the activity of defining the commercial manufacturing process that will be reflected in planned master* *production and control records*. The goal of this stage is to design a process suitable for routine commercial manufacturing that can consistently deliver the product that can meet its quality attributes.

Building and Capturing Process Knowledge and Understanding

Generally, early process design experiments do not require to be performed under the cGMP conditions required for drugs intended for commercial distribution that are manufactured during.

Stage 2: (process qualification) and

Stage 3: (continued process verification).

Table 3.2 Authorities responsible for validation.

Designation/ Department	Responsibilities
Manager Production	Responsible for manufacturing of batches and review of protocol and report.
Manager QC	Responsible for samples collected
Executive QC	Responsible for analysis of samples collection and submission to QC
Manager Maintenance	Providing utilities and engineering support
Executive Production	Responsible for preparation of protocol and manufacturing of validation batches
Manager QA	Responsible for protocol authorization and preparation of summary report.

These should be conducted in accordance with sound scientific methods and principles, including good documentation practices. Decisions and justification of the controls should be sufficiently documented and internally reviewed to verify and preserve their value for use or adaptation later in the lifecycle of the process and product. Product development activities give important inputs to the process design stage, such as the intended dosage form, the quality attributes, and a general manufacturing pathway. Process information available from product development activities can be leveraged in the process design stage. The functionality and limitations of commercial manufacturing equipment should be considered in the process design, as well as predicted contributions to variability posed by different component lots, production operators, environmental conditions, and measurement systems in the production setting. However, the full spectrum of input variability typical of commercial production is not generally known at this stage. Laboratory or pilot scale models designed to be representative of the commercial process can be used to estimate variability. Designing an efficient process with an effective process control approach is dependent on the process knowledge and understanding obtained. Design of Experiment (DOE) studies can help develop process knowledge by revealing relationships, including multivariate interactions, between the variable inputs (component characteristics or process parameters) and the resulting outputs (in-process material, intermediates, or the final product).

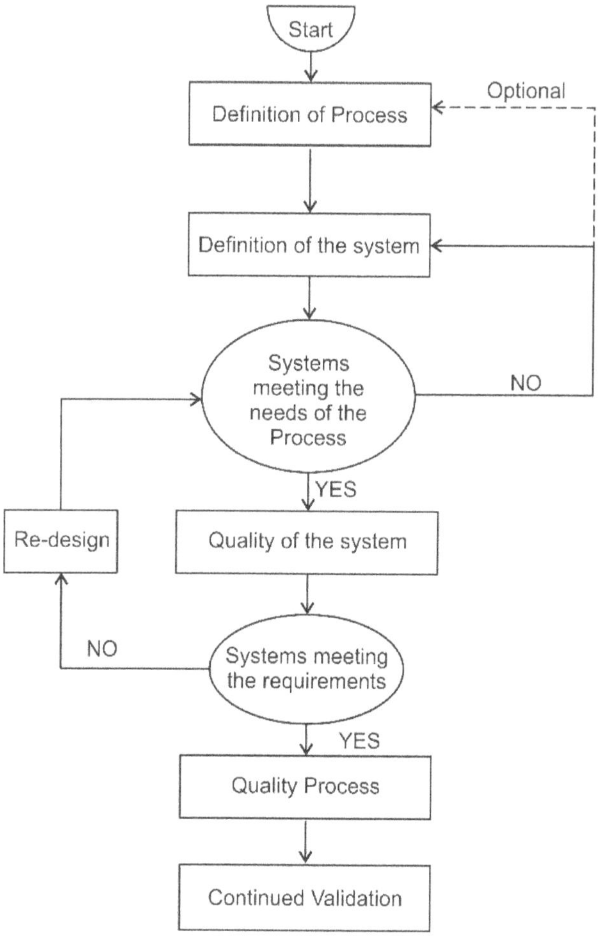

Fig.3.3 Life cycle of validation program.

DOCUMENTATION OF VALIDATION

Documentation at each phase of the process validation lifecycle is essential for effective communication in complex, lengthy, and multidisciplinary projects. Documentation is important so that knowledge gained about a product and process is accessible and comprehensible to others involved in each phase of the lifecycle. Information transparency and accessibility are fundamental tenets of the scientific method. They are also essential to enable organizational units responsible and accountable for the process to make informed, science-based decisions that ultimately support the release of a product to commerce. A written protocol should be established that specifies how qualification and validation will be conducted. The protocol should be reviewed and approved. The protocol should specify critical steps and acceptance criteria. A report that contain references, the qualification and/or validation protocol should be prepared, summarizing the results obtained, commenting on any deviations observed, and drawing the necessary conclusions, including recommending changes necessary to correct deficiencies. Any changes to the plan as defined in the protocol should be documented with appropriate justification. After completion of a satisfactory qualification, a format release for the next step in qualification and validation should be made as a written authorization.

VALIDATION MASTER PLAN (VMP)

A validation master plan is a document that summarizes the company's overall philosophy, intentions and approaches to be used for establishing performance adequacy. The Validation Master Plan should be agreed upon by management. Validation in general requires meticulous preparation and careful planning of the various steps in the process. In addition, all work should be carried out in a structured way according to formally authorized standard operating procedures. All observations must be documented and where possible must be recorded as actual numerical results. The validation master plan should provide an overview of the entire validation operation, its organizational structure, its content and planning. The main elements of it being the list inventory of the items to be validated and the planning schedule. All validation activities relating to critical technical operations, relevant to product and process controls within a firm should be included in the validation master plan. It should comprise all prospective, concurrent and retrospective validations as well as re-validation. The Validation Master Plan should be a summary document and should therefore be brief, concise and clear. It should not repeat information documented elsewhere but should refer to existing documents such as policy documents, SOP's and validation protocols and reports The format and content should include:

- *Introduction:* validation policy, scope, location and schedule.
- *Organizational structure:* personnel responsibilities plant/process/product description: rational for inclusions or exclusions and extent of validation.
- Specific process considerations that are critical and those requiring extra attention.
- List of products/ processes/ systems to be validated, summarized in a matrix format, validation approach
- Re-validation activities, actual status and future planning
- Key acceptance criteria

- Documentation format
- Reference to the required SOP's
- Time plans of each validation project and subproject[35].

ANALYTICAL METHOD VALIDATION

The most important objective of any pharmaceutical industry is to manufacture products of requisite attribute and quality consistently, at the lowest possible cost[36]. Although validation studies have been conducted in the pharmaceutical industry for a long time, there is an ever increasing interest in validation owing to their industry's greater emphasis in recent years on quality assurance program and is fundamental to an efficient production operation. Validation is a concept that has evolved in United States in 1978[37].

The process of confirming the analytical testing strategy utilized for a particular test that is reasonable for its expected use is referred to as method validation. The results which are gained by the process of validation of the method are utilized for passing a judgment on the consistent outcomes of the analysis. Then ensure for the quality and reliable product. For the reliable testing procedure, the well-developed method is regarded as the fundamental process. The requirement of the testing method is characterized by this. The reliability for the requirement of the process is affirmed by the performance capacities of the considered. The analytic testing process is proposed for the insurance of the identification, purification, and potential action of the medicine. The physical characteristics are also studied in this process. A stable study for a longer time is assured by the well-developed method. It also confirms the quality of the drug during the manufacturing of the drug. Likewise, the developed process may bolster the evaluation of the performance of the drug. It ensures the safety parameters and the study of physical characters[38]. Method development is a consistent procedure that arises in parallel accompanied by the development of pharmaceutical products. When talking about the cost, time, productivity, and effectiveness of the drug product, the idea of suitable method development is basic or essential. For the drug development phase, the objective and purpose of the method should be reflected. The characteristic of the API was concentrated in the initial phase of the development of the drug. The safety evaluation for the pre-clinical trial is a vital step. After that pre-formulation studies should be performed. This is followed by stability studies. Analytical method validation is reasonable to help these parameters. After that by studying the nature and characters of API, the analytical testing method is verified and extended during the process of progressing the development of the drug. The method must not be complicated. It must be robust. The suitable regulatory guidelines must be followed[39]. A well-developed method guarantees the goal which is essential during every step of the development of the drug. It ensures improved equipment in the lab. For the accomplishment of excellent quality and accurate testing outcomes, a significant job is performed by a validated analytical process. Subsequently, the guarantee of assurance of QC instrument is focused on by everyone in the chemical lab. Analysis methods can be of different types such as electrochemical analysis, chromatography analysis, spectral analysis[40]. A well-developed method helps in drug testing against specification during manufacturing and quality release operations; similarly, it promotes the studies regarding characters of chemical, safety examination, and analysis of activities of the medicine. The development of an analytical process is utilized for assisting the procedure of synthesis of drug. The formulation studies assist to screen the drug with potential activities. The finished pharmaceutical drug should be stable from the phase of raw material to the final formulation. So stability studies should be regularly monitored. The identification, purification, physical specification, and potential activities of the medicine are set up by these methods[41]. The purpose behind the analytical method from the development of a product to the manufacture of a product is to give information on the point given below

1) Product degradation indicates the stability.
2) Analysing and evaluating the properties of API for instance uniformity of drug, crystalline property of chemical, release API, etc. It helps in the study of bioavailability.
3) The study of impurities which in the identification of drug profiles for safety.
4) The study of the potential activities of the finished product deals with the calculation of the correct dose.

The validation of a specific method must be demonstrated through laboratory experiments by routinely analysing samples. The preparation and execution have to follow a validation protocol, preferably written in a step-by-step instruction format. Possible steps for a complete method validation are listed in Table 2.3. This proposed procedure assumes that the instrument has been selected, and the method has also been developed. It meets criteria such as easy to use, ability to be automated and controlled by computer systems, costs per analysis, sample throughput, turnaround time, environmental, health, and safety requirements. Successful acceptance of the validation parameters and performance criteria by all involved parties requires a cooperative effort of several departments, including analytical development, quality control, regulatory affairs, and individuals requiring the analytical data. The operating procedure or Validation Master Plan (VMP) must clearly define the rules and responsibilities of each involved department in the validation of analytical methods.

Table 3.3 Strategies and steps in analytical method validation.

Sl. No.	Particulars
1.	Develop a validation protocol, an operating procedure, or a validation master plan for the validation
2.	For a specific validation project, define owners and responsibilities
3.	Develop a validation project plan
4.	Define the application, purpose, and scope of the method
5.	Define the performance parameters and acceptance criteria
6.	Define validation experiments
7.	Verify relevant performance characteristics of equipment
8.	Qualify materials, e.g. standards and reagents for purity, accurate amounts, and sufficient stability
9.	Perform pre-validation experiments
10.	Adjust method parameters and/or acceptance criteria if necessary
11.	Perform full internal (and external) validation experiments
12.	Develop standard operation procedures for executing the method in the routine
13.	Define criteria for revalidation
14.	Define type and frequency of system suitability tests and/or analytical quality control checks for the routine
15.	Document validation experiments and results in the validation report

There are no official guidelines on the correct sequence of validation experiments, and the optimal sequence may depend on the method itself. Based on the experience of, the following sequence has proven to be very helpful:

1) Specificity (optimizing separation and detection of standard mixtures if selectivity is insufficient).
2) Linearity, range, limit of detection, and limit of quantitation.
3) Precision (Repeatability, short-term precision, intermediate precision, and re-producibility).
4) Accuracy at different concentrations.
5) Robustness.

The time-consuming experiments, such as accuracy and ruggedness, are included toward the end. Some of the parameters, as listed under (2) to (6), can be measured by combining experiments. For example, when the precision of peak areas is measured over the full concentration range, the data can be used to validate the linearity. During method validation, the parameters, acceptance limits, and frequency of ongoing system suitability tests or quality control checks should be defined. Criteria must be defined to indicate when the method and system are beyond statistical control. The aim is to optimize these experiments so that, with a minimum number of control analyses, the method and the complete analytical system will provide long-term results to meet the objectives defined in the scope of the method.

According to ICH Q2 (R1), validation of method can be defined as, "*Establishing a documented proof, which provides a high degree of assurance that a specific process will consistently produce a desired result at its prearranged specifications and quality characteristics.*" In other words, it is the process of indicating that analytical procedures are suitable for their planned use and that they support the identity, quality, purity, and potency of the drug substances and drug products. Method Validation is requiring when a new method has been developed and when established methods are used in different laboratories and different analysts. The performance characteristics required to validate various methods by using various guidelines such as USP, ICH, FDA, European guidelines etc.[42,43]

According to USP

The analytical parameters such as accuracy, precision, specificity, detection of limit, quantitation limit, linearity, range, ruggedness and robustness can be validated. According to ICH The analytical parameters can be validated are accuracy, precision, specificity, detection of limit, quantitation limit, linearity, range, system suitability and robustness.

According to FDA The analytical parameters can be validated are accuracy, precision, specificity/selectivity, detection of limit, quantitation limit, linearity, range, system suitability, reproducibility, sample solution stability and robustness.

According to European guidelines

The analytical parameters can be validated are accuracy, precision, specificity, detection of limit, quantitation limit, linearity and range. Analytical methods need to be validated, verified, or revalidated in the following instances:

- Before initial use in routine testing
- When transferred to another laboratory
- Whenever the conditions or method parameters for which the method has been validated change (for example, an instrument with different characteristics or samples with different matrix).

Types of analytical procedures to be validated

The following types analytical procedures to be validated[44].

- Identification tests
- Quantitative tests for impurities content
- Limit tests for the control of impurities
- Quantitative tests of the active moiety in samples of drug substance or drug product.

Identification tests are used to ensure the identity of an analyte in a sample. This is normally achieved by comparison of a property of the sample (e.g., spectrum, chromatographic behaviour, chemical reactivity, etc.) to that of a reference standard.

Quantitative tests and Limit tests for impurity control Testing of impurities can be performed by using a quantitative test or a limit test for the impurity in a sample. Different validation parameters are required for a quantitative test than for a limit test;

Quantitative tests of the active moiety in samples of drug substance or drug product In this type, assay procedures are used to measure the analyte present in a given sample. The assay represents a quantitative measurement of the major component(s) in the drug substance.

CLEANING VALIDATION

Validation is documented evidence which provide a high degree of assurance that a specific process will consistently produce a product meeting its predetermined specification and quality attributes[45]. Cleaning validation is documented evidence with high degree of assurance that one can consistently clean a system or piece of equipment to predetermined and acceptable limits. Cleaning validation is primarily applicable to the cleaning of process manufacturing equipment in pharmaceutical industry. It is necessary to have effective cleaning programs in place because of regulatory requirements. However more fundamental reason is that to produce products that are as pure and free from contamination to extent that is possible and feasible[46].

To verify the effectiveness of cleaning procedures and to ensure no risks are associated with cross contamination of active ingredient or detergents/ sanitizer.

The objectives of equipment cleaning and cleaning validation in an Active Pharmaceutical Ingredient (API) area are same as those in pharmaceutical production area. In both these areas efforts are necessary to prevent contamination of a future batch with the previous batch material. The cleaning of 'difficult to reach' surface is one of the most important consideration in equipment cleaning validation. Equipment cleaning validation in an API facility is extremely important as cross contamination in one of the pharmaceutical dosage forms, will multiply the problem. Therefore, it is important to do a step-by-step evaluation of API process to determine the most practical and efficient way to monitor the effectiveness of the cleaning process. It is necessary to validate cleaning procedures for the following reasons[47]

1. It is a prime customer requirement since it ensures the purity and safety of the product.
2. It is a regulatory requirement in Active Pharmaceutical Ingredient product manufacture.
3. It also assures the quality of the process through an internal control and compliance.

Types of contaminations

1. Cross contamination with active ingredients Contamination of one batch of product with significant levels of residual active ingredients from a previous batch cannot be tolerated. In addition to the obvious problems posed by subjecting consumers or patients to unintended contaminants, potential clinically significant synergistic interactions between pharmacologically active chemicals are a real concern.
2. Contamination with unintended materials or compounds While inert ingredients used in drug products are generally recognised as safe or have been shown to be safe for human consumption, the routine use, maintenance and cleaning of equipment provide the potential contamination with such items as equipment parts, lubricants, chemical cleaning agents and pieces of cleaning tools such as brushes and rags.
3. Microbiological contamination such as maintenance, cleaning and storage conditions may provide adventitious microorganisms with the opportunity to proliferate within the processing equipment.

According to the requirements of FDA[48]:

1. FDA expects firms to have written standard operating procedures (SOP) detailing the cleaning process used for various pieces of equipment.
2. If firms have a specific cleaning process for cleaning between different batches of the same product and use a different process for cleaning between product changes, FDA expects the written procedures to address these different scenarios.
3. If firms have one process for removing water-soluble residues and another process for non-water soluble residues, the written procedure should address both scenarios and make it clear when a given procedure is followed.
4. It is required by the FDA, in the general validation procedure, that the personnel responsible for performing and approving the study should comply with the acceptance criteria and the revalidation data.

5. FDA expects firms to prepare specific written validation protocols in advance for the studies to be performed on each manufacturing system or piece of equipment which should address such issues as sampling procedures, and analytical methods to be used including the sensitivity of those methods.
6. It is expected that firms conduct the validation studies in accordance with the protocols and document the result of studies.
7. Final validation report is to be approved by the regulatory board which states whether or not the cleaning process is valid.

Current approaches in determining the acceptance limits for cleaning validation

Acceptance limits for pharmaceutical manufacturing operation[49-51]

1. Approach 1 (Dose criterion) Not more than 0.001 of minimum daily dose of any product will appear in the maximum daily dose of another product. Milligrams of active ingredient = I x K x M in product A permitted per J x L 4 inch2 swab area I = 0.001 of the smallest strength of product A manufactured per day expressed as mg/day and based on the number of milligrams of active ingredient. J = Maximum number of dosage units of product B per day K = Number of dosage units per batch of final mixture of product B L = Equipment surface in common between product A & B expressed as square inches. M= 4 inch2 /swab.
2. Approach 2 (10 ppm criterion) Any active ingredient can be present in a subsequently manufactured product at a maximum level of 10 ppm. Milligrams of active ingredient = R x S x U in product A permitted per T 4 inch2 swab area R = 10mg active ingredient of product A in one kg of product B S = Number of kilograms per batch of final mixture of product B T = Equipment surface in common between product A & B expressed as square inches. U = 4 inch2 /swab.
3. Approach 3 (Visually clean criterion) No quantity of residue should be visible on the equipment after cleaning procedures are performed.

Cleaning Procedures

Standard cleaning procedures for each piece of equipment and process should be prepared. It is vital that the equipment design is evaluated in detail in conjunction with the product residues which are to be removed, the available cleaning agents and cleaning techniques, when determining the optimum cleaning procedure for the equipment. Cleaning procedures should be sufficiently detailed to remove the possibility of any inconsistencies during the cleaning process. Following parameters are to be considered during cleaning procedures.

A. Equipment Parameters to be evaluated
   1. Identification of the equipment to be cleaned
   2. 'Difficult to clean' areas
   3. Property of materials
   4. Ease of disassembly
   5. Mobility
B. Residues to be cleaned
   1. Cleaning limits
   2. Solubility of the residues
   3. Length of campaigns
C. Cleaning agent parameters to be evaluated
   1. Preferable materials that are normally used in the process
   2. Detergents available (as a general guide, minimal use of detergents recommended unless absolutely required)
   3. Solubility properties
   4. Environmental considerations
   5. Health and safety considerations
D. Cleaning techniques to be evaluated
   1. Manual cleaning
   2. CIP (Clean-in-place)
   3. COP (Clean-out-of-place)
   4. Semi-automatic procedures
   5. Automatic procedures
   6. Time considerations
   7. Number of cleaning cycles Sampling Technique[52-55]

Generally, there are two types of sampling that are accepted. The most desirable is the direct method of sampling the surface of the equipment, another method being the use of rinse sampling.

1. Direct surface sampling

It involves the determination of the type of sampling material used and its impact on the test data to check the interference of the sampling material with the test. Therefore, early in the validation programme, it is crucial to assure the sampling medium and solvent if they are satisfactory and be readily used. Advantages of direct sampling are that, areas hardest to clean and which are reasonably accessible can be evaluated, leading to establishing a level of contamination or residue per given surface area.

Additionally, residues that are "dried out" or are insoluble can be sampled by physical removal.

2. Swab sampling

After cleaning the equipment, product contact surfaces could be swabbed to evaluate surface cleanliness. Swabs used should be compatible with the active ingredients and should not interfere with the assay. They should not cause any degradation of the compound. The solvent used for swabbing should provide good solubility for the compound and should not encourage degradation.

3. Rinse sampling

Sampling and testing of rinse samples for residual active ingredient is a commonly adopted method to evaluate cleanliness. This is a fairly convenient method in many cases and requires control over the solvent used for rinsing, the contact time and the mixing involved. The solvent used should be selected based on the solubility of the active ingredient and should either simulate a subsequent batch of product or at least provide adequate solubility. A disadvantage of rinse samples is that the residue or contaminant may not be soluble or may be physically occluded in the equipment. An analogy that can be used is the 'dirty pot.' In the evaluation of cleaning of a dirty pot, particularly with dried out residue, one does not look at the rinse water to see that it is clean; one looks at the pot.

Testing methods

The basic requirements of the analytical methods should have the following criteria.

1. Testing method should have the ability to detect target substances at levels consistent with the acceptance criteria.
2. Testing method should have the ability to detect target substances in the presence of other materials that may also be present in the sample.
3. The testing analytical method should include a calculation to convert the amount of residue detected in the sample to 100% if the recovery data generated indicates a recovery outside the allowed range.

Analysing cleaning validation samples

There are many analytical techniques available that can be used in cleaning validation[56]. But choosing the appropriate analytical tool depends on a variety of factors. The most important factor is to determine the specifications or parameters to be measured. The limit should always be established prior to the selection of the analytical tool.

Specific and non-specific methods

A specific method detects unique compounds in the presence of potential contaminants. Ex: HPLC. Non-specific methods are those methods that detect any compound that produces a certain response Ex: Total Organic Carbon (TOC), pH and conductivity

High performance liquid chromatography

Almost every pharmaceutical company has an HPLC instrument, utilising a variety of detectors. These include UV, fluorescence, electrochemical, refractive index, conductivity, Evaporate light scattering detector (ELSD) and many others. The vast majority of techniques described in the literature are for the determination of surfactants in concentrated products. Therefore, the limits of quantitation and the limit of detection are rather high. Analysis of anionic and cationic surfactants is done by HPLC and Capillary electrophoresis (CE), whereas amphoteric surfactants are analysed by HPLC, CD and ELSD23-25.

Capillary electrophoresis

Capillary electrophoresis can be used for many different types of analysis, viz; separation, detection and determination of sodium lauryl sulphate in cationic, anionic and non-ionic surfactants[57]. Another technique known as Micellar electro kinetic capillary chromatography is used for the separation of non-ionic alkyl phenol polyoxyethylene type surfactants.

Total organic carbon (TOC)

Presently total organic carbon is used widely in the pharmaceutical industries for various purposes. TOC is determined by the oxidation of an organic compound into carbon dioxide. The oxidation can occur through a number of mechanisms depending on the instrument being used. TOC is used for the analysis of detergents, endotoxins, biological media and poly ethylene glycol. Ion chromatography Ion chromatography can be used for the analysis of inorganic, organic and surfactants present in the cleaners. Most cleaners contain sodium and/or potassium. The ion chromatography detection technique of suppressed conductivity is more sensitive to potassium ions than to sodium ions. Very low levels of cleaning agents can be detected by using this technique.

Others

1. Thin layer chromatography (TLC) is widely used for the qualitative determination of surfactants.
2. Atomic absorption spectroscopy (AAS) is used for the determination of inorganic contaminants.
3. Bioluminescence: It is useful for biologicals. This type of analysis usually uses ATP-bioluminescence.

4. Optically simulated electron emission (OSEE)

   In some cases the limits of residue are very less that they can't be detected by conventional methods. OSEE is a very sensitive method that can be used for both qualitative and quantitative manner in this regard.

5. Portable mass spectrometer

   Portable mass spectrometer can be used to detect ultra-sensitive measurements and identification of the residue.

Additional techniques

Apart from the above mentioned techniques the biopharmaceutical industry utilises a wide variety of techniques. These include Enzyme-Linked Immuno Sorbent Assay (ELISA) and Limulus amoebocyte lysate (LAL) technique.

Method validation

It is very important to scientifically establish the residue limit prior to choosing the method of analysis. This includes the limit in the analytical sample and the limit in the next product. This will ensure the ability of the chosen method to detect and quantitate the limit present. Once the technique for analysis has been chosen, it is very important to validate the method used. The validation of a method is very different from validation of recovery. A validated method is one that is rugged and robust enough to measure the residue limit established. Whereas, the validation of a recovery helps to determine the amount that can be recovered from a surface.

VENDER QUALIFICATION

Good Manufacturing Practice (GMP) is that part of quality assurance which ensures that products are consistently produced and controlled to the quality standards appropriate to their intended use. GMP are aimed primarily at diminishing the risk inherent in any pharmaceutical production. Such risks are essentially of two types: cross contamination (in particular of unexpected contaminants) and mix-ups for example false labelling.

Excipients are those materials that when combined with the Active Pharmaceutical Ingredients (API) result in a drug product. Whereas an API has only one function-albeit an extremely important one, that of providing a therapeutic effect – the excipients contained in a drug product play a multitude of roles. Excipient ingredients enable an APIs to be compounded into a stable drug dosage form that can be safely stored and administered with assurance of a consistent bioavailability profile[58]. Most formulations (70–80%) contain excipients at a higher concentration than active drug. Consequently, the excipients contribute significantly to a formulation's functionality and processability[59]. Now a days purity, safety and standardization become extremely important, as excipients are critical to delivering drug actives. In the past, excipients were merely regarded as the inactive part of formulations and relatively unimportant from a specification perspective. It has recently become obvious that controlling the quality and consistency of excipients will have a major impact on dosage form development. They are a key aspect of product Quality by Design (QbD). Excipients are an intrinsic part of nearly all medicinal products and therefore they have an impact upon the quality, safety and efficacy of drug products. Under current GMP rules and regulations, it is the pharmaceutical manufacturer who is responsible for overall operations including the quality of components: the active ingredient(s), the excipients and the packaging materials.

Current status of GMP for pharmaceutical excipients

Many regulatory agencies provided GMP guidelines for APIs. Unlike APIs, excipients receive least oversight from regulatory authorities. In the United States, FDA is responsible for enforcing the requirements of 21 CFR Parts 210 and 211 for the manufacture of drug products from APIs, excipients, and other components. Over the years, the agency has issued numerous guidance documents concerning the manufacture of drug products. In the past several years the agency has also focused on the manufacture of APIs, which has led to an additional series of guidance documents. However, to date, no FDA guidance exists that deals solely with the requirements of the excipient quality system. The Drugs and Cosmetics Act, India has not provided a discrete GMP guideline for manufacture of excipients.

The World Health Organization (WHO) published GMP Guidelines specifically for excipient manufacturers in 1999 and industry bodies have evolved GMP guidelines previously over many years. In the UK, the Pharmaceutical Quality Group (PQG) developed "PS 9100:2002 Pharmaceutical Excipients" which includes both a GMP guide and an audit standard based on ISO 9001:2000. In 2006, the International Pharmaceutical Excipient Council (IPEC) of Europe and America jointly published "Good Manufacturing Practices Guide for Pharmaceutical Excipients". U. S. Pharmacopeia 31-NF 26 also mentioned discrete chapter for GMP for Bulk Pharmaceutical Excipients. The regulatory environment for excipients is subject to change in Europe as part of the new legislation amending the existing pharmaceutical laws that was introduced in 2005. This new legislation requires from API manufacturer to adhere to GMP requirements. Directive 2004/27/EC specifically mandated the implementation of GMP for "certain excipients" including[60]:

- Excipients prepared from materials derived from a Transmissible Spongiform Encephalopathy (TSE) relevant animal species, with the notable exception of lactose
- Excipients derived from human/animal material with potential viral contamination risk

- Excipients claimed to be sterile (or sold as sterile) and used without further sterilization
- Excipients with the specification or claim that they are endotoxin/pyrogen controlled; or
- Specific excipients, namely propylene glycol and glycerol.

  In addition to GMP regulatory expectations and requirements mentioned above, the excipient vendor qualification is particularly important
- In the product approval process, where bioequivalence comparisons are made between clinical bioequivalence (bio batch) production and commercial scale-up batches.
- to provide adequate assurance of drug product performance in vivo, the excipient used in commercial batches should not differ significantly from that used in biobatches and in case of significant differences, additional testing is required to establish the bioequivalence of the product.
- to avoid the potential risks mentioned below
  - Presence of extraneous matter e.g., metal, paper, particles
  - Cross contamination with other chemicals (either excipients or APIs or breakdown products)
  - Contamination with TSE & melamine risk materials which is not permitted by legislation
  - Inconsistent manufacture such that the quality of final products cannot be assured
  - mis-labelling of containers leading to product mix-up
- Concept of Quality by Design (QbD) involves understanding of product variability in which contribution of excipient also needs special consideration

  Product variability[61]: Current requirement of GMP, Quality by Design and Process Analytical Techniques demands thorough understanding of a process and the impact on that process of all the input variables and their effect on that process. Following variables affect the consistency of the product:
- Variable Manufacturing Techniques
- Manufacturing Equipment Variables
- Manufacturing Process Conditions
- Environmental Conditions
- Formulation (API and Excipient) chemical & Physical property Variation Figures 2.4 and 2.5 indicate that variation in excipient manufacturing/ supply/quality has a significant effect on consistency of drug product manufacturing.

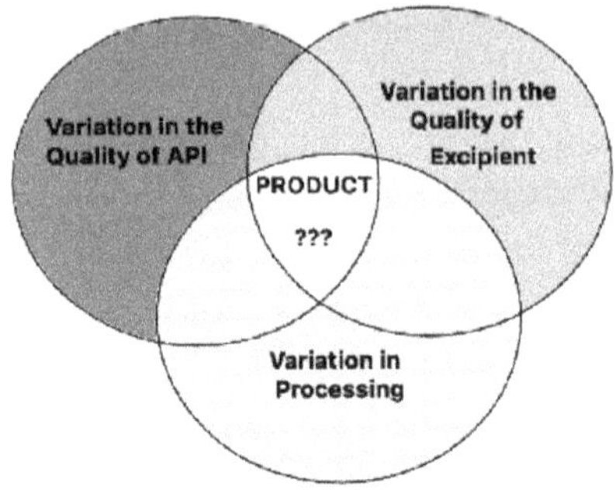

Fig.3.4 Factors affecting the product's quality

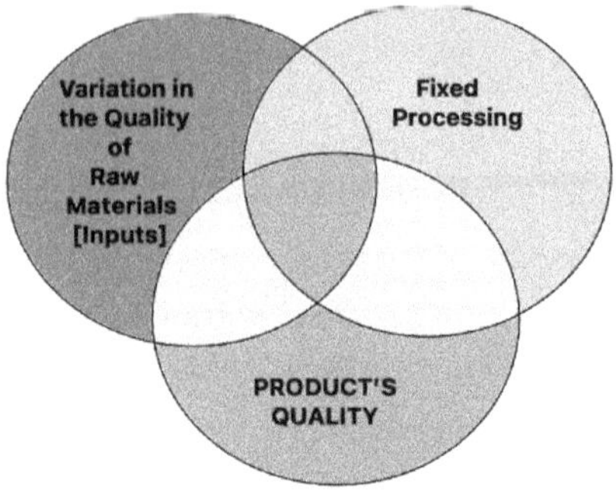

Fig.3.5 Validation in the product's quality with variable RM and fixed process.

Methods used for excipient vender qualification

The qualification process is defined by the American Society for Quality Control (ASQC) as "the process of demonstrating whether an entity is capable of fulfilling the specified requirement." Vendor qualification is the process by which a vendor is evaluated to determine if it can provide the necessary goods or services to the standards that the purchasing company requires. Quality systems are defined as "the processes, organizational structure, procedures and resources that are used to control variables associated with producing a product of consistent quality and that meets predefined specifications." In simpler words, an organization's entire operation is a measure of a product s quality and not simply the testing of its finished product. For effectiveness of the quality systems and to assure continual quality of excipient to be used for drug product manufacturing, following approach may be helpful. Design the SOP for "Excipient Vendor Qualification" which includes following:

- Excipient vendor selection criteria
- Procedure for evaluation of criticality of excipient for consistent output of drug product
- Procedure for Qualifying Non-Critical Excipients
- Procedure for Qualifying Critical Excipients
- Onsite audit requirement and frequency of periodic audit for assurance of consistent supply
- Procedure for preparation of audit report and verification of observations made during audit
- Procedure for pre-shipment sample analysis
- Procedure for manufacturing trial batches and evaluation of stability data for preliminary screen
- Procedure for alternate vendor development
- Procedure for Trend analysis

- Criteria for Rejection of approved vendor
- Agreement with vendor

Q.U.E.S.T. approach[62] Q = Question phase: What type of excipient is required for the drug product manufacturing to fulfil the drug product characteristics, safety and efficacy of the product. The defined specification for raw material required should be prepared with scientific rationale behind its proposed usage. U = Understanding phase: The specific requirement related to particle size, special functionality. Based on the preliminary trials taken at laboratory scale and outcome of compatibility, stability and development activity, the requirement of excipient can be finalized. Scientific rationale shall be available in form of the laboratory trials or through published literature E = Evaluation phase: Identification of the best potential vendor Based on the requirement, the potential vendor can be identified. S = Site audit phase: Onsite and offsite verifications Based on the criticality of excipient, the onsite audit shall be carried out.

T = Track phase: Monitor and requalify

The vendor's performance must be monitored on a continuous basis. The monitoring process involves a review of any problems associated with the good or service supplied by the vendor. A schedule is determined so that each qualified vendor is requalified on a periodic basis.

Following checkpoints / checklist may help to assess the GMP compliance during vendor audit of pharmaceutical excipient manufacturer.

Table 3.4 Checklist to assess the GMP compliance.

Sl. No	Checkpoints
General Information of the company	
1.	Name of the organization
2.	Address of manufacturing site
3.	How long has the company been manufacturing pharmaceutical excipients?
4.	No of Products and range being manufactured by the organisation
5.	% of supply to the pharmaceutical industries
6.	Approximate turn over
7.	Strength of the organization
8.	Approximate area of the manufacturing facility
9.	Type of pharmaceutical formulation
10.	Details of National/international accreditations
Quality Management System	
11.	Is Quality manual available?
12.	Is Quality policy in place?

Table 3.4 *contd...*

13.	Is system for documentation control available to include following? • Indexing • Document numbering • File numbering • Storage of documents
14.	Are all documents pass through appropriate review and approval procedure?
15.	Is distribution records maintained for all documents?
16.	Is there any procedure for assurance of current version of documents being used?
17.	Are all documents impacting quality of final product reviewed by quality units? e.g., specification, Batch Records...
18.	Is responsibility assigned for issuance and control of documents?
19.	Is history of changes made in documents are maintained?
20.	Is electronic signature being used?
21.	Is procedure available for "correction of entries"?
22.	Is retention period of documents defined in procedure? Is it appropriate?
23.	Is procedure available for change control management?
24.	Is independent unit like QA/RA responsible for review and approval of changes?
25.	Is there any procedure to inform customers for process related changes?
26.	Is independent quality unit available?
27.	Is a defined job responsibility available for all personnel?
28.	Is approved organization chart is available?
Management Responsibilities	
29.	Is there a defined programme for review of quality objectives?
30.	Is there procedure to permit customer audits and records are maintained?
31.	Is there procedure for upgradation of system based on customer demand?
32.	Is there system for periodic review of quality systems? (Internal audit)
33.	Is there system in place for periodic management review? If yes, following details covered under the scope? • Results of internal and external audits • Customer feedback • Customer complaints • Status of CAPA • Changes that affect the quality
Resource Management	
34.	Are sufficient personnel with appropriate qualification available to carry out assigned responsibilities?
35.	List of personnel available with their experience and qualification status?
36.	Is there system to maintain personnel file which includes • Job description • CV • SOP training record • Record of external training and certificates

Table 3.4 ***contd...***

37.	Is record of consultants maintained? which includes • Name • Address • Qualification of consultants • Type of service they provided
38.	Is there procedure for periodic training?
39.	Is the appropriate documents available for training of the personnel?
40.	Is there a system to train person on job-specific task before allocation of job? Documents available for the same?
41.	Is the training SOP covers the training on GMP and health and hygiene on periodic basis?
42.	Is appropriate gowning procedure available and followed?
43.	Are protective wears available in the applicable locations?
44.	Is there any policy available for periodic health-check up for employee?
45.	Is there procedure to re-evaluate health condition of the personnel suffering from an infectious disease before re-assigning task?
46.	Is premises situated in appropriate location to prevent cross contamination?
47.	Is toxic/sensitizing material being produced in the premises?
48.	Is facility permits easy cleaning?
49.	Is SOP for cleaning available?
50.	Is record of cleaning maintained with type of disinfectant / sanitizing agent used?
51.	SOP for pest control available?
52.	Is list of equipment available with • Capacity • Id. No. • Preventive maintenance frequency • Material of construction
53.	Are SOPs available for operation, cleaning and preventive maintenance of equipment?
54.	Is there a system to maintain equipment file containing all details of equipment containing IQ,OQ,PQ, Preventive maintenance, details of breakdown and re-qualification?
55.	Are Equipment logs maintained properly?
56.	Is any equipment attached with computerized system? If yes, • Record available for proper functioning of software? • Periodic check-up procedure for proper functioning? • Retention at suitable location for back up? • Change control system for programme?

Table 3.4 ***contd…***

57.	Is there procedure for checking quality of utilities? (Compressed Air, Steam, Nitrogen gas used in production are certified for its quality?)
58.	Is water being used in the production? If yes, • Is type of water appropriate for its intended use? • is there procedure for periodic testing of bore-well water? • Are specification of bore-well water and process water available and followed? • Is facility for water testing is appropriate?/ Is contract available for testing of water? • Is microbial control is part of specification?
59.	Is purification of excipient is carried out in controlled environment?
60.	Is there system for qualification of AHU/HVAC? Collect the following details. • Type of filter • % of Recirculation Is the type of filter and system for recirculation of air is justifiable for its intended use?
61.	Are pipework identified with its content and flow direction?
62.	Is the location of piping/ducts appropriate for minimizing contamination?
63.	Is there adequate lighting available?
64.	Are drain provided with an air break to prevent back-siphoning?
65.	Washing & toilet facilities are adequate and equipped with following? • Hot & cold water • Soap or detergent • Air dryers • Single service towels • Clean toilet facility • Showering/changing cloths
Product Realisation	
66.	Is there a system for purchasing agreements for quality critical materials? It shall include: • The name, type, class, style, grade, item code number or other identification and packaging specifications • Drawings, process requirements, inspection instructions and other technical data along with procedures, process equipment and personnel. • A statement to notify the excipient manufacturer of significant changes in quality critical raw material
67.	Is there SOP for receipt, identification, testing and release of materials being used for manufacturing of excipients?
68.	Specification for all incoming material is available?
69.	Is testing procedure for all incoming material available?
70.	Is there SOP for sampling of material?

Table 3.4 ***contd…***

71.	Is there system to approve the suppliers/manufacturers of raw material? (It is required for consistency in product quality)
72.	Is there SOP available to follow controls for bulk deliveries? ▪ Bulk deliveries should have additional control to assure material purity and freedom from contamination e.g., dedicated tankers, temper-evident seals, a certificate of cleaning, analytical testing and / or audit of the supplier)
73.	Is there procedure for customer communication?
74.	Is master production record available?
75.	Is batch production records includes following? • Date/time each step was completed or date/time log of key parameters • Identification of major equipment and lines used • Material inputs to enable traceability, for example batch number and quantities of raw material/intermediate, time it was added etc. • In-process and laboratory control results • The quantity produced for the defined batch and a statement of the percentage of theoretical yield, unless not quantifiable • Inspection of the packaging and labelling area before and after use • Labelling control records • Description of excipient product containers and closures • Description of sampling performed • Failures, deviation and their investigations • Results of final product inspection
76.	Is the detailed cleaning procedure? Is the SOP has mention of following details? • Schedule • Cleaning agent • Procedure for disassembling and re-assembling • Cleaning verification • Time frame after cleaning and before usage for next product • Cleaning procedure for • Product change over • Batch changeover
77.	Is there SOP / Policy available for recovery of solvents, mother liquors and second crop crystallization?
78.	Is there procedure to check appropriateness of recovered solvents prior to reuse?
79.	Is the use of mother liquors or filtrates containing recoverable amounts of excipients is being documented in batch records?
80.	Is there procedure for In-process inspection at defined locations and times?
81.	Is in-process sampling carried out according to approved sampling procedure?
82.	Is in-process sampling carried out according to approved sampling procedure?

Table 3.4 ***contd…***

83.	Is there SOP available for issuance and control of labels?
84.	Is there procedure for reconciliation of packaging and labelling materials?
85.	Is there procedure for process validation? OR product review reports? (Process consistency can be determined through process capability studies, development and scale – up reports etc.)
86.	Customer property Is there procedure for verification, storage and maintenance of customer-supplied materials intended for incorporation in to the customer's excipient?
87.	Is there procedure for handling, storage and preservation of the raw materials? • Appropriate storage condition • Outdoor storage also acceptable provided containers give suitable protection against deterioration and identifying labels remain legible and container cleaned prior to opening and use
88.	Packaging system Is there specification and testing methods available for packaging materials?
89.	Is cleaning procedure available in case of re-use of container?
90.	Is there adequate warehouse for proper segregation of material?
91.	Is there a system to record temperature and humidity at warehouse?
92.	Is there procedure to maintain distribution records? -what is the retention period for distribution records?
Measurement, Analysis and Improvement	
93.	Is specification and testing procedure available?
94.	Are all instruments qualified?
95.	Are SOPs available for calibration of instruments / equipment?
96.	Are SOPs available for operation of instruments / equipment?
97.	Is there a system for labelling of calibration status?
98.	Are reagents/volumetric solutions are labeled for identity & used before date?
99.	Is there procedure for standardization of volumetric reagents?
100.	Is there written procedure for recording analytical data? Are Laboratory control records written with sufficient details as mentioned below? • Description of sample, batch number, date of sampling • Statement referencing each test method used • Records of raw data including chromatograms, graphs, spectra etc. • Calculation record Comparability with specification • Date of analysis • Analysed by
101.	Is document of reference standard available? Following details shall be in place • COA • Storage location and temperature record • Reconciliation record

Table 3.4 ***contd...***

102.	Is document of working standard (secondary reference standard) available? Following details shall be in place • COA • Storage location and temperature record • Reconciliation record • Labelling • Characterization of Working standard
103.	Is there documented procedure available for qualification of working standard?
104.	Re-evaluation period is defined for working standard?
105.	Is there procedure to carry out microbial analysis of final excipients? If yes, • Adequate facility available? • Contracted out? • Written contract available? • Contract lab audited for competency?
106.	Are scientifically sound and validated analytical methods available to carry out testing of different excipients?
107.	Are following details available on certificate of analysis? • Batch No. • Retest date • Address of manufacturer • Product name • Acceptance criteria and results
108.	Is any repacking / re-processing activity contacted outside? If yes, re-packers / re-processor's details mentioned in COA
109.	Is there approved procedure available for conducting stability studies? • Carried out in final container? • Procedure reflects to include re-process batch or re-work batch in stability?
110.	Is appropriate back-up data available to support the re-test / expiry date assigned to the product? If no, What is the procedure to assign re-test / expiry date?
111.	Is there defined procedure for release of material?
112.	Is there procedure for investigation of OOS?
113.	Is there procedure for retained sampling? It should include • Quantity to be retained • Retention time
114.	Is back up for impurity limit is available? OR system for impurity profiling?
115.	Is there SOP for control of nonconforming product to prevent inadvertent use?
116.	Is there procedure for reworking or reprocessing?

Table 3.4 ***contd…***

117.	Is there system to perform risk assessment during approval of reworking to include following • New impurities that may be introduced as a result of reworking • Additional testing to control the reworking • Records and traceability to the original batches • Suitable acceptance criteria for the reworked excipient • Impact on stability or the validity of the re-evaluation interval • Performance of the excipient
118.	Is separate space available for storage of returned products?
119.	Is there procedure for handling return goods? Are following details part of the record for returned goods? • Name and address of consignee • Batch No. • Quantity returned • Reason for return • Use / disposal decision

Exercise

Multiple Choice Questions

1. Fill in the blanks with appropriate words given below.
2. ...., ..., ... are designed or built into the product.
   a) Validation, Specification, and Calibration
   b) Quality, Safety, and Efficacy
   c) Quality, Cost, and Waste
   d) Process, Product, and Quality
3. Fill in the blank with appropriate word given below.
4. The word .... means 'evaluating validation actions or proving effectiveness'.
   a) Evaluation b) calibration
   c) Validation d) specification
5. Which of the following statement is correct?
   a) Validation is an integral part of quality assurance system.
   b) Validation is an integral part of quality control system.
   c) Quality assurance is an integral part of validation.
   d) None of the above.

6. Which of the following statement is correct?
   a) Validation involves systematic study of the systems.
   b) Validation involves systematic study of the facility.
   c) Validation involves systematic study of the processes.
   d) All the above

7. Which of the following statement is correct?
   a) In prospective validation, the validation protocol is executed before the process is put into commercial use.
   b) The concurrent validation involves in-process monitoring of critical processing steps and product testing.
   c) Retrospective validation of the processes should be based on historical data.
   d) All the above

8. Fill in the blank with an appropriate word given below.

   .... gives the evidence that changes in a process and/or the process environment that are introduced do not adversely affect process characteristics and product quality.
   a) Prospective validation
   b) Retrospective validation
   c) Revalidation
   d) Concurrent validation

9. Under which circumstance revalidation is NOT necessary?
   a) Changes of source of active raw material manufacturer.
   b) Changes of equipment which involve the replacement of equipment on a "like for like" basis.
   c) Changes in the plant/facility.
   d) Changes in raw materials.

10. Which of the following statement is correct?
    a) Pharmaceutical Process Validation is the most important and recognized parameters of quality assurance.
    b) Pharmaceutical Process Validation is the most important and recognized parameters of cGMPs.
    c) Pharmaceutical Process Validation is the most important and recognized parameters of quality control.
    d) None of the above.

11. Fill in the blank with an appropriate word given below.
12. Calibration, preventative maintenance, ... schedules are considered in installation qualification.
    a) cleaning
    b) production
    c) maintenance
    d) purchase
13. Fill in the blank with an appropriate word given below.
14. The proposal for .... control should be properly documented through the change control procedure.
    a) Quality
    b) managing
    c) change
    d) None of the above
15. Which of the following statement is correct?
    a) Process Development Designee shall review the product development report.
    b) Process Development Designee shall review the data from pilot scale, scale up batch.
    c) Process Development Designee shall review the proposed master formula document of product intended for manufacturing.
    d) All the above.
16. Which of the following statement is correct?
    a) The initial on-site validation is performed to validate technical benchmark data.
    b) The initial on-site validation replicate the benchmark performance data before improvements funded through the project.
    c) The initial on-site replicates the benchmark process details and techno-economic information.
    d) All the above
17. Which of the following statement is NOT correct?
    a) Batches should be manufactured in the equipment and facilities designated for eventual commercial production.
    b) Critical process variables should be set within their operating ranges and should not exceed their upper and lower control limits during process operation.
    c) Output responses should not be well within finished product specifications.
    d) Batches should be run in succession and on different days and shifts.

18. Which of the following statement is NOT correct?
    a) Process validation includes the installation qualification.
    b) Process validation includes the process design.
    c) Process validation includes the process design.
    d) Process validation includes the continued process verification
19. Which of the following statement is correct?
    a) The supplier should understand the sources of variation.
    b) The manufacturer should understand the presence and degree of variation.
    c) The supplier should understand the impact of variation on the process and ultimately on product attributes.
    d) The supplier should control the variation in a manner commensurate with the risk it represents to the process.
20. Fill in the blank with an appropriate word given below.
21. Documentation at each phase of the process validation lifecycle is essential for effective .... in complex, lengthy, and multidisciplinary projects.
    a) Connection b) connectivity
    c) Communication d) communicative
22. Fill in the blank with an appropriate word given below.
23. A validation master plan is a .... that summarizes the company's overall philosophy, intentions and approaches to be used for establishing performance adequacy.
    a) notice b) notification
    c) information d) document
24. Which of the following statement is correct?
    a) The process of confirming the analytical testing strategy utilized for a particular test that is reasonable for its expected use is referred to as method validation.
    b) The process of denying the analytical testing strategy utilized for a particular test that is reasonable for its expected use is referred to as method validation.
    c) For the unreliable testing procedure, the well-developed method is regarded as the fundamental process.
    d) The analytic testing process is proposed for the identification, purification, and potential action of the medicine.

25. Which of the following statement is NOT correct?
    a) Analytical method validation confirms the quality of the drug during the manufacturing of the drug.
    b) The safety evaluation for the pre-clinical trial is a vital step in analytical method validation.
    c) The safety evaluation for the pre-clinical trial is an important step in analytical method validation.
    d) The guarantee of assurance of QC instrument is focused on by everyone in the chemical lab.
26. Which of the following statement is NOT correct?
    a) Product degradation indicates the stability.
    b) Sampling and testing of rinse samples for excipient is a commonly adopted method to evaluate cleanliness.
    c) The most important factor is to determine the specifications or parameters to be measured.
    d) Excipients are those materials that when combined with the Active Pharmaceutical Ingredients (API) result in a drug product.

Short Questions

1. Who are the two FDA officials, who spoke about validation? Write down the definitions of validation as per different authorities.
2. Write about the technical performance verification.
3. What is meant by process design and cost validation?
4. What do you know about 'documentation at each phase of the process validation lifecycle is essential for effective communication in complex, lengthy, and multidisciplinary projects.'
5. 'The process of confirming the analytical testing strategy utilized for a particular test that is reasonable for its expected use is referred to as method validation.' – what do you understand by this?
6. What are the strategies and steps in analytical method validation? What are the types of analytical procedures to be validated?
7. Why the cleaning validation is documented? Why the evidence with high degree of assurance is required in pharmaceutical industries?
8. What do you know about the current status of GMP for pharmaceutical excipients?
9. What are different types of contaminations found in pharmaceutical industries? What are the parameters to be considered during cleaning procedures?
10. Why vendors' qualification is important in pharmaceutical industries?

Long Questions

1. Write down in brief different types and timing of validation?
2. 'The concept of process validation came through the regulatory aspects associated with cGMP regulations.' – explain about requalification.
3. 'The validation process is intended to assess technical performance and cost improvements within the context of the FOA goals, as defined in the negotiated award.' – write about the protocols of validation.
4. 'A validation master plan is a document that summarizes the company's overall philosophy, intentions and approaches to be used for establishing performance adequacy.' – explain.
5. Discuss on 'any validation demonstrations do not meet the agreed validation criteria during a site visit, the recipient discusses the options for addressing the failure.'
6. What are the current approaches in determining the acceptance limits for cleaning validation? Explain standard cleaning procedures for each piece of equipment and process.
7. What is meant by total organic compound?
8. What is meant by quality by design? What are the methods used for pharmaceutical excipient vendors qualification?
9. How can you assess the GMP compliance in pharmaceutical industries?
10. Explain the importance of cleaning validation in pharmaceutical industries. What are the analytical techniques available that can be used in cleaning validation?

Answers

1	2	3	4	5	6	7	8	9	10	11	12	13	14	15	16	17	18	19	20
b	c	a	d	d	c	d	b	a	c	d	d	c	a	b	c	d	a	c	b

Reference

1. Sharma A, Saini S; Process Validation of Solid Dosage Form: A Review. International Journal of Research in Pharmacy and Science, 2013; 3 (2): 12- 30.
2. Kaur H, Singh G, Seth N; Pharmaceutical Process Validation: A Review. 2013; 3 (4): 189-194.
3. Thaduvai R, Rao BS, Jeybaskaran M; Process Validation of Pantoprazole 40 mg Tablets: The Pharma Innovation. 2012; 1 (5): 50-52.
4. Kavita, Khurana G, Chaudhary S; Process Validation of Solid Dosage Form: A Review. Pharma Science Monitor, An International Journal of Pharmaceutical Sciences, September 2013; 4 (4): 390- 391.

5. Agalloco J., Validation: an unconventional review and reinvention, 49(4), 2011, 175-179
6. Sarvani V, Elisha Raju P, Sreekanth Nama, Leela Madhuri Pola, Chandu Babu Rao, PROCESS VALIDATION: AN ESSENTIAL PROCESS IN PHARMACEUTICAL INDUSTRY, Sarvani V. et al. / IJMCA / Vol 3 / Issue 2 / 2013 / 49-52.
7. Keyur B. Ahir, Khushboo D. Singh, Sushma P. Yadav, Hetal S. Patel, Chetan B. Poyahari, Overview of Validation and Basic Concepts of Process Validation, Sch. Acad. J. Pharm., 2014; 3(2): 178-190
8. Chapman K. G: A History of Validation in the United States, Part I, Pharma Technology. November 1991; 39-98.
9. Kaur H, Singh G, Seth N; Pharmaceutical Process Validation: A Review. 2013; 3 (4): 189-194.
10. CARDONE J.M.J. Assoc. Off. Anal Chem, 66, 1983, p. 1257
11. MILLER J.N., Analyst, 116, 1991, p. 3.
12. ALEXANDROV, Yu I. Analyst, 121, 1996, p. 1137.
13. Lakshmana Prabu S, Suriyaprakash TNK, Ruckmani K, Thirumurugan R (2014) Concepts of Process Validation in Solid Dosage Form [Tablet] – An Overview. SAJ Pharma Pharmacol 1: 103.
14. Chapman K. G: A History of Validation in the United States, Part I, Pharma Technology. November 1991; 39-98.
15. Nash R. A., Wachter A. H: In Pharmaceutical Process Validation. Third Edition; Revised and Expanded, Marcel Dekker Inc., New York, 1993.
16. Potdar MA; Pharmaceutical Quality Assurance. 2nd Edition, Nirali Prakashan, 2009: 8.6-8.20.
17. WHO Expert Committee on Specifications for Pharmaceutical Preparations. WHO technical report, series no. 863 – 34th report, Annex 6 – GMP: Guidelines on the validation of manufacturing processes: 4-7.
18. ICH Q7A Good Manufacturing Practice Guidance for Active Pharmaceutical Ingredients: 33.
19. Potdar MA; Current Good Manufacturing Practices for Pharmaceuticals. 2nd Edition, Pharma Med Press Publication, Delhi, December 2007: 8.2-8.3.
20. Validation of Solid Dosage Forms the FDA view, 1989; 15(6-7): 1119-1133.
21. Guidelines for Process Validation of Pharmaceutical Dosage Forms. Saudi Food and Drug Authority, Kingdom of Saudi Arabia, 2010; 9-15.
22. Chaitanya Kumar G, Rout RP, Ramtake S, Bhattacharya S. Process Validation, The Indian Pharmacist, 2005, 14-19.
23. Potdar MA; Pharmaceutical Quality Assurance. 2nd Edition, Nirali Prakashan, Pune, 2007: 8.1- 8.44.
24. Nash R. A: Process Validation of a 17- Year Retrospective Study of Solid Dosage Forms. Drug Development Industrial Pharmacy 1966; 22 (1): 25-34.

25. Guideline on general principles of process validation. Centre for drug evaluation and research, FDA.
26. Guidance for Industry: Process Validation: General Principles and Practices. U.S. Department of Health and Human Services, Food and Drug Administration, Centre for Drug Evaluation and Research (CDER), Centre for Biologics Evaluation and Research (CBER), Centre for Veterinary Medicine (CVM), January 2011.
27. Oechslein C, Lazar MS; Process Validation from view report of the FDA. Maas and Peither AG – GMP Publishing, Logfile No. 3/ February 2012.
28. Guidance for Industry on general principles and practices of process validation; US Department of Health and Human Services, Food and Drug Administration, 2011;
29. Validation Guidelines for Pharmaceutical Dosage Form; Health products and Food branch Inspectorate, Canada, December 2009; 8-13.
30. Singh H, Rana AC, Saini S, Singh G; Industrial Process Validation of Solid Dosage Form: A Review. International Journal of Research Pharmacy, 2012; 3 (4): 63-70.
31. Patel RC, Bhuva CK; Pharmaceutical Process Validation: Pharmatutor, ART – 1053
32. Mohammed. SA; Pharmaceutical Process Validation: An Overview. Journal of Advanced Pharmacy Education and Research, 2012; 2 (4): 186-200
33. DOE-BETO (U.S. Department of Energy Bioenergy Technologies Office). 2008. Managing Design and Construction Using Systems Engineering for Use with DOE O 413.3A. Accessed June 6, 2017
34. DOE (Department of Energy). 2016. 2015 Peer Review Report: Review Panel Summary Report and Project Results. Accessed June 6, 2017
35. Health Canada: Health Products and Food Branch Inspectorate. Validation Guidelines for Pharmaceutical Dosage Forms, 2009 [Dated 7 Aug 2009, cited 2018 Apr 10].
36. Naga G. R., Vignesh K., Analytical Method Validation: An Updated Review, IJAPBC- Vol.1 (1), Jan- Mar, 2012.
37. G. Lavanya, M. Sunil, and M. Eswarudu*, Analytical Method Validation: an updated review. IJPSR, 2013; Vol. 4(4): 1280-1286.
38. Shah.K, Kumar.S, Upmanyu.N and Mishra.P, Review Article on, "Evaluation of an Analytical Method" IJPCR, Vol.1 issue 1, 2012.
39. T.A.Phazna Devi, Aravind Setti, S. Srikanth, original article on Method development and validation of paracetamol drug by RP-HPLC. 18 Feb 2013.
40. Beckett A.H and Stenlake J.B, In: Practical Pharmaceutical Chemistry, 3rd edn. Vol.II, CBS Publishers and Distributors, New Delhi; 1986.P. 131.
41. G. Lavanya, M. Sunil, and M. Eswarudu*, Analytical Method Validation: an updated review. IJPSR, 2013; Vol. 4(4): 1280-1286.

42. Reddy V.P, Rajan T.V.S, Kumar A. N, A review on analytical method validation. Int J Rev Life Sci 1: 141-144.
43. Chinmaya K. S, Muvvala S., Nalini k. S., Validation of Analytical Methods: A Review, International Journal of Chromatography and Separation Techniques, Volume 2018; Issue 01, 19 January, 2018,
44. Ravichandran. V, Shalini s, and Harish Rajak, Validation of analytical Methods-Strategies and Importance. Vol.2, 3 May 2010.
45. Amit Kailaschand M. Process validation of cephalosporin antibiotics cefuroxime axetil 500 mg tablets. Karnataka: Rajiv Gandhi University of Health Sciences; 2011.
46. Kumar V S, Sanjeev T: Overview of cleaning validation in pharmaceutical manufacturing unit. International Journal of Advanced Research in Pharmaceutical & Biosciences. 2012; 1(2): 154-164.
47. Cleaning Validation in Active Pharmaceutical Ingredient manufacturing plants by Active pharmaceutical ingredients committee. September 1999.
48. FDA, Guide to inspections of validation of cleaning process division of investigations, Office of regional operations & Office regulatory affairs. July 1993.
49. Fourman GL, Mullen MV. Determining cleaning validation acceptance limits for Pharmaceutical manufacturing operations. Pharm Tech. 1993; 54-60.
50. Vitale KM. Cleaning validation acceptance criteria, 15th Annual Pharm Tech conference, East Brunswi New jersey, September 1995.
51. Brewer R. Regulatory aspects of cleaning validation, ISPE seminar, Rockville, Maryland, March 1996.
52. FDA, Guide to inspection of validation of cleaning process, July 1993.
53. Hyde JM. Cleaning validation strategies, ISPE CIP/SIP seminar, Atlanta-Georgia, June 1994.
54. Leblane DA. Rinse sampling for cleaning validation studies. Pharm Tech. 1998; 22(5): 66-74.
55. James A. Points to consider in the validation of equipment cleaning procedures. J Parental Sci Tech. 1992; 46 (5): 163-168
56. Gavlick WK, Ohlemeier LA, Kaiser HJ. Analytical Strategies for Cleaning Agent Residue Determination. Pharm Tech. 1995; 19: 136-144.
57. Heinig K, Vogt C. Determination of Surfactants by Capillary Electro-phoresis. Electrophoresis. 1999; 20: 3311-3328
58. Silverstein I (2002) Excipient GMP quality standards: One is enough. Pharm Technol 26: 46–52
59 Nachaegari SK, Bansal AK (2004) Co processed excipients for solid dosage forms. Pharm Technol 28: 52–64.
60. Taylor P (2008) Pharmaceutical Excipients: Where Now for GMP?; RAJ Pharma December 2008.

61. Morris K (2006) Understanding Critical Material Properties for Pharmaceutical Dosage Forms, Summary of workshop – Physical and Mechanical Properties of Excipients, April, 2006.

62. Cafmeyer N, Lewis, JM (2009) How to develop a practical (and compliant) vendor qualification program, May 4th, 2010.

CHAPTER - 4

Equipment Qualification

Importance, Autoclave, Membrane Filter, Rapid Mixer Granulator, Cone Blender, Fluidized Bed Dryer (FBD), Tablet Compression Machine, Liquid Filling Machine, Liquid Sealing Machine, Aseptic Room Validation, Air Velocity and Air Changes, Differential Pressure Test, HEPA Filter Leakage Test, Air Flow Visualization (Non-unidirectional flow), Airborne Particle Count Recovery/decontamination Rate Test, Environmental Conditions - Temperature and Relative Humidity, Viable Count Monitoring - Settle Plate and Air Sampling

IMPORTANCE

Calibration of equipment is to be carried out on a regular basis. This is done because the instruments are likely to deviate due to hard operating conditions, mechanical shocks or exposure to extreme temperature or pressure. Frequency of calibration would depend on the tolerance level. When the objective becomes critical, the calibration would require to be carried out more frequently and with great accuracy[1]. When such informal checks are advantageous to ensure that performance requirements are met, it is of much greater advantageous to conduct this process on a formal, documented basis, known as Equipment Qualification. In addition, to check the performance during the commissioning of a measuring system, equipment qualification also should be documented on regular performance checks conducted throughout the equipment's operational life. The regulatory requirement for some industries, equipment qualification gives the following benefits to all analysts:

- New equipment should be made fit for their intended use. This is achieved fully when all of the required characteristics of the measuring system are done. This proves that the selected equipment meets these requirements before using these for analysis.
- Incorrect test may be considered as 'the equipment's performance has been reduced and proved to be suitable for their intended purpose.' It is used for sample analysis during their working life.
- A template for troubleshooting any problem that may occur while the conductivity measuring system is in service.

The documentation of equipment qualification can be used as a checklist for determining and rectifying the source of any measuring problems. Equipment qualification plays a fundamental role in the quality system of a laboratory. It helps the development and validation of suitable test methods. It also helps identifying the quality control and quality assurance measures that will be required to ensure the test measurements, fit for the purpose[2].

The ICH Q7(a) guideline demonstrates[3] that the facilities, systems, equipment and utilities are properly qualified and maintained to assure data and product integrity. Additional guidance is given by the PIC/S: "*While it is not possible to conduct the details of neither an Installation Qualification for established equipment nor the detailed approach for an Operational Qualification, nevertheless there should be data available to support and verify the operating parameters and limits for the critical variables of the operating equipment. Additionally, the procedures such as calibration, cleaning, preventative maintenance, operating procedures and operator training for the use of the equipment should be documented and in use kept as standard operating procedures (SOPs).*"

This has been mentioned earlier that equipment qualification is critical in the pharmaceutical industry. The equipment does not only include the manufacturing equipment but testing and sampling equipment also to name a few. Even the slightest error or misuse can pose a costly risk and time delay for the pharmaceutical product owner and their manufacturer. The equipment qualification is a series of inspections, tests, and assessments to ensure that a given piece of equipment is compliant and ensures reliable performance. Equipment validation is required to prove that a given piece of equipment works, consistently, what it is supposed to do. As an important component of quality assurance, equipment qualification is important to consistently produce the high-quality products.

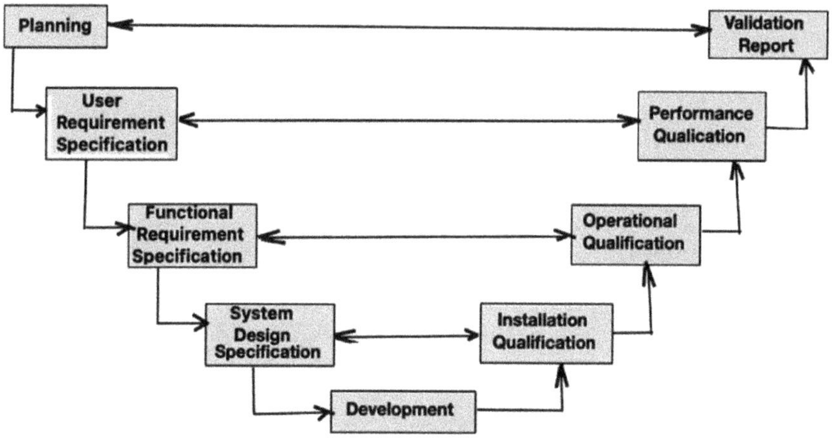

Fig.4.1 Relationship among different qualification documents with one another.

Qualification of utilities and equipment generally include the following activities[4]:

- Based on their specific uses, the selection of utilities, materials used for construction of equipment, operating principles and performance characteristics is done.
- In compliance with the specifications of design, verification of utility systems and equipment are built and installed, such as built as designed with proper materials, capacity, and functions, and properly connected and calibrated.
- Verifying that utility systems and equipment can operate in accordance with the process requirements in all anticipated operating ranges. This should include challenging the equipment or system functions while under load comparable to that expected during routine production. It should include the performance of interventions, stoppage, and start-up as is expected during routine production. During routine production, operating ranges should be shown capable of being held as long as would be necessary.

The prerequisites for the quality of drug product has been shown in Fig.4.2 below.

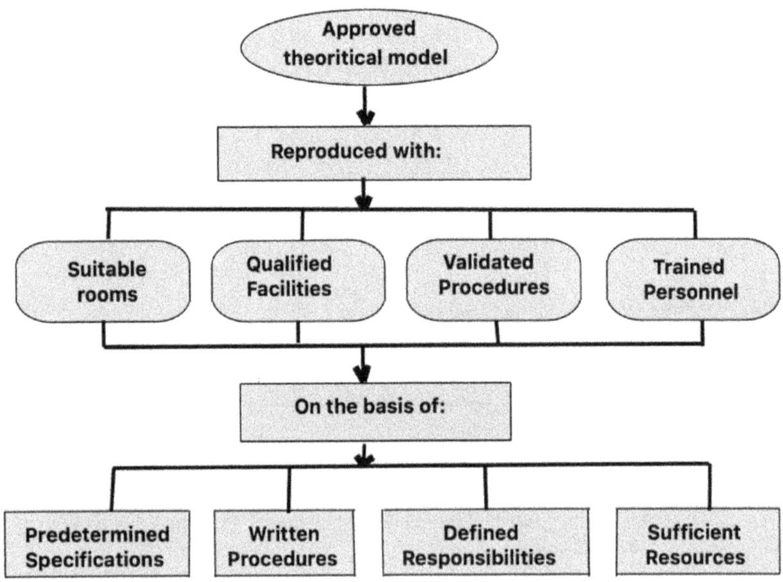

Fig.4.2 Prerequisites for quality of drug product.

Therefore, qualification of instrument is a normal process in pharmaceutical industries.

IQ (Installation Qualification)

The Qualification protocol is actually *intended to be used with new or relocated instruments. It is written to help the end-user in validation of predetermined specifications*. The use of this document does not replace the necessity for the pre-user's manual. Information within the user's manual is required to complete this IQ/OQ protocol. If the manual has been misplaced, copies can be obtained from the manufacturer or downloaded from their website. Qualification of instruments is a normal process of documenting. This is an instrument fit for its pre-planned use and that it is kept maintained and calibrated.

The Installation Qualification (IQ) protocols described below are prepared for initial qualification and/or for requalification. Installation qualification tests should be performed[5-7],

1) when the system is installed,
2) when the system is moved to a new location,
3) prior to running OQ tests.

This describes the procedure how to receive, unpack, and install a pre-instrument. The purchased instrument undergoes the qualification or is located as:

Name of the Company:...

Department:...

Address:...

....

....

City:...
State:... ....

Country:.. ....

Zip code/Postal Code:..

Phone Number:...

- **Equipment identification**

Fill out this section after unpacking the AquaLab instrument and corresponding accessories. Manufacturer:..

Model Number:................................ Serial Number:.....................

Name:...
Date:...

Signature:...

Initials:..

- **Receiving and Unpacking**

Verify that the external packaging was not damaged during shipment in a way that the internal package content might be damaged.

External package condition.. ....

Satisfactory ☐ Not Satisfactory ☐

Remarks: ☐ N/A

....

....

....

Compare shipment list with supplied items to ensure completeness of order.

Water Activity Instrument	☐ Complete	Not ☐ Complete	☐ N/A
Quick Start Guide	☐ Complete	Not ☐ Complete	☐ N/A
User's Manual	☐ Complete	Not ☐ Complete	☐ N/A
Certificate of Calibration	☐ Complete	Not ☐ Complete	☐ N/A
Trial Verification Standards	☐ Complete	Not ☐ Complete	☐ N/A
SDS Documents	☐ Complete	Not ☐ Complete	☐ N/A
Power Cable	☐ Complete	Not ☐ Complete	☐ N/A
USB/Serial Cable	☐ Complete	Not ☐ Complete	☐ N/A
Filters (Volatiles only)	☐ Complete	Not ☐ Complete	☐ N/A
Cleaning Kit	☐ Complete	Not ☐ Complete	☐ N/A
LDPE Sample Cups and Lids	☐ Complete	Not ☐ Complete	☐ N/A

Remarks: ☐ N/A

....

....

....

All parts were received as ordered and the delivery is complete ☐ Yes

No ☐

Any parts that are missing at the time of the supply verification and reported as Not Complete must be delivered to complete the shipment. Any parts marked as Not Complete must be indicated and reviewed with the customer. Minor parts or accessories that do not impact the installation or qualification procedure or the functionality of the instrument can be accepted, if agreed upon by the customer, to complete the remainder of the IQ/OQ process. Completed IQ/OQ should be marked after the item has been received.

Item:.......................... Date .... Initial......................

☐ Accepted ☐ Completed

☐ Accepted ☐ Completed

☐ Accepted ☐ Completed

☐ Accepted ☐ Completed

☐ Accepted ☐ Completed

☐ Accepted ☐ Completed

Remarks: ☐ N/A

Qualified by:..

Date:......................................
Initials:...

- **Visual Inspection**

After unpacking, verify whether there is no physical damage to the instrument, cables, and accessories. Note all observed damage in the remarks section. Minor defects that do not affect the functionality can be marked as accepted, if approved by the customer.

Name of the Instrument ☐ Satisfactory ☐ Not Satisfactory ☐ Accepted

Documentation ☐ Satisfactory ☐ Not Satisfactory ☐ Accepted

Other ☐ Satisfactory ☐ Not Satisfactory ☐ Accepted

Remarks: ☐ N/A

....

....

Qualified by: ....

Date: ....Initials:.......................

Severe damage to any of the parts delivered, interrupts the installation qualification until the part is replaced. Completion of the installation qualification after replacement should be documented below.

Instrument ☐ Satisfactory ☐ Not Satisfactory ☐ N/A
Documentation ☐ Satisfactory ☐ Not Satisfactory ☐ N/A

Other ☐ Satisfactory ☐ Not Satisfactory ☐ N/A

Remarks: ☐ N/A

Qualified by: ....

Date:...
Initials:...

- **Environmental Conditions**

Installation of any instrument includes placing the instrument on a level surface in a location where the temperature remains fairly stable[8-10]. This location should be well away from air conditioner and heater vents, open windows, outside doors, or other items that may cause rapid temperature fluctuation.

Location	☐ Satisfactory	☐ Not Satisfactory
Adequate Power	☐ Satisfactory	☐ Not Satisfactory
Stable Surface	☐ Satisfactory	☐ Not Satisfactory
Temperature	☐ Satisfactory	☐ Not Satisfactory

Remarks: ☐ N/A

....

....

....

Qualified by:..

Date..Initial....................

Remarks: ☐ N/A

....

....

....

....

Qualified by:..

Date............................

Initial...

- **Completeness of Installation Qualification (IQ)**

Installation Qualification is completed and documented according to manufacturer's guidelines.

☐ Initial Qualification ☐ Requalification

Authorized Representative of the Devices

Name: ....

Function: ....

Company:...

Date: .... Signature: ....

Initials: ....

Installation Qualification is reviewed by the representative of the system owner.

Reviewed and approved by:...

Name:..

Function: ....

Company: ....

Date: ....

Signature:....................................

Initials: ....

Remarks: ☐ N/A

....
....
....
....
....
....

OQ (Operational Qualification)

Operational qualification (OQ) is *the process of testing to ensure that the individual and combined systems function to meet the agreed performance criteria and to check how the result of testing is recorded.* The purpose is to ensure that all the dynamic attributes comply with the original design. Each of the instrument's function is checked to ensure that they conform to the manufacturer's specifications. This includes the use of certified, traceable electrical simulators and standards to verify that the equipment is processing input signals correctly.

The purpose of the operational qualification protocol is to define the requirements and acceptance criteria for the operation of the instruments spreadsheet. The spreadsheet will reside on the manufacturer/ supplier. After successful completion of the supply, the OQ should provide the necessary documented evidence[11] to assure that the validation spreadsheet has been properly operated in accordance with the manufacturer's procedures and complies with all cGMP requirements.

The OQ protocol verifies the operation of the validation spreadsheet. Functional requirements for the validation spreadsheet are detailed in the functional requirements specification for the validation spreadsheet (FRS-001). Design requirements for the validation spreadsheet are detailed in the software design specification for the validation spreadsheet (SDS-001).

The validation is performed by the manufacturer/ supplier on a properly functioning systems workstation.

OQ Acceptance criteria

OQ Tests		**Acceptance criteria to be performed**	
		☐ Yes	☐ No
		☐ Yes	☐ No
		☐ Yes	☐ No
		☐ Yes	☐ No
		☐ Yes	☐ No
		☐ Yes	☐ No
Test result			
Acceptance criteria / criteria met? (see deviation report no.:		☐ Yes	☐ No
	Date	Name	Signature
Test conducted			
Test conducted			

Performance qualification (PQ), also called process qualification, *is the process of testing to ensure that the individual and combined systems function to meet agreed performance criteria on a consistent basis and to check how the result of testing is recorded.* The purpose is to ensure that the criteria specified can be achieved on a reliable basis over a period of time. The performance of the equipment for its routine analytical use is checked to ensure that this complies with its specification. The temperature sensor readings are compared with a certified reference thermometer. After calibration, the conductivity sensor readings are compared using certified, traceable control standards.

Control standards of similar values to the intended test samples must be used for PQ. Performance qualification (PQ) is the process of demonstrating that an instrument consistently performs according to a specification appropriate to its routine use. It is important here that the word should be consistently. The test frequency is much higher than for OQ. Another difference is that PQ should always be performed under conditions that are similar to routine sample analysis.

PQ should be performed on a daily (or at least a weekly) basis, or whenever the instrument is used. The test frequency depends not only on the stability of the equipment/ instrument but also on everything in the system that may contribute to the analysis results. PQ specification should contain the following three information.

1. Definition of the performance criteria and test procedures.
2. Selection of the critical parameters.
3. Definition of the test intervals.

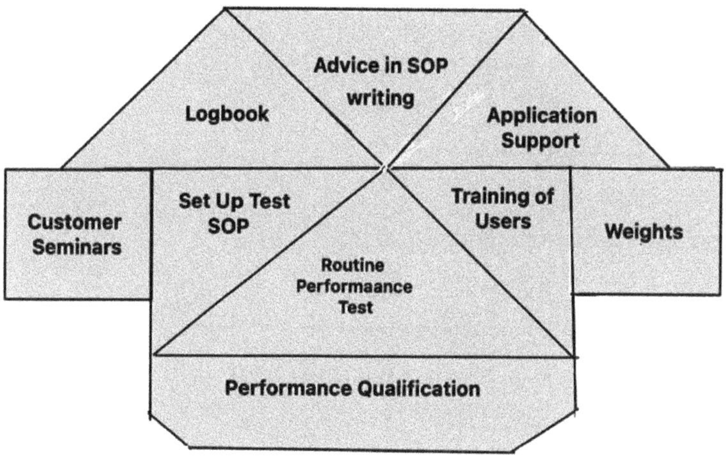

Fig.4.3 Performance qualification.

PQ (Performance Qualification) FOR EQUIPMENT

In manufacturing facilities, validation test procedures are used to validate the equipment and processes that may influence the quality of product. The tests for validation are used according to the approved and written qualification procedures. All necessary activities and responsibilities for the qualification and validation are controlled and specified in the Validation Master Plan. Every step of the described validation program for facilities[12-14], equipment, processes, process controls, and cleaning is according to the current European Community Guidelines for GMP and FDA, and the cGMP guideline for finished pharmaceutical products.

Qualification: *Action of proving and documenting that the equipment or ancillary systems are properly installed, work correctly, and actually lead to the expected results.* Qualification is part of a validation, but the individual qualification steps alone do not constitute the process validation.

1) Design Qualification (DQ)
2) Installation Qualification (IQ)
3) Operational Qualification (OQ)

4) Performance Qualification (PQ)
5) Maintenance Qualification (MQ)

The vendors or the users have the ultimate responsibility for the accuracy of the analysis results and also for equipment qualification. DQ should always be done by the user. While IQ for a small and low cost instrument is usually done by the product manufacturer (user). IQ for large, complex and high cost instruments should be done by the vendor. OQ can be done by either the product manufacturer (user) or the vendor. PQ should always be done by the user because it is application specific, and the vendor may not be familiar with these. As PQ should be done on a daily basis, this practically limits the task to the user[15].

Importance of validation

- Increased throughput
- Reduction in rejections and reworking
- Reduction in utility costs
- Avoidance of capital expenditures
- Fewer complaints about process-related failures
- Reduced testing in-process and in finished goods
- More rapid and reliable start-up of new equipment
- Easier scale-up from development work
- Easier maintenance of equipment
- Improved employee awareness of processes
- More rapid automation

- *Design Qualification (DQ):* Design qualification (DQ) defines the functional and operational specifications of the instrument and details for the conscious decisions in the selection of the supplier. The steps should be considered for inclusion in a design qualification are description of the analysis problem, description of the intended use of the equipment, description of the intended environment, preliminary selection of the functional and performance specifications, preliminary selection of the supplier, final selection of the equipment, final selection of the supplier, development and documentation of final functional and operational specifications.

- *Installation Qualification (IQ):* Installation qualification establishes that the instrument is received as designed and specified. It is properly installed in the selected environment, and this environment is suitable for the operation and use of the instrument. The qualification involves the coordinated efforts of the vendor, the operating department. The project team provides the input into the purchase, installation, operation and maintenance of the equipment.

- *Operational Qualification (OQ):* Operational qualification (OQ) is the process of demonstrating that an instrument will function according to its operational specification in the selected environment. The proper operation of equipment is verified by performing the test functions specified in the protocol. A conclusion is always drawn regarding the operation of equipment after the test functions are checked and all data have been analysed. A sample contents of an equipment operation qualification are:

1. Application S.O.P's,
2. Utilization List,
3. Process Description,
4. Test Instrument Utilized To Conduct Test,
5. Test Instrument Calibration,
6. Critical Parameters,
7. Test Function (List),
8. Test Function Summaries.

- *Performance Qualification (PQ):* Performance Qualification (PQ) is the process of demonstrating that an instrument consistently performs according to a specification appropriate for its routine use. PQ should always be performed under conditions that are similar to routine sample analysis. PQ should be performed on a daily basis or whenever the equipment is being used[16-18]. In practice, PQ can mean system suitability testing, where critical key system performance characteristics are measured and compared with documented.
- *Maintenance Qualification (MQ):* The MQ describes and documents whether any maintenance required for the equipment. This includes routine servicing and any repairs necessary. Details of whether any maintenance contracts is required or done should also be documented in this section, together with a list of authorized service engineers. Moreover, the MQ includes the routine cleaning of the equipment and also its ultimate disposal.

AUTOCLAVE

Sterilization can be defined as *a process that effectively kills or eliminates transmissible agents (such as fungi, bacteria, viruses) from surface, equipment, foods, medications or biological culture medium.* A sterility assurance level (SAL) of 10-6 means that there is less than or equal to one chance in a million of that particular item is contaminated or unsterile following sterilization process. These events raised awareness across the regulatory agencies, but soon after among companies that something was seriously amissing the production of sterile product. But the United Kingdom speaks of something new validation. Validation is the attaining and documentation of sufficient activities that give reasonable assurance, given the state of science, which is the process under consideration, does, and/or will do, what it purport to do. This definition has changed minimally over the year and prevailing USFDA definition in use today is quite similar. Validation is establishing documented evidence which provided a high degree of assurance that a specific process will consistently produce a product meeting its pre-determined specification and quality characteristics.

Sterilization methods

- **Dry heat sterilization**

  Heat is most reliable and rapid method of sterilization. The killing of dry heat is due to protein denaturation, oxidative damage and toxic effect of elevated level of electrolytes. Microorganism is more resistant to dry heat as compared to moist heat. So, this process requires higher temperature and longer exposure time. This method of sterilization can be applied only to thermo stable products but it can be used for moisture-sensitive materials for which dry heat (350°-360°C) sterilization, such as Hot air oven.

- **Moist heat sterilization**

  Sterilization by moist heat means killing of microorganism with hot water or steam. The lethal effect of moist heat is due to denaturation and coagulation of protein. Moist heat sterilization involves the use of steam in the range of 121-123°C, such as Autoclave

- **Chemical sterilization**

  The chemically reactive gases such as formaldehyde (HCHO) and ethylene oxide $(CH_2)_2O$ possess biocidal activity. Ethylene oxide is colourless, odourless, and flammable gas.

- **Radiation sterilization**

  Many types of radiation are used for sterilization like electromagnetic radiation (e.g. gamma rays and UV light) particulate radiation (e.g. accelerated electrons).

- **Filtration (Cold sterilization)**

  Filtration process does not destroy but removes the microorganisms. It is used for both the clarification and sterilization of liquids and gases as it is capable of preventing the passage of both viable and non-viable particles.

Responsibility of the department

Production

Ensures implementation of BPR and protocol, sample withdrawal and sending to QC for testing as per specification. Ensures all the equipment used during process validation was documented in respective equipment usage log.

Validation

Prepare the protocol and review

Quality Assurance

Review and approval of protocol report and raw data generated were in accordance with protocol and expected result achieved.

Quality control

Testing of sample

Basic Qualification approach

Users Requirement Specification (URS) User or customer of equipment has certain expectations about the equipment which is wanted to be used. These expectations are generally in the form of his requirements. It is called as user requirement specifications.

Design Qualification (DQ)

Design qualification may verify that design of equipment, system/facility is according to requirement of user and current good manufacturing practices.

Installation Qualification (IQ)

Installation qualification is conducted to prove that equipment/system has been installed as per user and manufacturer recommendation and verifying that all required utilities have provided safe operation of equipment/system.

- Utilities specification
- Drawing specification(electrical, mechanical)
- Construction material in product contact
- Operating and maintenance manual

Operational Qualification (OQ)

The operational qualification process is intended to demonstrate that the components are operating properly and ready for performance or load testing. Operational qualification shall be done “without load.

Performance qualification (PQ)

Performance qualification is documented evidence to prove that equipment/system is performing under specified condition. It involve in taking trial under "loaded condition.

Dry heat sterilization

Qualification of equipment Steam Sterilizer (Autoclave)

Steam sterilization can make the articles sterile using saturated steam and is equipped specifically for application in the pharmaceutical field. Sterilizer is an effective equipment to ensure the sterilization of the garment, cleaning aids filter, utensil, vial filling m/c parts, rubber, etc. The set of main activities for treating the processed materials in order to sterilize them is termed as sterilization process/cycle.

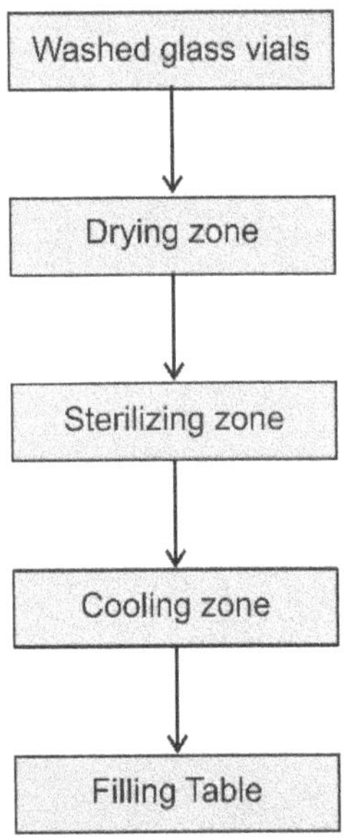

Fig.4.4 Process for flow of sterilization tunnel.

Performance of autoclave

It involve in taking trial under *loaded condition*. The calibration of instruments, apparatus carried out at suitable intervals in accordance with an established written program containing specific directions, schedules, limits for accuracy and precision. Operating range, approval standard operating procedure is used or verification. Performance qualification is integrate, procedure, personal, system and material verify pharmaceutical grade utility, and environment, equipment, and system produce required output.

The following main activities can be distinguished in the sterilization process

- Autoclave preparation
- Load sterilization
- Load cooling
- Final phase

Different tests are follows

Vacuum leak test

Objective

To prepare master chart of sterilization cycle for reference during normal production cycle and demonstrate that autoclave is leak proof and there no leakage from the chamber.

Procedure

- Ensure that the chamber temperature is stable at ambient and compressed air is on at pressure of 6 bar
- Ensure gasket lubrication is proper and switch provided on panel board
- Start the vacuum leak rate test cycle
- Observe the pressure in the pressure gauge of steam sterilizer
- Cycle allow the pressure to drop up to 450-470 mmHg
- Machine will close all the valves connected to the chamber and stop the vacuum pump and note the time and pressure (P_1)
- Wait for stabilization period of 5 minute (±10 second) and note down the pressure again (P_2)
- Wait for another 10 minute (± 10 second) and note down the pressure third time (P_3)
- Return to atmospheric pressure and continue to run for next cycle of Bowie Dick test.

Acceptance criteria

The vacuum leak test should not more than 1.0 mmHg

Air removal test (Bowie Dick test)

Objective

If commercially available Bowie-Dick test pack is used, make sure that all tests are conducted with test pack of the same manufacturer's specification. If you are at this point and have not identified the source of the problem, inform and request assistance in resolving the problem

- by contacting the sterilizer manufacturer, the maintenance or service provider, the Load the tray in the autoclave chamber
- Place the bowie dick test pack on the bottom shelf of the sterilizer just above drain point (100mm over the drain)
- Air removal study shall be performed in empty chamber by placing the Bowie Dick test kit. This shall be reusable or disposable Bowie Dick test kit manufactured by standard manufacture. it consist of standard paper pack and indicator sheet
- Start the cycle by pressing enter key
- After the cycle is over open the door from control area side and take the sterilized test pack from the autoclave and check the indicator paper/strip for uniform colour change
- As Bowie Dick test kit is designed to simulate the garment pack, it used to test the efficiency of the air removal from the steam sterilizer
- Three cycle of air removal study shall be performed (initially) by using fresh indicator kit pack and only one cycle during re-validation

  This test shall be performed by using Bowie Dick test cycle. To fulfil the maximum exposure requirement, the sterilization cycle shall have 10 minutes at 121°C test pack manufacturer and facility engineering department. Procedure to 123°C sterilization period.

Acceptance criteria

The indicator paper/sheet should be uniformly changed in colour (brown) over the entire pattern of indicator sheet when compared with control.

Heat distribution study (empty chamber)

Objective

The chamber provides a uniform sterilizing environment and verifies the temperature stability.

Procedure

- Connect the thermocouple with SIM to the kaye validator and distribute these thermocouple throughout chamber
- Pass the probes into the chamber through validator port by using Kaye 'feed thru' and seal the port properly to avoid any steam leakage
- Place the external temperature sensor, one each, geometrically and equally distributed in the sterilizer chamber
- Fix 10 pre-calibrated thermocouple (type T) with in chamber in different location for mapping the distribution temperature with in empty chamber
- As in-built control temperature sensor is fixed, locate the external temperature sensor at the pre- determined location

- Theoretically the drain point is considered to the coldest point because steam condensate and air is removed through this point
- It shall ensure that temperature probes/sensor do not touch any metal surface or walls of chamber. In case sensor touches the metal surface, it may show steam sterilizer body part temperature, and not the chamber temperature. Set the data logger.
- Start the data logger and steam sterilizer simultaneously. Stop the data logger when the entire sterilization cycle of the sterilizer is over.
- Check both the profile against the acceptance criteria for compliance.
- Change the location of the remaining external temperature sensor to different location to cover the maximum area.
- Attach the temperature profiles of data logger and in-built temperature recorder of all run in report.

Acceptance criteria

Temperature distribution within the chamber must be between 121°C to 123°C at all location during the sterilization period (dwell time). There should not be any slowest heating point (cold spot) in the autoclave chamber and equilibrium time should not be more than 30 second.

Heat distribution study (loaded chamber)

Objective

It identifies the cold spot in the loaded steam sterilizer Procedure

- Connect the thermocouple with SIM to the kaye validator and distribute these thermocouple throughout chamber
- Pass the probes into the chamber through validator port by using Kaye 'feed thru' and seal the port properly to avoid any steam leakage
- Fix minimum 10 pre-calibrated thermocouple (type T) with in chamber in different location for mapping the distribution temperature with in loaded chamber
- Load the article as per loading pattern in the autoclave chamber
- Loaded chamber heat distribution study shall be performed separately for all loading patterns. One cycle shall be performed for each loading type for loaded chamber heat distribution study
- Place the external temperature sensor in the chamber as far as possible, near to the location as in the empty chamber heat distribution study trials at the outside of article
- It shall be ensure that temperature probes/sensor do not touch the object surface or walls of chamber. The probes shall remain suspended in the chamber

- One external temperature sensor shall be placed at identified cold point as per empty chamber heat distribution
- One external temperature sensor shall be placed near inbuilt drain point temperature sensor and set the data logger
- Start the data logger and steam sterilizer simultaneously. Perform the cycle as per set parameter and stop the data logger when the entire sterilization cycle of the sterilizer is over then check both the profile against the acceptance criteria for compliance

Acceptance criteria

Temperature distribution within the chamber must be between 121°C to 123°C at all location during the sterilization period (dwell time) There should not be any slowest heating point (cold spot) in the autoclave chamber and equilibrium time should not be more than 30 second.

Heat penetration study

Objective

Biological indicator and thermo chemical indicator along with external temperature sensor shall be placed at drain point in all three cycle (at the time of initial validation or when any new load pattern introduces)

- Place one control probe on the identified cold spot of heat distribution study
- Perform the sterilization by operating the program specified for each load type as per standard operating procedure
- Start the data logger and steam sterilizer simultaneously
- After the sterilization cycle is completed, stop data logger and open the sterilizer
- Take out challenge biological indicator and thermo chemical indicator from load and send to microbiological lab for testing
- Challenge biological indicator shall aseptically inoculate into sterile soyabean casein digest media (SCDM) and incubated at 55 - 60°C and liquid load at 35 – 39°C for 7 days
- Check the thermo chemical indicator for the compliance as per manufacturer recommendation for colour change (i.e. Brown)
- Take out temperature chart/data logger and inbuilt temperature recorder, report of biological indicator. Check against acceptance criteria for compliance
- Determine the F_0 value and compare against acceptance criteria. Take out external temperature sensor from the chamber and perform vacuum leak rate test.

Acceptance criteria

Temperature distribution within the chamber must be between 121°C to 123°C at all location during the sterilization period (dwell time). Sterilization temperature should be maintained for NLT 15 minute for minimum 10 thermo couple during hold time. Biological indicator (*Geobacillus stearothermophillus*) should show complete sterilization (i.e. no growth after incubation).

Depyrogenation tunnel (Sterilization tunnel)

Depyrogenation can be defined *as the elimination of all pyrogenic substances, including bacterial endotoxin and is generally achieved by removal or inactivation.* The sterilization tunnels have been designed to continuously sterilize dehydrogenated glass vial containers in a class 100 and environment. The tunnel is comprised of the In feed chamber, Sterilizing chamber and Cooling chamber. In feed chamber (where the vials enter) creates thermal barrier between the vial washing room and the sterilizing chamber to protect the vials from contamination and to pre heat the vials. The vial is heated up to 85-90°C. Sterilizing chamber is responsible for sterilization and depyrogenation. The sterilizing chamber is fully insulated and can be heated up to temperature 350-390°C for (3-4 min). Heaters generate heat, the sterilizing time of the vials depends upon the temperature and air velocity. If the temperature is high and air velocity is available as required then less time will be required for sterilization. After passing through the conveyor, the air taken up by fan with continuous speed adjustment to required f_H value.

The cooling chamber, depending upon the tunnel size, comprises of one or two cooling coils, which assist in the cooling of the vials to ambient temperature. Regular chilled water may be used, vials stay in the cooling chamber for 15-20 minutes.

Different tests are performed as follows

Air velocity

Procedure

- This test shall be performed by trained person and training record should be attached in report.

  Performed at least 30 minute.

- Measure the velocity above the conveyor for the different zone of tunnel sterilizer and measure the air velocity 6 inches below filter.
- Take the velocity of air at five locations (on centre and four corners) of each zones of sterilizer tunnel. Calculate average velocity for each filter
- If velocity is not within the limit, inform the manufacturer of the sterilizing tunnel for corrective action. Acceptance criteria

Air velocity should be maintained within 90 fpm ± 20% of mean unit velocity for even distribution of temperature.

HEPA filter integrity test

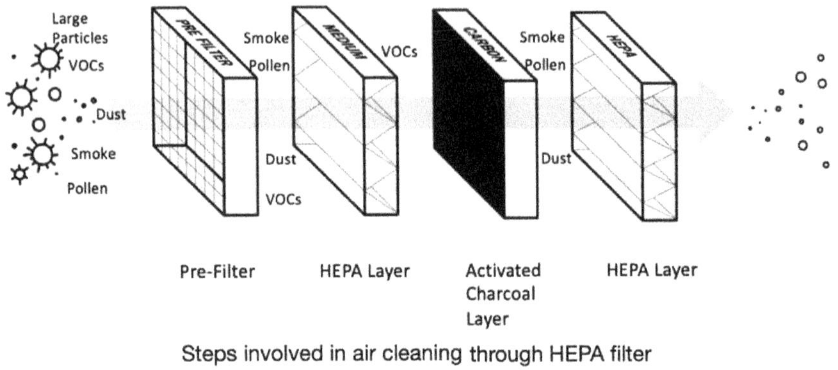

Fig.4.5 Steps involved in HEPA filter.

Objective

To verify the integrity of HEPA filter installed in the sterilization and depyrogenation tunnel. HEPA filter installation has been done properly and qualifies the filter integrity test.

Equipment

Aerosol photometer Procedure

- Place the aerosol generator to introduce an aerosol challenge upstream of the HEPA filter in zone wise manner in concentration of 80- 120mg/cubic m of air by opening appropriate number of nozzles
- Measure upstream concentration of aerosol by using zone wise upstream (in feed zone, hot zone 1, hot zone 2 and cooling zone)
- Adjust the photometer gain/span control for full scale deflection on 100% range
- Scan the downstream side of the HEPA filter, its perimeter, the seal between the filter frame and grid structure including its joints using overlapping strokes with the photometer probes
- The photometer probes should move at transverse rate not more than 10ft/minute with sample flow rate of 1cft/min ±10%
- If any leak is more than the specified limit, the above test should be repeated after taking the recommended corrective action

Acceptance criteria

Photometer reading downstream of the HEPA filtration unit caused by the leakage should be less than 0.01% of the upstream challenge concentration of the aerosol 100%.

Air flow visualization study

Objective

To determine the air flow pattern of HEPA filter installed in sterilization and depyrogenation area.

Procedure

- Take the glass rod with cotton or sponge tied to it
- Take a smoke pencil/titanium tetrachloride swab and bring it near to infeed of tunnel sterilizer.
- Check the air flow direction at the downstream of the filter face
- Observe and record the same with video camera

Acceptance criteria

- The direction of flow should be from in- feed area to vial washing zone
- Away from all the opening i.e. from the sterilization tunnel to washing area from sterilization zone to in feed/drying zone from sterilization zone to cooling zone
- Vial filling room to the cooling chamber of sterilization tunnel

Non-viable borne particulate count

Objective

To establish that at different location within the tunnel, count size of particle per cubic meter is within the limit.

Procedure

- The particle count test should be performed by qualified or trained person
- Start blower of the sterilizing tunnel
- Calculate the number of location by the following formula
- Number of sampling location $N_L = \sqrt{A}$
- Whereas; the minimum number of sampling locations
- Switch on particle counter and place the iso-kinetic suction probes at specified location under the filter of conveyor belt of tunnel and observe the reading, record in reports
- Take the particle counts for all zones of sterilizing tunnel Acceptance criteria

- The particle counts taken under the HEPA filter in the different zones of sterilizing tunnel should meet the requirement of ISO 5/class A.
- Maximum permitted no. of Grade/class particle/cubic m 0.5μm 5μm

Heat distribution study (empty tunnel)

Objective

The sterilizing and depyrogenation tunnel when operated with empty chamber is capable of producing the temperature profile as per temperature set point set in PLC of the equipment. The temperature distribution is uniform throughout the sterilization period.

Procedure

- Place 10 temperature indicating probes across the width of the conveyor of an empty tunnel, in such a way that probes junction do not touch solid surfaces as to determine the air temperature profile
- Use zig to hold the probes in place as the probes travels through the tunnel
- Attach the connecting cable of probes to data logger, which can scan the date, time and temperature of probes at every 10 seconds
- Set the temperature/cycle condition as per set parameter
- Record the set parameter for the sterilization cycle operated during test
- Operate the tunnel as per the standard operating procedure and start the data logger to record the actual temperature within the sterilization zone of tunnel by passing the zig plate holding the external temperature sensor through the sterilization zone
- When the probes cross the sterilization zone stop the conveyor belt of sterilizing tunnel, switch off the data logger and pull out the probes
- When the validation is completed, collect the batch report of sterilizer
- Record the observation from the data logger in to the computer and take printout for analysis of the data collection. Also record temperature observation at different location
- Report the time for each probes for which the vial are exposed to temperature of 300 ^{O}C or above

Acceptance criteria

The temperature at each temperature probes should be $\geq$ 300°C during the cycle.

Heat distribution study (loaded chamber)

Objective

The sterilizing and depyrogenation tunnel when operated with empty chamber is capable of producing the temperature profile as per temperature set point set in PLC of the equipment. The temperature distribution is uniform throughout the sterilization period.

Procedure

- Place 10 temperature indicating probes across the width of the conveyor of tunnel, in such way that probes junction do not touch solid surfaces but remain in hanging condition inside the vials
- Use zig plate to hold vial with the probes (sensor) in place as it help smooth travel through the tunnel
- Attach the connecting cable of probes (sensor) to data logger, which can scan the date, time and temperature of probes at every 10 seconds
- Set the temperature/cycle condition as per set parameter
- Record the set parameter for the sterilization cycle operated during test
- Operate the tunnel as per the standard operating procedure and start the data logger to record the actual temperature within the sterilization zone of tunnel through probes (sensor). Allow the zig plate having vials containing the external temperature probes (sensor) to travel along with other washed vials through the sterilization zone. Operate vial washing machine continuously to fill the tunnel chamber back to back
- When the vials having probes cross the sterilization zone stop the conveyor belt of sterilizing tunnel, switch off the data logger and pull out the probes along with zig
- Take one validation run for loaded chamber heat distribution studies for each type of load.

Acceptance criteria

The temperature at each temperature probes should be ≥ 300°C during the cycle.

Heat penetration studies

Objective

To ensure that heat is sufficiently penetrating into the inner most portion of the vial subjected for sterilization and dehydrogenation to achieve desired temperature during the sterilization and depyrogenation cycle. The recovery of endotoxin concentration after exposing to depyrogenation tunnel should show more than 3 log reduction.

Procedure

- Get the 9 spiked vial with approx. 10,000 EU/vial of bacterial endotoxin from microbiology
- Place minimum 10 number of probes, one probe each inside the endotoxin spiked 8 vials and 3 without spiked vials at the junction of the bottom of the container and side wall. The containers inner surface should be in contact with the probe because for sterilization and depyrogenation of the inner walls of the container as well as inner space. Tie the probes firmly with the vial and place these vial inside the washed vial load

- Use zig to hold the spiked vials containing probes in place, as vial travel through the tunnel
- Set the temperature/cycle condition as per set parameter
- Record the set parameter for the sterilization cycle operated during test
- Operate the tunnel and pass the endotoxin spiked vials along with the washed vials as per standard operating procedure and start the data logger to record the actual temperature inside within the sterilization zone
- When the vial attached with temperature indicating probes cross the sterilization zone, stop the conveyor belt of sterilizing tunnel, switch off the data logger and pull out the probes. Wrap the exposed endotoxin indicator vials with aluminium foil and label properly
- Send the exposed vials to microbiology lab for testing of residual endotoxin in the vials after sterilization as per standard procedure
- Record the result and take validation run for each set of vial normally used in routine production with complete load and re-validation one run on rotation for different type of vial size
- Record the temperature observation at different location.

Acceptance criteria

All temperature measured in the chamber is ≥ 300°C. The recovery of endotoxin concentration after in sterilization and dehydrogenation should at least 3 log reductions.

Rubber Stopper Washer

Rubber stopper are washed to make free from particulate contamination in this machine prior to sterilization. The cycle is controlled by microprocessor through different solenoid valves, washing is done in two vessels M1 and M2 which can be programmed separately. The process cycle can be run separately or at same time.

Different test are follows

Removal of soluble and insoluble matter

Objective

To ensure that the vial washing machine meets the acceptance criteria for washing efficiency when challenged with sodium chloride spiked vial.

Procedure

- Prepare 0.5% w/v slurry of sodium chloride and talc/lycopodium slurry solution by adding 5g of sodium chloride and talc/ lycopodium in 1000 ml of purified water.

- Transfer 5000 numbers i.e. 1 bag each rubber stopper in two stainless steel (SS) container
- Contaminate the rubber stopper of each container (i.e.5000) with the above 0.5% slurry.
- Allow to air dry the rubber stopper over-night.
- Transfer the rubber stopper of each stainless steel (SS) container (5000) in to washing bucket (vessel m1 and m2) of rubber stopper washing machine.
- Sample 10 rubber stoppers (contaminated, before washing) from each bucket in separate clean conical flask containing 100 ml of water for injection (WFI). This will be used for positive control.
- Run the rubber stopper washing cycle as per standard operating procedure keeping all the process parameter identical to routine washing cycle.
- After completion of washing cycle take out 3×10 washed rubber stopper each from both the washing bucket into separate clean conical flask containing 100 ml of water for injection (WFI) in each flask. These will be used as test sample after washing. Take out sample for soluble and insoluble matter
- Send all the sample to quality control lab/microbiology lab for soluble matter (sodium chloride) and insoluble particulate matter (by liquid particle counter) analysis
- Inspect the washed rubber stopper visually with magnifying glass for presence of any particulate matter

Acceptance criteria

All challenged vials shall show negative test for presence of chloride.

Endotoxin challenge test

Objective

It ensure that the rubber stopper washing machine meets acceptance criteria when challenged with endotoxin

Procedure

- Send 10 washed rubber stopper of different colour to microbiology lab for inoculation spiking of endotoxin one day prior to test
- Get 7 numbers of coloured rubber stopper spiked with known amount of endotoxin i.e. 1000 (I.U)/rubber stopper in properly closed Petri dish from microbiology lab, number them from 1 to 7 Charge 5000 rubber stopper and 7 spiked rubber stoppers in each process in each washing vessel in such way that both washing bucket the spiked rubber stopper are kept at different layer respectively

- Run the washer as per standard operating procedure with all the process parameter kept identical to keep in normal production run
- After the cycle is over take out the spiked rubber stopper and send them to microbiology lab for determination of residual endotoxin

Acceptance criteria

There should minimum of 3 log reduction of endotoxin content in all spiked vials.

Steam Sterilizer (Autoclave)

All the tests were carried out as per procedure and parameter were found meeting the acceptance criteria. Hence steam sterilizer (autoclave) is successfully validated.

Depyrogenation Tunnel

All the test was carried out as per procedure and parameter were found meeting the acceptance criteria. Hence sterilization tunnel is successfully validated.

Rubber Stopper Washer

All the test was carried out as per procedure and parameter were found meeting it's the acceptance criteria. Hence rubber stopper washer is successfully validated.

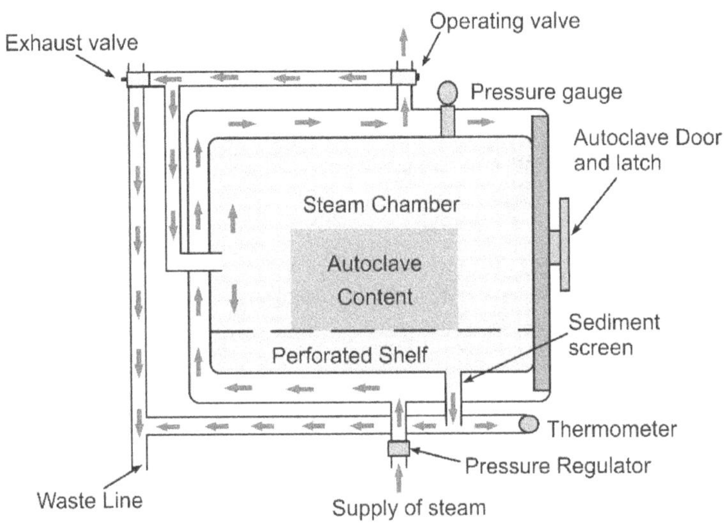

Fig.4.6 Flow of steam.

Horizontal autoclave

Fig.4.7 Horizontal autoclave.

MEMBRANE FILTER

The removal rating of a given membrane filter type refers to the size, or narrower dimension, of microorganisms and particles removed by the filter, rather than the actual size or shape (*i.e.,* morphology) of the filter pore structure. The industry- accepted rating for a sterilizing grade filter is 0.2 or 0.22 μm, depending on the manufacturer, which is validated as capable of removing $>10^7$ cfu/cm^2 *B. diminuta* under certain extreme processing conditions. Tighter filters such as 0.1 μm filters that demonstrate the same bacterial retention also may be rated as sterilizing grade.

In validating and performing sterile filtration, it is essential to identify the bioburden or endemic microorganism(s) in a given process, to use the grade of filter that quantitatively removes the microorganism(s), and to demonstrate quantitative removal by test before using the filter in production. This is the essence of filter validation.

Performance Qualification

Filters must be qualified by the user to demonstrate that their performance in processing. This will meet or exceed minimum process requirements.

Performance Qualification Requirements	
• Flow rates • Throughput • Pressure and temperature resistance • Hydrophilic or hydrophobic • Composition of membrane	• Compatibility • Membrane support layers, core, or cage • O-rings • Housings

The filter must be tested to verify that it provides the flow rates re- quired by the pharmaceutical process. The filter system must be sized to provide flow rates and volumes adequate to keep pace with filling machines or other production equipment requirements, with some reserve capacity for use in case of batch contaminant variability and premature plugging. The total liquid volume passed through the filters, its throughput, should be adequate to process a complete batch without interruption.

Small-scale sizing or *filterability* tests are used as the basis for extrapolating or scaling-up filtration systems. Sizing of final, sterilizing filters, and any upstream prefilters used to remove coarse contaminants and thereby extend the life of the final filters, is based upon anticipated flow rates and throughput in a given pharmaceutical liquid.

Sterilizing filters and filter housings, stainless steel, or disposable plastic, must be rugged enough to withstand the pressures and temperatures of normal process conditions, occasional runaway process conditions, and the temperature ranges of processing (minimum to maxi- mum) and steam or autoclave sterilization, including both temperature ranges and duration of the sterilization cycle(s).

Sterilizing-grade filters for aqueous pharmaceutical liquids are normally hydrophilic, or water- wettable, membrane filters. In the case of solvent or chemical liquids to be filter-sterilized, hydrophobic, or non-water-wetting, filters may be used. They can be wetted by a low- surface-tension liquid.

Compatibility

The filter system must be qualified to ensure that all product-contact surfaces of the filter and its constituent parts (mem- brane, support layers, core, cage, and end caps), O-rings, piping, hoses, seals, pumps, gaskets, and any other components of the sterilizing filtration system can withstand the hydraulic, thermal, and chemical challenges of the sterilization and production processes. None of these should extract into the filtered pharmaceutical product in any significant amount.

Generally, chemical compatibility is resolved by reference to compatibility tables generated by the manufacturers of elastomers or polymers used in O-rings, gaskets, and seals. Membrane compatibilities generally are well established for the commonly used membrane materials. Any specific questions can readily be resolved by testing during the qualification stage.

Sterilization of sterilizing filters

Sterilizing grade filters can be sterilized in a number of ways. Capsule filters can be gamma irradiated or autoclaved. Disk filter holders are autoclaved with the wetted filter in place. Cartridge filter installations frequently are sterilized by steam-in-place (SIP) operations.

Common steaming temperatures used in the United States are 121– 135°C, sustained for 30–60 min in the filter installation. Whatever time–temperature parameters are specified, it is critical that these parameters be validated by the pharmaceutical manufacturer under operating conditions.

Validation

There are four major elements of the filtration validation process:

- physical/chemical compatibility, usually established during the qualification phase before validation, is confirmed during the validation process
- binding and adsorption filter characteristics are measured in the qualification phase
- bacteria retention capability of the filter, which is established by challenging the filter with *B. diminuta*
- integrity of the process filtration installation, as verified by the filter integrity test.

Concerning integrity testing, the user must demonstrate that they know how to install, sterilize, and integrity test the filters. Filter integrity test values provided by the filter manufacturer are correlated to the bacterial challenge in the manufacturer's validation guide. Product integrity test values are correlated to the water or model solvent values.

Bacterial retention

The bacterial challenge test validates the ability of a filter to provide sterile effluent in a specific pharmaceutical liquid. It is also the ultimate compatibility test, because the bacterial challenge simultaneously tests the physical-chemical interaction of the liquid product and the filter, under process conditions. Any filter inadequacy caused by this interaction will be detected by the bacterial challenge. Validation of bacterial retention normally is performed by the filter manufacturer or an independent lab- oratory, using 47-mm diameter disks to minimize the volume of pharmaceutical product required. Larger surface area filters also can be used.

Bacterial challenge tests are usually performed with an industry standard concentration of 10^7 cfu of *B. diminuta* per sq. cm, using pharmaceutical product, whenever possible, for the most realistic validation. The high bacterial concentration used in the challenge test constitutes a worst-case scenario. The manufacturer qualifies the filter using a similar challenge.

B. diminuta is grown to produce monodispersed cells capable of penetrating a 0.45-µm filter, typically in accordance with ASTM Standard F838. Following that standard, the organism is cultured in saline lactose broth (SLB) and either used freshly cultured or concentrated into a frozen cell paste that is thawed immediately prior to use. A 0.4-µm rated membrane filter is used as a positive control; if the organisms pass through this control filter, it proves that they are alive, small, and nonaggregated, thus verifying that the challenge is a stringent test.

Validation parameters for bacterial challenge using pharmaceutical product.

Validation Parameters	
• Product contact time	• Temperature
• Differential pressure	• Bioburden
• Flow rates per unit area	• Integrity test correlation

Key considerations for using pharmaceutical product liquid to validate sterile filters are listed in the following chart.

Product contact time. The bacterial challenge using pharmaceutical product must be run for at least the same duration as a product batch will be run in processing. If the batch requires eight hours to filter, the challenge must be run for at least eight hours. It is good practice to run the challenge for a little longer to anticipate unusual pro- cessing circumstances.

Differential pressure and flow rates per unit area

Maximum process differential pressures and flow rates should be incorporated into the protocol. Often, it is virtually impossible to match both simultaneously. At the start of the challenge, when the filter is clean, extremely high flow rates per unit area are necessary to generate process-level differential pressures (pressure drop across the filter). But, as the test filter disks accumulate bacteria and pressure builds, the flow drops. One solution is to match flow rates at the start of the challenge and pressures near the end. Another solution is to decide whether pressure or flow is more relevant, and then develop a technically sound rationale to support the decision and use it in challenge testing.

Temperature

If the liquid temperature is outside the viable range of the challenge bacteria, it may be necessary to recirculate the product at process temperature, conditioning the filter first, and then challenge the filter at a temperature at which the bacteria survive.

Bioburden

Bioburden levels can influence process filtration efficacy. The probability of passage increases when the bioburden is high. The area-specific bioload (B_a) is the bioburden per unit area of filter (cfu/cm^2) or $B_a = BV/A$, where B is the bioburden in cfu/mL, V is the total volume to be filtered (mL) and A is the surface area of the filter in cm^2. It is therefore best to control the bioburden of the raw materials to avoid approaching or exceeding the validated limit.

Integrity test correlation

Filters used in the bacterial challenge must be integrity tested to form the correlation to retention. Because the user can- not use a destructive challenge test in processing, the filter manufacturer must supply a correlated, non-destructive integrity test that reliably assesses the integrity of a given filter installation. In performing the challenge test, three lots of filters typically are chosen, including a low-bubble-point lot, one with a bubble point specification that approximates the manufacturer's pro- duction limit. This is important because the end user is limited to using filters in their process that match or exceed the lowest bubble point validated in product.

Establishing the challenge protocol.

The above chart highlights the steps needed to develop a suitable challenge protocol. After the filter is qualified and selected, filter extractables and microbial retentivity are validated. Physical parameters such as sterilization and integrity test methods also are validated. Viability of the test microorganism, *B. diminuta*, in the pharmaceutical product is compared to a control over time. If there is less than one log difference in the counts, the organism is considered viable under those conditions. Results are documented. If a pharmaceutical product is toxic, has high potential for abuse, or is in limited supply, a non-bactericidal surrogate fluid with very similar properties may be developed. It is recommended that the user consult with local FDA inspectors before developing this approach.

If the microbe is viable

If *B. diminuta* is found to be viable in the pharmaceutical product, it is directly inoculated into the product as the challenge microorganism.

If the microbe is nonviable

If *B. diminuta* is found to be nonviable under process conditions, the test filter is preconditioned with pharmaceutical product liquid, and one of several options can be followed, prior to conducting the bacterial challenge.

Options are to:

- Modify the process by adjusting temperature or otherwise
- Modify the formulation, by adjusting pH, removing bactericidal components, or using a product surrogate liquid
- Use the bacteria for a brief enough time such that the challenge microorganism retains its viability during the test period
- Switch the test organism from *B. diminuta* to a process isolate, or native bioburden endemic to the actual pharmaceutical process.

It is recommended to consult first with FDA inspectors on this option. If the product is bactericidal, the volume and time required to thoroughly rinse the filter free of the product must be established, after the product has been recirculated, prior to adding the bacteria and challenge solution. This is documented in an inhibition test.

Bacterial challenge

The challenge procedure typically consists of integrity testing the filters, autoclaving the apparatus, integrity testing post-sterilization and recirculating product through the filters at process flow rates or pressures. Bacteria are added according to the results of the viability study. In non-bactericidal products, the microorganisms are added at intervals throughout the challenge. Before introducing the bacteria, analysis membranes are installed downstream of all test and control filters. Analysis filters must have a pore size of at least 0.45 µm or tighter. Membranes that are 0.45 µm will retain 10^4–10^6logs of *Brevundimonas*, which generally is accepted as adequate for a valid test.

RAPID MIXER GRANULATOR

1) Homogenous mixing of dry and wet powders, deagglomeration of wet mass and fast dispersion of binding agent.
2) Dust free, high free flowing dosing particles, high uniformity of granule size.
3) Frequency control for bottom driven Impeller Mixer with 3 or 4 blades with exclusive scrape side design and Chopper positioned to make granules.

Installation Qualification

An IQ establishes confidence that the equipment is properly installed. The installation must meet the manufacturer's specified guidelines, along with design changes at installation. Also the supporting electrical utilities must meet all electrical codes[19].

Equipment identification

Record the equipment identification number, with equipment manufacturer, purchase order, model number, and equipment number.

Required Documentation

The manufacturers operation and maintenance manual and SOPs that cover the set up.

- Utility requirements
- Power
- Water
- Compressed air, spraying, impeller movement, pneumatic discharge port.

Calibration Requirements

- Ammeter
- Voltmeter
- Water pressure gauge
- Air pressure gauge

Equipment major specifications

- Mixing bowl material of contact,
- surface finishing,
- dimensions,
- capacity.
- Two motors are required
- Discharge port
- Lid
- Liquid air dispersing system
- Nozzle
- Components coming in contact with product
- Lubrication/ filter

Equipment Safety Features

- Emergency stop button,
- Barrier guard,
- Electrical inter locking system,
- Alarms Control Functions:
- Regulators,
- Discharge port opening,
- Spraying button

Operational Qualification

- Calibration requirements for temperature,
- Timer,
- Pressure gauges,
- Ammeter.

Fig.4.8 Schematic diagram of Rapid Mixer Granulator.

Equipment control functions

- Impeller, timer, bowl on/off & slow/fast buttons.
- Emergency, discharge port on/off
- Alarm, wash down walls on/off Equipment operation:

Equipment operation

An empty impeller should run at low speed and also check direction and speed.

Performance Qualification

By using placebo max/min conditions are verified.

CONE BLENDER

Installation Qualification

- Verify approved purchase order.
- Verify invoice.
- Check manufacturer and supplier.
- Verify model number and serial number.
- Check for any physical damage. Confirm location and installation requirements per recommendation of manufacturer.
- Verify that the required utilities are available.

- Installation shall be conducted per the instructions provided in the manual.
- Ensure that all relevant documentation is received:
- User manual
- Maintenance manual
- List of change parts
- Electrical drawings
- Mechanical drawings

Calibration of the control and recording equipment

Instruments for measuring temperature, pressure, time, mixing chamber slope, and mixing velocity, as well as recording devices for these variables, should be calibrated[20].

Operational Qualification

- Verify alarm control.
- Perform calibration requirements, identified in the manual or established by the validation team.
- Operate the equipment at low, medium, and high speed per operations manual to verify the operating control.
- Verify that all switches and push buttons are functioning properly.
- Establish procedures for operation, maintenance, and calibration.
- Establish training program for relevant staff.

Net capacity of the mixing chamber

Procedure

Fill the mixing chamber with reweighed quantities of water. The available net capacity should be equal to the supplier specification.

Mixing or stirring velocity:

Measure velocity three times at low, medium, and high speed and compare the average and deviation from the average of the single measurements with the supplier specification.

Requirements
Compliance with the supplier specification

Performance Qualification

Product homogeneity:

Mixing process

Procedure
Fix the mixing or stirring velocity, load the mixer with the product and switch the mixer on. After previously fixed intervals, the mixer should be switched

off and samples should be taken from different locations of the product surface. The samples should be analysed for their active content.

Unloading

Procedure

After determination of the suitable mixing time to achieve product homogeneity, the influence of the unloading process on the homogeneity should be evaluated. Samples should be taken and sent to QC for analysis[21,22].

Requirements

Homogeneity should remain consistent. Water content of the product:

Take samples of the product prior to mixing, after mixing, and after unloading (begin, mid, end). Determine the water content of all samples.

Fig.4.9 Schematic diagram of a Cone Blender.

Test Functions

1) Perform Installation Qualification. Verify equipment identification, required documents, utilities, manual, and drawings.
2) Verify components material.
3) Verify equipment safety features.
4) Operate the blender throughout the range of operating design specifications or range of intended use direction, and motor fixed speed.
5) Verify equipment switches, push-buttons, and rotation
6) Perform the assay to check the content uniformity on blended granules at different locations.

Acceptance Criteria

- The system is installed in accordance with design specifications, manufacturer recommendations, and cGMPs. Instruments are calibrated, identified, and entered into the calibration program.
- General alarms and controls operate in accordance with design specifications.
- The system operates in accordance with design specifications throughout the operating range or range of intended use.
- The safety devices operate as specified in the manual.
- The quality of lubricants is adequate and the lubricants are properly stored.
- Unauthorized changes to cycle parameters are not allowed without supervisory control or password.
- Assay results should be within the specifications.

FLUIDIZED BED DRYER (FBD)

Design Qualification

- In FBD, the fluidizing air stream is introduced by a fan or blower. The air is heated to the required temperature in an air heater and flows upward through the wet materials, which contained in a drying chamber fitted with a wire mesh supported at the bottom[23].
- Capacity : 5-200kg
- Drying time: 20 to 40 min

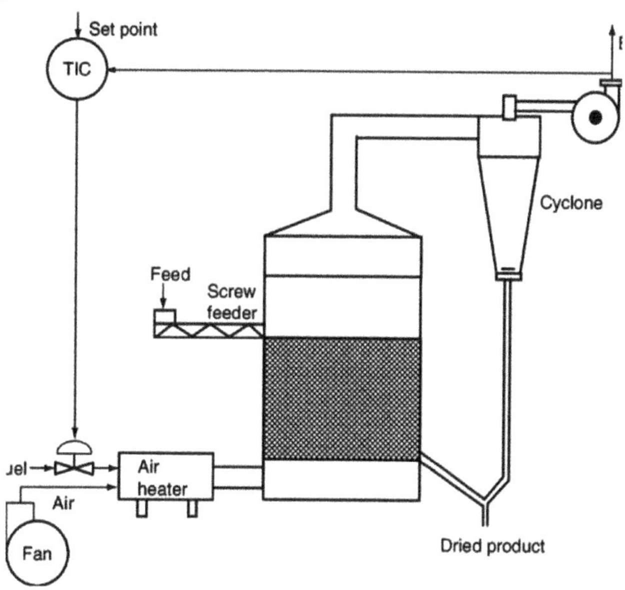

Fig.4.10 Schematic diagram of an Fluidised Bed Dryer.

Fig. 4.11 Fluidised Bed Dryer.

Installation Qualification

- An IQ establishes confidence that the equipment is properly installed. The installation must meet the manufacturer's specified guidelines, along with design changes at installation. Also the supporting electrical utilities must meet all electrical codes.
- Verify approved purchase order.
- Verify invoice.
- Check manufacturer and supplier.
- Verify model number and serial number.
- Check for any physical damage.
- Confirm location and installation requirements per recommendation of manufacturer.
- Verify that the utilities required are available.
- Installation shall be conducted per instructions provided in the manual.
- Ensure that all relevant documentation is received:
- User manual
- Maintenance manual
- List of change parts
- Electrical drawings

Instruments for measuring

Humidity, time, air volume and pressure, as well as recording devices for these variables, should be calibrated.

Air temperature distribution:

Place several thermocouples at different locations in an empty fluid bed drier:

- Inlet air channel below product container mesh bottom
- Product container
- Below filter bag
- Above filter bag
- Exhaust air channel

Measure the temperatures, letting in air of a constant temperature (e.g., 60°C).

Inlet air installation

Delay time for achieving constant air conditions

Determine, by use of a thermocouple and hygrometer, the necessary delay time required at an adjusted inlet air temperature (in relation to drying processes) for reaching constant air conditions. Determine these figures for the first use of the equipment at the working day, as well as for further use of the equipment at the same working day[24].

Also calculate from the obtained data the water content of the inlet air (g water per kg air) and compare with the previously fixed requirements.

Microbiological quality of the inlet air

Determine, by use of a bio test RCS centrifugal air sampler, the microbiological quality of the inlet air. Sampling time 5 min = 8:1 air

Requirements

- 200 CFU/m inlet air

Influence of weather on inlet air conditions

Inlet air installation

Delay time for achieving constant air conditions

Procedure

Determine, by use of a thermocouple and a hygrometer, the necessary delay time required at an adjusted inlet air temperature (in relation to granulating processes) for reaching constant air conditions. Determine these figures for first use of the equipment at the working day, as well as for further use of the equipment at the same working day.

Also calculate from the obtained data the water content of the inlet air (g water/kg air) and compare to the requirements.

Equipment identification

- Record
- The Equipment identification number,
- Equipment Manufacturer,
- Purchase order
- Model number
- Equipment number

Required documentation

The manufacturers operation and maintenance manual and SOPs that cover the set up.

***Equipment Utility Requirements*:**

- Compare the manufacturer's specified requirements to their as found conditions at the time of qualification testing.
- Power
- Steam
- Compressed air
- Calibration
- Ammeter
- Air/ water Pressure gauge
- Temperature gauge
- Major component specifications:
- Motor
- Fan: mfg., location, no of blades, rotation, capacity
- Ducting systems:
- Material, type, welding, type of welding, no of weld spots
- Heater: voltage/ capacity
- Air heaters: coils
- Product container: housing, material, type of discharge port.

Equipment Safety Features

- Barrier guard, alarm, emergency stop button, interlock with housing, positive pressure differential with flow regulators for fluid air regulation
- Positive high temperature alarm device
- Control functions:

- Process control like temperature, timer, on/off bath, product discharge port buttons, filter bag, cleaning button

Operational Qualification

An OQ evaluation should establish that the equipment can operate within specified tolerances and limits.

- Verify alarm control.
- Perform calibration requirements, identified in the manual or established by the validation team.
- Operate the equipment at low, medium, and high speed per operations manual to verify the operating control.
- Verify that all switches and push buttons are functioning properly.
- Establish procedures for operation, maintenance, and calibration.
- Establish training program for relevant staff.

Procedure

Run three batches of each product and analyse for:

- Active ingredient homogeneity
- Moisture content
- Particle size distribution
- Percentage fines
- Tap density

Based on these data try to fix a drying end point of the process (e.g., correlation between moisture content of the product and the product bed temperature).

Calibration requirements

- All the critical instruments on the equipment must be calibrated with calibration procedures. The equipment's calibrated are temperature probes, pressure gauges for air/steam, timer, air flow rate and volume.
- Equipment control functions
- In this the ON/Off switches and discharge port are verified and also the LED buttons.

Equipment Operation

1) Drying cycle
2) Air flow
3) High temp
4) Filter test
5) Feeding inlet/outlet

6) Air volume
7) Damper control
8) Humidity control
9) Drying time

All these parameters are recorded before operation

Performance Qualification

- After the equipment proper installation it's functioning and operating parameters must be verified.
- Calibrated equipment like hydrometer, temp probes, air flow monitors are required.
- Using placebos the PQ is verified
- The drying cycle parameters are fed charge at min & max load

As drying proceeds check temp, RH, fluidization pressure, differential air pressure parameters, after drying timer is set back to "O" to stop. All these parameters are recorded before operation. After drying the product check weight and also sampling is done at varied time and location.

Test Functions

1. Perform Installation Qualification. Verify equipment identification, required documents, utilities, manual, and drawings.
2. Perform general operational controls verification testing. pressure, timer operations, circulation air flow, exhaust Verify calibration requirements.
3. Operate system throughout the range of operating design specifications or range of intended use. Verify switches and push- buttons, open-door leaks, differential air flow, and high-temperature limit.
4. Verify that all safety devices are operating as specified in the manual.
5. Verify that recommended lubricants are used during machine operation.
6. Perform controller security challenges to verify that specified parameters cannot be altered without appropriate supervisory control.
7. Perform studies to check the moisture removal on each product as per SOP.
8. Perform the study for establishing the drying time as per acceptable moisture level.

Acceptance Criteria

- The system is installed in accordance with design specifications, manufacturer recommendations, and cGMPs. Instruments are calibrated, identified, and entered into the calibration program.
- General alarms and controls operate in accordance with design specifications.

- The system operates in accordance with design specifications throughout the operating range or range of intended use.
- The safety devices operate as specified in the manual.
- The quality of lubricants is adequate, and their storage is dry and cool.
- Unauthorized changes to cycle parameters must not be allowed without supervisory control or password.
- The moisture level should meet specifications.

TABLET COMPRESSION MACHINE

A 45-Station Tablet Press The press is automatic, high speed rotary press. A motor drives the press at speeds that vary from 410 to 1630 tablets per minute (rpm). The material being tableted is fed from a hopper by gravity through the feed frame into dies. Regulating the weight adjusting cam controls the weight of material in each tablet can be adjusted[25].

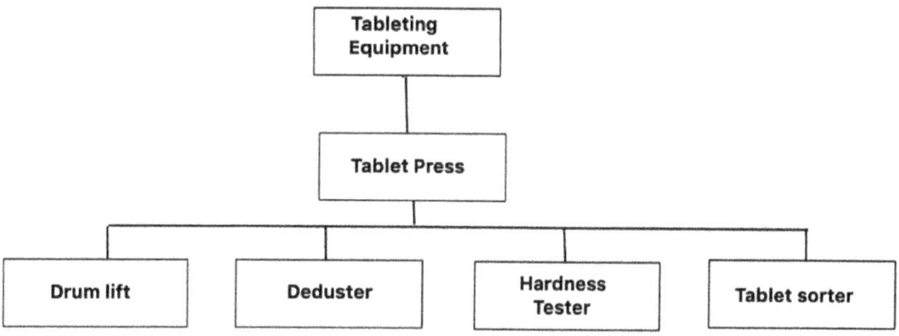

Fig.4.12 Components of tableting equipments.

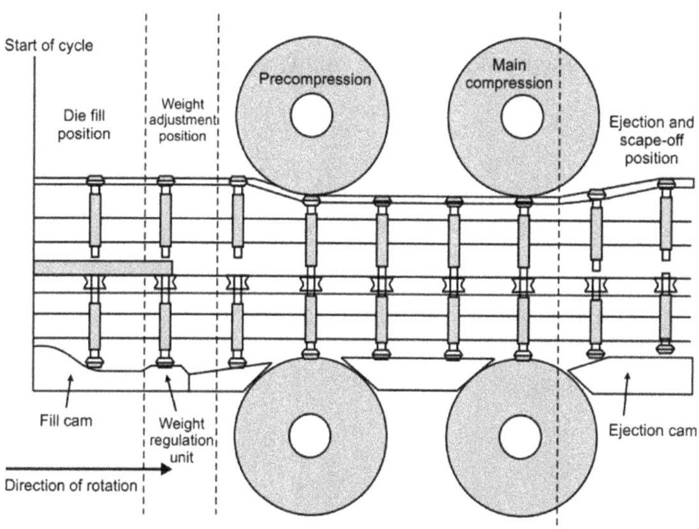

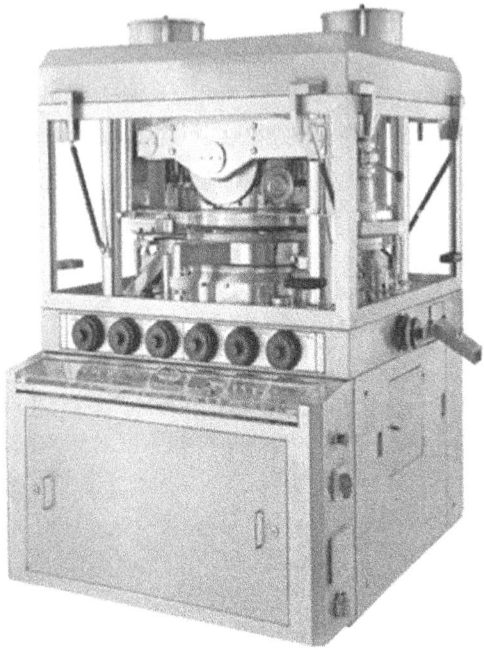

Fig. 4.13 Schematic diagram of a Compression Process.

Installation Qualification

The supporting electrical utilities must meet all electrical codes. The information required for an IQ evaluation is equipment identification, required documentation, equipment utility requirements, major component specifications, component material, lubricants and equipment safety features.

Equipment Identification:

Record the equipment identification numbers, along with the following information:

- Model number
- Serial number
- Company assigned equipment number and
- Location of the equipment

Required Documentation: Record the equipment manufacturer's operation and maintenance manual and drawings. Record the SOP that cover the setup, operation and cleaning of the tablet press.

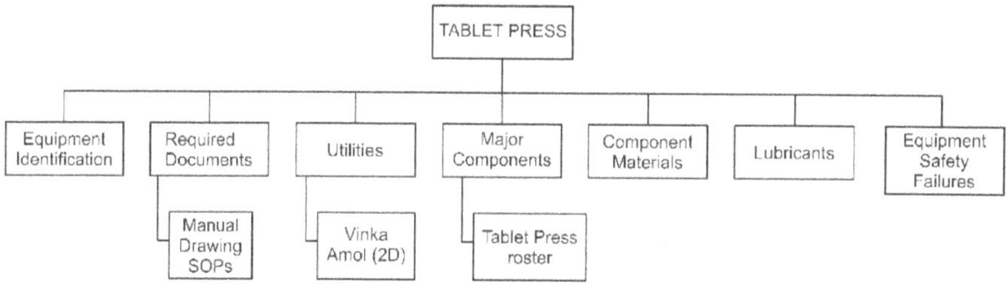

Fig.4.14 IQ elements of a tablet press.

Equipment Utility Requirements

Compare the manufacturer's specified volts (V) and amps (A) requirements to their as found conditions at the time of qualification testing and record. Also record the location of the power supply source.

Major Component Specifications

The component specifications section of the protocol verifies that the tablet press components purchased were delivered and installed.

Component material

Record the material of each component that contacts the product.

Lubricants

Record the lubricants used to operate the tablet press and indicate if they make contact with the product.

Equipment Safety Features

The objective of testing equipment safety features is to verify that the safety features on the tablet press function according to the manufacturer's specifications. This test is performed with the tablet press empty. Verify that all of the guards are present and record the results.

Operational Qualification

An OQ evaluation should establish that the equipment can operate within specified tolerances and limits. The mechanical ranges of the tablet press are challenged, along with the basic tablet press operations. The tablet press will be validated for its operating ability, not how well it makes tablets. Information required for the OQ evaluation is: calibration of the instruments used to control the tablet press, equipment control functions (switches and push buttons) and equipment operation (cam tracks, upper punches, lower punches, feed frames, take off bars, rotor head direction, tablet press speed).

Calibration requirements

Verify that all the critical instruments on the equipment have been logged into the calibration system, have calibration procedures in place and are in calibration at the time of qualification testing. Record all information for calibrated instruments used to control the tablet press.

Equipment Control Functions

The objective of testing equipment control functions is to verify that the switches and push buttons on the tablet press operate per the manufacturer's specifications. The tests will be performed with the tablet press empty. Operate each control and verify its proper position.

Equipment Operation

a) Cam Tracks Test

The objective of the cam track test is to verify that the upper and lower cam tracks make contact with the upper punches according to the manufacturer's specification. Use the following procedure and record the results.

- Install the punches and verify that the cams are contacting the punch head angles on the both the sides of the double-sided cams.
- Verify that the punches are contacting one side of the single-sided came through a full cam track, upper and lower.

b) Upper Punch Test

The objective of the upper punch test is to verify that the upper punch penetration is according to the manufacturer's specification. A vernier calliper is required for this test, which is performed as follows:

- Attach a piece of tape to mark the depth of penetration of an upper punch when it is set to a standard depth.
- Remove the upper punch and use a calibrated vernier calliper to measure the depth of penetration into the die. Record the results and instrument used to measure the depth.

c) Lower Punch Test

The objective of the lower punch test is to verify that the lower punch height is set according to the manufacturer's specification. A dial indicator test is required. Measure the height of the lower punch above the die with a dial indicator and record the results and the instrument used to measure the height.

d) Feed Frame Test

The objective of the feed frame test is to verify that the feed frame distance above the rotor head is according to the manufacturer's specification. Feeler gauge test: Measure the clearance between the feed frame and the motor head with a feeler gauge and record the results and the instrument used to measure the clearance.

e) Take Off Bar Test

The objective of the take-off bar test is to verify that the take-off bars do not make contact with the lower punches. Turn the tablet press by hand and verify that the take-off bars do not make contact with the lower punches. Record the results.

f) Tablet Press Rotation Direction

The objective of the rotation direction test is to verify that the rotor head rotates in the proper direction. The tests will be performed with the tablet press empty. Press the start switch and observe the direction of the rotation of the rotor head as viewed from front of the press and record the results.

g) Tablet Press Speed

The objective of the speed test is to verify that the measured speeds are within ± 10 % of the manufacturer's specification of a minimum of 9 rpm and a maximum of 36 rpm. This test will be performed with the press empty. A stop watch is required for this test. Measure the speed of the rotor head with a calibrated stopwatch. Verify that the measured speeds are within ± 10 % of the manufacturer's specification and record the results and the instrument used to measure the speed.

Performance Qualification

Once the equipment is properly installed and functioning within is properly installed and functioning within specified operating parameters, it must be shown that the tablet press can operate reliably under routine, minimum and maximum operating conditions.

The objective of the weight and hardness test is to verify that tablet weight and hardness can be maintained consistently throughout the entire weight and hardness setting range.

The materials and instruments required for this test are a placebo and a weight, hardness, and thickness gauge. Compress tablets using placebo granulation. Record the placebo used. Obtain the average weight and hardness of 5 tablets at start up, 10, 20 and 30 min and record the results and the instrument used to measure the weight and hardness.

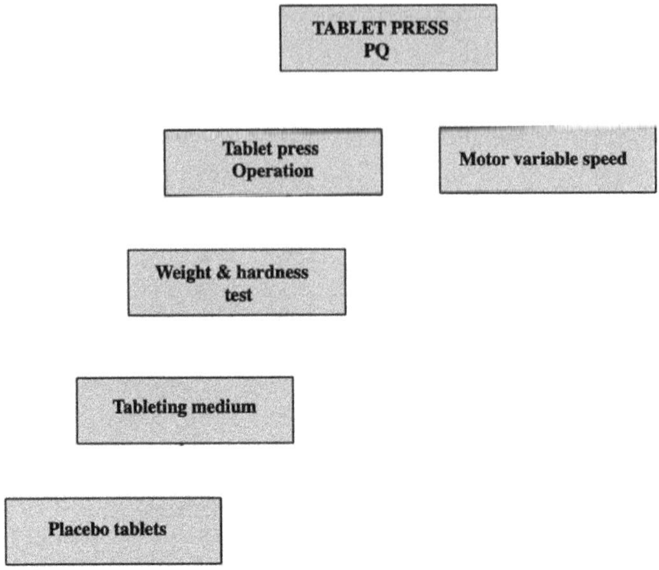

Fig.4.15 PQ elements of a tablet press.

Test Functions

a) Perform Installation Qualification.
b) Perform general operational controls verification testing.
c) Operate system throughout the range of operating design specifications or range of intended use.
d) Verify that all safety devices of the tablet press are operating as specified in the manual.
e) Verify that recommended lubricants are used during machine operation.
f) Perform controller security challenges to verify that specified parameters cannot be altered without appropriate supervisory control.
g) Perform capability and consistency studies to check the weight variation of each product as per SOP.

Acceptance Criteria

1) The system is installed in accordance with design specifications, manufacturer recommendations, and cGMPs. Instruments are calibrated, identified, and entered into the calibration program.
2) General controls and alarms operate in accordance with design specifications.
3) The system operates in accordance with design specifications throughout the operating range or range of intended use.
4) The safety devices must operate as specified in the manual.

5) The recommended lubricants must be used as specified in the manual.
6) The storage location of the lubricants must be according to manufacturer recommendations.
7) Unauthorized changes to cycle parameters must not be allowed without supervisory control or password.
8) The machine must be in statistical control as per capability and consistency studies.

LIQUID FILLING MACHINE

Importance of Liquid Filling Machines

Liquid filling machines are important equipment in various industries like cosmetics, pharmaceutical, food and beverages industries where liquids are to be packed in various types of containers. With liquid filling machines liquids, can be easily and efficiently packed into containers without much wastage and that too faster. Imagine, if this process is to be done manually in industries. Much of the liquids would be wasted due to spillage and much of time would be required to do such bulk packing applications.

The modern liquid filling machines come in advanced forms with user friendly controls and features. The best machines can fill liquids in industries in less time and with less labour. A liquid filling machine can accomplish the huge liquid filling tasks in industries easily and fast can replace the work of number of human beings who were to do the process in absence of these machines. It is mainly used for liquids like- syrup, oil, wine, etc. that have high viscosity and hence, require this method to fill up the containers. The liquid filling machine provides a very effective solution for filling such liquids into their respective containers. The filling machine fills the liquid due to gravity. The liquid gets filled in the bottle due to their own weight. The machine is capable of using tank, bottle or a container to fill the liquid. These containers move in a cycle in which after getting filled up with liquid, they are processed further for packaging[27].

Types of Liquid Filling Machine

Liquid filling machines come in different forms depending on degree of their automatic functioning, the containers in which the liquid is to be filled and number of heads the machine has to enable the specific number of bottles or container filling at a time. Some of the commonly used forms of liquid filling machine for industries may be fully automatic liquid filling machine, semi-automatic liquid filling machine, twin head liquid filler machine, four head liquid filling machine, six head liquid filling machine, eight head liquid filling machine. Liquid filling machine is used for vials, for bottles, electronic liquid filling machine, liquid filling machine with capping feature and liquid filling with rubber stoppering machine. Even machines for filling viscous liquids like oils are also available in markct, for example there are machines like oil filling machine for filling edible oil, cooking oil fillers, oil fillers for lube oil filling and much more[28].

- **Liquid Filling Machine**

  It is a device that has been used in several industries to load raw materials into containers and pack them to create a final product. Different packaging companies have been benefited from this machine. In liquid filling machine, the tanks, container, or vessel can move in a cycle, is loaded by the machine, and is then prepared for packaging. There are several liquid filling machines worthy to mention.

- **Injectable Liquid vial filling machine**

  This is widely used to fill vials with medications. It operates on the volumetric concept, using dividing nozzles and a pneumatic mechanism with rubber stoppers on the top of the containers. The injectable liquid vial filling system contains a stainlesssteel flat conveyor belt, so that the vials can move on. The vials are then transported to the filling station, which has 2 to 12 heads. After the precise filling, the station places a closure on the head. The basic components of the vial filling machine are a conveyor belt on which the bottles are transported and a filling and stoppering machine on which the vials are loaded and rubber stoppered so that no medical material is wasted and precision is preserved.

- **Prefilled syringe filling machine**

  This machine is best suited for usage in the pharmaceutical industry since it is used to fill a prefilled syringe. A stainless hopper is used to hold syringes. On top of the structure is the pre-filled syringe slot. Piece by piece, syringes are transported to the filling station, where an automated pump is installed. The syringes go to an outfeed plate of the syringe filling equipment once they have been injected to the correct quantity.

- **Liquid bottle filling machine**

  Bottles are filled with a variety of viscous liquids, like oil, which is utilised for both food and industrial properties. The volumetric or gravimetric method can be used to fill the containers. For filling the bottles, there is a funnel alternative. To impart force to denser fluids, pumps or pistons can be utilised if the liquid is thick or viscous. The liquid bottle filling machine is used to fill lotions and creams. The swift nozzles enable a quicker and more efficient discharge.

- **Linear Liquid filling machine**

  The linear liquid filling machine works on the volumetric basis and can fill up to 1000 ml bottles. The driving nozzle contains a suck back configuration and is used to prevent foam.

- **Oil filling machine**

  Automatic liquid filling machines, particularly fast-moving ones, frequently perform several advances. The oil filling machine is one such machine, it uses the same line to line outward and inward filling ideas. For bulk manufacturing and packaging, the oil can be put in containers, bottles, and jars. The automated 8 head twin-track liquid filling with rubber stoppering machine is a high-speed, high-efficiency liquid filling with sturdy construction. The Automated Rotary Piston Filling and Capping Machine is also a great option, having a rotary valve for drip-free filling. Other machines in high demand are the Engine Oil Filling machine, Volumetric Oil Filling Machine for Lube and Oils utilised for gastronomic and medicinal purposes.

- **Manual Liquid filling machines**

  These rely on manual operations and require no electricity. These are suitable for small-scale industries.

- **Semi-Automatic Liquid Filling Machines**

  These use syringe, piston, and nozzle so that there is no drip in operation. This is used for cleaning detergents and pharmaceutical products.

- **Fully Automatic Liquid Filling Machines**

  These can fill liquids with all viscosity and can handle large-scale operations. This is used for food products.

- **Inline Liquid Filling Machines**

  This machine pours all types of liquids in containers that are arranged in a single line along with the conveyor system. This is ideal for food, dairy, and cosmetics products.

- **Rotary Liquid Filling Machines**

  It moves containers along different circular stations, with each one performing a specific function such as filling, sealing, and capping. This type of liquid filling machine is commonly used in the beverage, food, automotive, and personal care industries. These machines also come in variants like twin head liquid filler machine, four head liquid filling machine, six head liquid filling machine, eight head liquid filling machine, liquid filling machine for vials, liquid filler machine for bottles, electronic liquid filling machine, a liquid filling machine with capping feature and liquid filling with rubber stoppering machine. Oil filling machines are also available for filling edible oil, cooking oil fillers, oil fillers for lube oil filling, and much more[29].

A liquid filling machine typically has the following features

1. **Volumetric or Gravimetric Filling**

   Liquid filling machines can use either volumetric or gravimetric methods to fill containers with a precise amount of liquid.

2. **Adjustable Filling Speeds**

   Liquid filling machines have adjustable filling speeds to accommodate different products and production rates.

3. **Accurate and Repeatable Fill Volumes**

   Liquid filling machines are designed to dispense consistently, the accurate volumes of liquid into containers, with repeatable results.

4. **Container Compatibility**

   Liquid filling machines are designed to accommodate various container sizes and shapes, including round, square, oval and flat-sided containers.

5. **User-friendly Controls**

   Liquid filling machines often come with user-friendly controls, such as touch screens and intuitive interface, to make operation simple and efficient.

6. **Automatic Container Handling**

   Liquid filling machines can be equipped with automatic container handling systems to streamline production, including conveyors and bottle unscramblers.

7. **Sanitary Design**

   Liquid filling machines can be designed with sanitary features, such as stainlesssteel construction, to meet the requirements of food and pharmaceutical applications.

8. **Integration with Other Equipment**

   Liquid filling machines can be integrated with other production equipment, such as capping machines and labelling equipment, to form a complete packaging line.

Liquid filling machine manufacturers are able to market their machines because they are adaptable, flexible, and waste-free. The machines are made to satisfy the user's requirements and preferences, as well as the form and size of the receiving containers.

Process of liquid filling machine

The inline or horizontal type piston filling machine is the first step in our bottle liquid filling machine's procedure. The fluid in the apparatus is directed and measured by this piston filler. After the vial filling machine's initial procedure of measurement and pouring is complete, the output (liquid) is immediately pumped into a vessel using a stainless filler with one or more heads. The liquid filling machine's process is fast, the liquid within the machine is fully safe, and it can be handled without any problems. After the basic process of the bottle filling machine is completed, the secondary phase of the equipment processing begins, and the filling machine can fill a large number of deposits in a minute. The liquid filling machine also ensures that the entire process runs smoothly without any disruptions. After all of the operations are completed, the finished product (filled bottles, containers, and vials) is collected. As a result, here is the full procedure that describes how the vial filling and packing technology works.

The objective of the PQ of the liquid filling machine is to establish that the documented proofs will provide a high degree of assurance and reliability of the performance of the liquid filling machine and to demonstrate that the equipment/ system is working reproducibly and consistently within its operating range of operation and fill the weight according to the manufacturer's specification.

The liquid filling machine is installed in the liquid filling room.

The machine is built on sturdy welded frame of S.S.304 completely enclosed in stainless steel sheet.

The filling unit is necessary for process simulation study, working on the basic principle of simple piston mechanism. The liquid will be sucked from the liquid holding tank with the help of a syringe during downward movement of the piston. The piston delivers the liquid into the filling container during its upward movement. The bottom end of the syringe is fitted with an eccentric shaft. The provided mechanical setting will vary its volume. The volume of the liquid to be filled in can vary up to 1000 ml[30].

Responsibilities and identification of the execution team

The group of people representing each of the following departments shall remain responsible for overall compliance with this protocol.

Department	Responsibility
Production	Execution of the validation activity and providing the necessary support.
Engineering and utility	Participation and providing the necessary support for successful completion of the validation activity.
Quality Assurance	Monitoring, sampling, and reviewing the validation activities.

The personnel involved in the execution of this protocol must bee recorded as: Name, Designation, signature and date.

The following test procedures are performed to qualify the equipment for its performance.

Six fill weights are selected ranging from the minimum and maximum based on the product list proposed (used in production) to evaluate the performance range of the filling machine.

Container size	Target Fill volume	Machine speed	Container size	Target Fill volume	Machine speed
55 ml	50 ml	Minimum	500 ml	450 ml	Minimum
		Medium			Medium
		Maximum			Maximum
105 ml	100 ml	Minimum	700 ml	650 ml	Minimum
		Medium			Medium
		Maximum			Maximum
205 ml	200 ml	Minimum	1000 ml	1000 ml	Minimum
		Medium			Medium
		Maximum			Maximum

- …………………. has been used as drug for performance qualification of the filling machine.
- Before the experimentation, the tap density………
- After the experimentation, the tap density………

Test procedure

- Required machine parts are assembled on the liquid filling machine,
- Indent and receipt of the drug, ……………………. and charged into the respective hopper,
- The sterilized and depyrogenated contained (as required for injectable solution filling) are obtained on the scrambler of the liquid filling machine from the sterilizing tunnel.
- Operate the machine as per the Standard Operating Procedure (SOP) and adjust the nitrogen gas pressure and vacuum as required.
- For each fill volume the machine is operated at three speeds, minimum, medium, maximum, and at each speed the machine is run for 10 mins.
- Collect 20 containers at initial, middle and at end of the filling operation of a particular speed and test for physical appearance such as appearance, variation in volume, average volume filled.
- The above procedures are followed for each container size as per the qualification matrix.

Acceptance criteria

- There should not be any spillage of liquid during filling operation.
- Number of containers damaged during the test.
- Filled volume should be within ± 5% of the target fill volume.
- Average volume filled in should be within ± 2% of the target fill volume[31-33].

Recording of the observations

- The observations after execution of each test procedure should be recorded in prescribed format.

Discrepancy and corrective action report

- Record any discrepancy, if observed, during the performance qualification of the liquid filling machine. Include the corrective action of the same[34-36]. When all the discrepancies are satisfactorily resolved or an approved action plan is developed ensuring that discrepancy would be resolved.

Compilation, review and summary report

- Compile all the records and review that all the test functions have been completed, reconciled and attached too this protocol. Verify that approvals for deviations have been taken care of and resolved appropriately up to the satisfaction.
- Performance qualification shall be considered acceptable when all the conditions specified in the test procedures have been met.
- Prepare the summary report (Performance Qualification Report), submit for review, approval and authorization to validation core team[37-39].

LIQUID SEALING MACHINE

The objective of Performance Qualification is

- To confirm that the Liquid Sealing Machine is capable of consistently performing as it is supposed to perform.
- To demonstrate that the equipment/ system is working reproducibly and consistently within its operating range of operation and suitable for sealing of different types/ sizes of containers as per Standard Operating Procedures.
- To demonstrate that the sealing process is capable of consistently and reliably producing appropriate sealing of the containers with flip off seals on different types of containers at different speeds encountered in the routine production operations.

- To assure the container integrity of the filled and sealed containers at different speeds with different sets of containers[40-43].

Equipment Description

- Sealing machine is installed in the sealing room adjacent to the filling machine.
- Main action of sealing machine is accumulated on the turntable at the infeed of the machine and is carried towards the machine by a slat conveyor. A worm separates the containers are transfers them onto infeed star wheel. The stoppers and caps are accurately positioned by means of centring device.
- The crimping process is carried out gradually during transport of the containers through the machine. The cam driven crimping process ensures proper synchronization between the crimping tool and containers. When the capping process is completed, the containers are discharged with a starweel and transferred for inspection.
- Change over to different sizes of the containers or flange caps (seals) are affected by exchanging complete set of change parts[44-49].

Responsibility

Representative of the following departments constitute the PQ team

Department	Responsibility
Production	Preparation of Performance Qualification Record and Operation of Machine
Validation	Verification and Compilation of PQ Record
Quality Control	Sampling and Analysis
Quality Assurance	Review and Control the Documents

The personnel involved in the execution of this protocol must bee recorded as: Name, Designation, signature and date.

Test Procedure

Dye inside the vial or container method

- The sterilized and depyrogenated vials/ containers (as required) are obtained on the scrambler of the vial/ container filling machine from the sterilizing tunnel.
- After completion of successful Operational Qualification check the performance of the powder filling line by filling anhydrous Lactose to ensure that the machine is performing as per its intended use.
- Ensure that the area and machine are cleaned before operation.

- Ensure that the LAF unit is cleaned and sanitized and that the LAF unit pressure is within the limit.
- Turn ON the electrical connection.
- Record the Sealing details in respective section tables.
- Check the sealing quality as per the frequency mentioned given in the respective Table. Sealing quality will be only checked visually during the performance qualification run, the performance of sealing will be evaluated in terms of the successful media fill on the same line. The media fill report shall be an addendum to the qualification report.
- Check the sealing quality of vials and record the observation in the respective tables.

Note: In case of any deviation observed during Performance Qualification of the filling line with powder filling, inform to department head and quality head for necessary action.

1. Document the deviation detail in the observed deviation section.
2. The quality head and the department head will study the impact of deviation.
3. If the deviation is acceptable and it does not have an impact on operation as well as on the performance of the machine, provide final conclusion.
4. If the deviation is not acceptable, inform the quality head and department head for further action.

Frequency

- The performance qualification should be done for the new facility.
- Any major modification to any of the existing equipment after the validation activity must be documented through a change control system.

Acceptance criteria

- Weight variation observed at all levels of the hopper and at all speeds should be between 98% to 102% of the standard limit.
- Nitrogen flushing should be achieved throughout the performance qualification.
- Rubber stoppering should be achieved properly.

Validation Report

The interim report shall consist of a summary document, in narrative form, which briefly describes the steps and observations during performance Qualification.

Approval of Validation Report

The validation Executive shall evaluate the validation report before the Authorization of the General Manager of Quality Assurance and Quality Control (GM QA/QC) and General Manager Production.

ASEPTIC ROOM VALIDATION

Quality risk management is an important part of science based decision making essential for quality management of pharmaceutical manufacturing. The ICH Q9 guideline, quality risk management and other literature provide guidance on the principal of quality risk management. The FMEA model can be used to facilitate risk assessment for any system in the aseptic processing area of sterile products. It provides a tool to assess and evaluate different activities and conditions. Risk ranking system in FMEA model is given in Table 4.1. Risk in sterile product manufacturing and aseptic processing is relatively high when compared to other pharmaceutical process, making risk assessment particularly important[50].

The European Union GMP requirements place specific obligations on manufacturers of medicinal products to implement risk based qualification, validation and change control programs. In pharmaceutical manufacturing, validation is an important part of QA and is a requirement of cGMP and other guidelines.

Table 4.1 Risk ranking system.

Qualitative Ranking	Risk factor		
	Severity	**Occurrence**	**Detection**
High	Impact of unwanted event is severe	Occurrence is often	The process failure will almost certainly escape detection
Medium	Impact of unwanted event is moderate	Occurrence is periodic	Control may detect the existence of a process failure
Low	Impact of unwanted event is low	Occurrence is seldom	The process failure is obvious and readily detected

In the air handling system, special attention must be made to keep the environment clean and prevent product contamination. From a technical perspective, the role of the HVAC system is paramount in achieving and maintaining an acceptable manufacturing environment[51-53].

Experimental

Evaluate the overall risk of the qualification and validation steps by combining individual risk values. For the most of the direct impact system, the severity will always be high. The risk priority ranking (RPR) then becomes a combination of an occurrence and detection. If the level of risk is not acceptable, a recommendation must be made to modify the qualification and validation steps to reduce the risk to an acceptable level or enhance the method of detection to reduce the risk to an acceptable level. Preference should be given to reducing the occurrence rather than increasing the level of detection. Table 4.2 represented the risk priority ranking system as per the FMEA model. After completion of the risk assessment, the recommended action of unacceptable risk extended to qualification stages of HVAC system to have a high level of assurance and if the test result are not acceptable, carry out corrective action that may include modification in the existing controls and the system.

Table 4.2 Determination of RPR.

Occurrence	**Risk related to probability of detection**		
	Low	**Medium**	**High**
High	This is likely to occur, but when it does, it will be detected. If we are certain it will be detected, it is **Low Risk**, but if we are not certain then it should be a **Medium Risk**.	This is likely to occur and the detection is not certain. It is a **High Risk**.	This is likely to occur and the detection is not certain. It is a **High Risk**.
Medium	This could occur but if it did, it would be detected. Depending on the frequency of occurrence and the confidence in the detection, it is a **Low** or a **Medium Risk**.	This could occur and it could be detected. Depending on our confidence in the detection, its risk would be **Medium** or **High Risk**.	This may occur and it will not be detected The **Risk is High**.
Low	This is not likely to occur and if it does occur it will be detected. This is a **Low Risk**.	The cause is not likely to occur and if it did, it may be detected. Depending on the frequency of occurrence and the confidence in detection method, it would be a **Low** or **Medium Risk**.	The cause is not likely to occur but if it did occur, it probably would not be detected. The **Risk is Medium**.

AIR VELOCITY AND AIR CHANGES

Velocity at the inlet air grills was measured at 5 points in a plane parallel to filter face plane and at a distance of about 6 inches (~ 150mm) from the filter/opening face. The velocity was measured for at least 10 seconds from each point. It is performed by thermal anemometer and vane type anemometer and calculated by formula where, D is no. of air changes, B is air supply volume (CFM), R is volume of the room (ft^3), 60 is factor (for air change per hour)[54,55].

$$D = \frac{\sum B \times 60}{R}$$

DIFFERENTIAL PRESSURE TEST

Measure and record the pressure difference between the room to be tested and any surrounding ancillary environment.

HEPA FILTER LEAKAGE TEST

Position the aerosol generator to introduce an aerosol challenge upstream of the HEPA filter to a concentration of 20-100mg/m^3 (20 –100 µg/lit.) of air by opening appropriate number of nozzles. Measure upstream concentration of aerosol by using upstream port. Adjust the photometer's gain / span control for a full-scale deflection on 100% range. Scan the downstream side of the HEPA filter. The photometer probe should be about 1 inch from the surface and at a transverse rate not more than 10ft/minute with a sample flow rate of 1cft/min ± 10%.

AIR FLOW VISUALIZATION (NON-UNIDIRECTIONAL FLOW)

Generate the tracer particles by water for injection (WFI) fogger. Position the tracer at the appropriate place, such as at the downstream of supply air and the return air risers as well as at the doors opening and check for the indication of the airflow direction. Record the airflow pattern using photography/ videography[56].

AIRBORNE PARTICLE COUNT

Derive the number of sampling point locations by using the equation where, NL is the minimum number of sampling locations and √A is Area of the room in square meter.

$$NL = \sqrt{A}$$

Volume of sample (for grade A at rest and operation, grade B at rest) - 1m^3 equivalent to 35.3 ft^3

Volume of sample (for grade B at operation and other grades at both conditions) -1 ft^3

RECOVERY/DECONTAMINATION RATE TEST

Take the particle count in the area before aerosol generation under resting conditions. The sampling rate should be 1 CFM. Artificially generate DOP/PAO aerosol in the classified area and check the count (1000 times more than classified area "at rest"). Record the particle count and time. Stop the aerosol generator. The time at which the aerosol generator is stopped should be the starting time for establishing the recovery rate. Start the particle counting at the specified location at a sampling rate of 1 CFM. Establish the time required for attaining the "at rest" condition.

ENVIRONMENTAL CONDITIONS – TEMPERATURE AND RELATIVE HUMIDITY

Digital hygrometers and a Sling hygrometer were used to perform the test for 5 consecutive days for category A1 AHUs and for 3 consecutive days for AHUs of other categories. Readings should be for minimum 16 hours/day at 2 hour interval.

VIABLE COUNT MONITORING – SETTLE PLATE AND AIR SAMPLING

Settled plates should be of 90mm diameter and should be exposed for duration of 4 hours. Plates should be exposed at a height above 1 meter from the floor and also at work level for better exposure. For air sampling, $1m^3$ of air from specified locations should be sampled using Soybean Casein Digest Agar Incubate settle plate at 20 - 25°C for TFC and at 30 - 35°C for TBC.

Exercise

Multiple Choice Questions

1. Fill in the blank using appropriate word given below.
2. Calibration is done because the instruments are likely to deviate due to hard operating conditions, mechanical .... or exposure to extreme temperature or pressure.

   a) hazards   b) conditions

   c) pressures   d) shocks
3. Fill in the blank using appropriate word given below.
4. Possibility of incorrect test results as the equipment's performance has been reduced and proved to be suitable for their intended purpose both before it is used for test sample .... and during their working life.

   a) Conference   b) quality

   c) analysis   d) combination

5. Fill in the blank using appropriate word given below.
6. The .... guideline demonstrates[3] that the facilities, systems, equipment and utilities are properly qualified and maintained to assure data and product integrity.
   a) GMP b) ICH Q7(a)
   c) cGMP d) ICH
7. Fill in the blank using appropriate word given below.
8. As a key component of quality ...., equipment qualification is important to consistently produce the high-quality products.
   a) assurance b) control
   c) male d) care
9. Fill in the blank using appropriate word given below.
10. Based on their specific uses, the selection of utilities, equipment construction materials, operating principles and .... characteristics is done.
   a) Quality b) performance
   c) Equipment d) material
11. Which of the following statement is correct?
   a) Performance Qualification protocol is solely intended to be used with new or relocated instruments.
   b) Operational Qualification protocol is solely intended to be used with new or relocated instruments.
   c) Installation Qualification protocol is solely intended to be used with new or relocated instruments.
   d) Design Qualification protocol is solely intended to be used with new or relocated instruments.
12. Which of the following statement is correct?
   a) All necessary activities and responsibilities for the qualification and validation are controlled and specified in the Validation Master Plan.
   b) All necessary activities and responsibilities for the qualification and validation are controlled and specified in the Validation Master Plan.
   c) All necessary activities and responsibilities for the qualification and validation are not controlled and specified in the Validation Master Plan.
   d) All necessary activities and responsibilities for the qualification and validation are controlled and specified in the Validation Master Plan.

13. Which of the following statement is correct?
    a) Design qualification (DQ) defines the operational specifications of the instrument and details for the conscious decisions in the selection of the user.
    b) Design qualification (DQ) defines the functional and operational specifications of the instrument and details for the conscious decisions in the selection of the supplier.
    c) Operational qualification (OQ) is the process of demonstrating that an instrument will function.
    d) Performance Qualification (PQ) is the process of demonstrating that an instrument consistently performs.
14. Which of the following statement is correct?
    a) The MQ describes and documents any maintenance required on the equipment.
    b) The MQ describes the maintenance required on the equipment.
    c) The MQ confuses whether any maintenance required on the equipment.
    d) The MQ covers up any maintenance required on the equipment.
15. Which of the following statement is correct?
    a) A stability assurance level (SAL) of 10-6 means that there is less than or equal to one chance in million.
    b) A stability assurance level (SAL) of 10-6 means that there is less than or equal to one chance in million.
    c) A sterility assurance level (SAL) of 10-6 means that there is less than or equal to one chance in million.
    d) A sterility assurance level (SAL) of 10-16 means that there is less than or equal to one chance in million.
16. Which of the following statement is correct?
    a) Temperature is most reliable and rapid method of sterilization.
    b) Heat is most reliable method of sterilization.
    c) Temperature is most reliable for sterilization.
    d) Heat is most reliable and rapid method of sterilization.
17. Which of the following statement is correct?
    a) Sterilization by moist heat means killing of microorganism with hot water or steam.
    b) Sterilization means killing of microorganism with hot water or steam.

c) Sterilization by heat means killing of microorganism with hot water or steam.

d) Sterilization by hot air oven means killing of microorganism with hot water or steam.

18. Which of the following statement is correct?

a) The killing of moist heat is due to oxidation of protein and toxic effect of elevated level of electrolytes.

b) The killing of dry heat is due to protein denaturation, oxidative damage and toxic effect of elevated level of electrolytes.

c) The killing of moist heat is due to protein denaturation, oxidative damage and toxic effect of elevated level of electrolytes.

d) The killing of moist heat is due to protein denaturation, oxidative damage and toxic effect of elevated level of electrolytes.

19. Which of the following statement is correct?

a) Dry heat sterilization involves the use of steam in the range of 351-354°C.

b) Dry heat sterilization involves the use of steam in the range of 340-354°C.

c) Moist heat sterilization involves the use of steam in the range of 121-124°C.

d) Dry heat sterilization involves the use of steam in the range of 350-356°C

20. Fill in the blank using the word given below.

21. .... can be defined as the elimination of all pyrogenic substances, including bacterial endotoxin and is generally achieved by removal or inactivation.

a) Pyrogenation b. Sterilization

c) Oxidation d. Depyrogenation

22. Fill in the blank using the word given below.

23. The temperature at each temperature probes should be .... during the cycle.

a) $\leq$300°C b) 340 °C

c) 350 °C d) $\geq$ 300°C

24. Fill in the blank using the word given below.

25. Bioburden levels can influence process .... efficacy.

a) Filtration b) completion

c) manufacturing d) engineering

26. Fill in the blank using the word given below.
27. An .... Qualification establishes confidence that the equipment is properly installed.
    a) Performance
    b) Installation
    c) Equipment
    d) Operational
28. Fill in the blank using the word given below.
29. An empty impeller should run at .... speed and also check direction and speed.
    a) high
    b) medium
    c) low
    d) higher
30. Fill in the blank using the word given below.
31. Velocity at the inlet air grills was measured at 5 points in a plane parallel to filter face plane and at a distance of about 6 inches (............) from the filter/opening face.
    a) ~ 12cm
    b) ~ 150μm
    c) ~ 150nm
    d) ~ 150mm

Short Questions

1. What are the benefits of equipment qualification? What is meant by Qualification of utilities and equipment?
2. What are the importances of validation? What do you understand by design qualification and operational qualification?
3. What are the contents of equipment operation qualification? What is meant by performance qualification and maintenance qualification?
4. Define sterilization. What are different methods of sterilization? How can an autoclave perform, what are main activities to be performed using autoclave?
5. What is depyrogenation and sterilization tunnel? How can you verify the integrity of HEPA filter installed in the sterilization and depyrogenation tunnel?
6. Write down the steps of installation qualification and operational qualification of cone blender.
7. How can you determine the homogeneity of a mixture?
8. Write down the steps of installation qualification of a fluidized bed drier. How can you determine the air temperature distribution in a fluidized bed drier?
9. How can you determine the performance qualification of fluidized bed drier?

10. Once the equipment is properly installed and functioning within is properly installed and functioning within specified operating parameters, how can you qualify the performance of a rotary tableting machine?
11. What is Cam Tracks test? Mention the features of a liquid filling machine.

Long Questions

1. Explain in brief the Installation Qualification (IQ) protocols in pharmaceutical industry.
2. What is operational qualification? How can you perform the operational qualification in a pharmaceutical industry?
3. During steam sterilization how can you perform the heat distribution and heat penetration studies?
4. How can you determine the heat distribution and heat penetration study in a hot air oven?
5. Explain the statement, 'The removal rating of a given membrane filter type refers to the size, or narrower dimension, of microorganisms and particles removed by the filter, rather than the actual size or shape of the filter pore structure.'
6. Draw neatly a sketch of fluidized bed drier and write down the function of each component.
7. Discuss in brief the operation of each control and verification its proper position of a rotary tableting machine.
8. What is the importance of a liquid filling machine? What are different types of a liquid filling machine?
9. Write down the process of liquid filling. What is compilation, review, and summary report?
10. Explain the process of aseptic room validation. How can you determine the air velocity and air change?

Answers

1	2	3	4	5	6	7	8	9	10	11	12	13	14	15	16	17	18	19	20
d	c	b	a	b	c	d	b	a	c	d	a	b	c	d	d	a	b	c	d

References

1. Edward Simpson, Calibrating Specialist RSCalibration.com.
2. John J. Barron, Colin Ashton.; Qualification and its Application to Conductivity Measuring Systems, Journal for Quality, Comparability and Reliability in Chemical Measurement. 11(11): 554-561.

3. Sharanya N, Ramasubramaniyan P, Jeya shree P, Srinag T, Palanichamy S, Solairaj P. An Overview on Qualification of Equipment – An Ideal Approach for Equipment Validation. Indo American Journal of Pharmaceutical Research. 2013; 3(10): 9013-9018.
4. Guidance for Industry Process Validation: General Principles and Practices, U.S. Department of Health and Human Services, Food and Drug Administration, Centre for Drug Evaluation and Research (CDER), Centre for Biologics Evaluation and Research (CBER), Centre for Veterinary Medicine (CVM), January 2011, Current Good Manufacturing Practices (CGMP), Revision 1, p-14.
5. Syed Imtiaz Haider, Pharmaceutical Master Validation Plan: the ultimate guide to FDA, GMP and GLP compliance, CRC press, Florida; 2001
6. Syed Imtiaz Haider, Validation Standard Operating Procedures - A Step-by-Step Guide for Achieving Compliance in the Pharmaceutical Medical Device and Biotech Industry, CRC press, Florida; 2001
7. http://www.validation-online.net/process- qualification.html
8. http : //www . analytik-jena.com
9. http://www.chem.agilent.com/Library/ser vice/Public/Review%20Document_Stand ard_EQP_LCMS_01.71.pdf
10. http://www.askaboutvalidation.com/forum/showthread.php?1410-Cleaning validation-quot-Fuid-bed-dryer-quot
11. http://www.labcompliance.com/seminars
12. Phil cloud, Pharmaceutical equipment validation-The ultimate qualification guidebook, Interpharm/CRC press, Florida; 1998
13. James P.Agalloco, Frederick J.Carleton, Validation of Pharmaceutical Processes, Third edition, Informal Healthcare, New York;2007
14. Kenneth W. Sigvardson, Joseph A. Manalo, Robert W. Roller, F a t ieh S al,2011:http://pharmtech.findpharma.com /pharmtech/data/articlestandard//pharmte ch/502001/4496/article.pdf
15. Sharma A, Saini S; Process Validation of Solid Dosage Form: A Review. International Journal of Research in Pharmacy and Science, 2013; 3 (2): 12- 30.
16. Kaur H, Singh G, Seth N; Pharmaceutical Process Validation: A Review. 2013; 3 (4): 189-194.
17. Thaduvai R, Rao BS, Jeybaskaran M; Process Validation of Pantoprazole 40 mg Tablets: The Pharma Innovation. 2012; 1 (5): 50-52.
18. Kavita, Khurana G, Chaudhary S; Process Validation of Solid Dosage Form: A Review. Pharma Science Monitor, An International Journal of Pharmaceutical Sciences, September 2013; 4 (4): 390- 391.
19. Chapman K. G: A History of Validation in the United States, Part I, Pharma Technology. November 1991; 39-98.
20. Nash R. A., Wachter A. H: In Pharmaceutical Process Validation. Third Edition; Revised and Expanded, Marcel Dekker Inc., New York, 1993.

21. Potdar MA; Pharmaccutical Quality Assurance. 2nd Edition, Nirali Prakashan, 2009: 8.6-8.20.
22. WHO Expert Committee on Specifications for Pharmaceutical Preparations. WHO technical report, series no. 863 – 34th report, Annex 6 – GMP: Guidelines on the validation of manufacturing processes: 4-7.
23. ICH Q7A Good Manufacturing Practice Guidance for Active Pharmaceutical Ingredients: 33.
24. Potdar MA; Current Good Manufacturing Practices for Pharmaceuticals. 2nd Edition, Pharma Med Press Publication, Delhi, December 2007: 8.2-8.3.
25. Validation of Solid Dosage Forms the FDA view, 1989; 15(6-7): 1119-1133.
26. Guidelines for Process Validation of Pharmaceutical Dosage Forms. Saudi Food and Drug Authority, Kingdom of Saudi Arabia, 2010; 9-15.
27. Guideline on General Principles of Process Validation. Washington DC: Center for Drug Evaluation and Research, US Food and Drug Administration, May 1987; 9.
28. Good Manufacturing Practices for Pharmaceutical Products, WHO/Pharm./93.562/Annex: Guidelines on Validation of Manufacturing Process. Geneva: WHO.
29. Kumar NL, Moorthy DG, Kumar SR; An Overview of Pharmaceutical Validation: Quality Assurance view point. 2011; 1(4): 1003-1014.
30. FDA Guidance Update: Process Validation: General Principles and Practices; version 01; 2009. 17. Potdar MA; Pharmaceutical Quality Assurance. 2nd Edition, Nirali Prakashan, Pune, 2007: 8.1- 8.44.
31. Nash R. A: Process Validation of a 17- Year Retrospective Study of Solid Dosage Forms. Drug Development Industrial Pharmacy 1966; 22 (1): 25-34.
32. Guidance for Industry: Process Validation: General Principles and Practices. U.S. Department of Health and Human Services, Food and Drug Administration, Centre for Drug Evaluation and Research (CDER), Centre for Biologics Evaluation and Research (CBER), Centre for Veterinary Medicine (CVM), January 2011.
33. Oechslein C, Lazar MS; Process Validation from view report of the FDA. Maas and Peither AG – GMP Publishing, Logfile No. 3/ February 2012.
34. Guidance for Industry on general principles and practices of process validation; US Department of Health and Human Services, Food and Drug Administration, 2011; 7-9. 22. Validation Guidelines for Pharmaceutical Dosage Form; Health products and Food branch Inspectorate, Canada, December 2009; 8-13.
35. Von Doehren PJ, St. John; An Approach to the Characterization and Technology Transfer of Solid Dosage Form Processes: Pharma Technology, 1982; 6 (9): 139–156.
36. Patel RC, Bhuva CK; Pharmaceutical Process Validation: Pharmatutor, ART - 1053

37. Jatto E, Okhamafe AO; An Overview of Pharmaceutical Validation and Process Controls in Drug Development. Tropical Journal of Pharmaceutical Research, 2002; 2: 115-122.
38. Mohammed. SA; Pharmaceutical Process Validation: An Overview. Journal of Advanced Pharmacy Education and Research, 2012; 2 (4): 186-200.
39. Guide to Inspections of Oral Solid Dosage Forms pre/post Approval Issue for Development and Validation; issue (1/94); January 2010.29. Rockville MD; Guideline on General Principles of Process Validation. U.S. Food and Drug Administration., U.S. FDA: 2010.
40. Dashora K, Singh D; Validation- The Essential Quality Assurance Tool for Pharma Industries. www.pharminfo.net. 2005; 3: 45-47.
41. Patel VB, Rathwa MR, Patel K; Studies in Prospective Process Validation of Cimetidine Tablet Dosage Form. International Journal of Research in Pharmaceutical and Biomedical Sciences, 2011; 2 (4): 1823-1836.
42. Sharma PP; Validation in Pharmaceutical Industry. 6th Edition, Vandana Publication, New Delhi, 2008; 91-115.
43. Health Canada / Health Products and Food Branch Inspectorate Validation Guidelines for Pharmaceutical Dosage Forms (GUI – 0029) /December 2009.
44. Rockville MD; Guide to Inspections of Oral Solid Dosage Forms pre/post Approval Issue for D28. U.S. Food and Drug Administration.
45. Jeena S; Industrial Process Validation of Solid Dosage Form. An Overview. International Journal of Pharmaceutical Science and Research, 2010; 4: 145-154.
46. South African Guide to Good Manufacturing Practice. Pretoria: Medicines Control Council, 1996.
47. Good Manufacturing Practices for Pharmaceutical products, WHO Expert Committee on Specifications for Pharmaceutical Preparations, 32nd Report, WHO Technical Report Series no. 823, WHO, Geneva, 1992: 14-96.
48. Loftus BT; The Regulatory Basis for Process Validation. Pharmaceutical Process Validation. Vol. 23, Marcel Dekker, New York, 1984: 1–7.
49. Singh H, Rana AC, Saini S, Singh G; Industrial Process Validation of Solid Dosage Form: A Review. International Journal of Research Pharmacy, 2012; 3 (4): 63-70.
50. WHO. Annex 4, Supplementary Guidelines on Good Manufacturing Practices: Validation, World Health Organization. Technical Report Series, No. 937, 2006, 116– 121.
51. Swarbrick J. *Encyclopedia of Pharmaceutical Technology*, 3rd ed. vol. 1. USA: Informa health care, 127– 128.
52. Agalloco, JP, Carleton FJ. *Validation of Aseptic Pharmaceutical Process*. 2nd ed. New York: Marcel Dekker, Inc., 2– 3.
53. Potdar AM. *Pharmaceutical Quality Assurance*, 2nd ed. Pune: Nirali Prakashan, 2007, 8.6

54. A working group of the Scottish Quality Assurance Specialist Interest Group. *Guideline On Test Methods For Environmental Monitoring For Aseptic Dispensing Facilities*, 2nd ed. February 2004, 3– 6.

55. Akers JE, Agalloco JP. The simplified Akers–Agalloco method for aseptic processing risk analysis. *Pharm Technol* 2006: 1– 8.

56. Lander V. 21 CFR part 11 and risk assessment: adapting fundamental methodologies to a current rule. *Pharm Technol Eur* 2004: 1– 3.

CHAPTER - 5

Process Validation

Importance of Validation, Validation of Mixing, Validation of Granulation, Validation of Drying, Validation of Compression, Validation of Tablet Coating, Validation of Liquid Filling and Sealing, Validation of Sterilization, Validation of Water Processing System, Validation of Environmental Control.

IMPORTANCE OF VALIDATION

Validation is a documented evidence of the consistency of any process or system. In 1978, it was first appeared in the United States by the Food and Drug Administration (FDA) to investigate the failure of the product in sterility. Now it is very common concept in pharmaceutical industries throughout the world[1-2].

Nowadays, validation of all major pharmaceutical systems and processes are very essential. It ensures the quality of manufactured products and helps to manufacture the quality of products.

Following are the advantages of the validation of any system or process.

- Process parameters and controls are determined during validation of any process or system.
- It helps to determine the worst case and risks that may come out during the manufacturing of the quality products.
- Validation may help to investigate the deviations caused during the process development.
- Deep study and understanding of the system and equipment are made possible due to validation.
- The risk of the regulatory non-compliance is minimized after the validation.
- A validated process requires less process control and the finished product testing.
- Batch to batch variation is reduced due to the validation of the processes, systems and equipment.
- Reduces the cost of production of the product.
- Increases the production of manufacturing facility due to reduced rework or rejection.
- Decreases the chances of failure of the batches.

Thus, validation is an important part of the pharmaceutical industry. It can ensure that the processes and products are safe, effective, and consistent. This can help to mitigate the risks associated with the pharmaceutical products and processes, making sure that the products, produced are of high quality, meet specifications, and are manufactured using appropriate processes. The pharmaceutical industry often struggles with over-validation, with companies feeling that they must check off every item on a validation checklist to make sure the compliance[3]. This can lead to unnecessary and redundant validation activities, slowing down the validation process and increasing costs.

To overcome this challenge, companies should start the validation as early as possible in the developmental process. This takes the advantage of implementation of new system to revisit and improve validation processes, implement new validation models on new systems. Companies should also stay up-to-date with the latest advances in technology, to better understand how it can impact the pharmaceutical processes and products, and to identify potential risks and opportunities for improvement in validation processes[4]. Sometimes, fear becomes a powerful motivator, especially in an industry where patient safety is of primary interest. People may worry that if they do not validate a product or process enough, there could be negative consequences such as patient harm or regulatory non-compliance. While it is important to ensure that products and processes are validated adequately. It is also necessary to consider the efficiency and effectiveness of the validation process and to avoid unnecessary or redundant validation activities. There are four things which could be done to validate the pharmaceutical industry:

1) *Learn how the technology works:* In today's technological age, it is essential to stay up-to-date with the latest advances in technology. By learning how technology works, one can better understand how it impacts the pharmaceutical processes and products. This knowledge can help to identify potential risks and opportunities for improvement in the validation processes.
2) *Start validation as early as you can:* Validation should start as early as possible in the development process to identify and address any potential issues before they become more challenging and costly to fix. Starting validation early can also help to reduce the risk of project delays and ensure that products are delivered on time.
3) T*ake advantage of new system implementation:* Implementing new systems provides an opportunity to revisit and improve validation processes. By taking advantage of a new system implementation, you can identify areas for improvement in your validation processes and implement changes that can help streamline the validation process.
4) *Implement new validation models on new systems:* The pharmaceutical industry is continually evolving, and new validation models are emerging.

By implementing new validation models on new systems, you can take advantage of the latest advances in validation and improve the efficiency and effectiveness of your validation processes.

At the end of the day, validation is critical to the pharmaceutical industry, ensuring that products and processes are safe, effective, and consistent. By balancing the need for compliance with the efficiency and effectiveness of validation processes, companies can ensure that they are delivering products that meet the highest standards of quality, safety, and efficacy[5].

Therefore, the importance of validation in pharmaceutical industry can be summarized as:

- Regulatory requirement (GMP, FDA, MHRA, TGA and other regulatory agencies)
- To confirm the process design as capable of reproducing commercial manufacturing and make the process better understood.
- To identify Risk/Worst Case assessment.
- To provide ongoing assurance that the process remains in a state of control during routine production through quality procedures and continuous improvement[6].
- Quantitatively (quantity of something rather than its quality) determine the variability of a process and its control.
- The variability within and between batches can be evaluated.
- Safeguard and process against sources of variation which may not have been identified during the original process development.
- The reason to optimize and validate pharmaceutical productions and supporting processes and cost reduction.
- Decreases the chances of the product failure and assures the smooth running of the process.
- Investigate the deviations if any from established process and Analytical parameters.
- Result obtained in the validation helps to take decision for the manufacturer regarding repeat the batch manufacturing.
- Validation is legible through the documentation establishment and it guarantees a manufacturing process with assured product quality[7].
- Deep study and understand the system and equipment are made possible due to validation.

Quality is always an imperative prerequisite when considered any product. Therefore, drugs must be manufactured to achieve a predictable therapeutic response. A drug in a formulation must be capable of large scale manufacture with reproducible and highest quality levels in the finished product.

Nowadays, the validation has become one of the pharmaceutical industry's most recognized, discussed subjects and fond in number of pharmaceutical industries. It is a critical success factor in product approval to get commercialization of the product. Among the various reasons for process validation, the first and primary reason is a regulatory requirement for almost every process in the global health care industry like pharmaceuticals, biologics, and medical devices. Regulatory bodies in the various countries across the world expect that the organization needs to validate their manufacturing processes. Once a process/product is systematically validated, it could be easily justified for the reduced sample size and intervals, which provide a measurable return on the effort of validation. Aside from utility systems, this is hardly ever realized and represents one of the major failings relative to the implementation of validation in pharmaceutical industry[8-10]. Nowadays more sophisticated drug delivery systems are introduced into the market, but tablets are still by far the most widespread solid dosage form in the global world.

Elements of Validation

The validation activities are performed in accordance with pre-approved written protocols. The facility, utilities, major manufacturing equipment and laboratory instruments should be qualified by performing Design Qualification (DQ)/ Installation Qualification (IQ)/Operational Qualification (OQ)/Performance Qualification (PQ) as per the approved protocols. Protocol is either be designed by the user department or supplied by the vendor. Preferably the skilled personnel engaged internally or externally conduct equipment / instrument qualification.

Design Qualification (DQ)

The DQ is aimed to specify that the equipment, system or facility is designed in accordance with the requirements of the user and Good Manufacturing Practice (GMP) guidelines. A protocol should be made for design requirements/technical specifications with consultation of the supplier and a report is documented for the same.

Installation Qualification (IQ)

Upon arrival of the equipment in the plant, it is first checked to ensure that the equipment is supplied as per the design requirements/technical specifications. The Engineering Department verify that the equipment and components are supplied in accordance with the specifications mentioned in (DQ). The equipment is then shifted to its predetermined location and place as per the equipment floor Plan. The IQ procedure comprises the following activities. The activities are

Confirmation to the parameter specified in DQ

1) Equipment description and identification
2) Verification of major components
3) Material of construction
4) Utilities connections
5) Calibration Requirements
6) Installation verification
7) IQ certification

Installation Qualification (IQ)

It is considered after completion of proper installation of the equipment. All the above mentioned parameters are to be verified and documented according to the approved IQ protocol. The validation team check, identify and prepare the list of the appropriate safety features given for different service lines and prepare a preventive maintenance program.

Operational Qualification (OQ)

During documented evidence of Operational Qualification (OQ) are being completed, all the parts of the equipment work within their specifications and operational parameters.

The OQ procedure includes the following:

1) Brief identification information.
2) Visual inspection parameters
3) Functioning of switches and indicator lights
4) Check the calibration off sensor, probes, gauges, recorders, air flow rates, directions, pressures, temperatures etc.
5) Filter integrity and efficiency test
6) Cleaning procedure
7) Control panel testing
8) Safety features testing
9) Operational testing according to the process and system requirements and challenges.
10) Training for operators and supervisors for operation and cleaning of equipment.

The equipment is operated for each operating component to verify that all operating features are functioning in accordance with the specifications. A special attention is to be given to service line connections and safety features. Critical devices are identified and calibrated against a standard device.

The completion of a successful operational qualification allow the finalization of calibration, operating and cleaning procedures, operator training and preventive requirements. It shall permit the formal "release" of the facilities, systems and equipment[11,12].

Performance Qualification (PQ)

Performance qualification is the final stage of qualification. It demonstrates that how the equipment / system will work when challenged under simulated or actual production conditions. A series of tests are designed to demonstrate that the equipment / system is capable to work consistently meeting the required specifications under routine production operations.

Principles of process qualification

Process validation is defined as *establishing documented evidence which provides a high degree of assurance that a specific system, related equipment and process consistently meet the approved specifications and produce products meeting predetermined quality attributes*[13-15].

Process validation

Process validation is a basic factor for drug product safety and quality and thus a fundamental component of the quality assurance system used by pharmaceutical manufacturers. The basic principle of Quality Assurance is that a drug should be produced that is fit for its intended use. Effective Process Validation contributes significantly to assure the drug quality; this principle incorporates the understanding that the following conditions exist:

- Quality, safety, and efficacy are designed or built into the product.
- Quality cannot be adequately assured merely by in-process and finished-product inspection or
- Each step of a manufacturing process is controlled to assure that the finished product meets all design characteristics and quality attributes including specifications.

Types of Process Validation

1) Prospective validation
2) Concurrent validation
3) Retrospective validation
4) Revalidation[16-19].

Prospective validation

Prospective validation is carried out during the development stage of a product. It is required for new manufacturing formulae or methods of preparation where the latter are adopted. The purpose is to ensure that the defined process is being carried out with consistent results, using the materials and equipment specified. It should be shown that a product of consistently and required quality is being yielded and quantity is proposed to do based on the pre-planned protocols. In this phase, the extent to which deviations from the chosen processing parameters can influence in the product quality is also to be evaluated. In general, the final batch size should not be more than 10 times the batch size of the representative development batches. The process should include identification and evaluation of individual steps, identification of critical situations, design of trial plans and set of priorities, performance of trials, recording of results, assessment and evaluation of observed results. If the results are unsatisfactory then the processes are modified and improved until acceptable results are obtained. This is essential to limit the risk and errors that may occur on production scale[20,21].

Retrospective validation

Retrospective validation is based on a review of historical manufacturing and testing data, and the analysis of accumulated results from past production to assess the consistency of a process. It is assumed that the composition, procedures and equipment remained unchanged.

During retrospective validation the results of in-process and final control tests are evaluated. A total of 10-25 batches (or more), manufactured over a period of 12 months, is used for reviewing the results, to provide a statistically significant picture. Quality control charts could be used when performing retrospective validation. Failure investigations should however, be performed separately. All difficulties and failures recorded are analysed to determine limits of process parameters and product-related problems. These should include rejections, complaints and returns. As retrospective validation is not considered to be a quality assurance measure, it should not be applied to new processes or products. Steps during retrospective validation includes

- Choosing a critical quality parameter, for example, assay value, unit dose uniformity, disintegration time and dissolution rate.
- Extracting the analytical results from each batch, the results of batch are grouped or subgroups.
- Pooling the results from the batches.
- Calculating the grand average, process average and control limits, upper and lower control limits.
- Plotting the results on graphs or charts.

Concurrent validation

Concurrent validation is carried out during normal production. This method of validation can only be successful if the development stage has resulted in a proper understanding of the fundamentals of the process. It is carried out during normal production of products intended for sale. It should involve close and intensive monitoring of the steps and critical points for at least first three production scale batches. The in-process control results are used to provide some of the evidence required for validation but these have no substitute for validation. Validation in the production unit mainly comprises of the determination and evaluation of the process parameters of the facilities applied for the scale-up to final batch size. The control of all critical process parameters, the results of the in-process controls, final controls and stability tests should prove the suitability of the important individual steps of a procedure.

Revalidation

In general, revalidation is exploratory review the current performance of the validation effect to confirm the validated status of the facilities, systems, equipment, manufacturing processes, software and testing.

Reasons for performing the revalidation process includes

- Transfer of a product from one plant to another plant.
- Changes made in the manufacturing process or other changes which might have impact in the quality of the product.
- Systematic periodic checking of the validation results.
- Change in the batch size.
- Consecutive fail in the batch to meet the predetermined specifications with respect to process and product.
- Revalidation procedures depend on the extent of the changes made in the process and the effect upon the product.

Process Design

The goal of this stage is to design a process suitable for routine commercial manufacturing that can consistently deliver a product that meets its quality attributes.

Process Qualification

This stage has two elements:

(1) design of the facility and qualification of the equipment and utilities and

(2) process performance qualification (PPQ).

Continued Process Verification

The purpose of the third validation stage is to obtain a continual assurance that the process remains in a state of control (the validated state) during commercial manufacture.

This lifecycle approach emphasizes the importance among three stages are:

1) Product/ process design and development,
2) Qualification of the commercial manufacturing equipment and its process
3) Maintenance of the process in a state of control during routine commercial production.

Process validation lifecycle approach between the three stages is shown in Fig.5.1.

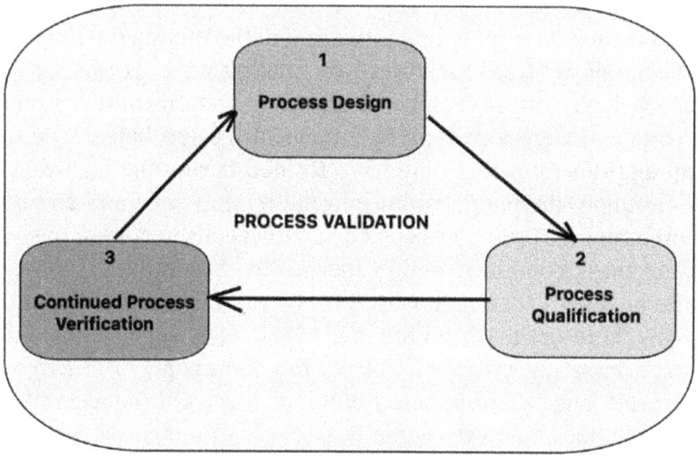

Fig.5.1 Process validation lifecycle approach between three stages.

VALIDATION OF MIXING

Mixing is a very critical and important step in preparation of various pharmaceutical substances. Tablet and capsules are the most commonly used and popular solid dosage form. In case of tablets or capsules, there may be continuous mixing process or traditional batch manufacturing process. The solid mixers are in general heterogenous. There is greater chance of separation of particles. However, this chance of separation can be reasonably reduced by reducing the size differences, shape differences and density differences. Since, density is a basic property of materials, shape and sizes are considered for modification. Nowadays, the former technique is in demand due to some definite advantages of the method. For example, smaller footprints of processing units and intermediate product storage, faster turnaround times and better control of quality parameters[22,23]. Continuous processing offers several advantages to improve the manufacturing efficiency of solid dosage forms: reduced costs through faster development and less scale-up, smaller equipment footprint and elimination of intermediate storage. Implementation of in-line process analysers allows to monitor continuous processes which improves process understanding. This enables the design of a process control and real-time-release strategy which should ultimately improve the quality of the end product [24,25]. Implementation of in-line process analysers allow to monitor continuous processes which improves process understanding. The simplest setup for a continuous tableting line is the continuous direct compression (CDC) process, consisting of three main unit operations: feeding of raw material, mixing of individual component streams and compressing the blends into the tablet dosage form. Various critical quality attributes (CQAs) of the final product, for example, the content and uniformity of content, are affected by the mixing step. Moreover, the tensile strength of final tablet depends on the extent of powder lubrication in the mixing device. Continuous Mixing Technology (CMT) features two rotating impellers stacked on top of each other in a cylindrical vessel with a conical section at the bottom. The top impeller rotates inside a delumping screen in the top half of the CMT and breaks up agglomerates that may have formed during the upstream process. After de-lumping, the particles fall into the mixing zone and are agitated by the bottom impeller. The CMT is placed on load cells to continuously measure the hold-up mass contained within the mixer. A control system constantly adjusts the opening of the motor-driven exit valve to control the outflow and to keep the hold-up mass within the CMT constant[26]. The initial study analysed the operating space of CMT at a low throughput (10 kg/h) with a free flowing blend and a formulation with a low API concentration. Such calibration method is known as the bulk calibration approach and is widely applied in the pharmaceutical field and beyond[27-30].

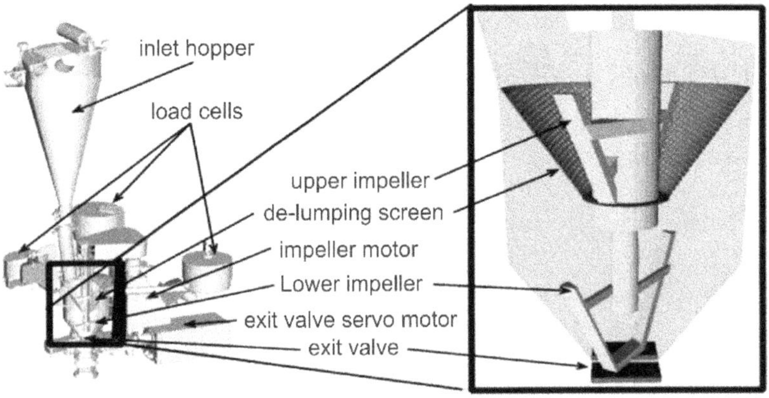

Fig.5.2 Continuous mixing technology: Comparison between a CAD drawing of the CMT and DEM model.

The bulk calibration approach has been applied to model vastly different types of granular media with different flow behaviour by adjusting the contact parameters. This implies that the change in flowability due to a different API particle size can also be modelled using different contact parameters, without the need to change the DEM particle size. The calibration routine reproduces small-scale characterization experiments: a compression and spring-back test for the plastic deformation and elastic recovery of the powder bed, and a shear cell test to measure the flowability, as already demonstrated in. Because previously calibrated contact models are available, the new formulations can be calibrated quickly by adjusting a limited set of contact parameters. This workflow is applicable as long as there are no fundamental changes in the powder behaviour, e.g. a segregation tendency or electrostatic charging. The obtained contact parameters are subsequently used in DEM simulations of the CMT, by replicating the experiments[31]. For validation, the raw residence time distributions (RTD) and the resulting predicted damping of feeder fluctuations in the DEM and tracer experiments are to be compared.

Validation experiments

For validation, 10 tracer experiments with two blends, two throughputs (15 kg/h and 30 kg/h) and varying hold-up masses, impeller speeds, mean residence times and total blade passes are performed. For example, the formulation contains API (Pfizer, Sandwich, United Kingdom); Microcrystalline Cellulose (MCC) (Avicel PH 102, FMC, Philadelphia, USA); Dicalcium Phosphate (DCP), Anhydrous, Granular (A-TAB, Innophos, NJ, USA); Sodium starch Glycolate (SSG), Type A (EXPLOTAB, JRS PHARMA GMBH & CO.KG, Rosenberg, Germany); and Magnesium Stearate (MgSt) NF VG (Impalpable Powder) Food Grade (HyQual, Mallinckrodt Pharmaceuticals, Saint Louis, USA). Details on the individual particle size distributions, experimental procedures and results are reported. The two blends of the same composition of microcrystalline cellulose, dicalcium phosphate, sodium starch glycolate and magnesium stearate and the API when prepared, the only difference between the blends is the API grade with a different particle size, resulting in blends with different flowability.

Characterization experiments

The blends were characterized in two experiments: (1) a compression test with spring-back (comparison in in the supplementary material) and (2) a shear cell test. Shear cell tests were performed using a pre-shear stress of 1 kPa and 4 kPa. The differences between the two blends vanish in a very confined flow regime at a higher normal stress of 4 kPa. At lower stresses, the large API blend had better flowability than the small API blend. In addition, lower stress states with 1 kPa are more representative for the conditions in the CMT. Thus, the shear cell results with 1 kPa were the basis for the calibration of the DEM parameters.

Homogeneity of mixer

Determination of homogeneous mixing of the active pharmaceutical ingredient (API) is an important in-process control within the manufacturing of solid dosage forms. The near-infrared (NIR) based methods can be used both for qualitative and quantitative analysis. Based on the calculation of net analyte signal (NAS) models which were very easy to develop, specific with respect to the API and required no additional reference analysis. This is used for monitoring the homogeneity of other batches with NIR.

A computer simulation model has been developed using finite element-based commercial software, to simulate the temperature distributions in wheat samples packed in a rectangular plastic container and treated in a 6 kW, 27.12 MHz RF system with and without mixing conditions. The developed model has then been experimentally validated by temperature distributions of three layers without mixing condition. The surface and interior temperature distributions of wheat samples under one, two and three times mixing conditions[32,33].

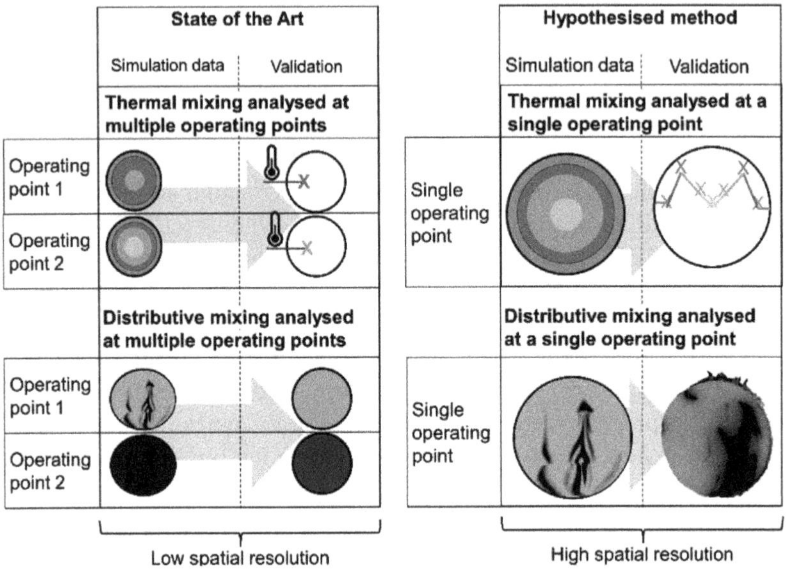

Fig.5.3 Validation of simulation of mixing elements in single-screw extrusion as done per state of the art (by comparing multiple operating points, with low spatial resolution) and as intended by the authors (at a single operating point with high spatial resolution).

VALIDATION OF GRANULATION

If the properties of a powder blend do not suit direct compression tabletting, manufacturers will turn to granulation processes to create the desired flowability and low dust ability. These characteristics are required to minimize tablet weight variations, and ensure high density for high tablet filling weight and high mouldability for hard tablet manufacture. However, granulation is a more time-consuming technique compared with direct compression and there is also a risk of product cross-contamination and product loss during the different processing steps (granulation, drying, sieving). All of these factors can increase costs compared with direct compression[34].

A. Wet Granulation

In wet-granulation, a liquid binder solution is combined with a bed of mixed powders to mass the particles together into granules. The damp mass is then screened, dried and milled to the desired size. The mass may also be dry screened, lubricated and compressed or extruded through a perforated screen and then dried.

I) What type of wet granulation technique will be used? Will it be low shear, high shear or fluid bed (e.g., Glatt, Fluid Air)? Each technique will produce granules with different physical properties and will require monitoring of different processing parameters.

II) *Binder addition:* Should the binder be added as a granulating solution or dry like the other excipients? Adding the binder dry avoids the need to determine the optimal binder concentration and a separate manufacture for the binder solution.

III) *Binder concentration:* The optimal binder concentration will need to be determined for the formulation. If the binder is to be sprayed, the binder solution needs to be dilute enough so that it can be pumped through the spray nozzle. It should also be sufficiently concentrated to form granules without over wetting the materials.

IV) *Amount of binder solution/granulating solvent:* How much binder or solvent solution is required to granulate the material? Too much binder or solvent solution will over wet the materials and prolong the drying time. The amount of binder solution is related to the binder concentration.

V) *Binder solution/granulating solvent addition rate:* Define the rate or rate range at which the binder solution or granulating solvent can be added to the materials. Can the granulating solution be dumped into the mixer or does it have to be metered in at a specific rate?

VI) *Mixing time:* How long should the material is mixed to ensure proper formation of granules? Should mixing stop after the addition of the binder or solvent solution or should additional mixing be required? Granulations that are not mixed long enough can form incomplete or weak granules. These granules may have poor flow and compression properties. On the other hand, over mixing the granulation can lead to harder granules and a lower dissolution rate.

VII) *Granulation end point:* How is the granulation end point determined? Is it determined or controlled by granulation end point equipment (e.g., ammeter or wattmeter)? Is it controlled by specifying critical processing parameters? For example, a drug or excipients mixture may be granulated by adding a predetermined amount of water (granulating solution) at a certain rate. The granulation is completed after mixing for a set time after the water has been added[35,36].

B. Dry granulation: In the dry granulation method the granulation is formed not by adding a binder. Here compacting large mass of the mixture and subsequently crushing and sizing these pieces into smaller granules takes place. The primary powder particles are aggregated under high pressure. There are two main processes. Either a large tablet (known as a slug) is produced in a heavy-duty tablet press (a process known as slugging) or the powder is squeezed between two rollers to produce a sheet of material (roller compaction). Wet Milling Does the wet granulation need to be milled to break up the lumps and enhance drying of the granulation? Wet granules that have a wide aggregate range can lead to inefficient drying (long drying times and partially dried large granules or lumps).

Factors to consider are

1) **Equipment size and capacity:** The mill should be large enough to de lump the entire batch within a reasonable time period to minimize manufacturing time and prevent the material from drying during this operation.
2) **Screen size:** The screen needs to be small enough to de lump the material, but not too small to cause excessive heating of the mill, resulting in drying of the granulation.
3) **Mill speed:** The speed should be sufficient to efficiently del ump the material without straining the equipment.
4) **Feed rate:** The feed rate of the wet granulation is interrelated to screen size and mill size and speed.

Drying

The type of drying technique (e.g., tray dryer, fluidized bed dryer, and microwave) required for the formulation needs to be determined and justified. The type of technique may depend on the factors such as (1) drug, (2) formulation properties, and (3) equipment availability. Changing dryer techniques could affect the tablet properties such as hardness, disintegration, dissolution, and stability. The optimal moisture content of the dried granulation needs to be determined. High moisture content can result in tablet picking or sticking to tablet punch surfaces and poor chemical stability as a result of hydrolysis. An over dried granulation could result in poor hardness and friability. Moisture content analysis can he performed using the conventional loss-on-drying techniques or near infrared (NIR) spectroscopy.

Factors to be considered are

- Inlet/outlet temperature
- Airflow
- Moisture uniformity
- Equipment capability/capacity[37].

Milling

The milling operation can reduce the particle size of the dried granulation. The resultant particle size distribution will affect such material properties as flow, compressibility, disintegration, and dissolution. An optimal particle size/size distribution for the formulation will need to be determined.

Factors to consider in milling are

- Mill type
- Screen size
- Mill speed
- Feed rate

Lubrication

1. **Selection of lubricant:** what kind of lubricant should be used? Grade of the lubricant used. Compatibility with other ingredients.
2. **Amount of lubricant added:** How much lubricant is required? Too much lubricant will form hydrophobic layer on the tablet resulting in dissolution problems.
3. **Mixing time:** How long should the material is mixed to ensure proper formation? Should mixing stop after the addition of the lubricant or should additional mixing be required? If not mixed long enough form problems like chipping, capping, etc[38].

Table 5.1 Control parameters for granulation process.

Fixed Parameters	Variable Parameters (to be monitored)	Response (Test to be conducted)
Name of the Equipment	Mixing speeds Amount of granulation Fluid feed rate granulation Time of Loading	Drug distribution Water/ solvent Appearance (size) Power consumption (amp/torque)

VALIDATION OF DRYING

The type of drying technique (e.g., tray, fluid bed, and microwave) required for the formulation needs to be determined and justified. The type of technique may depend on factors such as drug or formulation properties, equipment availability. Changing drying techniques could affect the tablet properties such as hardness, disintegration, dissolution, and stability. The optimal moisture content of the dried granulation needs to be determined. High moisture content can result in

(1) Tablet picking or sticking to tablet punch surfaces and

(2) Poor chemical stability as a result of hydrolysis.

An over dried granulation could result in poor hardness and friability. Moisture content analysis can he performed using the conventional loss-on-drying techniques or near infrared (NIR) spectroscopy.

- Inlet/outlet temperature

  The inlet temperature is the temperature of the incoming air to the dryer, while the outlet temperature is the temperature leaving the unit. The inlet temperature is critical to the drying efficiency of the granulation and should be set high enough to maximize drying without affecting the chemical/ physical stability of the granulation. The outlet temperature is an indicator of the granulation temperature and will increase toward the inlet temperature as the moisture content of the granulation decreases (vaporization rate).

- Airflow

  There should be sufficient airflow to ensure removal of moisture laden air from the wet granulation. Insufficient airflow could prolong drying and affect the chemical stability of the drug. Airflow and the inlet/outlet temperature are interrelated parameters and should be considered together.

- Moisture uniformity

  The moisture content could vary within the granulation. Heat uniformity of the dryer (e.g., tray), amount of granulation per tray, and incomplete fluidization of the bed are factors that could affect the moisture uniformity of the granulation.

- Equipment capability/capacity

  The load that can be efficiently dried within the unit needs to be known. A larger load will require more moisture to be removed on drying and will affect the drying time. In the case of fluid bed drying, a maximum dryer load is that load above which the dryer will not fluidize the material. Table 5.1 shows the control parameters for granulation process.

Table 5.2 Control parameters for drying in fluidized bed dryer and sizing process.

Fixed Parameters	Variable Parameters (to be monitored)	Response (Test to be conducted)
Bowl charge	Inlet/ exhaust air temperature	Particle size distribution
Porosity of filter bags	Product temperature	Densities
Bowl sieve	Drying time	Loss on drying
	Air volume Humidity of incoming air (dew point) Humidity of exhaust air	Assay (for heat sensitive materials)

When a tray dryer is used for drying the material the control parameters do not remain same. The Table 5.3 indicates those parameters. In this method the material to. be dried is sprayed in layer in the trays. The trays are then loaded in the dryer, the temperature is adjusted and switched on the dryer. After specific period, the material is checked for loss on drying to see whether drying has been completed.

Table 5.3 Control parameters for drying using tray dryer.

Fixed Parameters	Variable Parameters (to be monitored)	Response (Test to be conducted)
Tray dryer	• Inlet/exhaust air temperature • Thickness of the layer spreaded over • Drying period	Loss on drying

Table 5.4 Control of parameters for milling.

Variable parameters	Response
Screen size Milling speed Feed rate	Particle size distribution Loose/ tapped densities

Table 5.5 Control of parameters for powder blending.

Variable parameters	Response
Blending time Blender speed Intensifier bar Method of addition	Content uniformity Assay Particle size distribution Powder flow Tabletting characteristics (Friability, hardness)

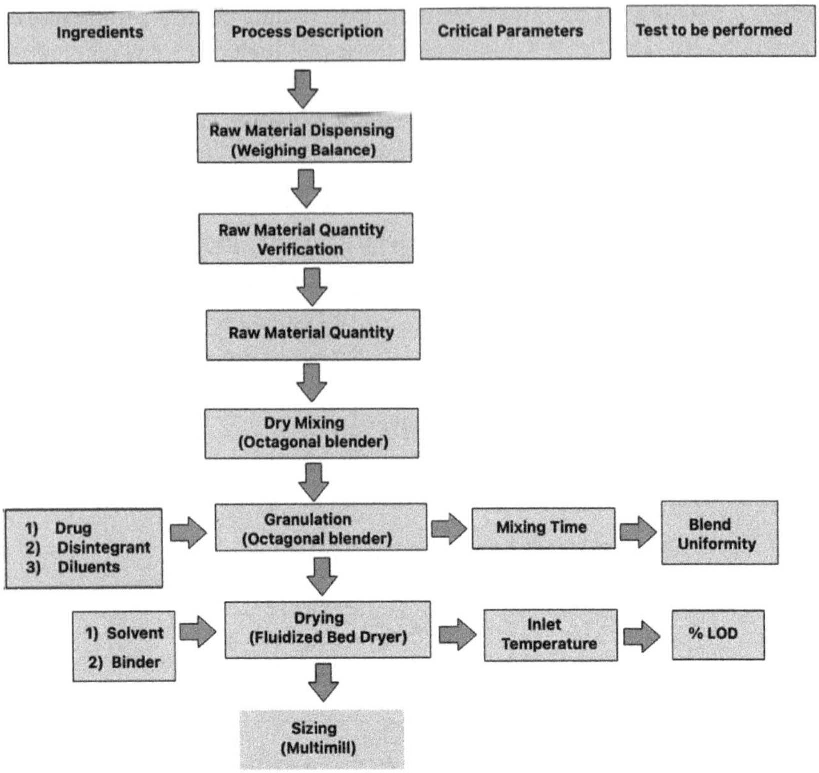

Fig.5.6 Process flow chart for granulation, drying and milling (sizing).

Stage	Sample Location	Sample Size	Test
Dry Mixing	Three sample of approx.. 1g each from top, middle, and bottom of the octagonal blender after 30 min of blending.	Approx. 300 mg per each Location	Blend uniformity Assay
Drying		Approx. 5 g per each location	Loss on drying
Lubrication	Unit dose samples shall be withdrawn from 11 different location of the blender comprising of upper, middle, lower layer, and bottom layer after 3 minutes mixing with lubricant in octagonal blender.	Approx. 1100 mg	Blend uniformity

Table ***contd...***

	Approx. 300 g of lubricated bulk blend to be sampled for evaluation Of physical characteristics.	Approx. 300 g	Physical Characteristics Description Tapped density Bulk density Angle of repose Particle size analysis Sieve analysis Assay
Compression Minimum speed Optimum Speed Maximum speed	During compression, samples to be collected and mixed from both sides of press (RHS and LHS) at initial, middle and at the end of compression operation.	150 tablets at each stage	Description Average weight Uniformity of weight Disintegration time Friability Hardness Thickness Dissolution Content uniformity Assay

VALIDATION OF COMPRESSION

Compression is a critical step in the production of a tablet dosage form. The materials being compressed will need to have adequate flow and compression properties. The material should readily flow from the hopper onto the feed frame and into the dies. Inadequate flow can result in "rat holing" in the hopper and/ or segregation of the blend in the hopper/feed frame. This can cause tablet weight and content uniformity problems. As for the compressibility properties of the formulation, it should be examined on an instrumented tablet press.

Factors to consider during compression are as follows:

Tooling:

The shape, size, and concavity of the tooling should be examined based on the formulation properties and commercial specifications. For intagliated (embossed) tablets, factors such as the position of the intagliation on the tablet and the intagliation depth and style should be examined to ensure that picking of the intagliation during compression or fill-in of the intagliation during coating does not occur.

Compression speed:

The formulation should be compressed at a wide range of compression speeds to determine the operating range of the compressor. The adequacy of the material's flow into the dies will be determined by examining the tablet weights. Is a force feeder required to ensure that sufficient material is fed into the dies?

Compression/ejection force:

The compression profile for the tablet formulation will need to be determined to establish the optimal compression force to obtain the desired tablet hardness. The particle size/size distribution or level of lubricant may need to be adjusted in order to have a robust process on a high-speed compressor.

The following in-process tests should be examined during the compression stage:

- Appearance
- Hardness
- Tablet weight
- Friability
- Disintegration
- Weight uniformity

VALIDATION OF TABLET COATING

Tablets may be coated for various reasons.

Stability

- Taste masking controlled release product identification.
- Aesthetics safety–material handling.

Tablet coating can occur by different techniques, such as, sugar, film, or compression. Film coating has been the most common technique over recent years and will be the focus of this section.

Key areas to consider for tablet coating include the following:

Tablet properties

Tablet properties such as hardness, shape, and intagliation (if required) are important to obtain a good film-coated tablet. The tablet needs to be hard enough to withstand the coating process. If tablet attrition occurs, the tablets will have a rough surface appearance. For tablet shape, a round tablet will be easier to coat than tablets will multiple sides or edges because of the uniformity of the surface. For intagliated tablets, the intagliation style and depth should be developed to prevent fill-in or chipping of the intagliation.

Equipment type

The type of coater will need to be selected. Conventional or perforated pan and fluid bed coaters are potential options.

Coater load

What is the acceptable tablet load range of the equipment? Having too large a pan-load could cause attrition of the tablets because of the overall tablet weight in the coater. In the case of a fluid bed coater, there may not be sufficient airflow to fluidize the tablets.

Pan speed

What is the optimal pan speed? This will be interrelated to other coating parameters, such as inlet temperature, spray rate, and flow rate.

Spray guns

The number and types of guns should be determined in order to efficiently coat the tablets. The spray nozzles should be sized properly to ensure even distribution over the tablet bed and to prevent clogging of the nozzles. The location and angle of the spray gun(s) should be positioned to get adequate coverage. Having the guns positioned too close together can lead to a portion of the tablets to be over-wet.

Application/spray rate

The optimal application/spray rate should be determined. Spraying too fast will cause the tablets to become over wet, resulting in clumping of tablets and possible dissolution of the tablet surface. Spraying too slowly will cause the coating materials to dry prior to adhesion to the tablets. This will result in a rough tablet surface and poor coating efficiency.

Tablet flow

The flow or movement of the tablets in the coater should be examined to ensure proper flow. There should be sufficient tablet bed movement to ensure even distribution of the coating solution onto the tablets. The addition of baffles may be required to provide adequate movement of tablets for tablet coating.

Inlet/outlet temperature and airflow

These parameters are interrelated and should be set to ensure that the atomized coating solution reaches the tablet surface and then is quickly dried.

Coating solution

The concentration and viscosity of the coating solution will need to be determined. The solution will need to be sufficiently diluted in order to spray the material on the tablets. The concentration of the coating solution will also determine the amount and volume of solution to be applied to the tablets. The stability of the coating solution should be investigated to establish its shelf life.

Coating weight

A minimum and maximum coating weight should be established for the tablet. Sufficient coating material should be applied to the tablets to provide a uniform appearance; however, it should not be great enough to cause fill-in of the intagliation.

Residual solvent level

If solvents are used for tablet coating, the residual solvent level will need to be determined.

Appearance testing of the tablets is critical during the coating operation. Items to look for include the following:

- Cracking or peeling of the coating Intagliation fill-in
- Surface roughness
- Colour uniformity

Coating efficiency should be determined for the coating operation. The efficiency will determine the amount of coating solution overage that may be required.

VALIDATION OF LIQUID FILLING AND SEALING

The production of liquid preparations should be carried out in clean areas, entry to which should be through airlocks for personnel and/or for equipment and materials. Clean areas should be maintained to an appropriate standard of cleanliness and supplied with air that has passed through filters of the required efficiency. The various operations of component preparation (such as those involving containers and closures), product preparation, filling and sterilization should be carried out in separate areas within the clean area. These areas are classified into four grades. Manufacturing operations are divided here into two categories:

— first, those where the product is terminally sterilized; and

— second, those which are conducted after filtration.

Quality Control

The test applied to the finished product should only be regarded as the last in a series of control measures by which quality is assured. The test should be validated for the product(s) concerned.

Samples should be taken for testing should be representative of the whole of the batch but should, in particular, include samples taken from parts of the batch considered to be most at risk of contamination, for example:

- for products that have been filled aseptically, samples should include containers filled at the beginning and end of the batch and after any significant interruption of work;
- for products that have been heat sterilized in their final containers, consideration should be given to taking samples from that part of the load that is potentially the coolest.

The finished product is assured by validation of the sterilization cycle in the case of terminally sterilized products. Batch-processing records and the environmental quality records, should be examined in conjunction with the results of the tests. The test procedure should be validated for a given product. Pharmacopeial methods should be used for the validation and performance of the test. In those cases where parametric release has been authorized in place of testing special attention should be paid to the validation and the monitoring of the entire manufacturing process.

For injectable products the water for injection and the intermediate, if appropriate, and finished products should be monitored for endotoxins, using an established pharmacopeial method that has been validated for each type of product. For large-volume infusion solutions, such monitoring of water or intermediates should always be done, in addition to any tests required by an approved monograph for the finished product. When a sample fails a test, the cause of the failure should be investigated and necessary action should be taken. Alternative methods to those in the pharmacopoeias may be used if they are validated, justified and authorized.

The use of rapid microbiological methods to replace the traditional microbiological methods, and to obtain earlier results on the microbiological quality of, for example, water, the environment or bioburden, could be considered if appropriately validated and if a comparative assessment of the proposed rapid method is performed against the pharmacopeial method.

Only the minimum number of personnel required should be present in clean areas; this is particularly important during aseptic processes. As far as possible, inspections and controls should be conducted from outside such areas.

All personnel (including those concerned with cleaning and maintenance) employed in such areas should receive initial and regular training in disciplines relevant to the correct manufacture of sterile products, including hygiene and the basic elements of microbiology. When outside staff who have not received such training (e.g. building or maintenance contractors) need to be brought in, particular care should be taken over their instruction and supervision.

Changing and washing should follow a written procedure designed to minimize the contamination of clean-area clothing or the carry-through of contaminants to clean areas. The clothing and its quality should be appropriate for the process and the grade of the working area. It should be worn in such a way as to protect the product from contamination.

Wrist-watches, cosmetics and jewellery should not be worn in clean areas.

Clothing used in clean areas should be laundered or cleaned in such a way that it does not gather additional particulate contaminants that can later be shed. Separate laundry facilities for such clothing are desirable. If fibres are damaged by inappropriate cleaning or sterilization, there may be an increased risk of shedding particles. Washing and sterilization operations should follow standard operating procedures.

A conveyor belt should not pass through a partition between a Grade A or B clean area and a processing area of lower air cleanliness, unless the belt itself is continuously sterilized (e.g. in a sterilizing tunnel).

Whenever possible, equipment used for processing sterile products should be chosen so that it can be effectively sterilized by steam or dry heat or other methods. As far as possible, equipment fittings and services should be designed and installed so that operations, maintenance and repairs can be carried out outside the clean area. Equipment that has to be taken apart for maintenance should be re-sterilized after complete reassembly, wherever possible.

When equipment maintenance is carried out within a clean area, clean instruments and tools should be used and the area should be cleaned and disinfected again, where appropriate, before processing recommences, if the required standards of cleanliness and/or asepsis have not been maintained during the maintenance work.

All equipment such as sterilizers, air-handling and filtration systems, air vent and gas filters, water treatment, generation, storage and distribution systems should be subject to validation and planned maintenance; their return to use should be approved.

Water-treatment plants and distribution systems should be designed, constructed and maintained so as to ensure a reliable source of water of an appropriate quality. They should not be operated beyond their designed capacity. Consideration should be given to including a testing programme in the maintenance of a water system. Water for injection should be produced, stored and distributed in a manner which prevents the growth of microorganisms, e.g. by constant circulation at a temperature above 70°C or not more than 4°C[45].

VALIDATION OF STERILIZATION

Whenever the products are intended to be sterile should be sterilized by any suitable method. There are various methods of sterilization. Depending on the type of product a particular method of sterilization is selected. The methods of sterilization are

1) Dry heat sterilization,
2) Moist heat sterilization,
3) Sterilization by radiation,
4) Sterilization by gases and fumigants.
5) Sterilization by filtration (Cold sterilization)

Sterilization can be achieved by the use of moist or dry heat, by irradiation with ionizing radiation (noting that ultraviolet irradiation is not normally an acceptable method of sterilization), by ethylene oxide (or other suitable gaseous sterilizing agents), or by filtration with subsequent aseptic filling of sterile final containers. Each method has its advantages and disadvantages. Where possible and practicable, heat sterilization is the method of choice. In any case the sterilization process must be in accordance with the marketing and manufacturing authorizations.

Before any sterilization process is adopted, its suitability for the product and its efficacy in achieving the desired sterilizing conditions in all parts of each type of load to be processed should be demonstrated by physical measurements and by biological indicators, where appropriate. The validity of the process should be verified at scheduled intervals, at least annually, and whenever significant modifications have been made to the equipment. Records should be kept of the results.

The dry heat sterilization is suitable for glassware, non-aqueous liquids or dry-powder products, etc. Of course the powders must be stable to heat, that is it should neither melt nor decompose. This means that the solids to sterilized by dry heat have melting point higher than the sterilizing temperature, which is about 170°C(350oF).

Next is sterilization by moist heat, that is, using boiling water or saturated steam. This method is suitable for sterilization of solution filled in pre-sterilized glass bottles or vials, media used for microbiology, bandages, etc. Since this method is used after filling and sealing, the method is called as terminal sterilization. Generally, such terminal sterilization is done at 121 – 123°C for 30 – 45 mins. Where it is not possible to carry out terminal sterilization by heating due to the instability of a formulation or incompatibility of a pack type (necessary to the administration of the product, e.g. plastic eye-dropper bottles), a decision should be taken to use an alternative method of sterilization following filtration and/or aseptic processing. The microbial contamination of starting materials should be minimal and the bioburden should be monitored before sterilization. Specifications should include requirements for microbiological quality when the need for this has been indicated by monitoring.

Normally, the microorganisms are arrested by filtering the solution through 0.22μ membrane filter. The solution is filtered through this filter under aseptic condition.

All sterilization processes should be validated. Particular attention should be paid when the adopted sterilization method is not in accordance with pharmacopeial standards or other national standards, or when it is used for a preparation that is not a simple aqueous or oily solution, for example, colloidal suspensions.

For effective sterilization the whole of the material should be subjected to the required treatment and the process should be designed to ensure that this is achieved.

Biological indicators should be considered only as an additional method of monitoring the sterilization process. The filled and sterilized containers should be stored and used according to the manufacturer's instructions, and their quality are checked by positive controls. Validated loading patterns should be established for all sterilization processes. Sterilization records should be available for each sterilization run. They should be approved as part of the batch-release procedure.

1) Sterilization by dry heat

Sterilization by dry heat may be suitable for non-aqueous liquids or dry-powder products. The process used should include air circulation within the chamber and the maintenance of a positive pressure to prevent the entry of non-sterile air. If air is supplied it should be passed through a microorganism-retaining filter, such as a HEPA filter. Where sterilization by dry heat is intended to remove pyrogens, challenge tests using endotoxins are required as a part of the validation.

- 170°C (340F) for 1 hour (total cycle time—placing instruments in oven, heating to 170°C, timing for 1 hour, and then cooling is from 2– 2.5 hours), or 160°C (320F) for 2 hours (total cycle time is from 3–3.5 hours).
- Exposure time begins only after the sterilizer has reached the target temperature.
- Do not overload the sterilizer. (Leave at least 7.5 cm [3 inches] between the items and walls of sterilizer.) Overloading alters heat convection and increases the time required to sterilize.

Sterile instruments and other items should be used immediately unless they:

- were wrapped in a double layer of muslin, paper or other appropriate material prior to sterilization; or
- can be stored in a dry, sterile container with a tight-fitting lid.

The material used for wrapping the instruments and other items must be porous enough to allow the steam to pass through but tightly woven enough to protect against dust particles and microorganisms. Wrapped sterile packs should remain sterile until the package or container become contaminated. In case of a tear or worn area in the wrapping, the package become wet or anything else that will allow microorganisms to enter the package or container.

Dry-heat sterilization is completed by thermal (heat) conduction. Initially, heat is absorbed by the exterior surface of an item and then passed to the next layer. Eventually, the entire object reaches the temperature required for sterilization. Death of microorganisms takes place with dry heat by a process of slow destruction of protein. Dry-heat sterilization generally, takes longer than steam sterilization, because the moisture in the steam sterilization process heat can significantly penetrates and shortens the time needed to kill the microorganisms.

To ensure correct operation, specific operating instructions supplied by the oven's manufacturer may be consulted. Otherwise, following steps are to be followed:

1) Decontaminate, clean and dry all instruments and other items to be sterilized.
2) If desired, wrap instruments in aluminium foil or place in a metal container with a tight-fitting, closed lid. Wrapping helps prevent recontamination prior to use. Hypodermic or suture needles should be placed in glass tubes with cotton stoppers.
3) Place loose (unwrapped) instruments in metal containers or on trays in the oven and heat to desired temperature.
4) After the desired temperature is reached, begin timing. The following temperature/time ratios are recommended (APIC 2002):

<table>
<tr><th>Temperature</th><th>Duration (Hours)</th><th>Total time-cycle</th></tr>
<tr><td>170°C (340°F)</td><td>1</td><td rowspan="5">Depending on the temperature selected, the total time- cycle will vary from about 2.5 hours at 170°C to more than 8 hours at 121°C.
Total time-cycle = preheating time + sterilization time + cooling down time.</td></tr>
<tr><td>160°C (320°F)</td><td>2</td></tr>
<tr><td>150°C (300°F)</td><td>2.5</td></tr>
<tr><td>140°C (285°F)</td><td>3</td></tr>
<tr><td>121°C (250°F)</td><td>overnight</td></tr>
</table>

5) After cooling, remove packs and/or metal containers and store. Loose items should be removed with sterile forceps/pickups and used immediately or placed in a sterile container with a tight-fitting lid.

Note:

(1) When using dry heat to sterilize instruments wrapped in cloth, be sure that temperature does not exceed 170°C/340°F.

(2) Use dry heat only for items that can withstand a temperature of 170°C (340°F).

(3) Needles and other instruments with cutting edges should be sterilized at lower temperatures160°C (320°F), because higher temperatures can destroy the sharpness of cutting edges.

2) Sterilization by moist heat

Of the methods currently available, steam sterilization is preferred. Steam is an effective sterilant for two reasons. First, saturated steam is an extremely effective "carrier" of thermal energy. It is many times more effective in conveying this type of energy to the item than is hot (dry) air. In a kitchen, potatoes can be cooked in a few minutes in a steam pressure cooker while cooking may take an hour or more in a hot-air oven, even though the oven is operated at a much higher temperature. Steam, especially under pressure, carries thermal energy to the potatoes very quickly, while hot air does so very slowly. Second, steam is an effective sterilant because any resistant, protective outer layer of the microorganisms can be softened by the steam, allowing coagulation (similar to cooking an egg white) of the sensitive inner portions of the microorganism. Certain types of contaminants, however, especially greasy or oily materials, can protect microorganisms against the effects of steam, thus hindering the process of sterilization. This reemphasizes the need for thorough cleaning of objects before sterilization.

Unless otherwise special instruction is given, the following steps are to be followed:

1) Decontaminate, clean and dry all instruments and other items to be sterilized.
2) All jointed instruments should be in the opened or unlocked position, while instruments composed of more than one part or sliding parts should be disassembled.
3) Instruments should not be held tightly together by rubber bands or any other means that will prevent steam contact with all surfaces.
4) Arrange packs in the chamber to allow free circulation and penetration of steam to all surfaces.
5) When using a steam sterilizer, it is best to wrap clean instruments or other clean items in a double thickness of muslin or newsprint. (Unwrapped

instruments must be used immediately after removal from the sterilizer, unless kept in a covered, sterile container.)

If a pressure cooker or kerosene-powered (nonelectric) gravity displacement steam sterilizer is used, bring the water to a boil and let steam escape from the pressure valve; then turn down heat, but keep steam coming out of the pressure valve.

6) Sterilize at 121C (250F) for 30 minutes for wrapped items, 20 minutes for unwrapped items; time with a clock.
7) Wait 20 to 30 minutes (or until the pressure gauge reads zero) to permit the sterilizer to cool sufficiently. Then open the lid or door to allow steam to escape. Allow instrument packs to dry completely before removal, which may take up to 30 minutes. (Wet packs act like a wick drawing in bacteria, viruses and fungi from the environment.) Wrapped instrument packs are considered unacceptable if there are water droplets or visible moisture on the package exterior when they are removed from the steam sterilizer chamber. If using rigid containers (e.g., drums), close the gaskets.
8) To prevent condensation, when removing the packs from the chamber, place sterile trays and packs on a surface padded with paper or fabric.
9) After sterilizing, items wrapped in cloth or paper are considered sterile as long as the pack remains clean, dry (including no water stains) and intact. Unwrapped items must be used immediately or stored in covered, sterile containers.

Ideally,

- a steam sterilizer log-book should be maintained wherein time is to be noted.
- heat begun,
- correct temperature and pressure achieved,
- heat turned down, and
- heat turned off.

Keeping a log can help ensure that the required amount of time will be observed, even when multiple, new or hurried workers are responsible for overseeing sterilization.

Note:

1) Devices and instruments that are not heat-resistant or are difficult to clean should be incinerated.
2) WHO recommends that contaminated instruments be steam sterilized while they are still soaking in NaOH. This practice, however, is not recommended because of the additional risk of sterilizer damage and exposure of health workers to chemical toxicity. A warning regarding this

practice has been posted on the CDC website (http://www.cdc.gov /ncidod /diseases/cjd/cjd_inf_ctrl_qa.hun).

3) NaOH is caustic and after use must be neutralized before being disposed of by diluting with large amounts of tap water or addition of an acid, such as hydrochloric acid.
4) To prevent dulling of sharp points and cutting edges, wrap the sharp edges and needle points in gauze before sterilizing. Repair (sharpen) or replace instruments, if required.
5) Do not allow to boil, dry steam should always be escaping from the pressure valve.
6) Do not store trays or packs until they reach room temperature. This usually takes about an hour.

3) Sterilization by radiation

Sterilization by radiation is used mainly for heat-sensitive materials and products. Many pharmaceutical products and some packaging materials are radiation-sensitive, so this method is permissible only when the absence of deleterious effects on the product has been confirmed experimentally. Ultraviolet irradiation is generally done by exposing the material to UV radiation for certain period of time. Of course, this method is done under aseptic condition.

If sterilization by radiation is done by an outside contractor, the manufacturer is responsible for ensuring that the requirements of section are met and the sterilization process is validated.

During the sterilization procedure the radiation dose should be measured. The dosimeters used for this purpose should be independent of the dose rate and should provide a quantitative measurement of the dose received by the product itself. Dosimeters should be inserted in the load in sufficient number and close enough together to ensure that there is always a dosimeter in the chamber. Where plastic dosimeters are used they should be used within the time-limit of their calibration. Dosimeter absorbance should be read shortly after exposure to radiation. Radiation-sensitive colour discs may be used to differentiate between packages that have been subjected to irradiation; they are not indicators of successful sterilization. The information obtained should constitute part of the batch record. Validation procedures should ensure that consideration has been given to the effects of variations in the density of the packages.

Material-handling procedures should prevent any mix-up of irradiated and non-irradiated materials. Each package should carry a radiation-sensitive indicator to show whether or not it has been subjected to radiation treatment. The total radiation dose should be administered within a predetermined period.

4) Sterilization by gases and fumigants

Sterilization by gases and fumigants should only be used for finished products where there is no suitable alternative.

Various gases and fumigants may be used for sterilization, such as, ethylene oxide and hydrogen peroxide vapour. Ethylene oxide should be used only when no other method is practicable. During the process-validation, it should be shown that the gas has no damaging effect on the product and that the conditions and time allowed for degassing are sufficient to reduce any residual gas and reaction products to defined acceptable limits for the type of product or material concerned. These limits should be incorporated in the specifications.

Direct contact between the gas and microorganisms is essential; therefore, precautions should be taken to avoid the presence of organisms likely to be enclosed in materials such as crystals or dried protein. The nature and quantity of packaging materials can significantly affect the process. Before exposure to the gas, the materials should be brought into equilibrium with the humidity and temperature required by the process. This requirement should be balanced against the need to minimize the waiting time before sterilization.

Each sterilization cycle should be monitored with suitable biological indicators, using the appropriate number of test pieces distributed throughout the load. The information thus obtained should form the part of the batch record. Biological indicators should be stored and used according to the manufacturer's instructions and their performance should be checked by positive controls.

For each sterilization cycle, records should be made about the time taken to complete the cycle, the pressure, temperature and humidity maintained within the chamber during the process and about the gas concentration. The pressure and temperature should be recorded on a chart throughout the cycle. The records should form the part of the batch record. After sterilization, the load should be stored in a controlled manner in ventilated conditions to allow concentrations of residual gas and reaction products to fall to their prescribed levels. This process should be validated.

The objective of aseptic processing is to maintain the sterility of a product that is assembled from components, each of which has been sterilized by one of the above methods. The operating conditions should be such as to prevent microbial contamination.

In order to maintain the sterility of the components and the product during aseptic processing, careful attention needs to be given to:

- the environment;
- personnel;

- o critical surfaces;
- o container/closure sterilization and transfer procedures;
- o the maximum holding period of the product before filling into the final container; and
- o the sterilizing filter.

5) Sterilization by Filtration

Certain solutions and liquids that cannot be sterilized in the final container can be filtered through a sterile filter of nominal pore size 0.22 micron (or less), or with at least equivalent microorganism-retaining properties, into a previously sterilized container. Such filters can remove bacteria and moulds, but not all viruses or mycoplasmas. Consideration should be given to complementing the filtration process with some degree of heat treatment. Filtration alone is not considered sufficient when sterilization in the final container is possible. Owing to the potential additional risks of the filtration method as compared with other sterilization processes, a double-filter layer or second filtration through a further sterilized microorganism-retaining filter immediately prior to filling may be advisable. The final sterile filtration should be carried out as close as possible to the filling point.

The fibre-shedding characteristics of filters should be minimal (virtually zero). Asbestos-containing filters should not be used under any circumstances.

The integrity of the sterilized filter should be verified before use and should be confirmed immediately after use by an appropriate method such as a bubble point, diffusive flow or pressure hold test. The time taken to filter a known volume of bulk solution and the pressure difference to be used across the filter should be determined during validation and any significant differences from these during routine manufacturing should be noted and investigated. Results of these checks should be included in the batch record. The integrity of critical gas and air vent filters should be confirmed after use. The integrity of other filters should be confirmed at appropriate intervals. Consideration should be given to increased monitoring of filter integrity in processes that involve harsh conditions, e.g. the circulation of high-temperature air.

The same filter should not be used for more than one working day unless such use has been validated. The filter should not affect the product either by removing ingredients from it or by releasing substances into it.

VALIDATION OF WATER PROCESSING SYSTEM

The water is extensively used substance and raw material for manufacturing, processing and formulation of pharmaceuticals. Therefore, it plays an important role in pharmaceutical processing. Purified water is obtained from consuming water through a typical water purification system. The validation of water processing system is essential to get water with all quality characteristics[46].

Validation Requirement

To reduce the batch variations. To acquire an efficient, good and pure product.

Water for Pharmaceutical Purpose

The quality characteristics of water for a specific purpose depends on the requirement of its usage. Sequential processing steps are given below accompanying for treating water for distinctive reason.

Material of Construction and Component selection

The installation technique is important because they can affect the mechanical, sanitary, corrosiveness of the system.

Valve installation characteristics

It promotes the gravity-drainage. Pipe support provide suitable slope for drainage and must be designed to help the piping appropriately under worst case thermal conditions.

Methods of connecting device

Component such as unit of operation, the tank and distribution piping, all require careful attention to prevent potential problem. Stainless steel welds must provide reliable joint which are internally smoothened and made corrosion free. Low carbon stainless steel, compatible with filter, wherein necessary inert gas, automatic welding machine and regular inspection, documentation assist to ensure the acceptable weld quality. Follow up cleaning and passivation are necessary for removing contamination and corrosion of the product to reset up the passive corrosion resistant surface. Plastic material are fused in some cases to get a required smooth, uniform internal surface. Adhesive should be avoided because it may create the chance of voids and chemical reaction. Mechanical technique of joining such as flange fitting, requires a sufficient care to avoid the creation of offset, gap, penetration. Void control measure includes good alignment, properly sized gasket, appropriate spacing, uniform sealing force[49].

It must be selected to be well suited with control measure consisting of cleaning, sanitizing, passivating. Temperature score is an essential factor in selecting suitable material due to the fact that surface can be improved by operating and sanitization temperature. Material must be able to handling turbulent flow and improve velocities without wear on the corrosive barrier effect such as passivation related chromium oxide surface of stainless steel.

Validation and Qualification of Water Purification, Storage and Distribution System

Establishment of the pharmaceutical water purification, storage, and distribution system required, depends on suitable duration of monitoring and observation.

Simply, few problems can be observed in preserving the chemical purity of purified water and water for Injection. However, it is more difficult to fulfil established microbiology, quality criteria consistently. Usually, a program involves extensive day by day sampling and checking out by major process point for at least one month after operational criteria have been established for every sampling point. The validation defines essential procedure parameter and their operating ranges.

A Validation plan for a water system usually consists of following steps,

- Establishing standard for quality characteristics and working parameter.
- Defining system and sub-system able to produce the desired quality attribute from the available source water.
- Selecting device, control and monitoring technologies.
- Developing a set up qualification level such as tool calibration, inspection to confirm that the drawing appropriately depicts the as Constructed configuration of the water system and wherein important, unique assessment to confirm that the set up meet the layout requirement.
- Developing an operational qualification stage consisting test and inspection to confirm that the equipment, system alert and control are working are reliably and that appropriate alert and action stage are established. This stage of qualification may also overlap with element of the subsequent step.
- Developing a performance qualification level to verify the appropriateness of critical parameter operating range. A concurrent or retrospective performance qualification is accomplished to illustrate the system reproducibility over an appropriate time period. During this phase of validation, alert and action level for key quality characteristics and working parameter are verified.
- Supplementing a validation renovation program that include the mechanism to control modification to the system and establish and carry out preventive maintenance consisting of recalibration of instrument. In addition, validation renovation consists a monitoring program for essential procedure parameter and a corrective action program.

VALIDATION OF ENVIRONMENTAL CONTROL

Clean areas for the manufacture of sterile products are classified according to the required characteristics of the environment. Each manufacturing operation requires an appropriate level of environmental cleanliness in the operational state to minimize the risks of particulate or microbial contamination of the product or materials being handled.

Detailed information about the methods for determining the microbiological and particulate cleanliness of air, surfaces, etc., is not given in these guidelines. ISO 14644-1[39] should be used for classification of cleanliness according to concentration of airborne particles (determination of number of sample locations, calculation of the sample size and evaluation of classification from the data obtained).

For the manufacture of sterile pharmaceutical preparations, four grades of clean areas are distinguished as follows:

- **Grade A:** The local zone for high-risk operations, such as. filling and making aseptic connections. Normally, such conditions are achieved by using a unidirectional airflow workstation. Unidirectional airflow systems should provide a homogeneous air speed of 0.36–0.54 m/s at a defined test position of 15–30 cm below the terminal filter or air distribution system. The velocity at working level should not be less than 0.36 m/s. The uniformity and effectiveness of the unidirectional airflow should be demonstrated by undertaking airflow visualization tests.
- **Grade B:** In aseptic preparation and filling, this is the background environment for the Grade A zone.
- **Grades C and D:** Clean areas for carrying out less critical stages in the manufacture of sterile products or carrying out activities during which the product is not directly exposed, that is, aseptic connection with aseptic connectors and operations in a closed system.

A unidirectional airflow and lower velocities may be used in closed isolators and glove boxes. To reach the B, C and D air grades the number of air changes should be appropriate for the size of the room and the equipment and personnel present in it.

High-efficiency particulate air (HEPA) filters should be subjected to an installed filter leakage test in accordance with ISO 14644-3 at a recommended interval of every 6 months, but not exceeding 12 months. The purpose of performing regular leak tests is to ensure the filter media, filter frame and filter seal are free from leaks. The aerosol selected for HEPA leak testing should not support microbial growth and should be composed of a sufficient number or mass of particles. HEPA filter patching is allowed at the filter manufacturer and in situ operation provided that the patch sizes and procedures follow the recommendations of ISO 1822-4[40]. Clean room and clean-air device classification Clean rooms and clean-air devices should be classified in accordance with ISO 14644[41-43].

Classification should be clearly differentiated from operational process environmental monitoring. The maximum permitted airborne particle concentration for each grade is given in Table 5.6.

Table 5.6 Maximum permitted airborne particle concentration.

	Maximum permitted number of particles per m³ greater than or equal to the tabulated size			
	At rest[a]		**In operation[b]**	
Grade	0.5 μm	5.0 μm	0.5 μm	5.0 μm
A	3 520	20	3 520	20
B	3 520	29	352 000	2 900
C	3 52 000	2 900	3 520 000	29 000
D	3 520 000	29 000	Not defined	Not defined

[a]The "at rest" state is the condition where the installation of the equipment is complete and operating in a manner agreed upon by the customer and supplier, but with no personnel present.

[b]The "in operation" state is the condition where the installation is functioning in the defined operating mode and the specified number of personnel is present. The areas and their associated environmental control systems should be designed to achieve both the "at rest" and "in operation" states.

For classification purposes in Grade A zones, a minimum sample volume of 1 m³ should be taken per sample location. Referring to Table 5.7, for Grade A the airborne particle classification is ISO dictated by the limit for particles ≥ 5.0 μm.

For Grade B (at rest) the airborne particle classification is ISO 5 for both particle sizes considered.

For Grade C (at rest and in operation) the airborne particle classification is ISO 7 and ISO 8, respectively.

For Grade D (at rest) the airborne particle classification is ISO 8. For classification purposes ISO 14644-1 methodology defines both the minimum number of sample locations and the sample size based on the class limit of the largest particle size considered and the method of evaluation of the data collected. The sample volume should be determined according to ISO 14644-1 clause B.4.2. However, for lower grades (Grade C in operation and Grade D at rest) the sample volume per location should be at least 2 litres and the sample time per location should be not less than 1 minute.

Portable particle counters with a short length of sample tubing should be used for classification purposes to avoid the loss of particles ≥ 5.0 µm. Isokinetic sample heads should be used in unidirectional airflow systems.

Clean rooms and clean-air devices should be routinely monitored while in operation and the monitoring locations based on a formal risk analysis study and the results obtained during the classification of rooms and/or clean-air devices.

For Grade A zones, particle monitoring should be undertaken for the full duration of critical processing, including assembly of equipment, except where justified by contaminants in the process that would damage the particle counter or present a hazard, for example, live organisms and radiological hazards. In cases of monitoring during routine equipment set-up, the operations should be undertaken before exposure to the risk. Monitoring during simulated operations should be performed. The Grade A zone should be monitored at a frequency and sample size such that all interventions, transient events and any system deterioration would be captured and alarms triggered if alert limits are exceeded. It is accepted that it may not always be possible to demonstrate low levels, ≥ 5.0 µm of particles at the point of fill when filling is in progress, due to the generation of particles or droplets from the product itself.

It is recommended that a similar system should be used for Grade B zones, although the sample frequency may be decreased. The importance of the particle monitoring system should be determined by the effectiveness of the segregation between the adjacent Grade A and B zones. The Grade B zone should be monitored at a frequency and with a sample size such that changes in levels of contamination and any deterioration of the system would be captured and alarms triggers, if alert limits are exceeded.

Airborne particle monitoring systems may consist of independent particle counters; a network of sequentially accessed sampling points connected by manifold to a single particle counter; or multiple small particle counters located near monitoring points and networked to a data acquisition system. Combinations of systems can also be used. The system selected should be appropriate for the particle size considered. Where remote sampling systems are used, the length of tubing and the radii of any bends in the tubing should be considered in the context of particle losses in the tubing. The selection of the monitoring system should consider whether any risk presented by the materials used in the manufacturing operation, for example, those involving live organisms or radiopharmaceuticals.

To demonstrate control of the cleanliness of the various clean areas during operation, they should be monitored for airborne particles and microbial contamination. In addition to "at rest" and "in operation" classification, airborne particles should be monitored periodically "in operation" at critical locations. The sampling plan need not be the same as that used for classification. Locations and sample sizes should be determined based on an assessment of the process and contamination risk.

The monitoring of Grade C and D areas in operation should be performed in accordance with the principles of quality risk management.

Other characteristics such as temperature and relative humidity depend on the product and nature of the operations carried out. These parameters should not interfere with the defined cleanliness standard.

Examples of operations to be carried out in the various grades are given in Table 5.7.

Table 5.7 Examples of operations to be carried out in the various grades.

Grade	Operations for terminally sterilized products
A	Filling of products when unusually at risk
C	Preparation of solutions when unusually at risk. Filling of products
D	Preparation of solutions and components for subsequent filling
Grade	**Operations for aseptic preparations**
A	Aseptic preparation and filling
C	Preparation of solutions to be filtered
D	Handling of components after washing

To control the microbiological cleanliness of Grades A–D zones in operation the clean areas should be monitored. Where aseptic operations are performed, monitoring should be frequent using methods such as settle plates, volumetric air and surface sampling, such as, swabs and contact plates. Surfaces and personnel should be monitored after critical operations. Limits expressed in colony-forming units (CFU) for the microbiological monitoring of clean areas in operation are given in Table 5.8.

The sampling methods and numerical values included in the table are not intended to represent specifications, but are for information only.

Table 5.8 Recommended limits for microbial contamination.

Grade	Air sample (CFU/m^3)[a]	Settle plates (diameter 90 mm) (CFU/4 hours)[b]	Contact plates (diameter 55 mm) (CFU/plate)	Glove print (5 fingers) (CFU/glove)
A	< 1	< 1	< 1	< 1
B	10	5	5	5
C	100	50	25	–
D	200	100	50	–

CFU, colony-forming units.

[a]These are average values.

[b]Individual settle plates may be exposed for less than 4 hours.

Appropriate alert and action limits should be set for the results of particulate and microbiological monitoring. If the action limits are exceeded or a trend is identified in the alert limits, investigation should be initiated and the appropriate corrective actions should be taken, as prescribed in the operating procedures.

Terminally sterilized products

Components and most products should be prepared in at least a Grade D environment to ensure low microbial bioburden and particulate counts before filtration and sterilization.

The filling of products for terminal sterilization should generally be done in at least a Grade C environment.

The preparation and filling of ointments, creams, suspensions and emulsions should generally be done in a Grade C environment before terminal sterilization.

Aseptic preparation

Components after washing should be handled in at least a Grade D environment. The handling of sterile starting materials and components, unless subjected to sterilization or filtration through a microorganism retaining filter later in the process, should be undertaken in a Grade A environment with a Grade B background.

The preparation of solutions which are to be sterile-filtered during the processing should be undertaken in a Grade C environment. Unless a closed system is used, in which case a Class D environment may be justifiable. If not sterile-filter is used, the preparation of materials and products should be undertaken in a Grade A environment with a Grade B background. This is called an aseptic manipulation.

The aseptic handling and filling of prepared products, as well as the handling of exposed sterile equipment, should be undertaken in a Grade A environment with a Grade B background.

The transfer of partially closed containers, as used in freeze-drying, before stoppering is completed, should be undertaken either in a Grade A environment with a Grade B background or in sealed transfer trays in a Grade B environment. The preparation and filling of sterile ointments, creams, suspensions and emulsions should be undertaken in a Grade A environment with a Grade B background when the product is exposed and is not subsequently filtered.

Processing

Precautions should be taken to minimize contamination during all processing stages, including the stages before sterilization.

In general, preparations containing living microorganisms should not be made, nor should containers be filled in areas used for the processing of other pharmaceutical products. However, if the manufacturer can demonstrate and validate the effective containment and decontamination of the live microorganisms, the use of multiproduct facilities may be justifiable. Vaccines consisting of dead organisms or of bacterial extracts may be dispensed into containers in the same premises as other sterile pharmaceutical products, provided that the inactivation procedure has been properly validated. When multiproduct facilities are used to manufacture sterile preparations containing living microorganisms and other sterile pharmaceutical products, the manufacturer should demonstrate and validate the effective decontamination of the live microorganisms, in addition to precautions taken to minimize contamination.

Validation of aseptic processing should include a process simulation test using a nutrient medium (media fill). Selection of the nutrient medium should be made based on dosage form of the product and selectivity, clarity, concentration and suitability for sterilization of the nutrient medium.

The process simulation test should imitate as closely as possible the routine aseptic manufacturing steps except where the activity may lead to any potential microbial contamination.

Process simulation tests should be performed as a part of validation by running three consecutive satisfactory simulation tests. These tests should be repeated at defined intervals and after any significant modification to the heating, ventilation and air-conditioning (HVAC) system, equipment or process.

The number of containers used for media fills should be sufficient to enable a valid evaluation. For small batches the number of containers for media fills should be at least equal to the size of the product batch. The target should be zero growth and the following should apply:

- when filling is fewer than 5000 units, no contaminated units should be detected.
- when filling is 5000 –10 000 units:
- one contaminated unit should result in an investigation, including consideration of a repeat media fill;
- two contaminated units are considered because of revalidation following investigation;
- when filling is more than 10 000 units:

- one contaminated unit should result in an investigation;
- two contaminated units are considered cause for revalidation following investigation.

For any run size, intermittent incidents of microbial contamination may indicate low-level contamination that should be investigated.

Care should be taken to ensure that any validation does not compromise the processes.

Water sources, water-treatment equipment and treated water should be monitored regularly for chemicals, biological contamination and contamination with endotoxins to ensure that the water complies with the specifications appropriate to its use. Records should be maintained of the results of the monitoring and of any action taken[45].

Activities in clean areas, especially when aseptic operations are in progress, should be kept to a minimum and the movement of personnel should be controlled and methodical, so as to avoid excessive shedding of particles and organisms due to over-vigorous activity.

The presence of containers and materials responsible to generate fibres should be minimized in clean areas and avoided completely when aseptic work is in progress.

Components, bulk-product containers and equipment should be handled after the final cleaning process in such a way as to ensure that they are not recontaminated.

The interval between the washing and drying and the sterilization of components, bulk-product containers and equipment, as well as between sterilization and use, should be as short as possible and subject to a time limit appropriate to the validated storage conditions. The time between the start of the preparation of a solution and its sterilization or filtration through a bacteria-retaining filter should be as short as possible. A maximum permissible time should be set for each product that takes into account its composition and the prescribed method of storage.

Any gas that is used to purge a solution or blanket a product should be passed through a sterilizing filter.

The bioburden should be monitored before sterilization. There should be working limits on contamination immediately before sterilization, which are related to the efficiency of the method to be used. Bioburden assay should be performed on each batch for both aseptically filled products and terminally sterilized products. Where overkill sterilization parameters are set for terminally sterilized products, bioburden might be monitored only at suitable scheduled intervals. For parametric release systems, bioburden assay should be performed on each batch and considered as an in-process test. Wherever appropriate, the level of endotoxins should be monitored. All solutions, in particular large-volume infusion fluids, should be passed through a microorganism-retaining filter, if possible sited immediately before filling.

Components, bulk-product containers, equipment, and any other articles required in a clean area where aseptic work is in progress, should be sterilized and wherever possible passed into the area through double ended sterilizers sealed into the wall.

The efficacy of any new processing procedure should be validated and the validation should be done at regular intervals. If any significant change is made in the process or equipment, must be recorded.

Exercise

Multiple Choice Questions

1. Which of the following statement is NOT correct?
   a) Validation increases the cost of production of the product.
   b) Process parameters and controls are determined during validation of any process or system.
   c) Validation helps to determine the worst case and risks that may come out during the manufacturing of the quality products.
   d) Deep study and understanding of the system and equipment are made possible due to validation.
2. Which of the following statement is correct?
   a) The production people check, identify and prepare the list of the appropriate safety features given for different service lines and prepare a preventive maintenance program.
   b) The quality control people check, identify and prepare the list of the appropriate safety features given for different service lines and prepare a preventive maintenance program.
   c) The validation team check, identify and prepare the list of the appropriate safety features given for different service lines and prepare a preventive maintenance program.
   d) The quality assurance people check, identify and prepare the list of the appropriate safety features given for different service lines and prepare a preventive maintenance program.

3. Fill in the blank using appropriate word given below.
4. The basic principle of ....is that a drug should be produced that is fit for its intended use.
   a) Factory Manager
   b) The Management
   c) Quality Control
   d) Quality Assurance
5. Fill in the blank using appropriate word given below.
6. During retrospective validation results of in-process and final .... tests are evaluated. A total of 10-25 batches (or more), manufactured over a period of 12 months, is used for reviewing the results, to provide a statistically significant picture.
   a) product
   b) control
   c) finished
   d) analytical
7. Fill in the blank using appropriate word given below.
8. .... validation is carried out during normal production.
   a) Concurrent
   b) Retrospective
   c) Prospective
   d) Revalidation
9. Fill in the blank using appropriate word given below.
10. Revalidation is an exploratory review the current performance of the validation effect to confirm the validated status of the facilities, systems, equipment, manufacturing processes, software and ....
    a) Production
    b) testing
    c) Purchase
    d) maintenance
11. Fill in the blank using appropriate word given below.
12. The goal of the process design is to design a .... suitable for routine commercial manufacturing that can consistently deliver a product that meets its quality attributes.
    a) product
    b) facility
    c) production
    d) process
13. Fill in the blank using appropriate word given below.
14. The purpose of the third validation stage is to obtain a continual assurance that the .... remains in a state of control during commercial manufacture.
    a) Product
    b) production
    c) Process
    d) technology

15. Fill in the blank using appropriate word given below.
16. The chance of separation can be reasonably .... by reducing the size differences, shape differences and density differences.
    a) Increased
    b) unchanged
    c) changed
    d) reduced
17. Fill in the blank using appropriate word given below.
18. Determination of homogeneous mixing of the active pharmaceutical ingredient (API) is an important in-process control within the manufacturing of .... dosage forms.
    a) Liquid
    b) solid
    c) semi-solid
    d) lotion
19. Which of the following is NOT a reason for performing the revalidation process?
    a) The extent of the purity made in the process and the effect upon the product.
    b) Systematic periodic checking of the validation results.
    c) Change in the batch size.
    d) Transfer of a product from one plant to another plant.
20. Which of the following is NOT a reason for performing the revalidation process?
    a) If the properties of a powder blend suits direct compression, manufacturers will turn to granulation processes to create the desired flowability and high dust ability.
    b) If the properties of a powder blend suits common compression, manufacturers will turn to granulation processes to create the desired flowability and low dust ability.
    c) If the properties of a powder blend do not suit direct compression, manufacturers will turn to granulation processes to create the desired flowability and low dust ability.
    d) If the properties of a powder blend do not suit direct compression, manufacturers will turn to granulation processes to create the desired flowability and high dust ability.
21. Which of the following statement is NOT correct?
    a) To confirm the process design as incapable of reproducing commercial manufacturing and make the process better understood.
    b) To confirm the process design as capable of reproducing commercial manufacturing and make the process better understood.

c) The ongoing assurance activity speaks that the process remains in a state of uncontrol during routine production through quality procedures and continuous improvement.

d) The assurance activity that has been recently completed speaks that the process remains in a state of control during routine production through quality procedures and continuous improvement.

22. Which of the activities confirm to the parameter specified in DQ?

a) Equipment performance and identification

b) Installation verification

c) Material of construction of building

d) Certification of PQ

23. Which of the following point is NOT included in OQ?

a) Cleaning procedure

b) Filter integrity and efficiency test

c) Installation verification

d) Safety features testing

24. Which of the following statement is NOT correct?

a) Performance qualification is the final stage of qualification.

b) Operational Qualification is the final stage of qualification.

c) Installation Qualification is the final stage of qualification.

d) Process Qualification is the final stage of qualification.

25. Which of the following statement is NOT correct?

a) In direct compression, a liquid binder solution is combined with a bed of mixed powders to mass the particles together into granules.

b) In wet-granulation, a solid binder is combined with a bed of mixed powders to mass the particles together into granules.

c) In wet-granulation, a liquid binder solution is combined with a bed of mixed powders to mass the particles together into granules.

d) In dry-granulation, a liquid binder solution is combined with a bed of mixed powders to mass the particles together into granules.

26. Which of the following statement is NOT correct?

a) The resultant particle size distribution will affect such material properties as flow, compressibility, disintegration, and dissolution.

b) Low moisture content of granulation could result in poor hardness and friability.

c) High moisture content of granules can result in tablet picking or sticking to tablet punch surfaces.

d) Low moisture content of granules can result in tablet picking or sticking to tablet punch surfaces.

27. Which of the following statement is correct?

a) The efficacy of any new processing procedure should be validated and the validation should be repeated at regular intervals thereafter or when any significant change is made in the process or equipment, if found is recorded.

b) The bioburden should be monitored after sterilization.

c) Care should not be taken to ensure that any validation does not compromise the processes.

d) Two contaminated units should result in an investigation.

28. Which of the following statement is correct?

a) For the manufacture of sterile products clean areas are not classified according to the required characteristics of the environment.

b) A unidirectional airflow and lower velocities may be used in closed isolators and glove boxes.

c) The water is not extensively used substance and raw material within inside manufacturing, processing and formulations of pharmaceutical.

d) Asbestos-containing filters can be used under any circumstances.

B. Short Questions

1. What are four things that are done to validate the pharmaceutical industry? Write down the importances of validation in pharmaceutical industry.
2. Write down the validation plan for a water system usually consisting of subsequent steps.
3. Describe what do you about validation of the sterilization by radiation and dry heat.
4. Explain the reasons for tablet coating and also discuss the important areas to be considered during tablet coating.
5. Draw the process flow chart for granulation, drying and milling for making a tablet. How the tablet compression can be validated?
6. What are the fixed and variable controlling parameters for drying in a tray dryer. Explain the factors that affect the particle size and blending of a powder mixture.

7. How can you determine the homogeneous mixing of the active pharmaceutical ingredient with excipients in solid state?
8. What are prospective, retrospective validation and revalidation?
9. What are validation and qualification? Explain different types of qualification.
10. Write down the importances of validation in pharmaceutical industry.

C. Long Questions

1. How can the water purification, storage, and distribution system be validated and qualified?
2. How the clean areas for manufacture of sterile products are validated?
3. Write down in short, the validation of the process of sterilization by dry and moist heat.
4. Briefly write down how the liquid filling and sealing process be validated.
5. For preparation of sterile preparations, the environment should be bacteria free. How can you validate the environment.
6. When sterilization is required to be validated, how the 'sterilization by gases and fumigants' can be validated?
7. Is considered that 'compression is a critical step in the production of a tablet dosage form',

   – why? Explain.
8. How can you validate the wet granulation technique for making the tablet? What are other prosses of granulation?
9. Explain the terms, validation, and its different types. What is revalidation?
10. Explain importance of validation. Discuss different types of validation.

Answers

1	2	3	4	5	6	7	8	9	10	11	12	13	14	15	16	17	18	19	20
a	c	d	b	a	b	d	c	d	b	a	c	a	b	c	d	c	d	a	b

References

1. Van de Ven, A. H.; Nothing is quite as practical as a good theory; Academy of Management Review; 14: 486-489, 1989.
2. March, J. G.; Exploration and exploitation in organizational learning; Organization Science; 2: 71-87, 1991.

3. Hinds, Pamela and Bailey, Diane; Out of Sight, Out of Sync: Understanding Conflict in Distributed Teams; Organization Science; 14, 615 – 632, 2003.
4. Borsboom, D., Mellenbergh, G. J., and Van Heerden, J.; The theoretical status of latent variables; Psychological Review; 110, 203–219., 2003.
5. Kane, M. T.; Current concerns in validity theory; Journal of Educational Measurement; 38, 319–342, 2001.
6. Jansen, B. R. J., and Van der Maas, H. L. J.; The development of children's rule use on the balance scale task.; Journal of Experimental Child Psychology; 81, 383–416, 2002.
7. Westen, D., and Rosenthal, R.; Quantifying construct validity: Journal of Personality and Social Psychology; 84, 608–618, 2003.
8. Agalloco J., Carleton FJ.; Validation of Pharmaceutical Processes (3rd edn.); Informa Healthcare, New York, USA,; 2008.
9. Tarun Virmani; Validation: An Essentiality In The Pharmacy; Pharma Info; 2007.
10. Patel RC, Bhuva CK, Singh RP, Abhishek D, Sharma A.; Pharmaceutical Process Validation Why to Do, When to Do and How to Do it.; Pharma Tutor; May, 2011.
11. Lambert J.; Validation Guidelines For Pharmaceutical Dosage Forms.; Health Canada/ Health Products and Food Branch Inspectorate; 7 – 15, 2004.
12. Peither TL.; Equipment and facility qualification Pharmaceutical process validation (3rd) edn.; Marcel Deckker; NY, USA, 443 – 63, 2003.
13. Chitlange, SS., Pawar, AS., Pawar, HI., Bhujbal, SS., Kulkari, A.; A Validation; 2006.
14. Guidance for Industry Process Validation; General Principles Practices; 2011.
15. Chao, AY., John Forbes, F.; Prospective process validation Pharmaceutical process validation, 3rd edn. Marcel Deckker, NY, USA.; 2003.
16. Trubinski, CJ.; Retrospective validation: Pharmaceutical process validation, 3rd edn.; Marcel Deckker, NY, USA, 2003.
17. Ahir, KB., Singh, KD., Yadav, SP., Patel, HS., Poyahari, CB.; Overview of validation and Basic Concepts of Process Validation.; Scholars Academic Journal of Pharmacy.; 3: 178 – 90, 2014.
18. Parashar, B., Gupta, R., Khurana, G.; A review on process validation as an essential Process.; International Journal of Research in Pharmaceutical Sciences.; 4: 226 – 9, 2013.
19. Chaitanya Kumar G., Rout, RP., Ramtake, S., Bhatacharya, S.; Process Validation.; The Indian Pharmacist; 14 – 9, 2005.
20. Varshney, P., Shah, M., Patel, P., Rohit, M.; Different aspects involved in process validation.; Innovate Journal of Science; 1: 16 – 9, 2013.
21. Calnan, N., Redmond, A., O'neill, S.; The FDA's draft process validation guidance – A perspective from industry.; Pharmaceutical Engineering; 10 – 6, 2009.

22. Peter Toson, Johannes G. Khinast.; A DEM model to evaluate refill strategies of a twin-screw feeder; International Journal of Pharmaceutics; 641, June, 2023.

23. Pooja Bhalode, SoniaM. Razavi, Andrés RomanOspino, James Scicolone, Ger ardo Callegari, Geng Tian, Abdollah Koolivand, Scott Krull Marianthi G. Ierapetritou, Fernando J. Muzzio.; Optimal quantification of residence time distribution profiles from a quality assurance perspective; International Journal of Pharmaceutics; 634, March, 2023.

24. B. VanSnick, J. Holman, C. Cunningham, A. Kumar, J. Vercruysse, T. DeBeer, J.P. Remon, C. Vervaet: Continuous direct compression as manufacturing platform for sustained release tablets; Int. J. of Pharmaceutics; 519, 1–2, 390-407, March, 2017

25. Aigner, I., Hsiao, W.-K., Dujmovic, D., Stegemann, S., Khinast,; J., Methodology for Economic and Technical Comparison of Continuous and Batch Processes to Enhance Early Stage Decision-making. In: Kleinebudde, P. (Ed.), Continuous Manufacturing of Pharmaceuticals. John Wiley & Sons, Ltd, Chichester, UK, pp. 485–505, 2017.

26. Blackwood, D.O., Bonnassieux, A., Cogoni, G., Continuous Direct Compression Using Portable Continuous Miniature Modular & Manufacturing (PCM&M). In: am Ende, D.J., am Ende, M.T. (Eds.), Chemical Engineering in the Pharmaceutical Industry. John Wiley & Sons, Inc., Hoboken, NJ, USA, pp. 547–560, 2019.

27. Dai, L., Sorkin, V., Vastola, G., Zhang, Y.W., 2019. Dynamics calibration of particle sandpile packing characteristics via discrete element method. Powder Technol. 347, 220–226.

28. Ghodki, B.M., Patel, M., Namdeo, R., Carpenter, G., 2019. Calibration of discrete element model parameters: soybeans. Computat. Particle Mech. 6 (1), 3–10.

29. Madlmeir, S., Loidolt, P., Khinast, J.G., 2019. Study of the capsule-filling dosator process via calibrated DEM simulations. Int. J. Pharm. 567, 118441.

30. Orefice, L., Khinast, J.G., 2019. A novel framework for a rational, fully-automatised calibration routine for DEM models of cohesive powders. Powder Technol. 361, 687–703.

31. Lee, K.T., Kimber, J.A., Cogoni, G., Brandon, J.K., Wilsdon, D., Verrier, H.M., Grieb, S., Blackwood, D.O., Jain, A.C., Doshi, P.; Continuous Mixing Technology: Characterization of a vertical mixer using residence time distribution. J. Pharm. Sci. 110 (7), 2694–2702, 2021.

32. S.S. Sekulic, H.W. Ward, D.R. Brannegan, E.D. Stanley, C.L. Evans, S.T. Sciavolino, P.A. Hailey, P.K. Aldridge, Anal. Chem. 68 (1996) 509–513.

33. Uniformity of dosage units, in: U.S. Pharmacopeia (USP), 2003. pp. 2227–2229.

34. Kandharkar Kaustubh, Sakhare Mayur, Akmar Nikhil. Review on Industrial Process Validation of Tablet Dosage Form. International Journal of Interdisciplinary and Multidisciplinary Studies. 2014; 1(4):112-124.

35. Sharma M, Agarwal S, Agarwal S, Sharma M. Prospective Validation: A Review. The Pharma Innovation. 2015; 4(3):1-7.

36. Zameeruddin M, Kale SS, Jadhav SB, Kadam VS, Chaware SS. Process Validation of Oral Solid Dosage Form: Tablet – An Overview. World Journal of Pharmacy and Pharmaceutical Sciences. 2015; 4(12):358- 373.

37. Patil SS, Ola M, Bhaskar R, Wagh DD. Process Validation of Critical Steps Involved In Manufacturing of Solid Dosage Forms in Pharmaceutical Industry. International Journal of Pharmacy and Technology. 2013; 5(1):2403-2420.

38. Sharma C, Rana AC, Bala R, Seth N. An Overview of Industrial Process Validation of Tablets. Journal of Drug Delivery and Therapeutics. 2013; 3(3):175-183.

39. ISO 14644-1. Clean rooms and associated controlled environments. Part 1: Classification of airborne particles. Geneva, International Organization for Standardization.

40. ISO 14644-3. Clean rooms and associated controlled environments. Part 3: Test methods. Geneva, International Organization for Standardization.

41. ISO 1822-4. High efficiency air filters (HEPA and ULPA). Determining leakage of fi lter elements (scan method).

42. ISO 14644-4. Clean rooms and associated controlled environments. Part 4: Design, construction and start-up. Geneva, International Organization for Standardization.

43. ISO 14644-2. Clean rooms and associated controlled environments. Part 2: Monitoring for continued compliance with ISO 14644-1. Geneva, International Organization for Standardization.

44. ISO 14644-5 Clean rooms and associated controlled environments. Part 5: Cleanroom operations. Geneva, International Organization for Standardization.

45. Good manufacturing practices for pharmaceutical products: water for pharmaceutical use. In: WHO Expert Committee on Specifications for Pharmaceutical Preparations. Thirty-ninth report. Geneva, World Health Organization, 2005 (WHO Technical Report Series, No. 929), Annex 3; and in Quality assurance of pharmaceuticals. A compendium of guidelines and related materials. Vol. 2. 2nd updated ed. Good manufacturing practices and inspection. Geneva, World Health Organization, 2007.

46. QA Guide, Third edition, 1996, volume-1 Organization of pharmaceutical producer of India(OPPI).

47. Nush, RA; validation of pharmaceutical process.; In Swarbrick J. Boylan JC (Ends); Encyclopaedia of Pharmaceutical Technology, second edition Marcel Dekker, 2002.

CHAPTER - 6

Industrial Safety

Introduction, Hazards, Mechanical, Electrical, Chemical, Pharmaceutical Monitoring, Prevention Systems, Industrial Effluent Testing, Industrial Effluent Treatment, Control of Environmental Pollution

INTRODUCTION

Industrial safety is *primarily a management activity which is concerned with reducing, controlling and eliminating hazards from the industries or industrial units.*

Industrial work environments are sometimes characterized by dynamic resources such as interactions between mobile equipment and pedestrian workers. When the industrial work environment (facilities) becomes hazardous, it is observed that the high rates of workplace injuries and fatalities are also found regularly. The high-risk industries include the industries of construction, steel manufacturing, oil and gas, aviation, agriculture, forestry, fishing, and hunting, etc. For example, in many countries, the construction industry remains one of the most hazardous and unsafe industry with fatality rates considerably higher than the all industry average [1-4]. Although the efforts have been taken to improve safety performance, still the construction sector has been facing the disproportionate injury rates accounting for the most on-the-job fatal injuries. Many innovative intervention strategies are being continuously explored by researchers and practitioners to increase the management controls as well as to modify human behaviour and work environment to improve construction safety. Another example is the steel manufacturing industry. It is one of the most hazardous industries because of its complex socio-technical system. The steel manufacturing process involves the use of high technology and physical labour, making safety management a complicated task[5]. Members of the U.S. steel manufacturing industry have now been experiencing a significant number of injuries, illnesses, and fatalities[6]. Many organizations have thought to develop the programs to identify and benefit from the alerts, signals, and prior indicators[7]. Traditional measures of safety performance depend on some form of accident or injury data[8]. Necessary actions are being taken in response to the adverse trends in injuries[9]. Many organizations depend heavily on failure data to monitor performance. The consequence of this approach is that improvements or changes are only determined after something has gone wrong[10]. Effective management of major hazards requires a proactive approach to risk management. Information confirming that critical systems are operating as intended is essential[11]. Accurate safety performance, measurement of facilitates, evaluation of ongoing safety management and the motivation of project participants can improve safety[12]. The ability to collect, analyse and disseminate safety information, using a large amount of useful data from leading indicators, can allow for hazardous events and conditions to be efficiently mitigated and controlled before a lagging indicator occurs. The existing and commonly used measurement methods of the safety performance are extensive.

The human life has been endangered and increased with advancement of scientific development in different fields. The importance of industrial safety has been realized. Every millions of industrial accidents occur due to either death or in temporary disablement or permanent disablement of employees. This involves large amount of losses resulting from loss to property, wasted man hours and wasted hours. Moreover, from the managerial perspective the importance of industrial safety in any organization may be concluded by following facilitation:

a) *Treatment:* Industrial safety management provides treatment for injuries and illness at the work place.

b) *Medical Examination:* It carries out medical examination of staff joining the organization or returning to work after sickness or accident.

c) Hazards identification.

d) Provision of protective devices.

e) *Consultancy:* It provides medical advice on other condition potentially affecting health, such as, working in canteen, etc.

g) *Education:* it provides safety and health training.

The objectives of industrial safety are

1) to prevent accidents in the plant by reducing the hazard to minimum.
2) to eliminate accident caused work stoppage and lost production.
3) to achieve lower compensation of workmen, insurance rates and reduction of all other direct and indirect costs of accidents.
4) to prevent loss of life, permanent disability and the loss of income of worker by eliminating causes of accidents.
5) to evaluate employee's morale by promoting safe work place and good working condition.
6) to educate all members of the organization in continuous state of safety mindness and to make supervision competent and intensely safety minded.

A safety programme includes mainly following four E's.

- *Engineering:* That is, safety at the design, equipment installation stage.
- *Education:* That is, education of employees in safe practices.
- *Enlistment:* It concerns the attitude of the employees and management towards the programmed and its purpose. It is necessary to raise the interest of employees in accident prevention and safety consciousness.
- *Encouragement:* That is, to enforce adherence to safe rules and practices.

HAZARDS

Industrial hazard may be defined as *any condition created by industries that will cause injury or death to personnel or loss of product or property.* Over the past decades, successive major accidents. More than two thousand deaths from the deadly toxic gas released in Bhopal, India in 1984 to the Bunce field fire in the United Kingdom in 2005, the Deepwater Horizon oil spill in the Gulf of Mexico in 2010, and the Bento Rodriguez dam disaster in Brazil in 2015, have caused deaths, numerous injuries, significant environmental pollution and massive economic loss. The world drew attention to serious chemical hazards in the industry [14,15]. Industrial safety refers to reduction of the risk of injury or loss and danger to persons, property from the industrial hazards[16]. Effective management of worker safety and health protection is a decisive factor in reducing the extent and severity of work-related injuries and sicknesses and their related costs[17,18].

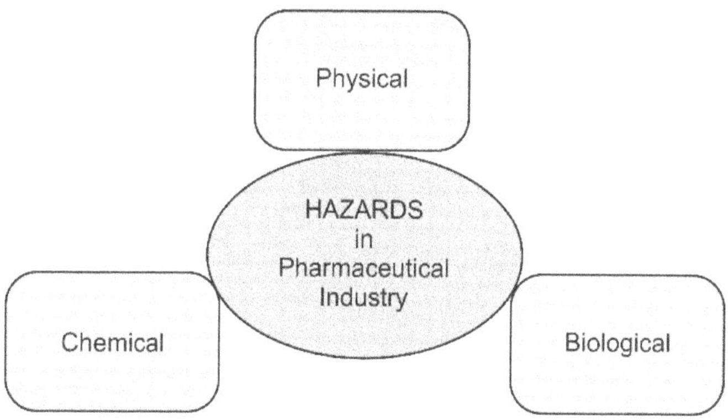

Fig.6.1 Types of hazards in pharmaceutical industries.

Routes of entry into the body of the industrial hazards

Working with chemicals will involve the chance of exposure, which is hazardous to a person's health. The health risks depend on the toxicity of the chemical, and types of effects[19,20]. Acute health effects develop soon after exposure whereas chronic toxic effects develop gradually over a prolonged period of exposure, many years after initial exposure[21]. There are four major routes through which the hazardous chemicals can enter into the body. Inhalation, skin or eye absorption, ingestion, and injection[22] as shown in Fig.6.2.

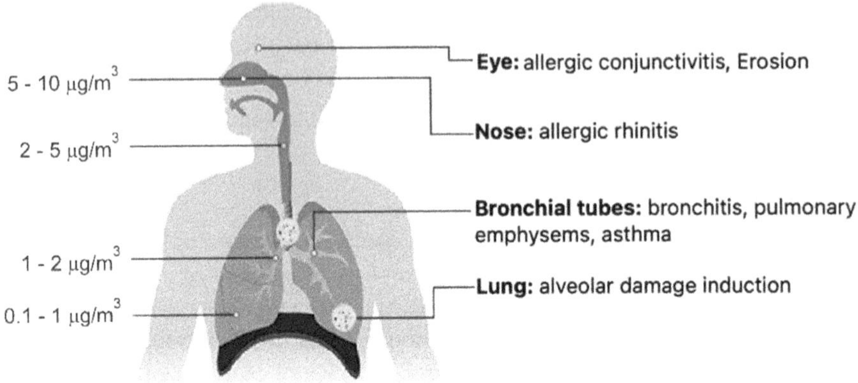

Fig.6.2 Dust size absorbed in the body and their effect on the body.

Inhalation

Hazardous chemicals enter the body through the respiratory tract through inhalation[23]. They enter the body in the form of vapours, gases, mists, or particulates (are shown in Figure.6.3). Once inhaled, the chemicals are deposited in the respiratory tract and damage the tissue, or they diffuse into the blood through the lung-blood interface. On contact with tissue in the upper respiratory tract or lungs, chemicals may cause health effects starting from simple irritation to severe. tissue destruction. Substances absorbed into the blood are circulated and distributed to organs.

Absorption

Chemicals pass through the skin and nearly always in liquid form. Solid chemicals and gases or vapours do not usually pass through the skin unless they are first dissolved in moisture on the skin's surface. The skin is the second most common route by which occupational chemicals enter the body[24]. Chemicals when crossing the skin barrier and absorbed into the blood system. Once absorbed, they may produce systemic damage to internal organs. Small amounts of chemicals may enter by dissolving in the liquid surrounding the eyes, may enter the eyes if they are splashed with chemicals. The eyes are rich in supplied blood, the blood vessels and many chemicals can penetrate the outer tissues and pass into the veins. Depending on the eye may or may not be damaged the corrosive nature of the chemical and its ability to penetrate the outer tissues.

Swallowed

Chemicals enter the stomach by swallowing (ingested) contaminated mucus. These can be expelled from the lungs or by eating and drinking contaminated food. Food and drink are usually contaminated by contact with unwashed hands, gloves or clothing, or by being left exposed in the workplace. Once the chemicals enter the mouth, it passes down the esophagus and then into the stomach. Alcohols can pass across the stomach wall and enter the bloodstream, but most of the chemicals move from the stomach through the small intestine. The small intestine has many hundreds of villi, it has very thin walls and is filled with tiny blood vessels (vein). Chemicals to pass from the small intestine across the walls of the villi and enter in the veins. The chemical is then carried around the body by the bloodstream.

Injection

Chemical substances enter the body if the skin is penetrated or punctured by contaminated objects. Though less common in most workplaces, it can occur when a sharp object (needle) punctures the skin and injects a chemical (or virus) into the bloodstream. When a chemical is sprayed at the body at high pressure. Effects can then occur as the substance is circulated in the blood and deposited in the target organs.

Toxic effect of industrial hazard

Toxicity is the relative ability of a substance or chemical to cause adverse effects in living organisms. One can reduce their toxic effects through the management of industrial waste. The chemical industry is important in many countries of the WHO. Many Member States are actively seeking to carry out the aims of the strategic approach, to deepen the involvement of their health sectors in the sound management of chemical safety to prevent the negative impacts of chemicals on health both directly and through the environment[25].

Effect on environment

Pharmaceutical industries also have many environmental problems, such as, the other chemical industries[24]. Environment safety is directly or indirectly related to human health, contaminated air in the environment or workplace can be inhaled. Air is drawn through the mouth and nose, and then into the lungs. An average person breathes in and out about 12 times a minute. Each of the twelve breaths brings in about 500 mL of air, corresponding to 6 litters of air per minute, together with any contaminants that the air contains. Over an 8-hour working day, more than 2,800 litters of air will be breathed in and out of the lungs. In conditions of hard physical work, up to 10,000 litters may be exchanged. Many tons and various types of pharmaceutical substances are used. They enter the environment through excretion of industrial waste. If they are not treated and degraded completely, they could contaminate the environment[26].

Effect on health

Hazardous gases (CO, CN^-) prevent the tissues from getting enough oxygen. Carbon monoxide binds to haemoglobin 200 times more readily than oxygen. Cyanide prevents the transfer of oxygen from the blood to tissues by inhibiting the necessary transfer enzymes. Carcinogen chemicals are associated with lung cancer. Long-term exposure to chemicals such as silica dust, engine exhaust or welding fumes has been shown to increase the risk of heart disease, stroke, and high blood pressure[27].

Types of industrial hazard

Hazard is a term *associated with a substance that is likely to cause injury to personnel or one which may lead to loss of property, products, etc.*[28]. Harmful chemical hazards in the Industry may be generally categorized into four different groups, and this is because the industries use many different processes involving a wide range of different raw materials, intermediates, waste products, and final products. The hazards encountered are fire, explosion, toxic release, and environmental damage.

Fire

Fire is a physical hazard. It is an *exothermic chemical reaction between oxygen and fuel at a certain temperature.* Most frequently it is the hazards however the consequences are generally less. People affected to fire usually take the form of skin burns and is usually dependant on the exposure time and the intensity of the heat. Physical structures can be damaged either by the intensity of the heat or combustion[27]. Three things essentials for the combustion of fire are Fuel (any combustible material), Oxygen (at concentrations above 23% in air, the situation becomes dangerous due to the increased fire hazard.) and Temperature[28].

The Fire is a process of burning that produces heat, light and often smokes and flames. The effect of fire on the people takes the form of skin burn due to the exposure to thermal radiation. The severity of the burns depends upon the intensity of the heat and exposure time. In general terms the skin withstands heat energy of 10kw/m^2 for approximately 5 seconds and that of 30kw/m^2 for 0.4 seconds before pain is felt. The effect of various heat radiation levels is given in table-6.I.

Table 6.1 Effects of radiation recommended (World Bank) Design Flare Radiation Levels (API 521).

Radiation Level (kW/m^2)	Observed Effect
37.5	Sufficient to cause damage to process equipment
25	Minimum energy required to ignite wood at indefinitely long exposures (non-piloted)
12.5	Minimum energy required for piloted ignition of wood, melting of plastic tubing
9.5	Pain threshold reached after 8s; second degree burns after 20s
4	Sufficient to cause pain to personnel if unable to reach cover within 20s; however blistering of the skin (second degree burns) is likely; 0: lethality
1.6	Will cause no discomfort for long exposure

Fire can take several different forms such as

- Flash Fire
- Jet fire
- Pool Fire
- Secondary fire

Flash Fire

A flash fire occurs when a cloud of flammable gas and air is ignited. The speed of burning is function of the concentration of the flammable component in the cloud and also the wind speed. Within a few second of ignition the flame spreads both upwind and downwind of the ignition source. Initially the flame is contained within the cloud due to premixed burning of the regions within the flammable limits. Subsequently the flame extends in the form of a fire plume above the cloud. The downwind edge of the flame starts to move towards the spill point after consuming the flammable vapor downwind of the ignition source. Typical flame propagation speeds are the order of 4m/s The flame velocity and dispersion increases with wind speed. The duration of this fire is very short and the damage is caused by thermal radiation and oxygen depletion.

Jet Fire

A jet fire occurs when a flammable liquid or gas is ignited after its release from a pressurized, punctured vessel or pipe. The pressure release generates a long flame, which is stable under most conditions. A flash flame may take the form of jet flame on reaching the spill point. The duration of the jet fire is determined by the release rate and the capacity of the source. Flame length increases directly with flow rate. Typically a pressurized release of 8kg/s would have a length of 35m. The cross winds also affects the flame length. An increase in the crosswind velocity increases the flame length.

Pool Fire

A pool fire occurs on ignition of an accumulation of liquid as a pool on the ground or on water or other liquid. A steadily burning fire is rapidly achieved as the flame vapor to sustain the fire is provided by evaporation of liquid by heat from the flames.

The maximum burning rate is function of the net heat of combustion and heat required fire its vaporization. Generally heat radiation dominates the burning rate for lame greater than 1m diameters.

Combustion of flammable materials those are not directly concerned with the process, and some time present unnecessarily. For example:

- Stored raw material and products, including packaging materials.
- Combustible insulation of vessels and pipelines and electrical cables.
- Combustible building construction and linings.

Protection is by elimination or segregation of combustible materials, use of incombustible materials of construction and insulation, and control of ignition sources. Careless or deliberate actions may defeat in-built precautions.

Fire Hazards

Fire damage occurs more frequently than losses by the explosion, the damage is generally less extensive. The jet fires mainly affect the mechanical properties of the structures. Material of construction loses mechanical strengths when exposed to high temperatures. Heat radiations emitted by the fires cause damage outside the fire. Human body may suffer the skin burns after its exposure to these thermal radiations. Other lethal effect that must be considered in case of fire is the depletion of oxygen by the consumption of oxygen in the combustion process generally in the vicinity of the fire. Of the importance also are the health effects arising from the exposure to the fumes generated as a result of fire. These fumes may include toxic gases, such as sulphur dioxide, nitrous oxides, oxides of carbon etc.

A BLEVE (Boiling Liquid Expanding Vapour Explosion) poses the following hazards:

- Fireball with thermal radiation with some rainout forming pool fires.
- Missiles and Major fragmentation
- Rocketing vessel parts
- Overpressure from minor shock waves

The past experience has shown that whenever there is BLEVE; it is only the heat radiation of the fireball and the over pressure, which do the offsite damages. The effects of both can be well understood by the following zones of the heat and over pressure generated by the BLEVE.

Radiation Zones

The very first zone for the heat effects of BEVE is the "Red Zone". It stretches from the release point to the contour representing radiation level of 37.5Kw/m^2. In this zone the radiation level varies from maximum (At the point of BLEVE) to the radiation level of 37.5Kw/m^2. In this zone complete burning of human body is likely to be occurred. The buildings and the industries may undergo the secondary fires. This radiation level of this zone can also damage the process equipment. The second zone is the "Orange zone". It spans from the contour representing radiation level of 37.5Kw/m^2 to the contour of radiation level of 12.5Kw/m^2. In this zone human body may suffer third degree burn injury. The buildings or the industries near to the point of BLEVE may suffer the local fire in celluloid materials like wood, paper, cotton and plastic etc.

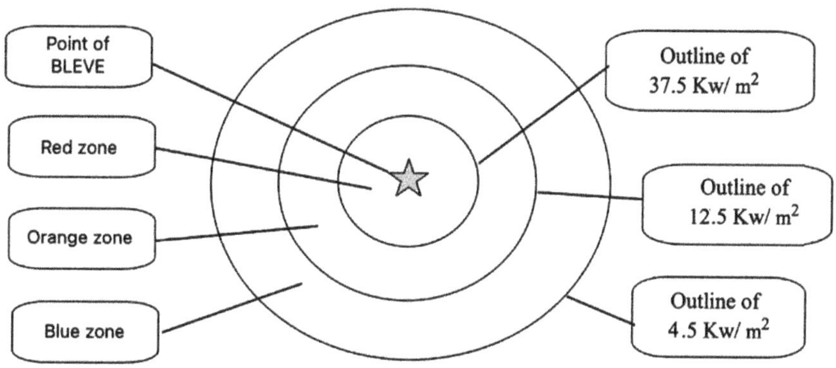

Fig.6.3 Radiation zones for boiling liquid expanding vapour explosion (BLEVE).

MECHANICAL

Almost every day, workers are injured on the job due to hazards of machines. In some cases, these injuries are fatal. Employers need to understand the dangers related to machines and take steps to protect the workers. Most machinery has the potential to cause injury to people. These injuries may range in severity from a minor cut or bruise, through various degrees of wounding and disabling mutilation, to crushing, decapitation, or other fatal injuries. It is not solely powered machinery that is hazardous, for many manually operated machines can still cause injury if not properly safeguarded.

Machinery accidents figure prominently in official accident statistics, and minimizing the risks posed by machinery in the workplace is important. Proper training, maintenance, and safety procedures can help to reduce the likelihood of an accident occurring, and effective safeguards can help to protect workers from injury if an accident does occur. By taking these precautions, we can help to make the workplace safer for everyone. In this blog post, we will discuss common machinery that can be taken to reduce the risk of injury.

Mechanical Safety is the practice of protecting workers from exposure to potential mechanical hazards. In the United States, Mechanical Safety Standard (29 CFR 1910.219) requires employers to protect workers from exposure to moving machinery and equipment parts.

Mechanical safety is important because it protects workers from injuries when exposed to moving machinery and equipment parts. Injuries that can occur include cuts, bruises, and fractures. Employers can prevent these injuries by protecting workers from exposure to these hazards.

When assessing the risks associated with machinery, it is important to consider all potential hazards, both those that are always present and those that can appear unexpectedly. All phases of the machine life cycle need to be considered, including transport, assembly, and installation; commissioning; use; maintenance; dismantling, disabling, and scrapping. By considering all possible hazards, it is possible to develop a comprehensive risk management plan that will help to keep workers safe and minimize the possibility of accidents.

Machinery generally refers to the machines that are used in industrial applications. These machines are usually powered by electricity and perform various industrial tasks. Some examples of machinery include lathes machines, milling machines, drill presses, and injection moulding machines.

Faulty machinery can lead to severe injury and/or death. This is why it's critically important that all machines be properly maintained, inspected, and used correctly. Machinery safety is important for several reasons, some of which include:

Moving machinery can cause injuries in many ways:

- People can be struck and injured by moving parts of machinery or ejected material. Parts of the body can also be drawn in or trapped between rollers, belts, and pulley drives.
- Sharp edges can cause cuts and severe injuries, sharp-pointed parts can cause stabbing or puncture of the skin, and rough surface parts can cause friction or abrasion.
- People can be crushed between parts moving together or towards a fixed part of the machine, wall, or another object, and two parts moving past one another can cause shearing.
- Parts of the machine, materials, and emissions (such as steam or water) can be hot or cold enough to cause burns or scalds, and electricity can cause electrical shock and burns.

- Injuries can also occur due to machinery becoming unreliable and developing faults or when machines are misused through inexperience or lack of training.

There are many potential hazards associated with machinery. Some of these hazards are always present, while others can appear unexpectedly. It is important to be aware of all potential hazards in order to develop a comprehensive risk management plan.

Some common hazards associated with machinery:

- Crushing Hazards

On construction sites, crushing hazards are often caused by excavators and other heavy machinery. If an employee is struck by a piece of machinery, it can result in serious injuries or even death. Employees should always be aware of their surroundings and clear areas where heavy machinery operates to prevent crushing hazards. Workers should wear personal protective equipment (PPE) to protect themselves from potential hazards if necessary.

Crushing hazards can also occur when workers are performing maintenance on machinery. If workers are not properly trained to safely perform maintenance, they could be seriously injured or killed. To prevent these hazards, it is important for employers to provide employees with proper training and safety procedures.

- **Shear hazards**

  Shear hazards are caused by moving parts that can cut or slice through skin and flesh. Shear hazards can occur when workers use hand-operated tools, such as knives, or when operating machinery with moving parts, such as saws. Employees should always use the proper safety equipment and procedures when working with hand-operated tools or machinery to prevent shear hazards.

- **Cutting/Severing Hazards**

  There are many types of cutting hazards, but the three most common contact with a moving sharp-edged part, contact with a rotating part, and contact with a moving part.

  The **first type** of cutting hazard is contact with a moving sharp-edged part. This can happen when using a machine with a blade, such as a bandsaw. If the blade is not properly guarded, your clothing or skin can come into contact with the blade and be cut.

  The **second type** of cutting hazard is contact with a rotating part. This can happen when you are using a drill press or lathe. If the chuck or bit is not properly secured, your clothing or skin can come into contact with the rotating part and be cut.

The **third type** of cutting hazard is contact with a moving part. This can happen when you are using a power saw or drill. If the blade or bit is not properly secured, your clothing or skin can come into contact with the moving part and be cut.

To avoid these hazards, always ensure that the blades on your machines are properly guarded and that the chucks and bits on your drill presses and lathes are properly secured. If you use a power saw or drill, ensure the blade or bit is not worn or damaged. Also, always wear proper protective clothing, such as gloves, when using machinery.

- **Drawing in or Trapping Hazards**

  This hazard can occur when clothing or body parts become caught in moving parts of a machine. The result can be severe injuries or even death. Always wear protective clothing, such as gloves and long sleeves, to prevent this hazard, when working with machinery. Also, keep your hands and feet away from moving parts and ensure that hair is tied back so it cannot become caught in machinery.

- **Stabbing or Puncture Hazards**

  Stabbing or puncture hazards can occur when using a machine with a pointy or sharp edge, such as a drill press. If the bit is not properly secured, your clothing or skin can come into contact with the pointy or sharp edge and be punctured. Always ensure the bit on your drill press is properly secured to prevent this hazard. Also, wear proper protective clothing, such as gloves, when using machinery.

- **Friction or Abrasion Hazards**

  Friction and abrasion hazards are often found in mechanical machinery. When contact is made with a fast-moving surface that may be smooth (e.g. touching a spin dryer) or rough (e.g. touching a belt sander), there is a potential for serious injury.

There are several ways to protect yourself from these hazards:

- Wear appropriate Personal Protective Equipment (PPE), such as gloves, safety glasses, and ear protection.
- Be aware of your surroundings and stay clear of moving parts.
- Follow the manufacturer's instructions for operating the machinery safely.

Entanglement Hazards

Entanglement hazards can occur when clothing or body parts become caught in moving parts of a machine. The result can be severe injuries or even death.

There are several ways to prevent this from happening

- Keep your hair pulled back and away from rotating machine parts.
- Wear close-fitting clothes that won't get caught on anything.
- Be aware of your surroundings and what you're doing at all times.

Turn off the machine and get help from someone who can safely release them. Entanglement is a very real hazard in any industry that uses machinery. By taking some simple precautions, you can prevent it from happening to you or anyone else.

- **Impact Hazards**

The most common type of impact hazard is when the body is struck by a powered part of a machine. This is similar to crushing, but there is no fixed structure to trap the person. The speed and weight of the object do the damage.

Impact hazards can also occur when two parts of a machine collide. This can happen when two machine parts are not properly aligned or when one part breaks and hits another. Impact hazards can also occur when a person is hit by a flying object thrown or ejected from a machine.

Impact hazards can be prevented by proper maintenance of machines, training of workers, and using safety devices. Impact hazards can also be minimized by the use of guards and barriers. When working with machines, it is important to be aware of the potential for impact hazards and to take precautions to avoid them.

- **High-Pressure Fluid Injection Hazards**

High-pressure fluid injection is a hazard that can occur when fluids are forced into the body at high pressures. This can happen when a person is cleaning a machine with high-pressure water and the nozzle breaks or when a person is hit by a high-pressure fluid from a ruptured hose. The high-pressure fluid injection can also occur when a person is welding, and the arc flashes back, injecting molten metal into the body.

The high-pressure fluid injection can cause serious injuries or even death. Always use proper safety equipment to prevent this hazard when working with high-pressure fluids. Wear goggles or a face shield to protect your eyes, and wear gloves and protective clothing to protect your skin. Wear a welding helmet to protect your face and neck if you are welding.

ELECTRICAL

Electrical hazards have always been recognized, yet serious injuries, deaths, and property damage occur daily. Organizations like the US Department of Labour and the National Safety Council compile statistics and facts on a regular basis. The following table demonstrates the importance of electrical safety. This has been noticed that

- 97% of all electricians have been shocked or injured on the job.
- Approximately 30,000 workers receive electrical shocks yearly.

- Over 3600 disabling electrical contact injuries occur annually.
- Electrocutions are the 4th leading cause of traumatic occupational fatalities.
- Over 2000 workers are sent to burn the centres each year with severe Arc-Flash burns.
- Estimates show that 10 Arc-Flash incidents occur every day in the US.
- 60% of workplace accident deaths are caused by burn injuries.
- Over 1000 electrical workers die each year from workplace accidents.
- Excess medical costs per person for severe electrical burns.

The moral obligation to protect workers who may be exposed to electrical hazards is fundamental, but there are legal and other factors that require every facility to establish a comprehensive Electrical Safety Program. Meeting OSHA regulations, reducing insurance costs, and minimizing downtime and repair costs are additional benefits of Electrical Safety programs. When electrical faults occur, the electrical system is subjected to both thermal and magnetic forces. These forces can severely damage equipment and are accompanied by fires, explosions and severe arcing. Such violent damage often causes death or severe injury to personnel. Costs of repairs, equipment replacements, and medical treatment can run into millions of dollars. Loss of production and damaged goods are also important considerations. Other major factors include the cost of OSHA fines and litigation. Severe electrical faults may shut down a complete process or assembly plant, sending hundreds or thousands of workers home for weeks while repairs are being made. It is also possible that one tragic event could close a plant permanently. Implementing and following a well-designed Electrical Safety Program will protect employees and employers against Electrical hazards occur when a person comes in contact with the conductor carrying current. Current level probable effect on human body 1mA slight tingling sensation. 5mA slight shock felt not painful but disturbing. 6-30mA painful shock, muscular control is lost. 50-150mA extreme pain, respiratory arrest, severe muscular contraction, and death are feasible, 1000-4300mA muscular contraction and nerve damage occurs and death is presumably. 10,000mA cardiac arrest, severe burns and probable death. Sources of Electrical Hazards are.

- Short circuits
- Electrostatic hazards
- Arcs and spark hazards
- Combustible and explosive materials
- Improper wiring

Types of electrical faults

- **Overloads**

  Together, current and voltage supply the power we use every day. Any electric current that exceeds the rating of the circuit is an Overcurrent. When the current exceeds the rated current carrying capacity of the conductor, it generates excess heat that can damage insulation. If insulation becomes damaged, personnel may be severely injured and equipment or property compromised or destroyed. Over currents can be divided into two categories[29]: (1) Overloads, and (2) Short Circuits. An overload is defined *as an overcurrent that is confined to the normal current path. Excessive connected loads, stalled motors, overloaded machine tools, etc. can overload a circuit.* Most conductors can carry a moderate overload for a short duration without damage. In fact, transient moderate overloads are part of normal operation. Start-up or temporary surge currents for motors, pumps, or transformers are common examples. Overcurrent protection must be selected that will carry these currents. However, if the overload persists for too long, excessive heat will be generated ultimately causing insulation failure. This may result in fires or lead to a short circuit.

- **Short Circuits**

  A Short Circuit is any current not confined to the normal path. The term comes from the fact that such currents bypass the normal load (i.e., it finds a "short" path around the load). Usually, when a current is greater than 6 times (600%) the normal current, it should be removed as quickly as possible from the circuit. Short Circuits are usually caused by accidental contact or worn insulation and are more serious than overloads. Damage occurs almost instantly. Examples of Short Circuits include[30,31] two or more conductors accidentally touching, someone touching or dropping tools across energized conductors or accidental connection between energized conductors and ground. Such ground faults may vary from a few amperes to the maximum available short circuit fault current.

  When the electric current passes through the human body as a result of contact with parts carrying the current, great harm is caused to humans. The electric current causes burns and other things that may lead to the analysis of blood and nerve cells, and from the risks that may also occur, Electric shock occurs when a person touches the electrified wires directly [32-34], or when he touches objects carrying an electric current as a result of not isolating them by indirect contact, which leads to severe damage that may reach the person, and the severity of the electric charge differs[35]. There are many factors:

- The intensity and type of the current passing through the body, the continuous current has less effect than the changing current. The duration of the current's flow in the human body.

- The greater the duration of the current's flow, the greater the damage. The organ in which an electric current flows, the heart and nervous system are two of the body parts most affected by electricity. In the case of skin, dry skin is more resistant to electric current, while wet skin that is wet with water has less resistance.
- Burns vary in severity, they may be simple and arise from weak currents, and they may be strong and severe that arise from strong currents of high pressure, and strong currents destroy most layers of the skin.
- Eye dazzle produces eye dazzle due to electric shock. As it leads to darkening of the lens of the eye due to the flow of electric current in the eye, in addition to the occurrence of infections due to the exposure of the eye to electric flash, as well as to the welding agent with electricity[35].

CHEMICAL

The Indian Pharmaceutical Industry is making enormous progress not only in the creation of excellence but also to meet the global requirements of providing APIs and quality medicines as well as getting into growing fields of research, production, and clinical trials as it is a highly regulated and R&D-driven industry. Pharmaceutical industries also have many environmental problems, like the other chemical industries, especially in API manufacture[36-39]. Hazard is a situation that poses a threat to life, health, property, or the environment. Industrial hazard can be defined as any condition produced by industries that can cause injury or death to personnel or loss of product or property[40]. Hazardous materials are chemicals that, if released or abused, can pose a threat to the environment or health. They include industrial chemicals, pesticides, agricultural chemicals, pharmaceuticals, cosmetics, and food chemicals that may be present at the workplace and 'have a negative effect on a worker's health as a result of direct contact or exposure to the chemical substance.' The first and fundamental step leading to the safe use of chemicals is knowledge of their identity, their health and environmental risks, and the means to control them. This knowledge must be available with an affordable cost and effort. In addition, this intrinsically complex knowledge must be organized in such a way that key information on relevant risks and protection measures can be identified and transmitted to the user in an easy-to-understand manner[41].

Several volatile and flammable liquids are employed in chemical industries. These liquids are vaporized when exposed to at room temperature or above causing air pollution. Sudden releases of toxic vapours have the potential to cause death and severe injuries several miles from the discharge point. They are carried by water and air. The vapour gets combusted causing fire accidents and explosions. Further, they spread rapidly into the surrounding area and result in the loss of life and property[42].

Combustible gases

- Explosion hazard
- Must maintain below lower explosive limit.

Toxic gases

- Hazardous to human health.
- Employee exposure must be limited.

Oxygen displacing gases

- Indirect human health hazard.
- Deficiency of breathing oxygen

Types of Chemical hazards

Chemical hazards may be toxic, corrosive, irritant, carcinogenic, flammable, and mutagenic. According to the nature of work hazardous materials information, or chemical hazards are classified as[43-44].

Class A

- Compressed gas
- Dissolved gas or Liquified gas

Class B

- Flammable gases.
- Flammable and combustible liquids.
- Flammable solid.
- Flammable aerosols.
- Reactive flammable material.

Class C

- Oxidizing materials- oxidizer and organic peroxide.
- Oxidizer: Chlorates, nitric oxide, peroxides, permanganates, perchlorates, nitrites, nitrates, and easily oxidize metal powder.
- Organic peroxide: Tetra hydro furan, diethyl ether, dioxane, and methyl isobutyl ether.

Class D

- Poisonous and infectious materials. e.g.: Cyanides, tea salts, and asbestos.

Class E

- Corrosive materials. e.g.: Inorganic acids and bases, hydrogen fluoride.

Class F

- Dangerous reactive materials. e.g.: Ethylene dioxide, organic azides, Na, Li, Ca.
- Pyrophosphoric materials. e.g.. White phosphorous, diethyl aluminium chloride, and lithium.

Routes of exposure to hazardous chemicals

To cause health problems, chemicals must get entry in the body. There are five main "forms of exposure" or ways in which a chemical can enter the body:

Inhalation

Hazardous chemicals in the air may be inhaled and may cause damage to the body.

Skin contact

Some hazardous chemicals may damage the skin directly or may be absorbed into the body through the skin.

Eye contact

Contact with some hazardous chemicals may cause serious eye injuries.

Ingestion

Hazardous chemical products may enter the body while eating or drinking food contaminated by chemicals.

Injection

Sharp objects can puncture the skin and inject chemicals or viruses into the body[45].

Effects on Health

The effects of toxic chemicals on the body can be categorized as acute or chronic. Acute (short-term) effects Appears immediately or soon after chemical exposure. They can be minor, such as irritation of the nose or throat, or can be severe, such as eye damage or chemical vapours. The only thing that is common with these effects is that they happen instantly. Chronic (long-term) effects They are usually caused by continuous or long-term exposure to harmful substances. These effects are generally irreversible. Some chemicals can cause both acute and chronic effects. For example, solvents vapor inhalation may cause immediate dizziness (acute effect). However, breathing the same vapours all the time for many years could cause liver damage (chronic effect[46]

Carcinogens

The identification of carcinogenic agents was based on the IARC classification and corresponding IARC monographs[47,48]. Only agents belonging to Group 1 were considered, i.e., agents for which there is sufficient evidence of carcinogenicity in humans, and therefore, a causal relationship between agent and increased incidence of malignant neoplasms has been established. The estimates of the number of specific exposures of a worker were taken from the database carcinogens exposure[49]. These estimates correspond to the exposure period 1990–1993 across 55 industrial sectors for the EU-15 countries[49,50]

Sensitizing and Reprotoxic Substances

The identification of sensitizing substances was based on the list of compounds published in 2013 by the German Commission for the Investigation of Health Hazards of Chemical Compounds (MAK-Commission)[51, 52], Sensitizing substances, i.e., substances capable of inducing an immunological response to an otherwise innocuous antigen, are classified either as "Sa," "Sh," or "SP." The label "Sh" designates substances that can cause allergic or irritant reactions of the skin and the mucosa close to the skin (skin sensitizing) such as irritant contact dermatitis, allergic contact dermatitis, protein contact dermatitis, and contact urticaria[53,54]. The label "Sa" designates substances causing airway sensitization. These involve allergic reactions such as bronchial asthma or rhinoconjunctivitis, and other effects associated with systemic reactions (anaphylaxis). The label "SP" designates substances causing photo contact sensitization, i.e., an allergic reaction of the skin due to the interaction of the substance with ultraviolet radiation[55]. In general, the classification of a substance as sensitizing is based on either sufficient empirical evidence of allergenic and/or irritant effects or in cases where the allergenic effect can be considered probable on the basis of appropriate empirical evidence[56].

Mutagenic

According to Annex 6 of the council directive 67/548/ECC mutagenic substances refer to substances giving rise to an enhanced occurrence of genetic mutations that may be transmitted to the offspring, that is, the permanent changes in the amount of the genetic material resulting in a change of the phenotypic characteristics of the organism and its offspring. Substances toxic to reproduction refer to substances causing either impaired fertility ("RF") or subsequent developmental effects in the progeny[57]. Chemical exposures are generally divided into two categories: Acute and chronic. Symptoms resulting from acute exposures usually occur during or shortly after exposure to a sufficiently high concentration of a contaminant[58-60]. The number of exposures for a given contaminant, the symptoms of an acute exposure may be completely different from those resulting from chronic exposure[61,62]. For either chronic or acute exposure, the toxic effect may be temporary and reversible or may be permanent (disability or death). Some chemicals may cause obvious symptoms such as burning, coughing, nausea, tearing eyes, or rashes. Other chemicals may cause health. Some clinical symptoms of the affected organs with the relative hazard causing agents are enlisted in the Table 6.2.

Table 6.2 Exposure limits of some commonly used chemicals.

Chemical	Exposure limit (ppm)
Ethyl Alcohol	1000
Acetone	1000
Methylene chloride	125
Isopropyl alcohol	400

Table 6.3 Clinical symptoms in affected body part and their causative chemicals.

Affected body organs/parts	Symptoms	Chemicals
Head	Dizziness, headache	Solvents, paint, ozone, smoke
Eye	Red, watery, irritated, grainy feeling Corneal and conjunctival disturbances Lens, iris, and anterior chamber disturbances Posterior segment and optic nerve disturbances Intra-ocular pressure elevation	Smoke, gases, various dusts, vapours from paint, and cleaners Sulphur dioxide, dimethyl sulphate, hydrogen sulphide Anticholinesterase agents, copper, phenylmercuric salts Carbon disulphide, ethylene glycol, warfarin Formaldehyde, ammonia
Nose	Sneezing, coughing, rhinitis, perforated septum	Smoke, ozone, solvents, various dusts, vapours, and fumes from paint and cleaners, acetic acetic acid, acetic anhydride
Mouth/throat, Chest and lungs	Green tongue, salivation, sore throat, Wheezing, coughing, shortness of breath, lung cancer	Vanadium, mercury, arsenic Metal fumes, various dusts, smoke, solvents, vapours from paint and cleaners
Breast	Gynecomastia	Oestrogens
Stomach	Nausea, vomiting, stomach ache, diarrhoea	Some metal fumes, solvents, paint vapours, long-term lead exposure

Table 6.3 ***contd...***

Affected body organs/parts	Symptoms	Chemicals
Skin	Redness, dryness, rash, itching, skin cancer	Solvents, chromium, nickel, detergents and cleaners, paint on skin
Skin	Yellow stains, acute eczematous dermatitis	Acetaldehyde, barium compounds, benzyl chloride, copper dust, epoxy resins
Nervous system	Nervousness, irritability, tremors, loss of coordination Drowsiness, disorientation Behavioural changes	Long-term solvent exposure, long-term lead exposure CNS depressants CNS depressants, convulsant
Reproductive system	Men: Low sperm count, damage to sperm. Women: Menstrual irregularities, miscarriage, damage to egg/foetus	Lead, toluene, some other solvents, ethylene oxide gas
Pulmonary system	Pneumonia Asthma Fibrosis	Ammonia, chlorine, oxides of N2 Phthalic anhydride, platinum salts Asbestos, kaolin, silica, talc
Cardiovascular system	Hypotension Hypertension Arrhythmia	CNS depressants, nitrites Diphenyl Trichloroethane, carbon tetrachloride
Digestive system	Nausea, vomiting Jaundice	CNS depressants, anticholinesterases Hydrazine, chloroform
Genitourinary system	Toxic nephrosis	Nephrotoxin (dioxane), oxalic acid, picric acid Picric acid

PHARMACEUTICAL MONITORING

Technical measures that can be used to prevent chemical dangers at the source and/or reduce staff exposure:

Substitution

It is an effective control method. A hazardous chemical substance is replaced by a less hazardous thing. It is particularly preferable if highly hazardous substances, such as carcinogens, can severely affect human physiological systems. However, it must be ensured that the substitution substance eliminates the danger of the above substance.

Engineering control (closed system)

In the absence of effective replacement, personnel must be safeguarded against any exposure. Steam and gas exposures should also be monitored and minimized if risks are involved in their use. A generally effective measure is to encircle the hazardous process or chemical. For example, sealed pipes should be used to transfer toxic or highly flammable solvents and other liquids (especially volatile) rather than pouring them outdoors. *Local ventilation systems*

If it is not possible to isolate experimental activities involving hazardous materials, then a properly designed local ventilation solution should be found, which generally helps remove contaminants at the source. A ventilation system consists of a hood, duct or pipe drain, a collecting system and contaminants are separated from clean and efficient air to create the fan suction force required. However, hazardous gases, fumes, and dusts from the ventilated air collection must be handled or treated before disposal. Inspection, proper maintenance, regular cleaning, and changing filters are essential for the protection against hazardous pollutants.

General ventilation

When it is difficult or impossible to avoid hazardous chemicals, fumes, dusts, fogs, or particles entering the laboratory air at the source, general dilution ventilation can be installed so that the maximum concentration of pollutants in the air does not exceed the TLV of the substance. At the best, it should consist of a clean air supply and a forced exhaust outlet in the right place. It can also be used in conjunction with other preventative measures.

Housekeeping

When working with hazardous chemicals, proper maintenance is required. The storage/stack/cabinet areas should be well organized and kept in order and along with the maintenance of premises and equipment should be planned. These tasks should be dedicated to individuals/laboratory workgroups. In addition, periodically check and repair the defective equipment. Cleaning efficiency should be monitored with adequate periodicity; this should involve the professors in charge/students/staff associated with a laboratory[63].

Maintenance of over exposure to chemicals

Although thousands of chemicals are commonly used in industry, the medical management of acute overexposure is not specific and includes four basic steps (with some exceptions).

1) Removal from exposure
2) Immediate removal of the person from the display site is the first step.
   - If a disabled victim is to be rescued; the rescue workers must protect themselves from contaminated atmosphere first.

- Respirators and rescue lines are compulsory first aid.
- Sometimes chemically impervious suits are also worn.

3) Resuscitation
   - Resuscitation means restoring the life of someone apparently dead (collapsed or shocked).
   - If the victim is apneic, resuscitation should start as soon as it is removed from the area.

   Sustainable care must be provided as with any other medical emergency.
4) Decontamination
   - A victim whose skin or clothing has been contaminated requires immediate removal of clothing and shoes. Then, a vigorous shower with soap and water is recommended, including attention to nails and scalp.
5) Symptomatic treatment
   - Acute overexposure can cause a series of signs and symptoms that require general medical support, regardless of the specific agent. Examples include convulsive seizure control, bronchospasm treatment, dehydration, and arrhythmias. There are some situations where specific antidotes or management strategies are available. The industry should prepare a list of medical management strategies for hazardous chemicals that it manages so that it can take corrective action and can attempt immediate rescue.

Workplace safety

Workplace safety is a joint responsibility of all individuals to create a healthy and safe workplace:

- Hazards of chemical substances exist and occur everywhere in the workplace. Students and professional workers must act by keeping safety in the mind all day, every day.
- Establish and clarify the rights and responsibilities of security in all workplaces.

However, it is the responsibility of the administration to:

- Educate workers and employers in the construction and maintenance of safe and healthy workplaces.
- Intervene when security responsibilities are not executed.
- Provide information and resources on a variety of security issues and to prevent injuries and workplace illnesses.

Any safety management system (SMS) is a constituent part of the overall management system of an organization/industry/establishment which reflects the overall management philosophy and system to achieve the goal. An SMS includes several important inputs such as:

- The purpose of inspections.
- Importance of workplace inspections.
- Plan of inspection.
- Types of hazards to be looked for in a workplace.
- Information needed to complete an inspection report.
- Time taken for an inspection.
- Frequency of inspections.
- The periodic audits, with routine monitoring of performance, should be carried out to determine the overall performance of the SMS in confirmation to requirements. The results are used to make necessary improvements for meaningful implementation of the work.
- The SMS requires periodic critical inspection of both workplace and workers to control and prevent the possible occurrences of injuries, accidents, and related problems for the necessary corrective action.
- Periodical workplace inspection by a qualified inspection team to know the real problems, if any, of the workers and workplace managers/supervisors. This help to identify jobs and tasks of the workers, the potential hazards that the workers are exposed to, and the possible reasons for occurrences of hazards[63].

Regulation for chemical hazards

The chemical management relies on a mix of national, regional, and international mechanisms, a range of multilateral environmental agreement, as well as voluntary initiatives including a globally harmonized system of classification and labelling of chemicals, the strategic approach to international chemicals management and responsible care. In many countries, legislative and administrative measures have been introduced to deal with chemical hazards. In 1992, the United Nations Conference on Environment and Development (the Rio Earth Conference) gave rise to the Agenda 21 Report 2. This report outlined the responsibilities of States toward the achievement of sustainable development and was adopted by heads of Government in over 150 countries. The management of toxic chemicals for all countries, including basic programs for:

1) Adequate legislation.
2) Information gathering and dissemination.
3) Capacity for risk assessment and interpretation.
4) Establishment of risk management policy.
5) Capacity for implementation and enforcement.

6) Capacity for rehabilitation of contaminated sites and poisoned persons.
7) Effective education programs.
8) Capacity to respond to emergencies.

Some international treaties related to chemical management and India's participation in them is represented in Table 6. The Indian Chemical Industry is poised for growth, and a clearly defined vision has been developed to enable it. The vision for Indian chemical industry is "To facilitate the growth and development of the chemical industry in an environmental friendly manner; with focus on innovation to meet local needs, sustainability, and green technologies and processes; so as to enable it to become a globally competitive major-player." The non-regulatory mechanisms adopted by industries in India, in addition to legislative control, play a very important role in the management of chemicals. Indian industries take several initiatives for environmental protection and chemical management, such as responsible care, corporate responsibility in environmental planning, ISO 14001, OHSAS 18001, ISI Marking (Indian Standards Institution), and eco-mark. Several awards related to chemical and environmental management are initiated on voluntary basis by industrial associations, who play an important role in encouraging industries to go for non-regulatory mechanisms for chemical management. Important industrial associations include Indian Chemical Council (formerly, the – Indian Chemical Manufacturer's Association), Confederation of Indian Industry, and Federation of Indian Chambers of Commerce and Industry[64,65].

The Republic of India enacted several legislations, rules, and regulations to exercise all the powers vested under the Act and Rules pertaining to the protection of environment and control of pollution. These are implemented and enforced in all environment legislation agency activities. The selected acts and Regulations include, but are not limited to, the following:

- Drugs and cosmetics act, 1940.
- The prevention of food adulteration act, 1954.
- Insecticides act, 1968.
- The water (prevention and control of pollution) act, 1974.
- Air (prevention and control of pollution) act, 1981.
- Narcotic drugs and psychotropic substances act 1985.
- The environment (protection) act, 1986.
- Manufacture, storage, and import of hazardous chemicals rules, 1989.
- Hazardous wastes (management and handling) rules, 1989.
- Water prevention and control of pollution act, 1974.
- Hazardous waste (management and handling) rules, 1989.
- Manufacture, storage and import of hazardous chemical rules, 1989.

- Rules for manufacture, use, import and storage of hazardous microorganisms, genetically engineered micro-organism or cells, 1989.
- Biomedical waste (management and handling) rules, 1998.
- The recycled plastic manufacture and usage rules, 1999.
- The ozone-depleting substances (regulation and control) rules, 2000.
- The noise pollution (regulation and control) rules, 2000.
- The batteries (management and handling) rules, 2001.

Our quality of life has significantly improved through chemistry since it has provided us with various useful products, but this has also provoked global environmental deprivation and the decline of non-renewable natural resources. Many pollutants end their path to the food chain and deteriorate the ecosystem. Green chemistry and its principles can change all of these negative aspects and impacts and through design, innovation, and green practices to restore the sustainable development. The ultimate goal is to develop and design non-conventional synthetic methodologies for important industrial chemicals to prevent/reduce environmental pollution[66].

PREVENTION SYSTEMS

The purpose of industrial safety is to understand the harmful effects of industrial hazards. It defines the relationship between hazard and risk. Industrial safety means the protection of workers from the major industrial accidents. The International Conference on Chemicals Managements has been convened in 2006 to work out how to ensure that all activities involving chemicals should be undertaken in such a way as to ensure the safety of human health and the environment. The chemical industry is important in many countries of the WHO. Many Member States are actively seeking to carry out the aims of the strategic approach, to deepen the involvement of their health in the sound management of chemical safety to prevent the negative impacts of chemicals on health, both directly and through the environment.

Reduction of accident

Industrial accidents and hazards have become the order of the day with new technologies evolving every day and few people knowing how to use these technologies. Such a dangerous trend is more likely by a low experience person. An accident is an unplanned event involving hazardous substances that cause or is liable to cause, harm to health, and environment. This excludes any long-term events (such as chronic pollution). There are some factors we should consider.

Design and premodification review

This involves correct layout, facilities, and material choice. Lesser chemicals should be stored, a reduction in inventory will automatically mean less damage if an accident is to occur.

Chemical risk assessment

Chemicals are assessed supported on compatibility, flammability, toxicity, explosion hazards and storage.

Process safety management

Before effecting, major process changes. Management should try to develop a culture of safety, reliability assessment of process equipment, incorporating safety trips and interlocks, scrubbing system, etc. in industrial organizations.

Safety audits

Periodical assessment of safety procedures and practices, the performance of safety systems and gadgets along with following up measures should be carried out.

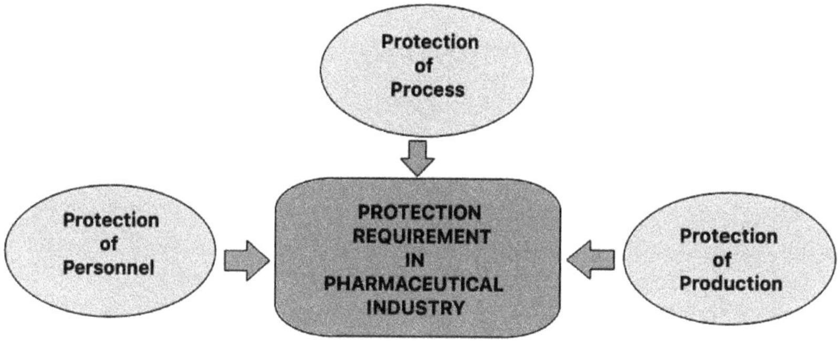

Fig.6.4 Protection requirement of pharmaceutical industry.

Training of employees

Proper training of staff and protective services should be arranged.

Proper storage

All chemicals and hazardous materials should be kept in proper storage temperature and in locked cupboards away from children and animals. Also, if reactive substances are stored, they should be stored is a water tight container.

Employer responsibilities

Employer remains fully responsible for the unauthorized activity. It is commonly observed that the management using 'Rule by Fear' method with employees (for example, employee do what employer are told). This leads to a culture of fear and blame and an inability of employees to challenge and not follow regulatory guidelines. An employee should be encouraged to avail advantage of an open-door route to organization top management when it comes to raising compliance issues and discussing potential compliance concerns pertaining to safety management. There are some responsibilities of the employer:

- To identify hazardous chemicals and to prepare a list of hazardous chemicals in their workplaces.
- To obtain Material Safety Data Sheets (MSDSs) and labels for each hazardous chemical, if not provided by the manufacturer, importer, or distributor.
- To implement a written Hazard program as well as labels, MSDSs, and employee training.
- To communicate hazard information to the staff through labels, MSDSs, and formal training programs.
- To review and if necessary, to revise all risk control measures already taken and maintained, and to revise the program for providing an environment that is without risk of health and safety[67].

INDUSTRIAL EFFLUENT TESTING

The production of bulk drugs has recently been identified as an important source for environmental pollution with active pharmaceutical ingredients (APIs) at certain locations. This has been shown that the effluent from a treatment plant receiving water from approximately 90 Indian bulk drug manufacturers contained very high levels (up to several milligrams per litre) of a variety of drugs. These findings were later confirmed by others. It also showed that the surface, ground, and drinking water in the region had become highly polluted with residual drugs. The treatment plant is located in an industrial area just outside the Hyderabad, and the bulk drugs produced in this area are primarily exported to the world market. It stressed the importance of this site in the global production chain for pharmaceuticals. Many of the drugs detected in the water are antibiotics, and the high concentrations of fluoroquinolones found in the effluent are expected to be highly toxic to bacteria. Concerns have also been raised about the possibility that the high environmental levels of fluoroquinolones may promote the development of antibiotic resistance. The occurrence of multi resistant pathogens is a serious global threat, and studies on the environmental microflora in have commenced.

Several drugs targeting a variety of human proteins were also detected at exceptionally high concentrations in the effluent. It is known that the PETL effluent can have a potent effect on aquatic vertebrates; as little as 0.2% of the effluent reduced the growth of tadpoles by 40%, whereas zebrafish (*Danio rerio*) growth was not affected according to an embryo toxicity test. The median lethal concentration (LC50) of effluent for zebrafish at 144 h after fertilization varied between 2.7 and 8.1% in different experiments. Concerns have been raised about the impact on both human health, wildlife ecology, and an impaired livelihood for local villagers. In the present study, focus begins on the potential effects on fish. Indeed, increased knowledge about how aquatic vertebrates are affected by effluent exposure, which substances in the effluent are causing the toxic effects, and at what dilutions of effluent fish are likely to be affected will aid in directing future efforts to improve the pollution situation in this area.

To achieve this end, gene responses and other biological effects characteristic of exposure to the PETL effluent could be useful as biomarkers for assessing how widely aquatic vertebrates are exposed and affected in the recipient environment. Patterns of gene responses could also generate hypotheses as to which compounds in the effluent are present at sufficiently high levels to affect gene expression and potentially become toxic to fish. Many useful environmental biomarkers of pollutant exposure are available (i.e., induction of vitellogenin in response to estrogenic compounds and induction of metallothionein in response to heavy metals), but few biomarkers of pharmaceutical exposure have been developed in wildlife species. The pharmacological and toxicological properties of drugs are, however, often well known in mammals and this knowledge might be useful in identifying the effects of pharmaceuticals in wildlife species. More than 80% of all human drug targets have homologs in zebrafish and western clawed frog (*Xenopus tropicalis*), and it is plausible that many drugs display similar modes of action in aquatic vertebrates and mammals. A microarray analysis of fish exposed to a high dilution of the PETL effluent (sublethal concentration) could identify useful biomarkers of exposure. Such an analysis could also provide information about affected functional pathways and might aid in the future identification of substances that are responsible for the toxic effects caused by effluent exposure. A microarray focused on genes relevant for both pharmacological and toxic responses was therefore developed for rainbow trout (*Oncorhynchus mykiss*). Using this array, the hepatic transcriptome was analysed in trout exposed to 0.2% of the PETL effluent. In addition, effects on higher levels of biological organization, such as hepatic and plasma enzyme activities and metabolite levels were measured.

Biological treatment of wastewater is frequently the most beneficial method for selecting various toxic compounds from the environment. Most of the organic compounds in industrial wastewaters are of natural origin and can be degraded by common bacteria in aerobic or anaerobic processes. "Due to its proven capacity to degrade certain toxic components as well as most common organic pollutants in industrial wastewater, anaerobic treatment today has advanced to a high level of usefulness in the restoration of many industrial effluents" (Donlon, Flores, Field & Lettinga, 1995). The pharmaceutical industry constitutes from the wastewaters containing toxic organic chemicals. The composition of these wastewaters is very variable. A great variety of organic chemicals can be determined among the principal components of these types of wastewaters. Antibiotics are the major group of pharmaceuticals. Among all the other pharmaceutical drugs and substances, antibiotics are important compounds due to its serious irreversible increase the release to the environment. Antibiotics are in effluent of treatment plants and receiver media due to difficult treatability with conventional treatment systems such as aerobic active sludge system. For that reason, they spoil ecological balance to form toxicity to organisms in ecosystem and biological treatment systems.

The purpose of this study is to provide the treatability of two types of antibiotics (Kemicetine and Sulfamerazine) in an up flow anaerobic sludge blanket (UASB) reactor/aerobic completely stirred tank (CSTR) reactor and an anaerobic baffled reactor (ABR)/aerobic (CSTR) reactor systems. There is not enough knowledge about the treatability of pharmaceutical wastewater in anaerobic conditions. Furthermore, no study about the treatability of wastewaters containing antibiotic was encountered using both UASB and ABR reactors. Therefore this thesis was designed to investigate these lacks in the literature. The major objectives of this research can be summarized as follows;

- to investigate the removal efficiencies COD and BOD5, VFA production, total and methane gas productions of synthetic wastewaters containing antibiotic in different Kemicetine and Sulfamerazine doses in sequential UASB/ CSTR and ABR/ CSTR reactor systems,
- to monitor the toxicity of synthetic wastewater containing antibiotic based on specific methanogenic activity (SMA) tests,
- to characterize the wastewater composition based on inert COD, slowly and readily biodegradable organic substances and BOD5 / COD ratios,
- to compare both systems according to their treatment efficiencies.

Descriptions of the PETL treatment plant, water sampling procedures, and chemical characteristics of the effluent were previously published. The effluent samples used in the present study were taken simultaneously with those used in the Larsson et al. study. The effluent was frozen on dry ice in India and was kept frozen until just prior to the exposure.

Physicochemical measurement

Temperature

Measured using pH and dissolved oxygen meter, or thermometer.

pH

The pH meter is used to measure the acidity of the water by comparing readings from a reference electrode and a sample electrode. The pH meter is used to measure the acidity of the water by comparing readings from a reference electrode and a sample electrode. To determine pH the output of these electrodes must be kept temperature constant, most pH meters also measure temperature.

Turbidity

The clarity of the water, measured using a portable turbidimeter. The turbidimeter measures the light transmittance of a sample in NTU's (Nephelometric Turbidity Units, a standard measure). It needs no field calibration. Handle the sample vials only by their ends (preferably the lid) so as not to affect the transmittance; wipe any fingerprints, spots, etc. from the outside of the vial; and be sure to close the vial-compartment lid when taking a measurement.

DO

Dissolved Oxygen content. Measured using a hand-held dissolved oxygen meter. The DO meter will measure dissolved oxygen, electrical conductivity, and salinity. DO is measured by the rate of consumption of oxygen at the tip of the probe, so it requires continual movement of water past the tip (an up-and-down motion seems to work best, keep the probe tip submerged). Stable readings are not possible while the temperature of the sample is changing. When performing analysis at multiple sampling locations, the DO meter calibration should be checked at the beginning, middle, and end of each analysis day. Oxygen from the atmosphere enters water through adsorption at its surface, a process enhanced by agitation (rapid moving water). In flowing water, oxygen-rich water at the surface is constantly being replaced by water containing less oxygen as a result of turbulence, creating a greater potential for exchange of oxygen across the air-water interface. Flowing water is more likely to have high DO levels than stagnant water Because still water undergoes less internal mixing, the upper layer of oxygen-rich water tends to stay at the surface, resulting in lower dissolved oxygen levels throughout the rest of the water levels DO can also enter water as a waste product of photosynthesis by aquatic plants, a process highly dependent on sunlight. The amount of oxygen that can be held by water depends on the water temperature, salinity, and pressure. Gas solubility increases with decreasing temperature and decreasing salinity Colder water can hold more oxygen than warm water and freshwater can hold more oxygen than saltwater. Gas solubility decreases as pressure decreases so the amount of oxygen absorbed in water decreases as altitude increases.

The Winkler method for the determination of dissolved O_2 involves adding an excess of 'white' $Mn(OH)_2$ which contains Mn^{2+} ions.

$$4Mn(OH)_2 + O_2 + 2H_2O \longrightarrow 4Mn(OH)_3$$

(White solid) (Brown solid)

This forms the brown manganese hydroxide containing Mn^{3+} ions. Addition of potassium iodide (I- ions) and an acid forms iodine.

$$2Mn(OH)_2 + 2I^- + 6H^+ \longrightarrow I_2 + 3H_2O + 2Mn^{2+}$$

For every molecule of O_2 two molecules of I_2 are formed. The quantity of iodine present can be found though titration of the sample with sodium thiosulphate.

INDUSTRIAL EFFLUENT TREATMENT

Bulk drug manufacturing industries use various processes such as chemical synthesis, fermentation, extraction, and other complex processes. The pharmaceutical industry also produces different products using different materials and different processes. Table 6.4 demonstrates some commonly prepared materials along with the typical examples.

Table 6.4 Classes of pharmaceutical products with typical examples.

Type of material	Sub classes	Common examples
Medicinal	Antibiotics Vitamins Anti-infective agents Central depressants and stimulants Gastro-intestinal agents and therapeutic nutrients Hormones and substitutes Autonomic drugs Antihistamines Dermatological agents - local anaesthetics Expectorants and mucolytic agents Renal acting and endema reducing agents	Penicillin, erythromycin, tetracycline Vit. B., C., E, A. Sulphonamides Antipyretics, analgesics, barbiturates Salicylic acid
Botanicals	Central depressants and stimulants Various alkaloids	Morphine, reserpine, quinine, curare Codeine, caffeine, etc.
Biologicals	Serums, vaccines, toxoids, antigens	

Hence, it is difficult to generalise its classification.

Most of the pharmaceutical industries in India are set up in Ahmedabad, Bangalore, Hyderabad, and Mumbai. These provides 20% generic medicines. However, a rather lenient regulatory for pharmaceutical waste disposal and irresponsible production have significantly affected the aquatic environment. The discharge from the pharmaceutical industries contains non-biodegradable recalcitrant organic substances, which have high toxicity toward the aquatic and human life. 60–80% of the prescribed pharmaceuticals are excreted, and they make their way to the sewage treatment plants and environment. Several researchers[68] have detected pharmaceuticals in the ground and surface water in the range of 15–1200 ng dm^{-3}. In recent studies, traces of pharmaceuticals were found in the lakes, rivers, and wells in Hyderabad. Although the amounts of pharmaceuticals were in the range of 90–31,000 μg dm^{-3}, the chronic effects of these compounds were caused by their long term exposure.

The current situation in USA predicts that the number of deaths (23,000 deaths per year) due to the anti-microbial resistance will surpass the combined number of deaths due to cancer and diabetes. Villages adjacent to the pharmaceutical industries are in alarming condition because of the highly contaminated groundwater, which leads to serious health problems such as cancer, miscarriage, and skin disorders. There are many confirmed cases of fish death in the water bodies and resistance developed in humans toward antibiotics[69]. In 2018, the National Centre for Disease Control (NCDC) of India raised the concern over antibiotic pollution in water and requested the ministry of environment to develop strict laws and to implement them for correct disposal and effective treatment by the antibiotic manufacturers.

The environment ministry of India has classified all pharmaceutical manufacturers in the "red category" because they release toxic and hazardous discharge into the environment. The existing policies are incredibly inefficient for regulating and enforcing the present laws. The conventional wastewater treatment plants have been found to be ineffective for removing the pharmaceuticals discharges due to the presence of refractory and selectively-active organic compounds. It has also been observed that the antibiotics present in the pharmaceutical wastewater show toxicity towards microorganism-embedded wastewater in the treatment plants. Thus, the overall efficiency is reduced.

In the past three decades, the advanced oxidation processes (AOPs) have proven to be a perfect tool for the removal of refractory organic compounds such as the pharmaceuticals[70] from synthetic wastewater. Most of the AOPs involve the generation of the hydroxyl radical as the main oxidant. The possibility of a high degree of mineralization and the non-selective nature of the AOPs have rendered them attractive. However, the commercial application of the AOPs is still scarce due to their high cost. To overcome the high cost, the AOPs are often integrated with other techniques such as biodegradation, adsorption, electro-coagulation, and membrane separation. AOPs are used in the pre-treatment stage for increasing the biodegradability and reducing the cost in the optimized integration for highly contaminated industrial wastewaters. Ozone alone has been recognized as a strong oxidant, and it is capable of degrading recalcitrant organic compounds. Ozone very selectively attacks organic compounds having a high electron density, whereas[71], OH is a non-selective oxidant, and the latter reacts with a variety of organic compounds.

CONTROL OF ENVIRONMENTAL POLLUTION

Environmental Pollution is one of the major problems that have been facing globally. To reduce our necessities is the biggest concern as it accumulates pollution. Pollution has many forms, the water that we drink to the sound that we hear can be considered as some aspects that contribute to environmental pollution which would, in turn, lead to health hazards, adverse effect on ecosystem and wildlife. Pollution can be stated as the introduction of harmful substances or any foreign particles that would have a bad effect on the environment.

Protection of our environment is one of our major responsibilities and a natural way of caring for self and for our future generations. There are several factors that would help reduce the impact of our consumption habits. Beneath are some of the practical ways that can be implemented in our daily life to reduce pollution.

- Avoid using a car for short-distance travel, instead, you can make use of a bicycle which will be beneficial in terms of health as well as in the reduction of air pollution.

Air pollution refers to any physical, chemical or biological change in the air. It is the contamination of air by harmful gases, dust and smoke which affects plants, animals and humans drastically.

There is a certain percentage of gases present in the atmosphere. An increase or decrease in the composition of these gases is harmful to survival. This imbalance in the gaseous composition has resulted in an increase in earth's temperature, which is known as global warming. There are two types of air pollutants:

- Primary pollutants

  The pollutants that directly cause air pollution are known as primary pollutants. Sulphur-dioxide emitted from factories is a primary pollutant.

- Secondary pollutants

  The pollutants formed by the intermingling and reaction of primary pollutants are known as secondary pollutants. Smog, formed by the intermingling of smoke and fog, is a secondary pollutant.

  Following are the important causes of air pollution:

- The combustion of fossil fuels emits a large amount of sulphur dioxide. Carbon monoxide released by incomplete combustion of fossil fuels also results in air pollution.
- The gases emitted from vehicles such as jeeps, trucks, cars, buses, etc. pollute the environment. These are the major sources of greenhouse gases and also result in diseases among individuals.
- Ammonia is one of the most hazardous gases emitted during agricultural activities. The insecticides, pesticides and fertilisers emit harmful chemicals in the atmosphere and contaminate it.
- Factories and industries are the main source of carbon monoxide, organic compounds, hydrocarbons and chemicals. These are released into the air, degrading its quality.
- In the mining process, the minerals below the earth are extracted using large pieces of equipment. The dust and chemicals released during the process not only pollute the air, but also deteriorate the health of the workers and people living in the nearby areas.
- The household cleaning products and paints contain toxic chemicals that are released in the air. The smell from the newly painted walls is the smell of the chemicals present in the paints. It not only pollutes the air but also affects breathing.
- As transporting the food across various parts of the country would lead to consumption of considerable fuel, we can minimize the consumption of excessive fuel by choosing food products that have been grown locally and naturally using viable methods. Hence reducing air pollution.
- Ensure that you switch off the lights and other electrical appliances when you are not in the room. Unplugging them when not in use would also help to save energy. Use energy-efficient light bulbs.
- Make use of eco-friendly chemicals because these are what we use for washing utensils, cars and homes get washed down into the sewage system that would, in turn, get collected as groundwater.
- Medicines with high dosage when end up in the sanitation system, are very difficult to isolate from the water system and would cause an adverse effect on people who would consume this water.
- Avoid excess unwanted usage of water. Some of the simple ways to prevent wastage of water include, to make use of water-saving apparatus, fixing leakage of taps and avoid washing utensils with running water.

Environmental pollution can be controlled or reduced by creating the awareness regarding the consequence of it. There are several ways that one could educate people on environmental pollution. Do some research online and get to know about the causes of pollution in your area. Share with many people as much as possible so that they are aware of the severity of pollution and the ways to prevent it. One can also create awareness by creating an environmental group.

With the urban development of society, environmental issues are getting increasing attention. In particular, the consequent harmful and toxic pollutants in the environment have aroused global concerns. Global efforts are underway to mitigate environmental pollution and protect human health. Nanotechnology is expected to contribute significantly to environmental protection. Over the past two decades, various nanomaterials have been researched in-depth for their potential of providing new solutions or enhancing the existing solutions to many of the pressing environmental problems from water pollution to air pollution[72]. Nanomaterials such as transition metal dichalcogenides, carbon-based nanomaterials, metallic nanoparticles, and metal-organic frameworks have versatile applications in contaminant monitoring, environmental decontamination, and energy production. Among them, carbon-based nanomaterials, including pristine graphene, graphene oxide, carbon nanotubes, as well as fullerene, have unique properties, such as high specific surface areas, excellent aqueous stability, and large pore volume. Therefore, they have been widely used for countless environmental applications such as sensing, adsorptive removal of contaminants, membrane-based separation, catalytic degradation, and energy conversion and storage.

Recently, the development of carbon dots (CDs) has also attracted enormous attention owing to their particular physical chemistry properties, ultra-small size, good biocompatibility, abundant and inexpensive precursor[73]. According to the Web of Science, the number of related publications on CDs has increased every year, and the application of CDs has been multidisciplinary. CDs show significant potential in the environmental field because of the following features:

- they possess a series of unique optical properties, such as continuous and wide absorption spectra, strong fluorescent activity, excellent photostability, highly tunable photoluminescence and excellent optoelectronic performances;
- CDs have a wide range of useful physicochemical properties due to the variety of raw materials and synthetic approaches, such as abundant surface functional groups, ultra-small sizes, large surface areas, excellent water dispersibility, superior ability in charge transport, and excellent electron donors and acceptors; and

- they are inexpensive, highly biocompatible, and environment-friendly. These peculiarities have enabled CDs to be used to monitor and remove pollutants assemble water treatment membranes, and serve as antibacterial material for pathogenic bacterium.

Previous reviews have detailed synthesis strategies, and different applications of CDs in bioanalysis, bioimaging, and energy conversion, which greatly improved our level of understanding and promoted the development of CDs. For instance, a review on the application of CDs in the photodegradation of organic pollutants, and heavy metal ion sensing was reported by Mehta *et al.* [20]. More recently, Abd Rani and co-workers summarized the use of CDs for applications in wastewater treatment and the biomedical field. With the development and integration of other nanotechnologies, CDs will have an increasing impact on the environmental technologies in the future. Consequently, it is imperative and timely to present a comprehensive and extensive review of the latest developments and application of CDs in environmental control and remediation. This review summarizes the recent developments of CDs in different environmental applications. First, the main synthesis methods and properties of CDs relevant to the environment are briefly outlined. Then, the recent progress in applications of CDs for pollutant sensing, contaminant adsorption, membrane-based separation, pollutant degradation, and antimicrobial control are discussed in detail. The potential use of CDs in environmental pollution control and remediation are also emphasized. Finally, the main knowledge gaps and future challenges to realize the full potential of CDs in environmental systems are also highlighted. We hope this review can offer referable directions for the environmental application of CDs, and provide guidance for the development of effective environmental pollution control and remediation technologies.

Exercise

Multiple Choice Questions

1. Fill in the blank using appropriate word given below.
2. Industrial safety is primarily a .... activity which is concerned with reducing, controlling and eliminating hazards from the industries or industrial units.

   a) quality control b) quality assurance

   c) production d) management

3. Fill in the blank using appropriate word given below.

4. Industrial safety can .... accidents in the plant by reducing the hazard to minimum.

    a) prevent   b) stop

    c) accelerate   d) nullify

5. Fill in the blank using appropriate word given below.

6. Industrial hazard may be defined as any condition created by industries that will cause injury or death to personnel or loss of .... or property.

    a) Profit   b) product

    c) Profitability   d) reputation

7. Fill in the blank using appropriate word given below.

8. There are four major routes, inhalation, skin or eye absorption, ingestion, and injection through which the .... chemical(s) can enter into the body.

    a) any   b) all

    c) hazardous   d) no

9. Fill in the blank using appropriate word given below.

10. Once the hazardous chemical is inhaled, it is deposited in the .... tract and damages the tissue, or diffusing into the blood through the lung-blood interface.

    a) Respiratory   b) oesophagus

    c) Lung   d) heart

11. Fill in the blank using appropriate word given below.

12. The skin is the .... most common route by which occupational chemicals enter the body.

    a) First   b) second

    c) largest   d) third

13. Fill in the blank using appropriate word given below.

14. One can reduce the toxic effects of hazardous chemicals through the .... of industrial waste.

    a) utilization   b) enlargement

    c) management   d) drainage

15. Fill in the blank using appropriate word given below.

16. .... is the relative ability of a substance or chemical to cause adverse effects in living organisms.

    a) Activity
    b) Effectiveness
    c) Lethality
    d) Toxicity

17. Which of the following statement is correct?

    a) Chemical substances enter the body if someone punctured the skin by contaminated objects.
    b) Chemical substances enter the body if the skin is penetrated or punctured by contaminated objects.
    c) Chemical substances enter the body if the contaminated object is penetrated the skin.
    d) Chemical substances enter the body if someone injects the skin with contaminated objects.

18. Which of the following statement is correct?

    a) Fire is an exothermic chemical reaction between oxygen and fuel at a certain temperature.
    b) Fire is an electrical hazards caused chemical reaction between electrical wiring and fuel at a certain temperature.
    c) Fire is an endothermic chemical reaction between oxygen and fuel at a certain temperature.
    d) Fire is a chemical hazard caused by a reaction between oxygen and fuel at a certain temperature.

19. Which of the following statement is correct?

    a) A jet fire occurs when a cloud of flammable gas and air is ignited.
    b) A pool fire occurs when a cloud of flammable gas and air is ignited.
    c) A flash fire occurs when a cloud of flammable gas and air is ignited.
    d) A secondary fire occurs when a cloud of flammable gas and air is ignited.

20. Which of the following statement is correct?

    a) A pool fire occurs when a flammable liquid or gas is ignited after its release from a pressurized, punctured vessel or pipe.
    b) A flash fire occurs when a flammable liquid or gas is ignited after its release from a pressurized, punctured vessel or pipe.

c) A secondary fire occurs when a flammable liquid or gas is ignited after its release from a pressurized, punctured vessel or pipe.

d) A jet fire occurs when a flammable liquid or gas is ignited after its release from a pressurized, punctured vessel or pipe.

21. Which of the following statement is correct?

a) A pool fire occurs on ignition of an accumulation of liquid as a pool on the ground or on water or other liquid.

b) A jet fire occurs on ignition of an accumulation of liquid as a pool on the ground or on water or other liquid.

c) A flash fire occurs on ignition of an accumulation of liquid as a pool on the ground or on water or other liquid.

d) A secondary fire occurs on ignition of an accumulation of liquid as a pool on the ground or on water or other liquid.

22. Which of the following statement is correct?

a) Jet fires are less dangerous to human life than flash fires but their longer durations results in greater structural damages.

b) Pool fires are less dangerous to human life than flash fires but their longer durations results in greater structural damages.

c) Flash fires are less dangerous to human life than flash fires but their longer durations results in greater structural damages.

d) Secondary fires are less dangerous to human life than flash fires but their longer durations results in greater structural damages.

23. Which of the following statement is correct?

a) In a flash fire, pressure release generates a long flame, which is stable under most conditions.

b) In a pool fire, pressure release generates a long flame, which is stable under most conditions.

c) In a jet fire, pressure release generates a long flame, which is stable under most conditions.

d) In a secondary fire, pressure release generates a long flame, which is stable under most conditions.

24. Which of the following statement is correct?

a) The orange zone spans from the contour representing radiation level of 12.5Kw/m^2 to the contour of radiation level of 37.5Kw/m^2.

b) The orange zone spans from the contour representing radiation level of 37.5Kw/m^2 to the contour of radiation level of 37.5Kw/m^2.

c) The orange zone spans from the contour representing radiation level of $37.5Kw/m^2$ to the contour of radiation level of $37.5Kw/m^2$.

d) The orange zone spans from the contour representing radiation level of $37.5Kw/m^2$ to the contour of radiation level of $12.5Kw/m^2$.

25. Which of the following statement is correct?
    a) Ozone very selectively attacks organic compounds having a high electron density.
    b) Ozone does not attack organic compounds having a high electron density.
    c) Ozone very selectively attacks organic compounds having a low electron density.
    d) Ozone selectively attacks inorganic compounds having a low electron density.

26. Which of the following statement is correct?
    a) The environment ministry of India has classified all pharmaceutical manufacturers in the "green category" because they release toxic and hazardous discharge into the environment.
    b) The environment ministry of India has classified all pharmaceutical manufacturers in the "red category" because they do not release toxic and hazardous discharge into the environment.
    c) The environment ministry of India has classified all pharmaceutical manufacturers in the "blue category" because they release toxic and hazardous discharge into the environment
    d) The environment ministry of India has classified all pharmaceutical manufacturers in the "red category" because they release toxic and hazardous discharge into the environment.

27. Which of the following statement is correct?
    a) The pH meter is used to measure the turbidity of the water by comparing readings from a reference electrode and a sample electrode.
    b) The pH meter is used to measure the alkalinity of the water by comparing readings from a sample electrode and a reference electrode.
    c) The pH meter is used to measure the acidity of the water by comparing readings from a reference electrode and a sample electrode.
    d) The pH meter is used to measure the salinity of the water by comparing readings from a reference electrode and a sample electrode.

28. Which of the following statement is correct?
    a) The low-pressure fluid injection can cause serious injuries or even death.
    b) The high-pressure fluid injection can cause serious injuries or even death.
    c) The high-pressure fluid injection cannot cause serious injuries or even bed ridden.
    d) The low-pressure fluid injection can cause serious injuries or even bed ridden.

Short Questions

1. What are the managerial perspective of the importance of industrial safety in any organization? What is meant by industrial hazard?
2. Briefly explain the electrical hazard.
3. Explain how it is a joint responsibility of all individuals to create a healthy and safe workplace.
4. Explain the statement 'The purpose of industrial safety is to understand the harmful effects of industrial hazards.'
5. Explain the statement, 'workers are injured on the job due to hazards of machines.'
6. 'Electrical hazards have always been recognized, yet serious injuries, deaths, and property damage occur daily.' – explain in detail.
7. What are the regulations for chemical hazards?
8. What are causes of air pollution? How can the environmental pollution be controlled?
9. 'The production of bulk drugs has recently been identified as an important source for environmental pollution with active pharmaceutical ingredients (APIs) at certain locations.' – explain the statement.
10. What are several legislations, rules, and regulations have been enacted by India to exercise all the powers vested under the Act and Rules pertaining to the protection of environment and control of pollution?

Long Questions

1. Explain the four major routes through which the hazardous chemicals can enter into the body.
2. Discuss different types of industrial hazard.
3. Explain different types of electrical faults.
4. Explain the regulations for chemical hazards.

5. What is fire hazard? Explain different types of fire hazards.
6. What are some common hazards associated with machinery?
7. Why the testing of industrial effluent is necessary? What is its relation to environmental pollution?
8. What is CD? How is it related to air pollution?
9. Explain how the industrial safety can be maintained with relevant example. How industrial safety is related to the human safety?
10. What is meant by workplace safety? Explain how can affect the human safety.

Answers

1	2	3	4	5	6	7	8	9	10	11	12	13	14	15	16	17	18	19	20
d	a	b	c	a	b	c	d	b	a	c	d	a	b	c	d	a	d	c	b

Reference

1. Bureau of Labor Statistics (BLS). 2018 Census of Fatal Occupational Injuries (Final Data)—Industry by Event or Exposure. U.S. Bureau of Labor Statistics, U.S. Department of Labor; 2019.
2. Health and Safety Executive (HSE). Construction Statistics in Great Britain, 2018. Health and Safety Executive. 2019.
3. China Labour Bulletin (CLB). China's most Dangerous Industry is Getting more Dangerous. China Labour Bulletin. 2019.
4. Hong Kong Occupational Safety and Health (HKOSH). Occupational Safety and Health Statistics 2017. Labor Department, The Government of the Hong Kong Special Administrative Region; 2017.
5. Verma A, Khan SD, Maiti J, Krishna OB. Identifying patterns of safety related incidents in a steel plant using association rule mining of incident investigation reports. Safety Science. 2014;70:89-98
6. Reimink H. Safety and Health. 2016. Available from: http://www.worldsteel. org/publications/position-papers/ safety-and-health.
7. Grabowski M, Ayyalasomayajula P, Merrick J, Harrald JR, Roberts K. Leading indicators of safety in virtual organizations. Safety Science. 2007;45(10):1013-1043.
8. Choudhry RM, Fang D, Mohamed S. The nature of safety culture: A survey of the state-of-the-art. Safety Science. 2007;45(10):993-1012

9. Hallowell MR, Hinze JW, Baud KC, Wehle A.; Proactive construction safety control: Measuring, monitoring, and responding to safety leading indicators. Journal of Construction Engineering and Management. 2013;139(10):04013010
10. Health and Safety Executive (HSE). Developing Process Safety Indicators: A Step-by-Step Guide for Chemical and Major Hazard Industries. London: Health and Safety Executive; 2006.
11. Awolusi I, Marks E. Near-Miss Reporting to Enhance Safety in the Steel Industry. Association for Iron and Steel Technology Publications: Safety First, Iron and Steel Technology; 2015. pp. 62-68
12. Han S, Lee S. A vision-based motion capture and recognition framework for behaviour-based safety management. Automation in Construction. 2013;35: 131-141
13. Dash DK. Industrial hazards and safety measures. Pharma tutor, March, 2020.
14. International efforts for industrial and chemical accidents prevention, preparedness and response. Interagency coordination. OECD & Unicef March, 2020.
15. Brock WE, Pendergrass JA. Safety & health guide for the chemical industry. Occupational safety and health administration, 2020. ml
16. Major hazard chemicals 8, International labour organization, 2020.
17. Herman AM. Hazard communication guidelines for compliance, U.S. department of labor occupational safety and health administration, 2000.
18. Shmmon Ahmad, Ashok Kumar and Dr. Abdul Hafeez. Importance of data integrity & its regulation in pharmaceutical industry. The Pharma Innovation Journal. 2019; 8(1):306-313.
19. Levit B. Chemical routes of entry. Levitt safety, 2015.
20. Prof Jonny Myers, Introduction to occupational hygiene. University of cape town, 2020.
21. Toxicology and exposure guidelines, University of nebraska lincoln, 2002 https://ehs.unl.edu/documents/tox_exposure_guidelines. pdf
22. Chemical Hazards, Australian OHS accreditation education board, 2012.
23. How workplace chemicals enter the body. Canadian centre for occupational health and safety, 2020.
24. Ciraj M, Vračko P. Chemical safety and protection of human health. World health organization, 2016.
25. Jeffress CN. Hazard communication guidelines for compliance. U.S. department of Labor, 2020.

26. Swedish council on health technology assessment, Occupational health and safety chemical exposure: a systematic review and assessment of the social, medical and ethical aspects, 2017.
27. Department of environmental health and safety. Chemical and hazardous materials safety, 2012, 29.
28. Office of disaster preparedness and management, Industrial hazards, 2020.
29. Bhattacharya, J. (2015). Quality Risk Management– Understanding and control the risk in the pharmaceutical manufacturing industry. International. Journal of Pharmaceutical Science Invention, 4(1), 29-4.
30. IEC 61241-10:2004-06- Electrical apparatus for use in the presence of combustible dust-Part-10; Classification of areas where combustible dusts area or many be present.
31. BS EN 60079-10:2003- Electrical apparatus for explosive gas atmosphere Part 20: Data for flammable gases and vapors, relating to the use of electrical apparatus.
32. Nawfel Muhammed Baqer Muhsin (2020). Review on Engineering Methods in Treatment of Chemical Rust. International Journal of Chemical and Molecular Engineering. 6 (2), 49-53.
33. Ali H. Mutaib, Noor H. Dhaher, Nawfel Muhammed Baqer, Nagham Mahmood Aljamali (2019). Review on Photoelectrical Cells and (ChemoEngineering)-Treatment of Corrosion in Machines. International Journal of Photochemistry, 5 (1), 37-48.
34. Nawfel Muhammed Baqer Muhsin, Hayder H K, Noor H. D., Nagham Mahmood Aljamali. (2019). Preparation of Chemical Inhibitors to Treat the Corrosion and Erosion of Machines. International Journal of Engineering, Applied and Management Sciences Paradigms, 54 (3), 89-93, Diaster management institute Bhopal. Types of major chemical/industrial hazards explosion, 2020,
35. Dubey R. Hazard Management in Pharmaceutical Industry. Event Report and Material. Bhopal: Disaster Management Institute, Sponsored by Disaster Management Institute, Bhopal and GIZAdvisory Service for Environmental Management (Cooperating Partner); 2010.
36. Shabaninejad H, Madani H, Amineh ZA, Doostzadeh E. A framework for evaluation of pharmaceutical industry development in developing countries: Evidence from Iran. Asian J Pharm Clin Res 2016;9:50-4.
37. Gupta AK, Nair SS. Chemical (industrial) Disaster Management, Trainer's Module. New Delhi: National Institute of Disaster Management (Ministry of Home Affairs); 2012.
38. Subrahmanyam CV. Pharmaceutical Production and Management. 1st ed. Delhi: Vallabh Prakashan; 2015.
39. Hazard Guidelines-Hazardous Material Spill. Ann Arbor: University of Michigan, Division of Public Safety and Security; 2011.

40. Pisaniello D, Tepe S. Chemical Hazards. In: HaSPA (Health and Safety Professionals Alliance), The Core Body of Knowledge for Generalist OHS Professionals. Australia: Safety Institute of Australia Ltd; 2012. content/uploads/2013/12/17-Hazard-Chemical.pdf?x71776. [Last cited on 2017 Oct 11].
41. Canadian Centre for Occupational and Health Safety. Canada: Canadian Centre for Occupational and Health Safety (CA).
42. Occupational Safety and Health Administration (WOSH Specialist Training Supplemental Module). Washington, DC (US): United States Department of Labor.
43. University of Medicine and Dentistry of New Jersey. Annual Refresher on Health and Safety for Hazardous Waste Site Investigation Personnel. New Brunswick, NJ: University of Medicine and Dentistry of New Jersey - School of Public Health, Office for Public Health Practice, Centers for Education and Training; 2001.
44. U.S. Food and Drug Administration, Office of Regulatory Affairs, Division of Field Investigations. (Current Edition). Investigations Operations Manual or the Website Address. Available from: http://www.fda.gov/ICECI/Inspections/IOM/default.html.
45. Subramanyam CV, Setty JT, Suresh S, Devi VK. Pharmaceutical Engineering Principals and Practices. 1st ed. New Delhi: M.K Jain for Vallabh Prakashan; 2003. p. 480-4.
46. Sambamurthy K. Pharmaceutical Engineering. New Delhi: New Age International Publishers; 2003. p. 440-9.
47. IARC: A Review of Human Carcinogens. Chemical Agents and Related Occupations. Vol. 100F. Lyon: IARC; 2012.
48. IARC: A Review of Human Carcinogens. Arsenic, Metals, Fibres, and Dusts. Vol. 100C. Lyon: IARC; 2012.
49. Kauppinen T, Toikkanen J, Pedersen D, Young R, Ahrens W, Boffetta P, et al. Occupational exposure to carcinogens in the European Union. Occup Environ Med 2000;57:10-8.
50. Raison-Peyron N. Occupational dermatitis diagnosis. Rev Fr Allergol 2006:46 Suppl 1:S45-50.
51. Deutsche Forschungsgemeinschaft (DFG). List of MAK and BAT Values 2013: Maximum Concentrations and Biological Tolerance Values at the Workplace. Weinheim: Wiley; 2013.
52. Schnuch A, Lessmann H, Schulz KH, Becker D, Diepgen T, Drexler H, et al. When should a substance be designated as sensitizing for the skin ('Sh') or for the airways ('Sa') ? Hum Exp Toxicol 2002;21:439-44.
53. Akan G, Lemanske R. Allergic disease. Pathophysiology and immunopathology. In: Lieberman P, Anderson JA, editors. Allergic Diseases. Totowa, NJ: Humana Press; 2007. p. 1-14.
54. Belsito DV. Occupational contact dermatitis: Etiology, prevalence, and resultant impairment/disability. J Am Acad Dermatol 2005;53:303-13.

55. Raison-Peyron N. Occupational dermatitis diagnosis. Rev Fr Allergol 2006;46 Suppl:S45-50.
56. Vocks E, Ring J. Lichtallergien under and lichtempfindlichkeitsreaktionen. Z Umweltchem Okotox 2002;14:237-44.
57. Bundesanstalt Für Arbeitsschutzund Arbeitsmedizin: Technische Regelnfür Gefahrstoffe TRGS 905; 2008.
58. Ferguson KK, O'Neill MS, Meeker JD. Environmental contaminant exposures and preterm birth: A comprehensive review. J Toxicol Environ Health B Crit Rev 2013;16:69-113.
59. Windham G, Fenster L. Environmental contaminants and pregnancy outcomes. Fertil Steril 2008;89 2 Suppl:e111-6.
60. Annual Refresher on Health and Safety for Hazardous Waste Sites Investigation Personnel 200. p. 45
61. Nawfel Muhammed Baqer Muhsin (2020). Review on Effects of Photo Processes in Environment. International Journal of Photochemistry, 6 (2), 15-19, Chemical Engineering, IIT Bombay. Chemical Hazard Control: Technical Measures. Mumbai (IN): Dept. of Chemical Engineering, IIT Bombay.
62. Dikshith TS. Hazardous Chemicals: Safety Management and Global Regulations. Boca Raton, Florida (US): CRC Press (Taylor and Francis Group); c2013.
63. Balaji G, Potdar A, Unnikrishnan S. Environmental legislation for chemical management in India: An agenda. J Environ Res Dev 2014;9:494-506.
64. Bhandari M, Raj S. Practical approach to green chemistry. Int J Pharm Sci 2017;9:10-26.
65. Department of Environmental Health and Safety. 800 West, Cambell Rd, SG No. 10 Appendix No. 6 Managing Risks of Hazardous Chemical in the Workplace Code of Practice Code-61. 2012.
66. Madureira, T. V.; Rocha, M. J.; Cass, Q. B.; Tiritan, M. E. Development and Optimization of a HPLC-DAD Method for the Determination of Diverse Pharmaceuticals in Estuarine Surface Waters. *J. Chromatogr. Sci.* 2010, *48*, 176– 182,
67. Dadgostar, P. Antimicrobial Resistance: Implications and Costs. *Infect. Drug Resist.* 2019, *12*, 3903– 3910,
68. Zhan, J.; Li, Z.; Yu, G.; Pan, X.; Wang, J.; Zhu, W.; Han, X.; Wang, Y. Enhanced Treatment of Pharmaceutical Wastewater by Combining Three-Dimensional Electrochemical Process with Ozonation to in Situ Regenerate Granular Activated Carbon Particle Electrodes. *Sep. Purif. Technol.* 2019, *208*, 12– 18,
69. Lee, Y.-G.; Park, Y.; Lee, G.; Kim, Y.; Chon, K. Enhanced Degradation of Pharmaceutical Compounds by a Microbubble Ozonation Process: Effects of Temperature, pH, and Humic Acids. *Energies* 2019, *12*, 4373,

70. B.E. Meteku, J. Huang, J. Zeng, F. Subhan, F. Feng, Yu. Zhang, Z. Qiu, S. Aslam, G. Li, Z. Yan.; Magnetic metal–organic framework composites for environmental monitoring and remediation; Chemical Engineering Journal; 406, 15, 2021

71. S.J., Park, J.Y., Park, J. W., Chung, H.K., Yung, B.K., Moon, S.S., Yi; Colour tuneable carbon quantum dots from wasted paper by different solvents for anti-counterfeiting and fluorescent flexible film; Chemical Engineering Journal; 383, 1, 2020

www.ingramcontent.com/pod-product-compliance
Lightning Source LLC
Chambersburg PA
CBHW071223230926
51849CB00001B/13
9789348734105